**WILLIAM GERALD SHADE** - Lehigh University

# BANKS OR NO BANKS

## THE MONEY ISSUE IN WESTERN POLITICS

# 1832-1865

Wayne State University Press, Detroit, 1972

Published simultaneously in Canada
by the Copp Clark Publishing Company
517 Wellington Street, West
Toronto 2B, Canada.

Library of Congress Cataloging in Publication Data

Shade, William G
    Banks or no banks.
    Bibliography: p.
    1.  Banks and banking—Northwest, Old.  2.  Northwest, Old—
Politics and government.  I.  Title.
HG2609.S33       332.1'0977       72-4229
ISBN 0-8143-1485-9

*To Lou, Alex and Chris*

# CONTENTS

## Maps

## Tables

# ACKNOWLEDGMENTS

Like all other historians I owe many debts to librarians, teachers, fellow scholars, and friends. I have found the staffs of the various libraries visited in the course of my research generally friendly and helpful. Particular thanks go to James Babcock and his staff at the Burton Historical Collection at the Detroit Public Library when this project was begun, and to the staff of the Linderman Library of Lehigh University, who have aided in the final stages of the work. Grants from the Society of Colonial Dames and the Lehigh University Office of Research facilitated the manuscript research.

This book began as a doctoral dissertation under the direction of Raymond C. Miller at Wayne State University. He has been an indulgent advisor and friend. At Wayne I had the good fortune of studying with Lee Benson, Edward Lurie, John Weiss, and William J. Bossenbrook. Sidney Glazer provided numerous suggestions at the early stages of the project and helped improve the dissertation. Forrest McDonald and Thomas Govan have been sources of much needed criticism and encouragement since I first met them over a decade ago. My friends James Curtis, Herbert Ershkovitz, James K. Flack, and Larry Leder have read all or parts of the manuscript and improved it with their suggestions. Roger Sharp has been generous with his information and expertise on the subject. Harvey L. Carter allowed me to read two helpful unpublished essays. Aletta Biersack of Wayne State University Press struggled to make the manuscript more readable. Mary Connell, Terry Racosky, and Virginia Frey have typed numerous drafts.

Special mention must be made of two excellent historians and fine friends, Lewis L. Gould and Ronald P. Formisano, who have

9

given me far more than I could repay. Finally, my wife, Mary Lou, has been a constant source of joy and encouragement.

William G. Shade

Bethlehem, Pennsylvania

April 1972

# INTRODUCTION

## NEW BOTTLES FOR OLD WINE

# 1

Financial and monetary questions have been near the center of the American political stage since the colonial period, and historians have often used these issues to characterize political developments. Most historians have insisted that the nature of Jacksonian democracy can be found in the "Bank War" and its aftermath, and that the conflict over Greenbacks, national banks and the silver issue holds the key to politics in the late nineteenth century. However, the years between the "Bank War" and the Civil War represent a distinct and poorly understood phase in the continuous political controversy over money, credit, and banking. During this period the states attempted individually to handle currency problems; and general histories of the two decades preceding the Civil War give the impression that such questions receded into the background following Jackson's retirement. While Manifest Destiny and the expansion of slavery overshadowed the bank issue in national politics, in an altered form it remained of primary importance in the states. In the years following the Panic of 1837, this question polarized the parties and epitomized their positions on economic policy.[1]

Nowhere was the contest over banks more bitterly fought than in the rapidly growing states of the Old Northwest: Ohio, Indiana, Illinois, Michigan, and Wisconsin. By examining the party press, ideas of party leaders, patterns of voting in state legislatures and constitutional conventions, and the popular response to referenda on the issue of "banks or no banks," this study attempts to unravel the complicated strands of the political history of the bank issue in the Old Northwest and to relate it to the social conflicts underlying the politics of the antebellum years.

# 2

The bizarre aspects of western banking have fascinated historians, but few have examined the role of the bank issue in state politics or the social roots of the animosity toward banks. No general study exists, and the story has to be pieced together from state studies often of dubious value. Three general and contrasting interpretations have gained a wide hearing because of their relation to the historiographical controversy over the Jacksonian era.[2]

In his famous paper "The Significance of the Frontier in American History," written in 1893, near the height of the demand for free silver, Frederick Jackson Turner argued that "each one of the periods of lax financial integrity [in American history] coincided with periods when a new set of frontier communities had arisen, and coincided in area with these successive frontiers." In describing "inflated paper currency and wild-cat banking" as a frontier phenomenon, Turner expressed a view commonly held by both sound money reformers, who dominated the writing of monetary history at the turn of the century, and the emerging school of "Progressive" historians, who associated easy money with debtor-farmers and "agrarian democracy."[3]

Thirty years later in his brilliant essay "The North Central States," appearing in *The United States, 1830-1850*, Turner altered his views in a longer and more sophisticated discussion of western banking:

> There are two distinct phases in the bank history of the section in our period: first, the years between the fall of the United States Bank and the Crisis of 1837 were a time of "wildcat" banking (for which Michigan was notorious), marked by a great increase of state banks, with enlarged circulation but inadequate

specie facilities; second, an anti-banking movement followed in most of the states.

During the first phase frontier finance dominated. But immediately following the Panic of 1837, local failures, together with sectional antagonism toward English and eastern capitalists and the Jacksonian sentiments of many settlers who had migrated from the South, made the area "a friendly field" for loco-foco influences from the East. Given their adherence to the "pioneer principles of freedom and equality" and their recent experiences, western farmers chose to abandon inflated currency and to adopt loco-foco remedies for their financial ills.[4]

Two decades after Turner's study, Bray Hammond presented a conflicting interpretation in the long essay "Banking in the Early West: Monopoly, Prohibition, and Laissez Faire," which later appeared as part of his Pulitzer Prize winning book, *Banks and Politics in America*. Hammond argued that "agrarian" opposition to banks and monetary expansion typified the agricultural West and that the push for easy money was more closely related to the needs of business enterprise. Loco-foco ideology was, for Hammond, little more than "agrarianism" transplanted to the city and adapted to the needs of small producers. As the title of his essay indicates, Hammond viewed western banking history as a series of phases, each of which was dominated by certain attitudes. In the years before 1837 state monopolies rather than wildcat banks dominated western banking. The Panic of 1837 ushered in a period of prohibition lasting until 1850. After this the western states turned to laissez-faire and adopted free banking. Hammond explained alterations in western attitudes on the bank issue as responses to the area's changing economic structure. "Prohibition and laissez faire—the extreme positions taken with respect to banking in the West—were products respectively of agrarianism and of enterprise." Until 1850 "agrarianism" dominated; but then, as "business interest . . . turned an economy originally agrarian into one that was industrial and monied, dominated by steam and credit," it gave way to "enterprise." While Hammond said little about partisan politics in the western states,

13

his assertion that free banking represented "the culmination of Jacksonian banking policy" would suggest that he saw free banking as the result of the emerging power of entrepreneurs within Jacksonian ranks in the Old Northwest.[5]

Hammond's views on the bank issue in the early West were in line with his adherence to the "entrepreneurial" interpretation of Jacksonian democracy. In 1970, James Roger Sharp vigorously disputed this interpretation in *The Jacksonians Versus the Banks: Politics in the States After 1837*. Sharp devoted significant portions of his book to the Old Northwest and studied Ohio in detail. His major thesis was that the conflict over banks after 1837 reflected the true nature of Jacksonian democracy and the essential difference between the parties in the following decade. Before 1837 the Democracy constituted a heterogeneous group. Gradually, however, in response to the economic crisis, the party took on the cast of "agrarian radicalism," moving against the banks in what amounted to a full-scale attack on the "increasing commercialization and vulgarization of American life." The party came to represent the interests of the lower orders of society, and the more wealthy elements faltered and deserted as one measure after another undermined their economic power.

> After the Panic of 1837, although the rhetoric of the two parties sometimes obscured their real positions, it is clear that the Whigs were the champions of the banks against the "radicalism" of the Jacksonians. Despite internal feuding the main body of the Democratic party supported reform of the banks and, in some cases, their destruction. The party reflected in both ethos and program the hard money position.

The hard money forces made their final attempts to centralize the banks in the constitutional conventions of midcentury. While Sharp admitted that free banking appealed to some Democrats, he insisted that most continued to adhere to hard money views and that it was their critique of the banking system that led to reforms making the country's banks "relatively stable and more responsible" during the decades of the 1840s and 1850s. "By the decade of the 1850s," he concluded, "banking was no longer a major

14

divisive issue in the states. The Panic of 1837 was but a distant memory to most Americans and the threatening clouds of Civil War already were on the horizon."[6]

# 3

While the present study owes much to these earlier works, it breaks with them in several ways. By extending the period of study, it shows that the partisan conflict over banks that arose after 1837 carried over into the decade of the 1850s and contributed directly to the monetary debates of the Civil War years.

Before the Panic of 1837 (particularly during the years from 1830 through 1836), neither free banking nor wildcat banks associated with it were common in these western states. Indiana and Illinois established state banks; but Ohio, Michigan, and Wisconsin Territory retained the system of individually chartered, privately owned banks. The erratic way in which these systems functioned makes generalizing dangerous, but the evidence supports the belief that these years witnessed a moderate expansion, which was held in check by quite fresh and unhappy memories of bank failures in the wake of the Panic of 1819. Although the nascent parties tended to align themselves either for or against the national policies of the Jackson administration during these years, in the Old Northwest there were few clear differences between them on the bank issue.

The Panic of 1837 accelerated the polarization of attitudes on the bank issue as parties emerged more distinctly in the late 1830s. Political necessity, together with the status fears of the groups constituting the Democratic party of the Old Northwest, moved the Democracy to support President Martin Van Buren's Independent Treasury program and attempts to reform the states' banks of issue. Although the Democracy of the Old Northwest gradually became dedicated to the elimination of these banks and to a return to the "constitutional currency" of gold and silver for everyday transactions, between 1837 and 1839 Democrats advocated a moderate program of "bank reform." Not until the early

15

and mid-1840s did the majority of the party in these states adopt a hard money stance. The Whigs opposed the Independent Treasury plan and struggled in Congress to revive the idea of a national bank, but in the states during these years they were not uncritical defenders of all banks and often censured what they believed to be excessive proliferation of banks. They were, however, less willing to abandon the "credit system" than the Democrats; and after proposals for a new national bank were defeated by the vetoes of John Tyler in the early 1840s, they supported demands for free banking. In the constitutional conventions of midcentury, these contrasting positions were debated. With the aid of a small number of "soft," or probank, Democrats, Whigs defeated hard money restrictions and wrote into these documents the acceptance of free banking.

In the 1850s all the states in the Old Northwest established free banking systems to answer their economic needs. Whigs took the initiative in the effort to institute these laws, and they succeeded because a minority of Democrats again split with party orthodoxy and voted for free banking. Although the Republican party ignored the issue in its platforms during these years, it took over Whig reformist attitudes on the bank issue. To eliminate weaknesses revealed by the economic crises of 1854, 1857, and 1861, Republicans proposed legal restrictions to protect bill holders and investors. At the same time the new party showed a willingness to establish state banks alongside free banks. Throughout the decade the Democrats reiterated the traditional opposition to banks of any kind.

At every turn, party, not section, was the most important determinant of attitudes on the bank issue. Within the Old Northwest, Whigs and Republicans favored banks, and Democrats supported their prohibition. The response of both parties to the Panic of 1857 reveals the tenacity with which people held on to the images and ideas forged in the crisis of the late 1830s, and the monetary legislation of the Civil War shows the degree to which these views affected Democratic and Republican outlooks on the financial problems posed by the war.[7]

A more intriguing and difficult question to which this study addresses itself involves the basis of this partisan response. Why did Whigs and then Republicans support banks, and why did Democrats oppose them throughout this entire period? Most often historians have explained partisan perspectives on economic matters in terms of the partisan's position in the economic structure. They have relied on the general theory that American parties offer alternative policies that clearly serve the needs of different economic groups, that the members of these groups clearly perceive their economic interest, and that they rationally act upon that interest. While this model may explain the behavior of certain elites, there is little evidence of its usefulness in accounting for mass political behavior.[8]

This study departs from these earlier studies in proposing a much broader social interpretation of the significance of the bank issue in western politics. Its assumptions are that "political life involves the origin, clash and resolution of all value conflicts within society" and that these conflicts must be related to the entire social environment that spawns them in order to be understood. It seeks to delineate the sources of dissension and relate particular issues to the values of the conflicting social groups. Political rhetoric is viewed not as a representation of external reality, but as a system of symbols embodying the values and reflecting the emotional and psychological perspectives of the relevant constituencies.[9]

Historians have generally acknowledged the enduring effects of the patterns of migration into the Old Northwest. These patterns brought the early settlers from the uplands of the southern states into religious, social, and economic conflict with Yankees, who poured into the area in ever-increasing numbers after 1830. Similarly, a thriving historical controversy over the importance of the German vote in Lincoln's victory in 1860 has revealed equally deep cultural animosities between foreign-born Roman Catholics from Ireland and the German states and "the older Americans, especially those of the Puritan tradition." Yet these same historians have for the most part either focused upon the

17

contributions of these various ethnic strains to the development of a distinctive western sectional culture or subjugated conflict between these groups to a general economic interpretation.[10]

A new frame of reference grounded in the realities of social discord can be found in Ronald P. Formisano's brilliant and detailed analysis of the context of partisan politics in Michigan during these years, *The Birth of Mass Political Parties*, which finds that "antagonistic . . . political subcultures," rather than opposed classes or occupation groups, formed the basic elements of the political structure.[11]

*The major thesis of the present study is that the antebellum fight over banks in the states of the Old Northwest cannot be understood simply as a conflict between the haves and the have-nots, but must be seen as an aspect of the broader conflict between political subcultures that structured partisan controversy within the area.* This is not to deny that government actions may alter the distribution of goods and services or that the importance of these changes may be clearly perceived by certain interest groups. It is to insist, however, that the focus of political behavior studies should be the more subtle area of issue perception among the voters and the symbolic aspects of economic issues. Because government actions on such issues can symbolize the acceptance by constituted authority of the economic style of one subculture rather than another, the political conflict over these issues may take on the form of a moral drama in which the group's values are justified. In this drama the voter's response is most often shaped by the combination of economic attitudes and behavior patterns sanctioned by his social peers.

Even in our secular, industrialized, and reasonably homogeneous society, religion and ethnicity operate as powerful variables influencing economic behavior and attitudes. Ethnoreligious subcultures within our society foster distinctive economic norms that function independently of class and that may either mute or reinforce the effects of the economic structure. In the fragmented society of nineteenth-century America, characterized by an absence of highly developed national institutions and a high degree of "social mobilization," with an increasingly heterogeneous popu-

18

lation, the effects of such allegiances were even more important. If the full significance of the bank issue is to be compre-
hended, it must be studied in these terms in order to explain the
ways in which a party system rooted in the conflict of subcultures,
rather than simple economic differences, could polarize around an
economic question, the bank issue. Essentially the bank issue had
both "real" and symbolic dimensions. Its outcome affected not
only the allocation of goods and resources within the economic
system but also the status of ethnoreligious groups and the dominance of certain values, particularly economic values, of the
Yankee-Protestant subculture.[12]

In a period when men were generally troubled by status fears
and anxious about the rapid changes that seemed to touch every
aspect of American life, when religious and ethnic hostilities were
pronounced and the institutional fiber of the society weak, the
bank issue served a symbolic function: to characterize, often in
highly moralistic terms, group differences, not only over the evolv-
ing economic order but also over the cultural identity of the society.[13]

# CHAPTER 1

## BANKS AND POLITICS IN THE OLD NORTHWEST DURING THE 1830s

### 1

It was not clear as the fourth decade of the nineteenth century opened that banking would be an issue in the politics of the Old Northwest. The Panic of 1819 and its aftermath had disrupted the area's banking systems, leaving a legacy of fear. But a scarcity of capital, an inadequate supply of currency to conduct day-to-day transactions, and the need for eastern exchange had led to demands for the establishment of banks within each of the states. A rapidly expanding area, the Old Northwest lacked the capital necessary to finance growth. The expansionist policies of the Bank of the United States after 1829 had helped alleviate this situation and had dispelled much of the earlier animosity toward that institution. Increased immigration and rising land values after 1830 spurred an economic boom, which subordinated antibank feelings to the general desire for expanded credit facilities.[1]

Between 1830 and 1840 the population of the Old Northwest nearly doubled, rising from 1,470,018 to 2,924,728. The most populous state, Ohio, grew by nearly 70%, while the population of Indiana doubled, and that of Illinois tripled. Particularly after the brief recession in 1834, land values zoomed. A young Illinois lawyer, Stephen A. Douglas, wrote a client in early 1836, "I am happy to inform you that I can now sell your Lots at from fifty to an hundred per cent advance . . . which by the by is pretty good interest."[2]

So great was this area's growth that the Bank of the United States, which had a branch in Cincinnati, could not supply sufficient credit to answer the area's needs. Agitation for expanded banking facilities increased. Experience dictated caution, but necessity demanded currency and credit. In the early and mid-1830s, Ohio rapidly expanded its banking system, Indiana and Illinois created new state banks with branches, and Michigan passed the nation's first free banking law. Throughout the Northwest this increase in banking facilities augmented a growing money supply and sent the economy spiraling upward. Although not intended by the Jackson administration, removal of federal deposits from the Second Bank of the United States to privately owned state-chartered banks (usually controlled by Democrats and called at the time the "pet" banks), along with the retirement of federal debt, neatly coincided with western expansion and contributed to the speculative psychology.[3]

Political parties of the Old Northwest were in their formative stage and dominated by factional bickering and personal politics. Not until the end of the decade did a fully functioning two-party system develop throughout the Old Northwest. During the years before 1837, personal or sectional ambitions rather than partisanship characterized responses to the bank issue, and there is little evidence that hard money antibank attitudes gained more than a limited hearing. Between 1832 and 1837 both parties struggled to establish banks in response to popular demands. Banking in these states was not a partisan issue, and the Democracy* of the Old Northwest was not a hard money party. The groups that formed the Democratic party were more hostile to banks than their opponents, and those men who harbored a dislike for banks of any variety were usually found within the Democratic fold. Yet opposition to state-chartered banks was hardly a test of party orthodoxy. Ardent bank expansionists marched side by side with hard money restrictionists under Democratic banners. The Whigs

---

* Contemporaries usually referred to Jackson's party as "the Democracy." In the 1840s its official name became the American Democracy.

advocated credit expansion through a moderate increase of banking facilities and were often caught between the factions of the Democratic party.[4]

# 2

During these years the idea of a state bank based upon public credit became popular in the capital-shy states of the Old Northwest. Traditionally banks in the states were privately owned chartered banks individually granted corporate privileges by the state legislature, which attempted to construct the charter so as to insure sound management and safety both for the investor and the noteholder. All too often such safeguards did not achieve their intended ends, and political influence was often more important than banking ability in obtaining a charter. State banks represented one alternative to chartered banks. These were banks with branches or systems of mutually responsible banks related to the state government through its ownership of a portion of each bank's stock. These could, at least in theory, be more tightly controlled by the state government, while their stock served as a solid investment for state funds. Sometimes, but not always, state banks were given a monopoly on banking within the state. Although their earlier experience with state banks had been unhappy, both Indiana and Illinois established new state banks in the 1830s. The fate of the state bank issue in Ohio was different. Between 1829 and 1834, Ohio debated and rejected the idea of a state bank in favor of an expansion of the number of chartered banks in the state.[5]

Ohio, the oldest state in the region, entered into one of its most dramatic periods of growth in the decade before 1837. Population increased rapidly and the value of taxable property nearly doubled. Every index of prosperity rose during these years, and villages grew into small cities. It was in this period that Cincinnati became the "Queen City" of the West and secured its domination as a mercantile and meat-packing center. British traveler James Silk Buckingham noted in 1833,

> Cincinnati is in every respect an extraordinary city; the only one, perhaps on record, which has, in the course of twenty-five years, sprung up from nothing to be a place of great consequence, with a population exceeding thirty thousand souls. Banks, University, Museum, Theatre, Athenaeum, Bazaar, and Hospitals, are now seen, where, a quarter of a century ago nothing but primitive forest was standing untouched.[6]

Partisan politics developed earlier in Ohio than elsewhere in the Old Northwest. From the election of Jackson in 1828, there was keen competition for control of the state, and power shifted repeatedly from one party to the other. Within this context a series of disputes relating to banking arose, but these do not lend themselves to any simple interpretation of partisan positions on banking in the state.

As the decade of the 1820s came to a close, Ohio's ten banks were sound but could not keep pace with increasing demands for currency and credit. Circulation of local banks remained what it had been ten years before, and interest rates were extremely high. To lure capital into the state, a legislative committee recommended a state bank in 1829; but the idea lay dormant for several years while the number of local banks grew slowly. Jackson's veto of the Bank of the United States led to the reconsideration of a state bank to meet the state's needs. Anti-Jackson governor Duncan McArthur suggested a state bank in 1832 as an alternative to the chartering of numerous local banks. In his message to the legislature, he warned,

> a depreciated paper currency, such as existed in this and other states of the Union a few years since is calculated to depress the spirit of commercial enterprise, lessen the confidence of the citizens in their pecuniary ability, check industrious efforts of the laboring and business men of the country and curtail improvement of individual possessions, and of course the general prosperity of the country.

McArthur believed that the working people of the state required a stable currency and urged that the legislature "guard as much as practicable against many of the impositions heretofore practiced by some of the local banks."[7]

23

During the legislative session of 1832–33, nearly everyone argued that some kind of bank had to be created "to take the place of the Branch of the Bank of the United States"; but the form such a bank should take remained in dispute. The most popular plan among Democrats was recommended by a senate committee and provided for a $7 million state loan to establish a mixed corporation partially owned by the state government and having a monopoly on banking in the state. Because stock subscriptions were to be secured by mortgages on real estate, the press referred to this project as a "property bank." Both the incoming Jacksonian governor, Robert Lucas, and Moses Dawson's pro-Jackson *Cincinnati Advertiser* supported the "property bank" idea. When it became apparent that no state bank bill could pass the divided legislature, the Democratic supporters of this proposal suggested that it be postponed until the next session of the legislature and that an independent bank be chartered in Cincinnati to provide the needed relief.[8]

The two leading Whig papers in the state, Charles Hammond's violently anti-Jackson *Cincinnati Gazette* and the *Ohio State Journal* at Columbus, favored a state bank but refused to support the Democrat's "property bank." Whigs generally viewed the proposal as "a grand scheme of speculation" for the benefit of a few and politically dangerous because of the control the party in office would have over it. The *Cleveland Herald*, which was shifting into the Whig camp, feared it looked "too much like giving a bounty to one class of the community to the prejudice of another." A Clarke County meeting favorably disposed to a state bank that was founded on "traditional principles" opposed the plan before the legislature as "novel and quite mischievous." Although the meeting believed the government should not be a banker and the state should not incur further debt, it emphasized the political danger of giving the dominant party control of such financial power. An indignant Whig in the *Ohio State Journal* opposed the "doubtful experiment" of a state bank and argued that

> it is not the farmer or mechanic nor the industrious and laboring
> classes of our citizens who are in favor of chartering the State

Bank . . . [but] men of desperate fortunes, spend thrifts, political gamblers and blacklegs of all parties—men who wear fine clothes, ride in carriages, give parties and sometimes *forget to pay their debts* even to the poor, hard working farmer, mechanic, and day laborer.

Yet a few Whigs opposed the chartering of a private bank in 1833 because it would endanger the state bank proposal, and the *Ohio State Journal* called upon the people to consider the matter carefully so that the next state legislature might

either incorporate a State Bank or adopt such other measures as shall then appear necessary in order to guard their constituents against the evils which may be apprehended from a deficiency of the circulating medium.[9]

Demands for legislative action increased in 1833, particularly following Jackson's announcement that the deposits would be removed from the Bank of the United States and that that institution would definitely be closed by 1836. The *Cleveland Herald,* which had opposed the state bank, shifted its position in November and noted that the idea was gaining friends. In the fall elections the Jacksonians won control of the legislature, with an overwhelming majority in the lower house.[10]

In his annual address to the legislature, Governor Lucas again called attention to the state's currency problems, which he blamed on the termination of the public works program. Believing that "the history of past events loudly admonishes us to guard the interests of the people against the deleterious effects of excessive local banking," Lucas recommended a state bank that would unite all the private banks in a single system to provide a uniform currency and safe investment for state funds. "It would secure us the control of all our resources; enable us to compete with foreign Banks, and relieve us from the influence of foreign capitalists."[11]

Although some Whigs supported the state bank proposal, it was sponsored by the Democratic Central Committee as well as the Democratic governor. In the legislature the Jacksonians split and an unusual coalition of advocates of a new national bank, backers of chartered private banks, and opponents of all banks defeated the measure. However, worsening economic conditions and an unprecedented number of petitions for bank charters forced the legislature to act. By the end of the 1833–34 session, it had created ten new banks, including the Ohio Life Insurance and Trust Company, and had revived two previously chartered institutions.[12]

An analysis of the votes in the 1833–34 session of the legislature helps clarify an often misunderstood situation and further validates the view that western Jacksonians had not yet taken an anti-bank stand in state politics. The overwhelming Democratic majority in both houses was badly split on the question. Most Democrats favored the state bank against fairly solid Whig opposition, but roughly one-third of the Jacksonians in each house defected and insured the bill's failure. The defectors numbered about equally chartered bank advocates and antibank men.[13]

Whig opponents of the bill included a few antibank men and a large number who feared that partisan control would make the state bank "a great political machine." Many of these Whigs also advocated local banks. One legislator argued,

> Local banks, properly guarded in the details of their incorporation with some additional securities to the public, quite limited in issue and under the supervision of Commissioners appointed by the legislature with powers to inquire into the state of their concerns, would answer best the demands of the people and best subserve the interests of the community.[14]

But it is clearly incorrect to portray the Jacksonians as opponents of banks and the Whigs as ardent bank expansionists. The increase in the number of local banks in Ohio from 1829 through 1833 had received Democratic support, and this support continued in the 1833–34 session, which nearly doubled the number of banks in the state. On ten of thirteen roll calls in the house, the majority of the Jacksonians favored banks. In the senate the majority of the party voted for five charters and opposed two charters of the seven such votes on which roll calls were taken. A large majority of those who opposed all banks were Democrats. But these Democrats, together with those generally opposed to banks but willing to accept a state bank made up less than 25% of the party in the house and an even smaller percentage in the senate. Actually a larger faction in the party was consistently probank, including half the Jacksonian senators and more than one-third the assemblymen. The small group of Democrats favoring all banks including the state bank was nearly three times as large as the group of Democrats opposed to all banks. Clearly, the Ohio Jacksonians were badly split on the question of banks in the mid-1830s.[15]

Ohio Whigs, like their opponents, tended to favor the establishment of banks, but rejected unlimited expansion and attacked the "Van Buren-Jackson party policy" of setting up "as many State Banks as you please." They had supported the limited expansion from 1829 through 1833, and the Whig record in the 1833–34 legislature was similar to that of the Democrats. In the house the majority of Whigs favored chartered banks ten times, opposed them twice, and split evenly on one vote. The senate roll calls reveal the Whigs less disposed toward banks than the Jacksonians. They favored four charters and opposed three. The increasing Whig desire for moderation can be seen in the progression of the votes. As the session wore on and the number of charters mounted, Whig opposition stiffened.[16]

Whigs as well as Democrats feared a repetition of their earlier experience. Hammond, the leading Whig editor in the state, urged a conservative policy. The party seemed to follow the editor's advice in the 1835 legislature, in which Whigs almost unanimously opposed demands for charters. Their opponents again split, with a slim majority of the Democrats advocating more banks, as they had in the previous session.[17]

The following year an intraparty feud developed among the Democrats over the repeal of the charter of the Ohio Life Insurance and Trust Company, which had banking privileges. The move to repeal the company's charter grew out of a rivalry among Cincinnati Democrats. It was initiated by Robert Lytle, who had supported the company earlier, but who blamed his defeat in the 1834 election on the influence of Micajah T. Williams. Lytle was joined in his opposition to the company by most of the Democratic press, which attacked the eastern capitalists owning its stock, and by vociferous antibank Democrats such as Benjamin Tappan. But

Williams, David Disney, Noah Swayne, and Daniel Kilgore, four leading Democrats among the company's directors, fought the repeal. They were aided by a small group of Democratic papers and a sizable minority of the party in the legislature. The Whigs, who believed the repeal merely a political maneuver, joined the opposition and generally voted with the successful defenders of the institution.[18]

The opposition to the Ohio Life Insurance and Trust Company was only an indication of growing antibank sentiment in Ohio. In his seventh annual message Jackson had recommended that the state should prohibit small notes as a step toward returning to the "constitutional currency" of gold and silver.* This was in line with his strict constructionist views on the Constitution and his fear of "an unchecked paper system." In 1836, Ohio Democrats forced through the legislature a prohibition of issuance of bank notes under $5. These moves were only intimations of future developments. Up to this point the demands for bank expansion had come from a bipartisan group of entrepreneurs "who realized the necessity of eastern capital to develop the financial system of the state."[19]

# 3

Constitutional restrictions limited both Indiana and Illinois to the establishment of state banks with branches. Earlier state banks had failed, leaving both states with a motley and depreciated "foreign" currency issued by the banks of other states, in addition to the notes of the Bank of the United States. Even before Jackson vetoed the rechartering of the national bank, the unstable currency had caused both legislatures to propose new state banks. Following the veto, the demand for such institutions to regulate

---

* The dogma of strict construction asserted that because only gold and silver are mentioned in the Constitution, they are the currency dictated by the Founding Fathers. This seems to have been based on a confusion of sections 8 and 10 of article 1. Section 8 gives Congress the power to coin money and regulate its value. Section 10 prohibits states from issuing bills of credit and making anything but gold and silver legal tender.

the local currency and fill the vacuum left by retirement of the national bank's notes proved irresistible. Indiana chartered a state bank in 1834 and Illinois created a similar institution the following year. In both instances support for a state bank was bipartisan.

In Indiana the Bank of the United States supplied most of the currency and was supported by all political factions. The bank's own notes were sound and the pressure it exerted on the banks in the states had a stabilizing effect on their issue. Many feared that without the national bank, the currency would go unregulated, "local paper would overflow the land and swindling [would] be in 'order' everywhere." Following Jackson's bank veto, Indiana's Whig governor, Noah Noble, called on the legislature to ease

> the severe pecuniary embarrassment under which, almost every class of our citizens are labouring . . . [and] prevent the further aggravation of the evils of a decreasing circulation . . . [by] the establishment of a State Bank.

In response John Ewing, a state senator from Vincennes, prepared a report that suggested several solutions. Among them was the creation of a state bank, and several such bills were introduced. Although all senators believed that something had to be done, none agreed on the form the legislation should take. After a vigorous debate, action was finally postponed by a single vote.[20] There was a general fear that the closing of the Bank of the United States would cause money to be tight and interest rates high. Members of both parties looked to a state bank to solve these problems. There was no party division on the issue in 1833. Throughout the year Democrats as well as Whigs worked to elect advocates of a state bank to the new legislature. Probank meetings were held throughout the state, and the *Indiana Democrat* urged voters to make sure that their candidates for the legislature supported a state bank. The 1833 election brought a large number of new faces into the legislature, and both parties interpreted the result as a mandate for a state bank. Noble again called for its establishment, and a new bill drawn up by Ewing quickly

29

passed. It created a mixed corporation composed of ten branches responsible to a bank board that met in Indianapolis. This "bank of branches," as it was called by its future president Hugh Mc-Culloch because it had no dominant parent institution, became one of the strongest and best-run banks in the country.[21]

Most of the proponents of the state bank took the position that the destruction of the Bank of the United States made the establishment of such an institution "absolutely necessary." Governor Noble believed it "rather a matter of necessity than choice." "If ever the state of society in a pecuniary point of view, demanded legislative interference," one supporter told the legislature, "it is the present." Legislators intended to create a conservative bank to serve the state's legitimate needs and generally showed a fear of "shaving shops," which dealt at a discount in the currency of other states.[22]

Yet the parties were badly split on the issue, and the state bank was not the exclusive creation of either party. Several Democratic legislators attacked the bill as forming the basis of a political machine; and there was also some hard money sentiment, which opposed all banks as unnecessary. However, these views represented only a minority of Democratic opinion. The leading organ of the Democracy, the *Indiana Democrat*, backed the bill and attacked its opponents as "low politicians," who either preferred wildcat banking or hard money. Thomas Brown, a Tippecanoe County Democrat, reasoned that a state bank would keep Indiana from paying "tribute to the [depreciated] paper of other states," and insisted the bill would aid "the farmer [more] than any other class in the community."[23]

Whigs were also divided on the issue. A small group favored free banking and opposed the bill. Others feared that a state bank would be a dangerous political machine, lead to a depreciated currency, or interfere with the rechartering of the national bank. But the majority of Indiana Whigs favored the state bank and hoped that it would "materially change the face of things by the impetus it will give to trade and relief it will afford to the needy and oppressed." The leading Whig paper, the *Indiana Journal*, constantly advocated a state bank from the time of Jackson's bank

30

veto; and the men most responsible for the successful establishment of the state bank, Governor Noble, John Ewing, George
Profitt, Samuel Bigger, and George Dunn, were all Whigs by the
mid-1830s.[24]

In the legislature the bill passed both houses easily, with the
majority of both parties supporting it. Contemporary observers
reported that representatives from rural constituencies were less
favorable to the bill than their urban counterparts, but the division ran across rather than along party lines. Even Joseph Wright,
later a leader of the radical, antibank faction of the Democracy
gave the bill his hearty support.[25]

Illinois was the most solidly Jacksonian state in the Old Northwest, and the same pressures at work in Indiana also operated in
Illinois. The state's political situation during these years was
fluid, but the state bank cannot be seen as either a party issue or
as an issue related to the Jacksonian factional conflict.

Hostility to the first state bank in Illinois led to Judge John
Reynolds's election as governor in 1830 as an antibank candidate.
A member of the moderate "milk and cider" faction of the Jacksonians, he appealed to both Jackson and anti-Jackson groups.
During his term in office, two bipartisan attempts to charter a
new state institution were narrowly defeated in legislatures dominated by the "whole hog" Jacksonian faction, who had been more
extreme in their support of the Old Hero in the 1820s.[26]

Both supporters and opponents of Jackson continued to advocate a state bank. Jacksonian leaders William May and William
Ewing called for a bank; and in the fall of 1833 the leading Jackson paper in the state, the *Illinois State Register*, joined those demanding the legislature to act. While somewhat more skeptical,
the anti-Jacksonian *Sangamo Journal* also supported a state bank
to replace the currency withdrawn by the closing of the Bank
of the United States and to free Illinois from dependence on the
paper of other states. It agreed with the *Alton American* that the
whole matter "should be examined with the utmost care."[27]

The bank issue played only a minor role in the gubernatorial
election of 1834, in which Lieutenant Governor William C. Kinney, who had been Reynolds's "whole hog" and probank oppo-

nent in 1830, was pitted against Congressman Joseph Duncan.
A third candidate, R. K. McLaughlin, warned against the repetition of the "bank mania" of 1816 to 1818. But neither Kinney nor
Duncan discussed a state bank, and the election turned on other
issues.[28]

Economic distress in 1834 and the increasing need for credit
and currency encouraged further demands for a state bank. Both
the *Illinois State Register* and the *Sangamo Journal* called for the
creation of a state bank, as did acting governor Ewing and the
newly elected governor, Joseph Duncan.[29]

Duncan, who eventually became a Whig, had been the Jacksonian congressman from Illinois during Reynolds's term as governor. A "whole hog" Jackson man in the 1820s, he continued to
call himself a "true Jacksonian" after he broke with the administration. He opposed Jackson's strict-constructionist attitudes on
internal improvements and supported the Bank of the United
States; yet he believed that all banks "were to some extent monopolies, and, therefore, inconsistent with the true spirit of our
free institutions." However, in 1834 he did suggest a state bank,
but with less confidence than his Jacksonian predecessor. He
feared Illinois could not construct a safe institution. (After the
bank bill passed, he opposed it in the Council of Revision. Had
he been able to veto the measure, he would have, because it provided insufficient security for the billholder.)[30]

In response to public pressure and the recommendations of
Ewing and Duncan, the 1834–35 legislature created a state bank
and revived two defunct chartered banks. An examination of these
votes shows that party lines were not observed on banking issues
during these years. The state bank bill, which had the support of
the leading newspapers of both parties and which had been introduced by Ewing, then a state senator, received bipartisan backing in both houses. But on this question and on the extension of
the charter of the Bank of Illinois at Shawneetown, established
when Illinois was still a territory, each party split between those
favoring *both* a state bank and the chartered bank and those opposing all banks. Exactly the same proportion (42%) of each
party in the assembly supported all banks, while a slightly higher

proportion of Whigs (42%) than Democrats (40%) opposed both the state bank and the Bank of Illinois at Shawneetown. Similarly, in the senate four Democrats and three Whigs supported both measures, while five Democrats and two Whigs opposed them. There were probably more antibank Democrats in Illinois than any other state in the Old Northwest, but antibank attitudes were shared by many Whigs. The antibank stance was related to the state's experience rather than to partisan attitudes. At the same time, it was the desperate needs of a growing state that undoubtedly led some who would later violently oppose banks to support them in 1835. Young Stephen A. Douglas explained, "I am no friend to the Banking System but on the contrary am in favor of real *Bentonian Shiners* [specie]; but under the existing circumstances a Bank may be necessary in this State in self-defense."[31]

## 4

Although overshadowed during this period by the idea of a single state bank, free banking presented a potential for financial expansion without the allegation of monopoly associated with state banks and without the inefficiency of the traditional chartering process. Free banks were established under general laws that extended corporate privileges to groups who met certain general requirements. Free banking promised added security to billholders while allowing the capital-shy states of the young nation to monetize their own debts since they were required to deposit collateral usually in the form of state stocks with a state official to redeem their issue in case of failure. Free banking would eventually dominate in nineteenth-century America, and it would become the way in which each of the five states of the Old Northwest attempted to answer their banking needs.

After a period of bank expansion through traditional means, Michigan chose to undertake the nation's first experiment with free banking. While it was generally unsuccessful, the Michigan free banking law was a response to many of the same needs that generated demands for state banks. A close analysis of the political maneuvering related to this law reinforces the thesis that opposition to local banks was not a major tenet of Democratic orthodoxy in the 1830s.

In the 1820s and 1830s Michigan was a booming frontier community passing from the territorial stage into statehood. Its population rapidly increased as a steady stream of immigrants poured in, drawn by "the prospect of speedy and golden fortunes." Cities of the future were laid out on paper complete with "Hotels, warehouses and banks . . . like places in a fairy land; piers projected into harbors, and steamboats were seen entering." There seemed every reason to believe that Michigan, with its excellent "water advantages," might become one of the richest states in the Union. The new state government acted to provide the necessities for such development. In the brief period between drafting its constitution and its final acceptance as a state, the Michigan legislature organized 57 townships, provided for 66 state roads, chartered 11 railroads, and permitted erection of 13 dams to provide water for manufacturing.[32]

The greatest need was for banks to provide the necessary currency and credit to finance both speculation and development. After the early speculative enterprise called the Bank of Detroit had closed, there had been no bank in the territory until 1817, when the governor chartered the Bank of Michigan. The influx of population after the Erie Canal opened led the Territorial Council to charter eight more banks and a new branch of the Bank of Michigan between 1827 and 1835. Up to this point there existed little antibank sentiment, and leading Jacksonians were deeply involved in these institutions. During the 1820s, John R. Williams, who would be a member of the Democracy for the next two decades, presided over the Bank of Michigan. After an altercation with the directors led to his removal, Williams was replaced by Peter Desnoyers, another leading Jacksonian. Williams then became president of the Farmer's and Mechanic's Bank of Michigan.[33]

The Bank of Michigan became a depository of federal funds in 1831 and remained one throughout the 1830s, although Desnoyers was succeeded in the presidency by two Whigs, Eurotas P. Hastings and C. C. Trowbridge. During this period out-of-state Whigs held the great majority of stock in the bank, but the largest local stockholder was Democrat Lewis Cass. In 1834, at the urging of the popular senator John Norvell, the Farmer's and Mechanic's Bank also became a federal depository. According to Norvell, Democrats at this time made up 90% of the directors. Interestingly, John Biddle, brother of the president of the Bank of the United States, eventually became president of this Democratic "pet."[34]

With the aid of Thomas Olcott and Erastus Corning, capitalists connected with Martin Van Buren's Albany Regency, John R. Williams founded the privately owned Michigan State Bank which was chartered in 1835. In the East the bank's stock eventually fell into Whig hands. However, in Michigan cashier and Democrat John Norton, a close friend of Governor Stevens T. Mason, controlled the bank; and it numbered among its borrowers most leading Jacksonians in the state. Eventually Whigs centered their attacks on this bank as the "pet" of the Democratic state administration.[35]

The debates over the new state constitution in 1835 showed little conflict concerning banking. The convention wished to eliminate the multiplication of banks, so it unanimously adopted the 1821 New York constitutional proviso that bank charters must receive a two-thirds majority in the legislature. An attempt by Peter Ferry of Monroe County to outlaw all corporations lost 56 to 9 in the Jacksonian-dominated convention. The 9 positive votes, moreover, did not all belong to Democrats, and included John Biddle! John McDonell, a Wayne County Democrat, tried to have the convention sanction, or at least leave the way open for, a state bank; but the convention soundly defeated this proposal 57 to 19.[36]

Little partisan conflict appeared on the question of requiring banks to provide collateral security to support their note issue. A committee dominated by Democrats and led by the Democrat Lucius Lyon prepared the report suggesting this reform. The convention vote defeating the proposal 48 to 27 defies partisan interpretation. There was no discernible split between the groups historians have termed the "radical" and the "conservative" Democrats; men who would be involved in nearly every faction of the subsequent party structure joined to defeat the motion.[37]

A Democratic administration, with Stevens T. Mason as governor and an overwhelming Democratic majority in both branches of the legislature, took office in late 1835. Historian Floyd Streeter characterized this administration as controlled by "the poor and radical element" and "hostile to monopolies and vested interests . . . [wishing] to break down the power of monied men in politics." While the rhetoric of Governor Mason lends support to this interpretation, the actions of the new government do not. In 1836, under the restrictive banking provision of the constitution, this antimonopoly legislature chartered nine new banks; and in no case did the governor, who warned against the multiplication of such enterprises, veto a charter. The thirst for credit was general and widespread, limited to no single party or faction.[38]

Various attempts to provide further security for billholders and to strengthen the state's banking system also revealed little anti-bank sentiment. A safety-fund law like that of New York, which required banks to contribute to a general fund to protect noteholders, received solid support from Jacksonians; but an attempt by "conservative" Democrats John Clark, Edward Ellis, and John Barry to extend the liability of both directors and stockholders was soundly defeated.[39]

In mid-1836 the *Detroit Democratic Free Press* began reprinting articles from New York papers advocating a repeal of restraining laws on banking and following the New York debate on free banking with some consistency. However, it can hardly be said that "the poor cried out against" banks and demanded free banking. Sometimes cast in antibank or loco-foco rhetoric, the pressure for free banks in Michigan came mainly from the entrepreneurial desire for extended credit facilities. The choice of articles reprinted by the *Democratic Free Press*, which was not hesitant in making clear its contempt for the rabid opposition to banks, revealed the party's purpose. Mostly from upstate Democratic papers, but also including a smattering of Whig editorials, these reprinted articles represented the entrepreneurial element of the New York controversy. They emphasized removal of restrictions that limited banking to large investors and excluded "the small capitalist . . . that is the mechanic with his $100." The supposed western distrust of banks often said to be typical of the frontier was completely absent.[40]

The state Whig organ, the *Detroit Daily Advertiser*, made little comment on the New York debate, and agreed for once with Governor Mason that banking privileges should not be extended. "We believe the people are opposed to it.—As for the importunate beggars of privileges," wrote the Whig paper, "there is no satisfying them. They must be refused first to last. Too many banks have been granted already."[41]

But the clamor for banks would not be stilled. Each new town, whether actually established or merely "on paper," demanded banking facilities. Further demands came from people deeply indebted by speculative and developmental enterprises, who hoped that additional banking resources would provide relief. A contemporary legislator later recalled,

> the public seemed imbued with the idea that to relieve them from the galling burden of indebtedness, and to restore activity and prosperity to the business world, nothing was needed but extensive bank issues.

In January 1837 the legislature was faced with 18 requests for new bank charters. This flood of demands for banking privileges led to the passage of Michigan's free banking law.[42]

After failure of an earlier senate bill, Edwin Lothrop, a Kalamazoo Democrat and chairman of the Committee on Banks and Incorporations, introduced the bill that eventually became Michigan's free banking law in the assembly. It easily passed, 39 to 4; and several weeks later it passed in the senate, 14 to 1. The main opposition in the lower house came from "conservative" Democrat Alpheus Felch, who feared its inflationary character. Its single opponent in the senate was John McDonell, a member of the supposedly "radical" Mason-Norvell fraction, who constantly advocated a state bank and believed free banking a "hazardous experiment."[43]

The free banking law of Michigan was passed, with little dissent, by a legislature in which, according to Streeter, "a majority of the members were Democrats representing poor and radical constituents." The only opposition came from individuals within the Democratic party who feared the inflationary consequences of the bill. As in the constitutional convention of 1835, no consistent partisan or factional consensus appeared in the voting. Such future antibank Democrats as John Barry and Kinsley Bingham favored the law. The Democratic press supported the law and the Whigs generally refrained from attacking it. The Whig *Daily Advertiser* announced the bill to its readers in an article that differed little from that in the *Democratic Free Press*, although it noted, "the associations thus authorized are fenced around with such restrictions as may, and we hope will serve for the security of the public." In the same issue the Whig paper supported the popular desire to change the New York banking system to remove "monopoly and the other political abuses which have grown up under it" by implementing free banking.[44]

# 5

During the 1830s, even after Jackson's bank veto, state banking in the Old Northwest met little opposition and the entrepreneurial spirit dominated. Nearly every portion of that area demanded banking facilities. Neither party was immune to these demands. Nevertheless, partisan division on the banking issue was beginning to form. Whigs tended to look favorably upon banking expansion, and the party harbored practically no hard money men. Most advocated moderate expansion of the number of banks through the traditional chartering process, although a number, at least in Indiana and Michigan, supported free banking. More often than their opponents, Whigs defended a national bank; but many Jacksonians in the Northwest also advocated such an institution. Some members of both parties therefore remained opposed to banks until the demise of the Bank of the United States left them no alternative. The majority of Democrats supported banking in some form. The hard money, antibank sentiment that did exist was lodged within the Democracy; but before 1837 this was a minority view within the party and within the Northwest generally. A hard money stance did not constitute Democratic orthodoxy at this time. Nearly every important party leader who would fight for the "constitutional currency" of gold and silver in the 1840s—John Barry, Moses Strong, Moses Dawson, Stephen A. Douglas, Joseph Wright—supported banks in some form in the 1830s.

The only connected issue that clearly divided the parties was the elimination of small bills, notes under $5. This was a reform urged by President Jackson. In Indiana and Illinois, Democrats added this restriction to laws creating state banks. Ohio Democrats passed a similar prohibition in 1836 over the Whigs' nearly unanimous opposition. In Michigan, a coalition of Democrats and Whigs defeated attempts to add such a prohibition to the free banking law. The demand for prohibition of small notes indicated an uneasiness in the Democratic party about paper money—even paper money easily convertible into specie—that would grow into open hostility. But hard money sentiments did not dominate the party until the Panic of 1837 and the subsequent depression, which altered the political and economic situation.

# CHAPTER 2

## PARTY PERCEPTION OF THE PANIC OF 1837

### 1

The Panic of 1837 and the subsequent depression significantly altered political attitudes toward banks as each party read its own meaning into the course of events. In order to exonerate Jackson, the Democrats found it necessary—and logical given the rhetoric of the "Bank War"—to blame the nation's banking system for the crisis. The Whigs developed a contrary interpretation of the causes of the crisis, which emphasized Jackson's responsibility. These interpretations originated with the national leaders of the party, but soon spread to the Old Northwest, where they formed the basis for the ensuing debate over banking in the states.

### 2

Although it had not been an issue in his election in 1828, Andrew Jackson, who had a long-standing distrust of banks and paper money, included a brief passage in his first annual message questioning the constitutionality and the expediency of the Bank of the United States. The following year he presented his own rather vague plan for an alternative to the bank; but his party was split, and cabinet members and some of Jackson's closest friends and advisors informed Nicholas Biddle, the president of the bank, that a modified charter might be acceptable. Although a revised charter passed both houses by healthy majorities in 1832, Jackson exercised the veto; then, following the nullification crisis, he "carried the war into Africa," ordering the removal of the government deposits from the Bank of the United States.[1]

The president's bank veto message, penned in the main by Amos Kendall, a long-time foe of the bank, was a masterpiece of political propaganda, which set the tone for Democratic rhetoric during the entire antebellum period. While in it the president said little about returning to a specie currency, he damned the bank as aristocratic, antirepublican, and a threat to the moral fiber of the society. Its destruction would mean a return to the true course of the Founding Fathers, a revival of "industry, economy and virtue" among the people, and simplicity and economy in government.[2]

While the veto message was successful in its intention to sway the emotions of the members of the diverse coalition making up Jackson's following, it provided no economic blueprint for the future. The destruction of the Bank of the United States left Jackson with no fully formed alternative policy. Gradually he and his closest advisers moved to reform and stabilize the nation's financial system by eliminating bank notes under $20 and by encouraging the wider circulation and use of specie. The administration's hard money policy was aided by the appearance of William Gouge's *Short History of Paper Money and Banking in the United States* in 1833. This book offered both a justification for hard money and the outlines of a program. The following year Secretary of the Treasury Roger B. Taney presented to Congress the Jacksonian program to rid the country of the "paper money system." All connection between the Bank of the United States and the government should be severed. Legislation should be enacted that revised the legal relationship of gold and silver to promote the circulation of gold. Legislation should also ban the issue of small notes by the deposit banks in order to restrain their issue and to place the fiscal affairs on a more nearly strictly specie basis.[3]

In achieving these goals the administration had only moderate success. In 1834, Congress passed the coinage act revaluing gold in terms of silver and prohibited government agents from making disbursements in currency that was less than par value. The following year the treasury established a policy of accepting no bills under $5 for land purchases and indicated that in the future this prohibition would be extended to bills under $10. In 1836 government disbursements were limited to bills over $10 and March 3, 1837, was set as the date on which this floor would be raised to exclude all bills under $20. At the end of 1836, Jackson praised this legislation, along with those state laws that eliminated small notes, for "restoring to the country the sound currency provided for in the Constitution." He hoped that more salutary legislation of this type would be forthcoming from both Congress and the states.[4]

Unfortunately for the administration, its proposals for further federal control of the deposit system were blocked in Congress. The "experiment" with the "pet" banks, which Jackson never really liked, inadvertently compounded the inflationary spiral of the mid-1830s and frustrated the long-range financial goals of the hard money Democrats. Perceiving this, Jackson acted to limit the expansion of the banking system and place the federal government's transactions on a specie basis. The Specie Circular issued by Secretary of the Treasury Levi Woodbury on July 16, 1836, provided that public lands must be paid for in either gold or silver. In this way "the monopoly of the public lands" would give way to settlements by "actual Settlers," and "the ruinous extension of bank issues and credits" upon which speculation was based would be discouraged. Jackson praised the Specie Circular in December because "it checked the career of the Western banks and gave them additional strength in anticipation of the pressure which has since pervaded our Eastern [financial centers] as well as European commercial cities." Jackson ignored the adverse effects of the Specie Circular.[5]

Certainly it is now clear that exterior circumstances account for both the inflation of the mid-1830s and the subsequent depression. Yet Jackson's policies made it difficult for the financial system to respond in any constructive way to the crisis. The

Specie Circular caused an increased demand for specie in the interior. The land offices there could only reply by attempting to draw specie from the eastern financial centers. But this pressure upon the eastern banks came at a time when they were faced with an unfavorable international situation, the primary cause of the nation's later financial problems. America's main creditor, England, underwent a rapid banking expansion in the 1830s. As loans to the "country banks" and investment houses increased, a drain on the gold reserve of the Bank of England forced that institution to raise its discount rate in July 1836 to 4½%. Eventually the bank moved to curtail the activities of merchants and bankers, particularly those deeply involved in American trade. This might have caused little alarm had it not been for the United States' unfavorable balance of trade at this time. The boom of the 1830s encouraged increased purchases of foreign goods by Americans; and the "mania" for internal improvements flooded the English market with state bonds. At the same time grain crops, which might have balanced this movement of goods and capital as exports, were so poor that the United States actually imported wheat in 1836. In this financial climate the most important effect of the Specie Circular was psychological. According to economist Peter Temin, "Even though the economic impact of the Specie Circular was small, it was still an important indicator of the government's attitude." Thus it fed the public distrust of banks and broke down mutual confidence within the banking community. In the West, far from strengthening the banks as Jackson had hoped by giving them a broader specie basis, it struck at the basis of bank circulation: the belief that the notes would be accepted at the land offices.[6]

The problems of the banking system were accentuated by the Deposit Act of 1836, which implemented restrictions on the deposit banks and proposed a distribution of surplus revenue of the federal government to the states. Although the consequences of this act have often been overestimated, they should not be totally discounted, particularly when dealing with the Old Northwest. At the time the structure of the American banking system was inadequate to make the necessary intersectional and intrasectional transfers without a serious disruption in the normal flow of business. The government responded by trying to keep intersectional transfers to a minimum and was partially successful. Enough specie was moved, however, to cause a decline in reserves and a general contraction.[7]

The Deposit Act, passed by a coalition of Whigs and Democrats against the advice of Jackson and Woodbury, stimulated state investments in internal improvements. Hoping to aid Van Buren in the West, where the bill was popular, Jackson refused to veto it, but he presented his objections in his December message. He based his opposition on strict construction of the Constitution, states' rights, and an abhorrence of a national debt. Jackson showed little or no awareness of the economic problems involved or the degree to which the western banks might be hurt. Yet Chief Justice Roger B. Taney had written to him in October that the mercantile community, which was indebted to the deposit banks, had been hurt when these banks were forced to call their loans to make the transfers of government deposits. Taney had added that the mercantile classes would foolishly blame Jackson's policies when it was in reality their own folly that had caused their distress.

> The currency will however be always liable to these ruinous fluctuations while it continues to be of paper, and nothing will cure the evil but the success of your great plan of restoring the Constitutional currency of Gold and silver.[8]

The whole financial structure suffered under the severe strains caused by the policies of the Bank of England and compounded by the Specie Circular and the Deposit Act. Against this background, the collapse of prices early in 1837 led to the commercial and financial panic that precipitated the suspension of specie payments by the nation's banks in May of that year. Although New Orleans and New York were hard hit in 1837, and business was dull everywhere, agricultural areas and some manufacturing areas were not badly hurt. The following year brought improved conditions and the resumption of specie payments based on British credit, which was again expanding. The situation, however, worsened in 1839. A reversal of the Bank of England's credit policies led to a second suspension of specie payments in October 1839. Depression had come to stay, and during the next four years the whole economy experienced one of the most severe setbacks in American history. A western editor wrote,

> Doubt, doom and despair seem to have taken possession of all classes—men of all parties are becoming alarmed at the state of things—one project after another is suggested to relieve the distress of the mercantile community; but without avail.[9]

Such financial disasters inevitably give rise to conjecture as to their causes. The keenest commentators of the day emphasized the effect of the Bank of England's credit policies, while they blamed the Jacksonian administration to a lesser or greater degree according to their general economic beliefs. Charles Francis Adams (who voted for Van Buren in 1836 and who later became a leader of the antislavery element of the Whig, then the Republican parties) presented a relatively nonpartisan analysis. The crisis of 1837, according to Adams, resulted from borrowing European capital. This could only have been handled adequately if the country had been free from the vast speculative debt caused by the undue expansion of the state banking systems. He held Jackson

> highly responsible, not for the present state of things, inasmuch as in this trading country it is always more or less likely to happen, but for the defenseless condition into which the government of the Union, intrusted to him for very different ends, has been thrown by it. It was the voluntary withdrawal of the *beneficial* inflence of the national power over currency which threw away all control over private and corporate cupidity, for which he must answer.[10]

Most contemporary analyses were not as balanced as that of Adams, and two conflicting conceptions of the causes of the depression were advanced by the parties contesting for power. Both parties asserted that there was some evil agent corrupting the proper functioning of the economic system. For the Democrats it was the "bank speculators," who sought to control the supply of currency and to expand and contract it to their own advantage. The Democrats defended the president's policies, thus having to fall back on a general theory of business cycles that laid the blame on the speculative expansion of banks. William Leggett and the loco-focos of New York offered this interpretation in moral terms well suited to explain political defeats as the result of "bank influence" and corruption. For the Whigs the depression was "the result of the wickedness, blunders and ignorance of our rulers." Jackson's policies had been like "setting a Blacksmith to mending a watch with a sledge hammer." The Whigs had all along warned that Jacksonian financial policies, in particular the destruction of the Bank of the United States, would be financially ruinous. They exploited the issue, laying the blame for the depression entirely on Jackson's policies and joining in a call for a national bank of some sort. Usually they interpreted electoral success as repudiation of the policies of the Democrats.[11]

Henry Clay made the classic statement of the Whig interpretation in his speech on the Independent Treasury bill. "Prior to that series of unfortunate measures" instituted by Jackson, "no people on earth enjoyed a better currency, or had exchanges better regulated, than the people of the United States." But in 1837 the country was endangered by the prospect of an irredeemable paper currency.

> Can it be doubted that it is the result of those measures to which I have averred? When at the very moment of adopting them, the very consequences which have happened were foretold as inevitable, is it necessary to look elsewhere for their cause? Never was prediction more distinctly made; never was fulfillment more literal and exact.

Clay attacked an argument advanced by Van Buren that because Europe, especially Britain, had also suffered "embarrassment," the crisis could not have been the result of Jackson's policies. For Clay the telling point was that the "degree of embarrassment has been marked, in commercial countries there by the degree of their connection with the United States." The great failures had been among those houses engaged in the American trade. Britain, which had been the most involved with the United States, had been worst hit, followed by France—"And so on in the order of their greater or less commercial intercourse with us." The fact remained that the intensity of suffering in the United States exceeded that of any other country. This, Clay argued, indicated that this country suffered from "some peculiar and more potent causes" than any operating in Europe. These were

> 1st. The veto of the bank. 2nd. The removal of deposits, with the urgent injunction of Secretary Taney upon the banks to enlarge their accommodations. 3rd. The gold bill, and the demand for gold for foreign indemnities. 4th. The clumsy execution of the deposit law; and 5th. The Treasury order of July, 1836.[12]

Clay's speech included most of the themes of the Whig interpretation. Vetoing the new charter of the Bank of the United States had meant the loss of its salutary effects on the currency and the abdication of federal control over the banks. Removing the federal deposits had resulted in the bank expansion of the mid-1830s. Although expansion had been encouraged, the mishandling of the distribution and the Specie Circular had struck at the entire banking system and had led to depression. It was a clear question of the misuse of power by the executive.

The Democratic conception of the causes of the panic and depression rested on a general theory relating the business cycle to bank issues. Gouge had formulated this theory in his *Short History of Paper Money*, which had influenced the administration's policies; but its most important and influential exponent was Jackson himself. While emphasizing the corruption of the Bank of the United States, the president censured *all* banks as harmful to the interests of the "producing classes,"* as "undermining the purity

---

* The phrase "producing classes" was standard fare in the political rhetoric of the period and was often used interchangeably with "useful classes" or "industrious classes." The emphasis was on productiveness or usefulness rather than on class, either in a Marxist or modern sociological sense. It was thus a very flexible term that could include nearly all occupational groups. Both parties upheld the sanctity of the "producing classes," but the Democrats increasingly defined bankers as unproductive parasites while the Whigs often used this rhetorical gambit to attack Democratic politicians and place-

and complicating the simplicity of our virtuous Government. . . ."
Taney had urged Jackson to attack the reckless expansions of the
"paper making corporations and speculators." Both Jackson's annual message in December 1836 and his Farewell Address in
March 1837 struck at the evils of the "paper system." The annual
message set forth the indictment of paper-issuing banks in its classic form:

> When thus, by the depreciation in consequence of the quantity of
> paper in circulation, wages as well as prices become exorbitant, it
> is soon found that the whole effect of the adulteration is a tariff
> on our home industry for the benefit of the countries where gold
> and silver circulate and maintain uniformity and moderation in
> prices. It is then perceived that the enhancement of the price in
> land and labor produces a corresponding increase in the price
> of products until these products do not sustain a competition with
> similar ones in other countries, and thus manufactured and agri-
> cultural productions cease to bear exportation for the cost. This is
> the process by which specie is banished by the paper of the
> banks. Their vaults are soon exhausted to pay for foreign com-
> modities. The next step is a stoppage of specie payment—a total
> degradation of paper as currency—unusual depression of prices,
> the ruin of debtors, and the accumulation of property in the
> hands of creditors and cautious capitalists.[13]

Jackson's personal animosity to banks and the paper system was
more visceral than his formal speeches would indicate. He re-
garded the suspension and the depression itself as part of the conspiracy by the monied interests, led by the president of the Bank
of the United States, Nicholas Biddle, to control the government
in their own interests and to undermine true republicanism. In
mid-1837 he wrote to his friend Moses Dawson, the Jacksonian
editor of the *Cincinnati Advertiser,*

> Is it possible that any true republican of talents and experience
> can have confidence in Banks as a safe repository of the public
> revenue after witnessing *their late* treacherous *conduct to the*
> government joining in league with Biddle and the Bearings to

men. The importance of this difference in usage will become clear in the
following chapters.

Bankrupt the government, degrade its character, both at home
and abroad. . . .

The only proper regulation of the currency could come from "a
strict specie policy."[14]

Although Martin Van Buren's inaugural address in March following his election hardly mentioned banking, his September,
1837 message to the special session of Congress set forth the official party position on the causes of the depression:

> The present condition is chiefly to be attributed to overaction in
> all departments of business—an overaction deriving, perhaps, its
> first impulses from antecedent causes, but stimulated to its de-
> structive consequences by excessive issues of bank paper and by
> other facilities for the acquisition and enlargement of credit.

"Redundancy of credit" and the spirit of speculation it engendered led to an increased foreign debt, unwise investments in
"unproductive public lands" at inflated prices, "improvident" expenditures of "immense sums" on internal improvements; "the di-
version to the pursuits of much of the labor that should have been
applied to agriculture," making it necessary to import grain; and
the encouragement "among all classes, and especially in our great
commercial towns of luxurious habits founded too often in merely fancied wealth, and detrimental alike to the industry, the resources, and the morals of our people."[15]

Van Buren's message was mildly worded and far from an antibank diatribe, but it contained all of the themes then current in
the Democratic literature. Business fluctuations, in general, and
the Panic of 1837, in particular, were caused by the paper money
system. In their greed for profit, banks expanded credit beyond
a "natural" amount. This led to a general rise in the price level,
which engendered a false sense of wealth. The spirit of speculation increased and undermined habits of thrift. Once this hap-
pened, the moral fiber of society was weakened. Formerly
virtuous young men left the professions of their fathers for the improvident life of the speculator and developed luxurious tastes
that could only be satisfied by the products of a depraved Europe.

This caused a decrease in the basic products of the United States and an adverse balance of trade, which led to the withdrawal of specie and, eventually, to economic embarrassment.

The *Democratic Review*, which had recently been formed as a vehicle of the "radical" wing of the Democracy, assented to the president's views and searched for "the Moral of the Crisis." Clearly the nation was suffering retribution for some "great national error." The crisis was the "fruit of the seed planted by sin." All the nation's suffering proceeded from the banking system. The crisis was "the legitimate consequence, and the just penalty, of our departure from the true principles of democratic *equality of rights* and *freedom of trade*, in the adoption of the system."[16]

# 3

In each of the states of the Old Northwest, the Democratic press and the Democratic politicians developed the Jacksonian view of the depression, although in some cases this Democratic interpretation of national events contradicted the Democratic policy on the local level. In Michigan, Democrats were intimately connected with banks and the multiplication of banks resulting from the free banking act they had sponsored. Nevertheless, the party's immediate reaction to the panic was to absolve Jackson by blaming the "pecuniary embarrassment" on the spirit of speculation the banks' "excessive" issuance of paper money had fostered. The 1837 Democratic platform supported a continuation of the national government's attempts "to introduce a greater amount of specie into our circulating medium." Governor Mason had warned against overbanking in January. In his message to the extra session of the legislature in June 1837, he ascribed the "crisis of the moneyed affairs of the country" to the "one fatal error into which the country has fallen . . . overbanking."[17]

The *Detroit Democratic Free Press* praised the opening of the new banks and attacked what it called the Whig "panic makers" in late 1836 and early 1837. On May 10, 1837, the paper somewhat prematurely announced that the panic was over. While con-

tinuing to defend Michigan's banks, particularly those set up under the free banking act, the *Democratic Free Press* slowly shifted
its ground. By mid-summer it asserted that "all sagacious men of
both parties have long been anticipating the difficulties in the
money market, in consequence of the unwise legislation of Congress and the states in regards to banking." The paper printed a
report of the Democratic members of the New York legislature
denying the Whig charges that the veto of the Bank of the United
States and the Specie Circular had been responsible for the panic.
The report blamed overtrading, speculation, the heavy foreign
debt, and the measures of the Bank of England. In July a discussion of the causes of the panic presented the standard Democratic interpretation, emphasizing overtrading, overbanking, speculation in land, and the distribution bill, which caused specie to
be retained in state treasuries, thereby forcing the state banks to
contract. Throughout the year Democratic papers attacked Nicholas Biddle and his "wildcat" bank and associated the Whigs
with those banks most responsible for the crisis. Although both
the *Democratic Free Press* and the *Constantine Republican* admitted that the Democrats had played an active role in granting
bank charters, both insisted that the Whigs made up a larger proportion of bank men and speculators, since Whigs were wealthy
while Democrats were farmers and workingmen. The *Democratic
Free Press* asserted,

> The truth is the spirit of stock-gambling and desperate specula-
> tion, in which the Whig aristocracy have borne the principal
> share, has been almost the exclusive cause of the multiplication of
> worthless local banks without specie capital, and without any
> substantial basis, for securing public confidence, on prompt re-
> demption of their bills.[18]

Only in Michigan was the Democratic response to the panic so
ambiguous. A sizable faction of the Ohio Democracy was antibank in the 1830s; but in general the party had supported state
banking, and most of the charters for Ohio banks were secured
from Democratic legislatures. Nonetheless, all factions of the
party accepted the Jacksonian interpretations of the causes of

51

the panic and unequivocally condemned state banks. In January the Democratic meeting of Delaware County blamed the depression on the Bank of the United States and state banks. Two months later the *Ohio Statesman* reprinted an article from the *Washington Globe*, "Democratic Creed in Relation to Banks, State and National," which blamed the state banks for the depression. In his annual message of 1839, Democratic Governor Wilson Shannon presented the party position on the cause of the crisis. An adverse balance of payments had resulted from an "overgrown system of banking," which had multiplied currency beyond "the real business wants of the community," inflating domestic prices and making importation favorable. The following year he expanded this to include the standard arguments concerning the relation between paper money and speculation, unnecessary debts, and extravagance. The importation of breadstuffs in 1836 had made the United States "tributary to Europe for the necessities of life by means of this artificial, anti-American system." Thomas W. Bartley, who served out Shannon's second term, echoed this interpretation in 1844.[19]

Throughout this period the leading Jacksonian editors presented Jackson's interpretation of the depression to the people and attempted to associate the Whig party with the banks. Ohio's *Newark Advocate* charged that "the Banks are Whig children"; and the *Ohio Statesman* referred to Whig Governor Vance and his associates as a "knot of Bankers." To prove these charges Samuel Medary, the editor of the *Statesman*, computed that of 405 bank officials in the state, 341 were Whigs and only 64 were Democrats.[20]

In Illinois, there was much the same pattern. "Long John" Wentworth's *Chicago Democrat* connected the banks with the crisis, and the Whigs with the banks. Governor Thomas Carlin charged that the banks had brought "gloom and desolation" where "prosperity and happiness had existed." The banking system, which was "unsanctioned by any principle of republican virtue," was the only way to account for the "fluctuations" of the economy, which had created fictitious value, engendered a spirit of speculation, and turned the people from honest industry. Earlier he had attacked the "pernicious and corrupting influence upon the morals of the people" exerted by the suspension of specie payments.[21]

The situation in Indiana differed from other states, giving rise to some variations on the standard pattern. The Whigs had solid control of the state throughout the 1830s, and the State Bank of Indiana was one of the soundest and best-managed banks in the country. In the state senate the Democrats defended Jackson's policies and attacked those of the Whig state administration. They denied that the national government was responsible, asserting that the "present collapsed state" was "a necessary consequence of our former inflated condition." This condition could hardly have been the result of Jackson's policies since England as well as the United States was affected. This inflation was the result of the "vicious paper system," in particular of the Bank of the United States, which by contracting its issue had forced the state banks to expand, extravagantly multiplying the currency. They then developed the standard Democratic arguments, that the expansion had led to prodigal foreign spending and had "induced men of all classes to drop their lawful callings and to turn out into the great Maelstrom of reckless speculation."[22]

Democratic politicians seldom mentioned the State Bank of Indiana but rather emphasized that local circumstances peculiar to the state had aggravated the general crisis. In particular, Democrats attacked the internal improvements system of the Whigs, which provided for simultaneous construction of all internal improvements. It was "a system in fact conceived in sin, brought forth in iniquity, and attempted to be sustained by deception." It had undermined the credit of the state and crippled the state bank. Democrats concluded,

> Our depressed financial system in short has been produced by our own unwise system of internal improvements, by our more unwise manner of prosecuting it, and by the *most unwise* course pursued by our fund commissioners in trusting our state bonds to so large an amount in the hands of irresponsible and swindling corporations [the New York banks], and *not* as modestly suggested by Governor Wallace is it owing to the measures of Andrew Jackson or Martin Van Buren.[23]

53

The Democratic press of Indiana was somewhat less delicate, although it also avoided direct attacks on the state bank. By mid-1837 the standard Jacksonian interpretation of the crisis was current and William Gouge was the accepted authority on banking. The *Indiana Democrat* even quoted Stevens T. Mason, Michigan's young governor, authoritatively on the relation of over-banking to the crisis. Democratic journalists contrasted the Biddle-Whig currency of paper with the Jacksonian-Democratic currency of gold and silver, and attacked the Whigs as the bank party. Attempts were made to prove that not just in Indiana but nationally the Whigs were the bank party, and Medary's figures from the *Ohio Statesman* on the political affiliation of Ohio bankers were widely circulated to support this contention.[24]

Throughout the Old Northwest the Whig press and the Whig politicians denied these charges and placed the blame for the crisis on Democratic financial policies. Whig governors joined in blaming the crisis on the "unhappy policy of the national government." Ohio's Governor Vance argued that

> it is not the amount of circulation that produces these evils, but the want of power to control, and judgment in the application of our means, by those who have the management of our financial system.

What was necessary was a well-regulated financial system capable of contraction and expansion according to the needs of a growing economy. Duncan, governor of Illinois, agreed that Congress should "regulate the currency, and restore it to its former sound condition and beneficent action" rather than try to escape the consequences of the Democratic policies "by amusing the people with the absurd and impracticable project of an exclusive hard money currency." In Indiana, Governor David Wallace's message on December 3, 1839, laid the blame for the "sudden blight which has come over our prospects" on the policies of Jackson's administration. His accusation touched off a lively debate over the causes of the depression. Democratic committees in the state senate and house answered Wallace, denying the administration's responsibility and urging the governor to tell the truth and to accept the consequences of his actions and those of his party. In the press Whigs countered these reports and asserted that the Democrats were completely wrong in their interpretation. The responsibility lay with Jackson. Samuel Judah, later to play a central role in the free banking movement, came to the defense of the Whig state administration. He argued that the distress was a national phenomenon; it could hardly be blamed on the Whig policies in Indiana.[25]

Although the Whigs emphasized the responsibility of the Jacksonian financial policies, they did not ignore the relationship of overbanking to the depression, and they were not uncritical of the state banks. In Illinois the Whigs constantly reminded the Democrats that they had voted overwhelmingly for the state bank but had tried as best they could to disconnect themselves from the institution. David Wallace in Indiana told his constituents that "experience teaches us the fearful lesson that there are limits beyond which if banking privileges and banking operations are carried, they cease to do good, and become engines of incalculable mischief." In Ohio, Governor Thomas Corwin readily admitted that banks, when not properly controlled, could cause dangerous fluctuations in the currency.[26]

It was in Michigan, however, that the Whigs vied with the Democrats in their damnation of banks. The *Detroit Daily Advertiser* believed that the spirit of speculation and overtrading had helped to produce the crisis, although "the great moving cause" had been the Specie Circular. The *Ann Arbor State Journal* condemned overbanking, connecting it with Jackson's policies not as "the cause of the present difficulties, but the effect, the legitimate and undeniable consequence of the fatuous acts of a party administration."[27]

In mid-1837 the *Daily Advertiser* began attacking Democratic policy, which, it argued, had caused the number of banks to increase, and turned the Jacksonian charges against the state's Democrats. A survey of bank presidents and cashiers showed the majority to be Democrats. The *Advertiser* added,

> The speculators are of all parties, but of one more than another, the most of the Van Buren party, because these had control of the

55

pet banks. Who form the great land companies of New York and of Washington? Ask the Butlers, ask Kendall, Blair and all that race.

According to the Whig paper, Michigan was suffering from a bank mania because the Democrats talked "gold humbug" but gave the people "a litter of infant monsters."[28]

The 1841 Whig platform in Michigan, three-fourths of which was devoted to banking and money questions, pulled together all the elements of the Whig interpretation. It set about to trace how the country that in 1829 had been "generally prosperous and happy" had come to its condition of "unparalleled embarrassment and distress." It argued that the causes were "the mismanagement, the improper and dangerous measures, the misconduct and corruption of our late rulers." It then noted:

> Our enemies say that all these things have been produced by the spirit of speculation which has prevailed, and by the great increase of Banks, and of a paper currency. But what stimulated this spirit of speculation and brought it into existence, and what caused the increase of Banks and paper currency? Who created these banks? . . . more than two-thirds of these banks were created by the loco foco party, mostly in the states of New York, Pennsylvania, Virginia, Ohio, Indiana, Louisiana, Alabama, Mississippi, Michigan, and a few others . . . the loco foco party created more than one hundred and fifty millions of dollars of State Bank capital, between the years of 1829 and 1838, and claimed to be the particular friends of State Banks. [They were in] opposition to a National Bank, until the general suspension and the great shock of 1837, when they suddenly renounced their own progeny, denounced all Banks and Bank paper, and became advocates of the Sub-Treasury, and specie currency.

What was needed was "a well regulated National Bank . . . to furnish the people of the United States a sound and uniform currency; to check the over issues of local State Banks, and to regulate the exchanges of the country. . . ."[29]

# 4

Each of these interpretations implied certain ideas about banks and their relation to a republican society. In the Jacksonians' view, the economic function of banks was subordinate to their social role. In the period following 1837, the structure of political symbolism that had been created during the "Bank War" was extended by the Democrats to cover all banks, so that the sins of the national bank became the sins of banks in general. The Jacksonians conceived of a republican social order in terms of simple decentralized government, "republican virtue," and the ultimate morality of agricultural labor. The United States represented all of these values in their minds, but they realized that the purity of their ideal had somehow been corrupted. It was banks that symbolized the corrupting influence in American society. They were the snake in the republican Garden of Eden.

Each of the positive values for which the Jacksonians stood found its negation in the banking system. Banks meant aristocracy rather than democracy. William Gouge had declared that "*a paper money aristocracy* [is] the only kind of aristocracy that can possibly exist in the United States" because of the impossibility of ecclesiastical, military, or landed aristocracies. The only aristocrats the Jacksonians saw were bankers. This "paper aristocracy" of bankers was the constant target of Jacksonian literature.[30]

Banks were said to endanger the existence of republican government. The purity of elections was soiled by "bank influence." Jacksonian defeats in the late 1830s and early 1840s, ascribed to bank influence, were proof of this. In particular, the allegation of bank influence in the New York elections of 1837 and 1838 was echoed throughout the Democratic press. Moreover, nearly all moral corruption was said to have its genesis in the banking system. By drawing laborers from agriculture and other virtuous occupations and employing them in nefarious activities Jacksonians subsumed under the rubric "speculation," banks undermined morality. They corrupted the youth of America and forced the most fertile land in the world to go begging among the potentates of Europe for foodstuffs.

This set of beliefs led to the demand for the "divorce of bank and state." The pure simplicity of republican government should no more be associated with the schemes of the bankers than with those of the clerics; the funds of the people should no more support the banks than the churches. Government would obstruct liberty once it became subservient to certain classes or interest groups. Only by purging from the government all such influences could republican simplicity be restored. "All communities are apt to look to government for too much," Van Buren told Congress. "The framers of our excellent Constitution . . . wisely judged that the less government interferes with private pursuits the better for general prosperity."[31]

The Whigs, on the other hand, viewed banks as a source of general prosperity for the community and an economic opportunity for the individual. Their main function was to supply the credit necessary for economic development. When properly used, they were valuable tools. Because they had been misused was no reason to discard them. In general this coincided with the Whig conception of the proper economic basis for a republican society. Whigs more readily accepted the function of business enterprise, emphasized the opportunity created by economic diversification and development, and saw the self-made man as the ideal citizen. While symbolic content was not absent, it was less central to the Whig than to the Democratic conception of banks. More important to the Whigs was the practicality of banks and the fact that through them the government shouldered its responsibility to aid enterprise. Most agreed with Webster:

> I feel as if I were on some other sphere, as if I were not at home, as if this could not be America when I see schemes of public policy proposed, having for this object the convenience of Government only, and leaving the people to shift for themselves.[32]

Although these interpretations and conceptions played a crucial role at the national level in the struggle over financial delays, they became more important when the Jacksonians succeeded in shifting the center of the banking struggle to what Van Buren called "the proper tribunal—the people of the States." The Democrats of the Old Northwest had not opposed state banks in the mid-1830s; and while they readily accepted the Jacksonian interpretation of the causes of the economic crisis, they were slow to embrace the administration's hard money policy. As political and economic problems multiplied, the logic of the Jacksonian interpretation of the depression eventually drove them to oppose all banks. In contrast, the Whig argument, which implicitly accepted governmental responsibility for economic progress and blamed presidential mismanagement for the crisis, led that party into a series of attempts at reform of the states' banking systems.[33]

# CHAPTER 3

## BANK REFORM, 1837-1839

### 1

The Old Northwest did not immediately feel the effects of the panic. Agricultural prices, while falling, held up fairly well throughout 1837 and 1838. Although the crisis of 1837 was basically urban and commercial, it forced all banks into suspension. In each state, however, bank commissioners affirmed the soundness of local banks and asserted that suspension was a defensive measure. In the main, the West was bothered by a shortage of adequate currency, but there were many individuals who believed that the misfortunes of the East would relieve those of the West. Michigan senator Lucius Lyon wrote from New York in May 1837,

> It is estimated that 4,000 mechanics were discharged here on Saturday last, and most of these, together with several thousands previously out of employment, will find their way to our country. This will do something toward counteracting the effect of the present scarcity of money, so far as we are concerned.[1]

With the resumption of specie payments, the year 1838 brought an increase in credit facilities and a tremendous rise in expenditures for internal improvements projects in all these states. Although land prices did not recover, optimism was hardly dampened. Lyon continued to praise the possibilities of Michigan. A recent immigrant to Illinois wrote a friend in the East, "All kinds of business are good [and a] good mechanik can get any kind of price and cash down."[2]

This resurgence of the economy continued until October 1839, when the suspension of specie payments by the Bank of the United States in Pennsylvania signaled a downturn into a full-fledged depression. By 1840 the depression had descended upon the Old Northwest. The banks of the area had again suspended specie payments, and by 1843 most of them had gone into liquidation. Illinois was entirely without authorized banking facilities; and Michigan was left with six rather shaky institutions, one of which closed voluntarily and two of which failed in the next three years. In Ohio, the most economically developed state of the Old Northwest, the charters of 15 of the state's 23 banks expired in 1843 and 1844. Only the State Bank of Indiana came through the period with its reputation intact.

The numerous exposures of fraud and malpractice during these years, along with the two suspensions of specie payments, built up a great deal of dissatisfaction with banks in general, as is illustrated in table 1 on p. 97. Regardless of how well deserved much of this censure was, banks and the banking system clearly served as a scapegoat for the economic disasters of the period. Men who had stood in the forefront of credit expansion became increasingly hostile in the years following the Panic of 1837. Good banks were attacked along with bad ones. Those that expanded were "reckless," while those attempting to curtail their operations were "oppressive."[3]

The political possibilities of such a flexible issue were clear. Hurt by the hard times, the Democratic party seized upon it. The rhetoric of the "Bank War" was easily, almost logically, extended to all banks. Jackson's policies were defended against Whig charges, and the embarrassing situation of the "party of the people" being beaten in state elections of the late 1830s and the federal election of 1840 was explained by "bank influence." In each of the states of the Old Northwest, banking became a political issue of the first importance during the depression years. Although there were certain local variations, a pattern emerged from this controversy that was remarkably similar in each state.

Throughout 1837 and 1838 party conflict over banking mainly concerned federal policy and Van Buren's Independent Treasury proposal. Although this policy was not hostile toward banks, the

61

Democratic diagnosis of the causes of the panic gradually led the party papers to associate the Whigs with state banks, depreciated notes—or "shinplasters," as they were often called at the time—and political corruption in the form of "bank influence." In some areas Democrats demanded the complete elimination of banks and the return to an exclusively hard money currency. But most Democrats continued to advocate a more moderate course: "Our object is not to destroy, but to preserve—to correct the errors of Banking and preserve the rights of the people. . . ." "TOTAL AND THOROUGH bank reform," not the elimination of banks, was the object of Democratic policy during these years. Yet the meaning of "bank reform" was unclear.[4]

In each state "bank reform" in some shape was debated, and reform projects varied from state to state depending on the local situation. The Democrats most loudly demanded reform, but these demands were not always implemented; and the initiative was sometimes seized by the Whigs, who in no state were content to merely defend the status quo.

During the depression years from 1837 to 1845, the logic of the Democratic interpretation of the economic crisis worked itself out in party policy. The Democracy of the Old Northwest gradually became dedicated to the extinction of banks of issue and a return to the "constitutional currency" of gold and silver. But this transformation took place in two stages. Between 1837 and 1839 anti-bank feelings grew, but the party still stood for "bank reform" rather than the elimination of banking. It denied any intention to "war on credit" or to destroy all banks. But after the second suspension of specie payments in 1839, the Democrats, spurred by political reverses, moved quickly to a hard money position, advocating the abolition of all banks. Their opponents also attempted reform and cursed bank failures, but Whigs generally refused to accept the hard money formula. When they held political power, the Whigs continued to search for ways to use banks safely so as to answer the region's economic needs.[5]

## 2

The situation in Michigan reached an advanced state of confusion. The economic crisis began in the East during the winter of

1836–37 and continued to mount throughout the next spring, leading to suspension of specie payments by eastern banks in May. Although some observers believed the West might benefit from this, the close commercial and financial relationship with New York forced Michigan banks to follow suit in order to protect their specie holdings. In reaction to news of the New York suspension, a public meeting in the Detroit City Hall, presided over by the mayor, resolved that the banks should be suspended and that the governor and the legislature should be requested to make provisions for the existing crisis. A committee of the city's political and economic leaders visited the governor and urged a special session to legalize the suspension. Governor Stevens T. Mason responded by calling a special session of the legislature for June 12. He also instructed the bank commissioner to prepare a detailed report on the state's banks for presentation to that body.[6]

Mason opened his message to the special session with an analysis of the "true sources" of the "present crisis" framed in typical Jacksonian terms; he placed the main responsibility on overbanking. The remedies he suggested included gradual curtailment of bank issues, curtailment of trade, cessation of "mad" investments in unproductive land, and a return to frugality and "honest industry." However, he recommended that the legislature sanction the admittedly "hazardous" suspension of specie payments for one year or until such time as the New York banks resumed and that it force Safety Fund banks to accept each other's paper during suspension, prohibit banks from selling specie at a premium, and restrict issues to "reasonable" needs of the public. The bank commissioner and the chancellor of the state, he further advised, should be given unrestricted authority to close any institution violating these provisions.[7]

While advocacy of suspension has traditionally been identified with the Whig party, this was not the case in Michigan. Not only did a Jacksonian governor propose legalization of suspension, but an overwhelmingly Democratic house approved it by a vote of 37 to 8. Even men who had originally voted against free banking, such as Alpheus Felch and Charles Whipple, favored suspension. The vote was much closer in the senate, but "conservative" Democrats John Barry, John Clark, and Edward Ellis failed to block passage. The *Calhoun County Patriot,* an avid Jacksonian paper, recommended allowing suspension:

> Although we are no great friend of banks, and are decidedly opposed to the substitution of a *rag money* currency, yet . . . we believe that the Michigan banks are as solvent and as well conducted as those of any other system.

The suspension bill, like the free banking act itself, was the work of Jacksonians. Opposition to either bill came only from the "conservative" faction of that party.[8]

On state banking policy, party differences were neither clear nor important. The opposing presses echoed party positions on national questions but showed few differences on state monetary policies. The Whig *Daily Advertiser* warned of a crisis, which it ascribed to overtrading and speculation occasioned by Jackson's "wild" monetary policies. It also attacked various Democratic legislatures in other states for establishing monied monsters and overextending bank issues. Yet it did not focus upon the policy of the local Democratic party. In fact, the Whig organ complimented the state legislature on its work, including the free banking law. Following the suspension it suggested legislation to sustain banks and safeguard the public, which was virtually the bill the Democrats had enacted in the special session in 1837. Party platforms written in late July and early August reflected these general attitudes. While Whigs and Democrats accepted their party's position on national policy, neither mentioned the state banking question.[9]

In the 1837 election the Whigs inadvertently made state banks a political issue by nominating Charles C. Trowbridge of the Bank of Michigan for governor. Democrats raised the specter of "bank influence," but the free banking law made them tread rather lightly. The official party position presented in the Democratic Address of that year chided overbanking and attacked the Bank of the United States, declaring, "Our motto in relation to the credit system is, LET IT BE PRESERVED AND LET IT BE REFORMED." Even though the legislature's special session had defeated a limitation on the size of bills, the address advocated reform laws limiting circulation to bills over $5. The Democrats also recommended the passage by all states of free banking laws and praised free banking as a system

> based upon the soundest principles, and which, with such further provisions for the public security as experience will soon suggest will render it the most safe and popular system of banking that has ever been adopted.[10]

The Whigs, on the other hand, generally denied Democratic charges that they favored an irredeemable paper currency and attacked Jackson's policies. They also decried what they sarcastically termed the "Tory Consistency" of Democrats who talked against a multiplication of banks and legislated them into existence. However, the Whig platform of 1837 again made no mention of banks.[11]

The first Whig attacks on the free banking law evolved out of campaign arguments concerning the inconsistency of Democratic rhetoric and policy that led the Whigs to denounce unethical practices of Democratic bankers. In July the *Daily Advertiser* charged that the Pontiac Bank was run by Van Buren men to lend to its own stockholders. The *Ann Arbor Journal* noted that the Ann Arbor Bank, which had defaulted, had been headed by leading Democrats, gibing, "This standing in the democratic ranks won't redeem their bills in circulation." The *Daily Advertiser* then commented that the Ann Arbor Bank represented "the first fruits" of the free banking law passed by a "Tory" legislature and fraud perpetrated against the people by "Tories" running the bank. In November the *Daily Advertiser* attacked the opposition as the "Rag Party." How could Democrats say they opposed paper currency while they supported the free banking law, "which now tends to fill our state with miserable rags"?[12]

Most Democrats defended the free banking law and attacked their critics as aristocrats. Their argument was clearly expressed in an article "The Aristocracy vs. the General Bank Law," which claimed that "Federalists" opposed the law because its antimonopoly features did not suit "the organs and retainers of the monied aristocracy." Free banks would drive down the value of bank stock, particularly that of Trowbridge, the largest holder of bank stock in Michigan. "Federalists" were aristocrats and the party of monopoly. Democrats favored "giving equal rights to all classes of investing their capital in that branch of business which had been heretofore monopolized by the few."[13]

Far from being opposed to banks, the Democratic press hailed the establishment of each new institution. The *Pontiac Balance* praised the Bank of Oakland as a true *"anti-monopoly bank,"* which would bring liberal discounts and prosperity. Pontiac had three banks for less than a thousand people; and the *Balance* proudly declared that "few eastern villages can boast of like means of enterprise." Similar statements came from Democratic papers all over the state. The *Grand River Times,* the *Ann Arbor Argus,* and the *Constantine Republican* all joined in welcoming new banks. This affluent praise even greeted the most famous of the wildcats, the Bank of Brest; and an irate editorial appeared in the *Tecumseh Democrat* defending the soundness of the banking system against Whig "libel."[14]

Mason and the Democrats won the 1837 election by 514 votes, but radical principles concerning banks were not at issue. Members of the Mason faction were almost all "men on the make." Mason's father and founder of this political clan, John T. Mason, was a spoilsman, a speculator, and an entrepreneur, a typical "Democrat by trade." John R. Williams combined his bank adventures with presidency of an insurance company and large land speculations. Nearly all leaders of this group borrowed heavily from the Michigan State Bank, and many were involved with other banks. Throughout the 1837 election, Democrats stood for a multiplication of banks in every corner of the state. They used antimonopoly arguments to attack chartered banks in general and their political opponent, who was president of one of them, in particular. But Democrats selectively employed party symbolism, rather than attacking all banks; in return, Whigs attacked Democratic banks, whether chartered or organized under the free banking law.[15]

Following the election, Democrats continued to defend the free banking law, but Whig criticism, public fear of fraud, and the urging of the bank commissioner in his yearly report led to the amendment of the law. Its provisions were tightened and a more thorough examination procedure was instituted. Yet there was no major revision of the law. Democrats hoped that these amendments would boost the credit of the free banks both within and without the state and add to public confidence.[16]

Despite these alterations in the law, bank expansion continued at a rapid pace. According to a leading Democrat, "The masses still looked to an increase in paper circulation as an unfailing remedy for all evils." Eventually 40 banks went into operation under the law. But as the system increased in size, objections were raised against it. Although Democrats sometimes complained of the depreciation of the currency, criticism generally came from Whigs, who charged that it was "an imperfect shin plaster system" and a "base deception" because specie capital was not being paid in properly.[17]

In his message to the legislature at the end of 1838, Mason was again equivocal. He warned that an excessive paper currency always disturbed the "natural laws of trade" and was "always attended with fluctuations and revulsions." He admitted that the free banks had multiplied beyond expectation, but he assured his audience that they were just as sound as the chartered banks and reaffirmed his belief that "competition is the best regulator of every branch of industry." He praised the free banking law for "destroying . . . the odious features of a bank monopoly and giving equal rights to all classes of the community."[18]

The Whigs were not as optimistic about the conditions of the free banks and opposed the further extension of bank capital at the time. The *Daily Advertiser* scored Mason for denouncing "with much apparent severity all private incorporations as dangerous monopolies which impair the equal rights of our citizens" while extending bank charters to all that would accept them. The state was suffering from "excessive use of bank facilities" for speculation. Most of the new banks were set up by borrowers rather than lenders. The *Daily Advertiser* quickly denied that it was hostile to "well conducted banks." Whigs publicly favored institutions that might aid persons of small means to rise in the world.[19]

In the legislature Whigs led by young Jacob Howard, who was later to become a power in the Republican party and a senator from the state, pushed for examination of the banks and for a one-year suspension of the free banking law. It seemed that fraud was rampant; but even if no fraud existed, the state simply did not require so many banks. "We shall one day see and feel these evils," declared Howard, "and the laboring productive classes of the community, will be those on whom the loss must fall most heavily." "Gentlemen," Howard told the legislators, "we are assaying bank institutions against the interests of the people." Howard was joined by other Whigs who advocated suspension of the law and could not see how the Democrats could agree that there were too many banks and still want to leave the law unaltered.[20]

Even though the *Democratic Free Press* assailed the motives of the Whigs, and a small group of Democrats in the legislature defended the free banks, the Democrats could not stay demands for an investigation. After a questionnaire failed to turn up irregularities, examinations were conducted personally by the three Democratic bank commissioners. The investigation revealed fraud and malpractice on a scale that even surprised the Whigs, who quickly charged the frauds to "Tory" bankers and "Tory" corruptionists.[21]

Democrats were forced to minimize the extent of malpractice and attempt to implicate their opponents. On the eve of the Detroit city election, the *Democratic Free Press* attacked the "Whig Panic Makers," who would destroy confidence in the free bank currency for political ends. Augustus S. Porter, who won the election, was attacked as the "Loco Foco Whig" candidate; and the epithet "loco-foco" was applied to the Whig party by the *Free Press*, which also charged that the only fraudulent banks were controlled by Whigs.[22]

The evidence of the extensiveness of fraud perpetrated under the free banking law given in the often-quoted Bank Commissioners' Report of January 1839 came as an anticlimax. A house committee of five Democrats and four Whigs reported that "The general banking law has received the disapprobation of the community, who seem not so much to condemn the principles, but the result flowing from the abuses." On April 16, 1839, the law was permanently suspended.[23]

Free banking was dead as a political issue in Michigan. The banking debate shifted to the struggle over a state bank that had begun in early 1838. Even before the free banking system had been tried and before its fraudulent operations had been uncovered, the Democratic press had made suggestions that Michigan establish a state bank. In January 1838, Mason recommended a state bank in addition to the free banks to help pay for internal improvements. It would also help sustain public credit, have a "salutary influence upon our currency," and aid the commercial community. Mason believed that such a bank should be a mixed enterprise, with the state holding majority control. It should be limited in its circulation and issue no bills under $10. As added security, the private stockholders should be made to place securities with the state equal to their holdings. Preferably these should be 6% bonds of Michigan.[24]

Although a great deal of the session dealt with the free banking system, a bill to establish a state bank passed the senate, then died in the house. The *Democratic Free Press* favored its establishment and charged the defeat to the Whig insistence that a majority of the directors be chosen by the private stockholders. This, thought the paper, was a perfect example of Whig distrust of the people.[25]

Yet the division of opinion on this issue did not so clearly follow party lines, and the Whigs had split. Those who opposed the state bank generally feared that with gubernatorial control of the bank, it would be used for political purposes. Isolated Whigs even opposed the bank on the grounds that no more bank capital was needed. Banker Trowbridge, who was consulted for expert advice by members of both parties, suggested the state bank be the sole bank and all other bank charters be abrogated, including that of his bank, the Bank of Michigan; but he believed it was best to leave control with those whose financial interests were involved. The *Daily Advertiser*, always eager to defend Whig views and chastise Democratic heresies, was silent on the issue.[26]

The house vote shows that the state bank was not a partisan

question, as the *Democratic Free Press* charged. Equal numbers of Whigs could be found on either side of the issue. The bill failed because 8 die-hard defenders of free banking among the 22 Democrats voted against the bill. The two-thirds clause in the Michigan constitution, rather than opposition from either party, killed the state bank.[27]

Throughout the summer of 1838, Democratic papers kept up demands for a state bank in which the state maintained control. They asserted that the Democrats favored "A People's Bank," and the "federalists" opposed it because of their distrust of the people. The Whigs were the corporation party, the "true Tories."[28]

The situation in 1838 remained confused. The *Democratic Free Press* attacked the Bank of Michigan and "bank Whigs," and at the same time  defended the Michigan State Bank against the "loco foco malignity" of the Whig *Daily Advertiser*. By the late fall the *Democratic Free Press* was more vehement in its attacks on bank influence and in its praise of the "constitutional currency," although it continued to attack the Whigs as loco-focos and to call for a state bank. But Mason disclaimed any Democratic "war against banks" and  urged the legislature "not to destroy, but to correct, the abuses incident to the present system of banking."[29]

The Whigs now attacked both the Independent Treasury system and the Michigan State Bank, but showed little hostility to the projected state bank. When the *Daily Advertiser* dealt with the question, it warned, as had Indiana Democrats, that control in the hands of the state would make the bank a "political engine." Would it be a bank controlled by the people or by the "executive and his tools"? After Mason opened the session calling for the establishment of a state bank, the Whigs gave the measure their solid support. The only opposition came from Democrats, but the report of the House Committee on Banks and the overwhelming vote indicate that "bank reform" rather than opposition to all banks dominated the Democratic party.[30]

# 3

While Michigan was attempting to solve its problems by setting up a state bank, New York passed a free banking law and the idea spread throughout the Old Northwest. Somewhat ironically, one of the strongest movements for free banking at this time developed in Indiana.

The Indiana Democratic party nearly ceased to exist during these years, and its remnants often joined politically with discontented Whigs against the state administration. In 1837 the *Indiana Democrat* supported *"The People's Candidate,"* John Dumont, a Whig, against the Whig governor David Wallace, *"The Speculators' Candidate."* Democrats had supported the state bank, but because of its connection with the Whig administration, "there was a disposition on the part of Democrats to find fault." Although the *Indiana Democrat* defended the soundness of the state bank and the suspension, Samuel Merrill, the Whig president of the state bank, was a constant target of Democratic gibes. He lamented to his brother that "On the one side the friends of specie would make the currency as strong as aqua fortes and many of the speculators deep in debt would be glad that it could be weak as milk and water." By the fall one banker believed there was "a settled determination to knock down the State Banks."[31]

Democrats blamed the economic crisis on a multiplication of banks and attacked their usual targets, Nicholas Biddle and the Whig bankers, for saddling the country with an irredeemable paper currency. "Biddle's bills are now at two per cent discounts . . . while the Jackson currency, the gold and silver, demands a premium of ten per cent." A few Democratic papers advocated the elimination of all banks. The vigorously antibank *Charleston Indianan* declared, "that state which first casts off her banks will be in the best financial condition—she will draw her supply of specie from the adjoining states." The *Indiana Democrat* suggested a less radical program of "bank reform" that included demands for a 33 1/3% specie reserve against note issue, deposits and liabilities, the elimination of all notes under $20 by 1842, and the extension of stockholder liability. These represented a rather typical set of Jacksonian reforms, but Democratic weakness in Indiana made their implementation impossible.[32]

The *Indiana Democrat* shifted its support to the free banking movement that developed in 1838. The demand for free banking in Indiana was a bipartisan response to the conservative policies of the state bank. One Democrat wrote,

71

> It does seem to me that our Legislators and the institutions they
> have chartered do not consider the country from Logansport to
> the Michigan line as forming an integral portion of their terri-
> tory, as entitled in any degree to their assistance or protection.

A number of Whigs had supported free banking at the time of the
creation of the state bank; and the movement in 1838 was again
led by Whigs, although a sizable number of Democrats and the
party's main newspaper gave their support.[33]

Indiana's leading advocate of free banking was a Whig, Samuel
Judah. "Sam the Jew," as one opponent called him, was born
in New York, educated at Rutgers, and was one of the leading
lawyers and businessmen in the state. Although he served several
terms in the state legislature, his vanity, his desire for office, and
his questionable political ethics—perhaps also his religion—limited his popularity. Like many Hoosiers he had been an ardent
Jacksonian in the 1820s but then had broken with the administration over economic policy. As the Whig party developed, he
emerged as one of its important figures. Judah was best known as
an advocate of internal improvements, but he was also a defender
of the Bank of the United States and an admirer of its president,
Nicholas Biddle. As an economic expansionist, a defender of bank
credit and convertible currency, and an advocate of the use of
government to promote economic development, Judah typified
the progressive element of the Whig party. Judah's policy recommendations were advanced for the day. Although not shared by
the majority of Indiana Whigs in 1839, his economic views would
dominate the party by mid-century and would eventually be
adopted by most Republicans.[34]

Judah, along with several other supporters of free banking, had
attacked the state bank for suspending specie payments, and
early in 1838 he suggested reform. At that time the attempt to
reform the state bank was bipartisan and moderate. Judah and his
colleagues were not hostile to the bank. They only wanted to extend the control of the legislature and the public directors over
the bank to better provide for the public welfare. One reformer
wrote, "The stockholders of the Bank seem to think the Bank was

erected for their exclusive benefit and not for the benefit of the people of the state."[35]

Under pressure from the state bank, the Whig legislature rejected the majority report and accepted the minority report, which saw little wrong with the institution as it was constituted. The bank's popularity at the time remained high, and those who wished to reform it were suspected of strictly political motives by members of both parties.[36]

There may have been some substance to these charges because the following year Judah led a reform movement of a somewhat different kind. In his report to the legislature recommending a free banking law, Judah argued that the legal restrictions on banking often failed to aid the public and merely conferred upon a few banks the advantages of monopoly. His free banking law would regulate their activities as the New York free banking law did. That law, he emphasized, was "the best yet devised" because of the safety it guaranteed to the billholder. "If ample security be given to the public for the notes," he told the legislators, "it is not easy to discover *any* well founded objection to free banking." Like nearly all of his contemporaries, Judah believed that business—including the banking business—should be constrained by few limitations and given as free a rein as possible. "All those varied regulations, by which Governments formerly attempted to restrain the freedom of commerce," he believed, were "fallacies of times past." Yet, there were limits to his advocacy of laissez faire. According to Judah, the laws of supply and demand would regulate banking, but they might not protect the public. This protection had to be extended by the state. Thus, under the free banking law banks were required to deposit state or federal stocks as security for their note issue. As an additional bonus, this requirement would create a demand for Indiana stocks and would "induce men of wealth and experience to embark in the business of Banking in this state."[37]

Judah more thoroughly developed his argument and more clearly revealed its essential spirit in the debate on his bill. Although he again asserted the constitutionality of his free banking law as merely "*a regulation of the present undoubted rights of individuals,"* Judah emphasized the need for added resources and the beneficial effects of bank expansion. Certain areas of the state that desired banks had been unable to obtain them. Adding new branches to old banks would just increase the risk of all other branches because of their mutual liability. Their directors could hardly be expected to assume such risks without some hesitation. Free banking would alleviate this problem, and "the extension of bank facilities to various parts of the state now destitute in our present system, would encourage commerce, stimulate agriculture, and bring forth and sustain manufacturers."[38]

In the debate Robert Dale Owen, the Democratic representative from Posy County, and Michael G. Bright, a Jefferson County Democrat, strongly supported Judah's bill. Owen, the radical reformer known for his involvement with the New York workingmen's movement, praised the antimonopoly aspects of free banking and the way in which it put "the security of the people first and the profit of the stockholders afterwards." Bright reiterated Judah's argument of the constitutionality of the measure and insisted that the currency would be better secured than that of the state bank.[39]

Partisan attitudes on free banking were unclear and often yielded to private desires and local interests. Indiana's leading Democratic paper had come out for free banking in mid-1838 and printed with favorable comment Samuel Young's reports to the New York legislature. The leading Whig paper had very little to say about the bill. In November it briefly asserted that such a law would be unconstitutional. While the bill was before the legislature, it printed the debates but refrained from an attack on the bill.[40]

The vote to table Judah's bill shows the issue was not clearly partisan. The majority of the Democrats, anxious to appeal to as many dissatisfied groups as possible and reflecting the growing antimonopoly feelings in their party, voted for the bill. Yet a sizable minority, 44% of the Democrats, continued to be satisfied with the state bank and opposed free banking. Judah, the Whig sponsor of the bill, was able to get the support of 30% of his party, even though the state bank was associated with the Whigs.[41]

The margin of defeat was supplied by the Whigs from the central and northern parts of the state. The two arguments most often appealed to by these Whigs were the unconstitutionality of the bill and the ability of the state bank to satisfy the state's needs through a moderate expansion. Nearly everyone, including the president of the state bank, acknowledged the necessity of expanded banking facilities. Governor David Wallace asked that the capital of the state bank be added to, but warned that this should not be done recklessly. "Experience teaches as the fearful lesson that there are limits beyond which if banking privileges and banking operations are carried they cease to do good, and become engines of incalculable mischief." He did not wish to see Indiana covered with "swindling shops." Other Whigs attacked Judah's bill as "a *private* measure; a measure for private speculation," one that subordinated state to local interests. "Pass this bill," declared one of its opponents, "and you put a dagger in the hands of private partners to stab the dearest interests of the state." In general, Whigs realized the need for banking resources, but preferred an expansion of the well-regulated state bank to the establishment of a new and possibly unconstitutional system.[42]

# 4

Because of the deep involvement of both parties in the formation of the Illinois State Bank and its close relation to the state's internal improvement system, the monetary struggle in Illinois during these years often centered on federal rather than state policy. Still, there was an undercurrent of Democratic opposition to the state bank. Opposition became overt in 1836 after the bank fell into Whig hands. Democrats insisted that the state bank had violated its charter in the mode of apportioning stock and was doing all in its power to block any investigation. Further, the bank's branches were interfering with elections and using their weight "against the candidate of the people," Martin Van Buren. "The State Bank was neither intended nor has it been used for the advantages of the people."[43]

The suspension of specie payments in May 1837 caused the *Chicago Democrat,* the *Jacksonville News,* and the *Illinois State Register* to renew their attacks. Throughout the summer most Democrats, including some former advocates of the state bank such as ex-Governor Ewing, turned against the bank; and the hard money element of the party, which was also interested in the Independent Treasury bill, became predominant. Although three Illinois congressmen were among the twelve Democrats who opposed the Independent Treasury, the local politicans and press gave the measure solid support.[44]

As in the other states, Democrats denied the responsibility of the administration for the crisis and asserted that "The True Cause" of the country's problems was "OVER-BANKING, OVER TRADING, EXTRAVAGANT LIVING and . . . deep and hazardous SPECULATION." At the heart of these problems lay the banking system. An anonymous article in the *Illinois State Register* argued that the system should be reformed in line with the plan of the *Richmond Enquirer,* which sanctioned suspension, but would require banks to give some form of security, extend penal laws to cover bank officers, and prohibit the payment of dividends until the resumption of specie payments. Democrats in the legislature followed this advice and joined the Whigs in sanctioning suspension with a series of restrictions on banking activities. Although several county organizations and a few prominent individuals called for the immediate end of banks and a return to hard money, most Democrats in 1837 agreed with the *Richmond Enquirer* that "we must correct or remove the system by degrees."[45]

During 1836 the Illinois Whigs criticized the banking systems of the other states for their instability in comparison to the Bank of the United States, but they said very little about the Illinois State Bank. Since Whigs tended to believe that Democratic attacks on the state bank were politically inspired, they opposed the form of the 1837 investigation. But Whigs were not adverse to reforming the system. Lincoln had favored periodic examinations earlier, Governor Joseph Duncan attacked the overexpansion of banks and proposed that the state bank secure with mortgages long-term low-interest loans to safely meet the needs of farmers and mechanics.[46]

When the crisis struck in May, the Whig *Sangamo Journal* ascribed the "present pecuniary distress" to the speculation and over trading encouraged by the Democratic policy of local banks, which flooded the country with paper money. The Bank of the United States had brought stability. The Democrats' "quackery upon the currency" had resulted in reckless local institutions "sucking the life blood" from honest industry. Throughout the summer Whig papers defended the Bank of the United States and attacked the system of local banks, but at the same time they defended the state bank from the loco-focos who would destroy it and have an exclusive metallic currency. "Does not common sense teach them, that should the paper of the State Bank be withdrawn from circulation that its place will be filled by the paper of the Banks of our neighboring states?" the *Sangamo Journal* queried. Illinois Whigs agreed that there must be reform, not by a "war upon the prosperity of the country," but by the establishment of a new national bank.[47]

To Whigs the Democratic flirtation with hard money was a product of their "total disregard of the welfare of the people when it comes into conflict with political objects." The Whig press took pleasure in the inconsistency of those Democrats who sanctioned suspension at the same time they supported a specie currency and the party's sponsorship of the state bank. The *Sangamo Journal* puzzled,

> They admit that they established this Bank, they know how intimately connected with it are the interests and welfare of the State; they know it has been the means of adding to the active capital of the State . . . yet as a "remedy" for the wretched state of the currency brought about by acts of the present administration, they call upon the party *"to put down the Bank."*

The Whig paper went on to suggest that the legislature's duty was not to destroy the bank but to *"regulate it* so as to render it useful to the government and the people."[48]

By the end of 1837, Whigs confidently predicted that "BANKS

OR NO BANKS" would become the test question separating the parties. As yet, though, the hard money advocates did not control the Illinois Democracy. As conditions improved, Democrats moderated their stand. In March 1838 the Democratic *Illinois State Register* supported a new branch of the Shawneetown Bank at Vandalia to meet the "fair demands of our businessmen" and praised the state bank. Even President Van Buren had modified his opposition: "Banks properly established and conducted are highly useful to the business of the country."[49]

The 1838 gubernatorial campaign centered on the internal improvements and the Independent Treasury plan, paying little attention to the state bank. Although there had been dissension within the Illinois Democracy, the newly developed convention system brought the feuding Democrats together behind the rather undistinguished Thomas Carlin, who was able to defeat Cyrus Edwards, the candidate of the "People's Party."[50]

The state bank per se was not discussed by the candidates nor by the partisan press, but candidates and press manifested contrasting attitudes on banks in general. Carlin declared the banking system unconstitutional and poor public policy. Although no further charters should be given, since banks were a curse to the producing classes, it was the governor's duty to make present banks as useful as possible. To do away with them suddenly would be an injustice to both the stockholders and the borrowers. He would "afford every aid in my power consistent with the public interest, in regulating our present Banking institutions." In contrast to the Democratic argument that banks were a necessary evil, Whigs defended the utility of banks and the credit system. According to the *Sangamo Journal* the Democrat motto was "perish credit, perish commerce" while the Whig motto was "encourage industry and reward virtue." Credit made it possible for the poor but industrious man to own his own business, and it placed him "on a footing with the wealthiest nabob in the land." The Whig credit policy would equalize opportunity while Democratic policy would make men "hewers of wood and drawers of water all their life."[51]

In his address to the legislature following his victory, Carlin espoused Democratic orthodoxy on the causes of the economic distress and the necessity of the Independent Treasury to "dissolve the connexion between the Government and Banks—a connexion as unnatural and dangerous as the union of church and state." He refrained from attacking the state bank directly but reasserted that the whole banking system was "radically defective" and that the legalization of suspension violated moral obligations and corrupted the people. He warned that the growing influence of banks, whether they were controlled by the state or private individuals, endangered freedom and liberty. Carlin made no specific suggestions and nothing was done to reform the Illinois banking system at that session of the legislature. Yet the direction in which the Democrats were moving was clear. Carlin's inaugural address shows how easily the Democratic diagnosis of the country's economic ills could lead to the distrust of all banks and prescription of "radical reform."[52]

# 5

Although no state in the Old Northwest can truly be considered typical of the area, Ohio, Indiana's neighbor to the east and the oldest state in the section, displayed most clearly the conflicting attitudes of Whigs and Democrats and the direction in which the parties were moving. Unlike its neighbors, Ohio had neither free banking nor a state bank. Its party system had developed early and was fiercely competitive. Perhaps because of these factors, the bank issue played a more important role in Ohio politics than elsewhere in the area.

The Whigs succeeded in the 1836 election, despite a Democratic gerrymander designed to unseat the popular senator Thomas Ewing. Ohio voters had given William Henry Harrison a majority in the presidential race and elevated Joseph Vance to the statehouse. Vance was a stout and energetic man of Scotch-Irish Presbyterian background. Although he had mercantile interests in Urbana, Ohio, he spent most of his adult life as a politician. Before he became governor, Vance had served in the state legislature and then six succeeding terms in Congress. He was a warm admirer of Clay, an advocate of the "American System," and a consistent opponent of the Jacksonians. Following his term as governor he remained active in politics, serving as a state senator, two more terms in Congress, and in 1851, just a year before his death, as a delegate to the state's constitutional convention. A colonizationist, a temperance advocate, and an economic expansionist, Joseph Vance was a representative Whig politician whose views typified the party.[53]

Vance perceived economic society in corporatist terms, emphasizing the interdependence rather than the antagonism of the various economic interests. "Agricultural, commercial, manufacturing and mechanical labor, are linked together by a strong common interest," he told the Ohio legislature in 1837, "and he who shall undertake to sever either branch of business from the others, strikes a blow at the prosperity of the whole." Believing that it was the government's responsibility to protect that prosperity and to establish the conditions for future development, he attacked Jacksonian financial policy and argued that it was not the "amount of circulation" that produced the economic crisis, "but the want of power to control, and judgement in the application of our means by those who have the management of our financial system." What was needed, was a well-regulated system capable of expanding and contracting to comply with commercial and agricultural needs.[54]

Vance believed the "credit system" was supported by all classes of society and defended it on two grounds. First, credit was the dynamic element in economic growth that encouraged the spirit of enterprise and insured high prices for Ohio's product. The state, according to Vance, had been built upon credit. With credit, the state had dug canals, erected churches, established colleges, "and put us into the possession of as large a share of rational freedom and solid comfort as has ever fallen to the lot of any people." Second, Vance insisted that credit was a source of opportunity as well as essential to economic progress. Through bank credit disadvantaged youth of high moral principles could compete with more fortunate members of society in the struggle for economic

80

success. "The distribution of loans among the enterprising class, who have not been favored by an inheritance of wealth, gives them a power to wield capital, not often possessed even by our wealthiest individuals." In contrast to his Democratic opponents, Vance argued that "the destruction of credit will make the rich richer and the poor poorer" by depriving the latter of the means to ameliorate their situation. Moreover, the quantity of money directly affected price levels. He claimed that bank credit meant high prices while an exclusively metallic currency would only lower prices, depreciate land values, and depress wages. But Vance was not simply an inflationist. He advocated an "elastic" bank currency that was at all times redeemable in specie, and he attacked the suspension of specie payments as "one of the greatest calamities that can come upon an industrious and enterprising people."

The country's economic problems in 1837 and 1838, Vance believed, required federal action. Yet the president and Congress promised no relief. "Our only reliance then must be on the state institutions." As a remedial measure, he suggested in 1837 that the prohibition of small notes instituted by the Democrats the previous year be removed on the condition that the banks resume specie payments and relinquish any rights to issue notes in denominations less than $1. The Whig majority in the legislature carried through Vance's proposals by a strict party vote, with every Democrat in the house and senate in opposition.

Vance was less enthusiastic about free banking, favored by many Ohio Whigs. In 1837 he called attention to the "great amount of local legislation and bestowment of corporate privileges" he believed to be a "growing evil in the state." But the following year the Whig governor discussed free banking as a possible way to reform the state's banking system. He reminded the legislators that it had failed in Michigan but was largely successful in New York. He left the question to the legislature and recommended "laborious and careful investigation." Whigs acted on this suggestion, but the free banking bill introduced in the 1839 session of the legislature was defeated by solid Democratic opposition.

81

During and after the panic Ohio Democrats generally opposed Vance and the Whigs on the bank issue. Although Samuel Medary's vehemently Jacksonian *Western Hemisphere* assured its readers that Ohio banks were "strictly solvent" so as to prevent hysterical reactions to suspension, it and other Democratic papers demanded the banks either forfeit their charters or resume. The Democratic press was quick to blame the Whigs for the crisis and depreciated "shinplasters." The *Newark Advocate* called on the Whigs to protect the people from the effects of the bank's misdeeds since "the Banks are Whig Children." Medary's estimate that 341 of Ohio's 405 bankers were Whig gained wide currency among Democrats.[55]

Throughout the state Democrats chastised Vance's suggestions. The *Ohio Statesman* thought his proposal to repeal the prohibition on small notes would flood the state "with nothing but trash." To the *Norwalk Experiment* his idea of an elastic currency was "an absurdity." The general Democratic response to free banking was only slightly less hostile. Both the *Cleveland Advertiser* and the *Statesman* followed the New York debate and praised the loco-focos. Medary wrote in the *Statesman*,

> The issue between Bank monopoly despotism, and free trade and equal rights had to be made sooner or later and we are rejoiced that the last strike has been struck and the standard of freedom has been raised.

However, while advocating "free scope for everything," the *Statesman* was initially skeptical about Michigan's free bank law and did not hesitate to attack the Whig free banking bill when it was introduced in the Ohio legislature in 1839. By this time other Democratic papers, such as the *Cleveland Gazette*, joined the opposition to the free banking "mania," as they termed it. In 1839 the Democratic governor who replaced Vance, Wilson Shannon, assailed free banking, and the Democrats in the legislature defeated a Whig-sponsored free banking bill.[56]

The Ohio Democrats wanted "bank reform," and they were quick to argue that they were not "contending for an exclusive metallic currency or the abolition of all credit." Their reform program called for the resumption of specie payments, making stockholders personally liable for all bank debts, swift punishment for "usurious practices," and annulment of bank charters that had been violated.[57]

The Ohio Democracy made "bank reform" the issue in the 1838 election. It attacked the "Shin-plaster Governor, Joseph Vance," charging that he and the Whigs were the advocates of the *"Bank Monopolists"* while Shannon and the Democracy stood for "bank reform." They would free Ohio from "bank domination and bank tyranny." Democratic speakers called upon the voters to decide if Ohio was to be governed by the people or the monied corporations. On July 7 at Ravenna, Shannon made his most important speech. In it he proposed unlimited liability, larger specie reserves, the prohibition of small notes, and the prohibition of loans to stockholders and directors.[58]

The Whigs attacked Shannon for making too much of the bank question, but they did not defend the banks. Vance believed that "ultraism in favor of vested rights" could only hurt the party. In his final message to the legislature, he continued to argue in favor of a national bank to control currency. The idea of allowing 26 states to regulate the currency was "totally impracticable and delusive." Banks, he believed, originally fulfilled a public function enabling small investors to share in their profits through the purchase of stock and allowing the poor but enterprising to borrow the necessary capital to compete with the wealthy. But this system had to be controlled so it served public advantage, not private profit. It had to be "subject to the control of the people through their representatives." If the state banks were not so controlled, "a few great bankers, doing business entirely on their own account, irresponsible to the people, and yet at critical moments, able, very seriously, to cripple their resources . . ." would dominate.[59]

Democrats looked upon Shannon's victory as a mandate for the bank reforms expressed in his Ravenna speech and suggested that provisions be inserted in bank charters allowing the legislature to amend, alter, or repeal them in the public interest. Under the leadership of young John Brough, who had helped write the Democratic platform attacking the Whig attitude toward banks, the Democrats in the legislature carried part of Shannon's bank reform plan into effect. They limited small notes, prohibited the issue of notes by unauthorized corporations, restricted issue to three times the specie on hand, and established a bank commission. While Brough's report assailed the evils of the banks and showed typical Democratic horror at the consequences of inflation, it insisted that "the people seek reformation, not destruction, and sooner or later it must be extended to them."[60]

## 6

The period between the Panic of 1837 and the second suspension of specie payments in 1839 was one of reorientation in which conflicting partisan attitudes on the bank issue began to coalesce. The *Democratic Review*, based in New York but widely read in the Midwest, attempted to show the states the way to reform. It blamed the economic crisis on banking excesses but denied the right of the federal government to interfere with banks established by the states, which were purely "local institutions." The state governments alone were responsible for "radical reform" to reorganize the banks on "correct principles" and to achieve their proper goals—the concentration of capital and the accommodation of credit. Banking should be simplified, small notes eliminated, and the whole matter freed from "legislative tampering and meddling, [and placed] under the vigilant guardianship of public intelligence, and the control [given over] to [the] two mutually corrective principles of free *association* and free *competition*." Free competition did not mean free banking for the *Democratic Review*. Early in 1838 the magazine attacked the free banking laws then being considered by several state legislatures as "a new mode of inflation" and "a very pernicious aggravation of the evils of the existing artificial paper-money system" because they created incorporated banks of issue. They represented a "partial and ill-directed application" of the great principle of reform, "liberty."[61]

84

In the Old Northwest, the Democrats were hesitant to follow all the *Democratic Review's* suggestions. A fairly consistent program for bank reform nevertheless eventually emerged. The party of Jackson constantly denied Whig charges that it wished to burden the country with an exclusively specie currency. Rather, it proposed to reform the banking system by prohibiting small notes, extending individual liability, and requiring resumption of specie payments. A small majority of Indiana Democrats supported free banking on antimonopoly grounds, while Ohio Democrats reflected the *Democratic Review's* opposition to free banks. A growing number loudly opposed banks of issue, but as of 1839 they could not control the Democratic party of any state. Regardless of specific proposals, nearly all Democrats agreed that inflation in any form was harmful and that the most important need of the economy was a stable measure of value.

The Whigs opposed the extension of liability and the prohibition of small notes but agreed with the Democrats on the importance of convertibility. The idea of free banking with a stock-based currency gained strength within the party. But the Whigs' basic commitment continued to be "reform" through the reestablishment of a national bank. They hoped that a national bank would form the basis for a sound expansion of credit and a stable currency, thus restraining the excesses of the banks chartered by the states. Whether they favored free banks, chartered institutions, or a state bank, Whigs, in contrast to their Democratic opponents, believed that the expansion of credit and currency would give "new impulses to industry and enterprise" and work "a mighty change in the condition of this country." Thus, they continued to search for a formula by which enterprise could be encouraged while the interest of the society and its citizens were protected.[62]

# CHAPTER 4

## THE REVULSION AGAINST BANKS, 1839-1845

### 1

The second suspension of specie payments in 1839 and a number of political reverses in the late 1830s and early 1840s signaled the shift in the Democratic party toward opposition to all banks of issue. To many Democrats suspension lent credence to the arguments of the hard money elements and discredited "bank reform." It was after 1839 that the antibank forces came to dominate the Democratic party. Antibank feelings rose as the economy sank. Moreover, bank corruption and bribery seemed to explain political reverses. How could the "party of the people" be defeated in an honest election? This shift took place over a period of years. The "hards" met opposition within their own ranks, but by the mid-1840s most Democrats agreed with the *Iowa Reporter* that "you might as well talk of well regulated DEVILS, as talk of well regulated banks. Their real object is to cheat and defraud the people." The only recourse was the prohibition of all banks of issue.[1]

Even before the second suspension, a few Democrats were not satisfied with the attempts at reform and demanded more radical measures. In May 1839, John Wentworth renewed his attack on the Illinois State Bank, accusing it of financing unwise speculations in pork and lead. During the following months, Moses Dawson of the *Cincinnati Advertiser* called for "a more radical reform of the banking system" allowing no new charters and providing for the gradual elimination of all notes under $20.[2]

The second suspension of specie payments in October triggered a redoubled effort by the antibank forces. Several Democratic county committees in Illinois passed antibank resolutions. Indiana Democrats attacked the state bank and called for a return to the "constitutional currency" of gold and silver. The Johnson County, Indiana, Democrats blamed the fluctuations of business on the "seizure of banks by the Whigs," who used them for political purposes only. Banks, they argued, merely facilitated the transport of the only true money, specie. A few bills of large amounts were all that would be necessary. The *Indiana Democrat* insisted that it did not oppose banks established on "correct principles," but rejoiced at the renewed suspensions because

> the time is now at hand when all the evils of the present banking system can be routed out . . . when paper promises, based upon nothing, will no longer be seen, and when the present vitiated and false credit system will be made to yield to a sound, safe and proper one.

The hard money system would be "steady and prosperous" and eliminate the disastrous fluctuations of the economy that characterized the paper credit system.[3]

The "perfect harmony" achieved in the Ohio Democratic party as a result of the 1838 election was shattered by the governor's message in early December 1839. A growing antibank sentiment in Ohio was no longer satisfied by Governor Wilson Shannon's renewed demand for "bank reform." Although there was some support for Shannon, the "exceptionable passage" in his message condoning banks generally met with disfavor among the Democratic politicians.[4]

The most violent opposition to Shannon came from Moses Dawson's *Cincinnati Advertiser*. At the time Dawson was in close correspondence with Andrew Jackson, who was shocked by Shannon's views and encouraged Dawson to attack the message. Dawson responded with a series of blistering attacks on Shannon and called for reform: unlimited liability, prohibition of all notes under $25, and the limitation of issue to $1 in paper for each held in specie. A meeting of Cincinnati Democrats in mid-December denounced the governor's "Whig views," proclaimed gold and silver as the only "constitutional currency," and resolved that the chartering of further banks was inexpedient.[5]

Thomas Carlin, the Democratic governor of Illinois, expressed similar views. He bitterly attacked all banks and opposed the legalization of suspension as "a fatal blow at the fundamental law of contracts." Further, the "incorporation of companies for the regulation of the financial operations of the country," he believed, was "at war with the genius of free government." He repeated his earlier charge that the banking system was defective and "unsanctioned by any principle of republican virtue," and rejected the arguments that the state bank had been forced to suspend in self-defense and that its destruction would harm the people of the state. "We indeed labored in vain," he said, "in overthrowing the Bank of the United States, if we should now draw to our embrace an institution above responsibility and capable of inflicting within its own sphere a still more deadly sting."[6]

The greatest shift in attitude came in Michigan. Up to 1839 the Democrats had often given lip service to the standard rhetoric concerning banks, but they had shown no reluctance to endorse a free banking experiment and to establish a state bank. The Democratic press often slurred the Whigs as loco-focos. The two parties were split, not on banks as such, but on their attitudes toward specific banks.

The Democrats were closely allied with the Michigan State Bank, which was the constant target of the Whig *Daily Advertiser*. The *Democratic Free Press* defended the Michigan State Bank but attacked the Bank of Michigan, which was associated with the Whigs because Charles Trowbridge, the Whig candidate for governor, was associated with it. When the Michigan State Bank failed in 1839 with $600,000 of the state's money on deposit, the *Daily Advertiser* gloried in exposing "Loco Fraud." It revealed that nearly every leading Democrat in the state owed the Michigan State Bank money.[7]

During that year the Democratic press shifted its ground. The

1839 election resulted in the victory of the "Democratic Whigs," led by William Woodbridge. The "radical" elements of the Democratic party, who had lost control to the "conservatives," deserted Elon Farnsworth, Woodbridge's opponent. By the end of the year the Democrats no longer held power, and within the party the element more generally opposed to banks had control.[8]

The Democratic press now attempted to associate the Whigs with the wildcat system. In September 1839 the *Democratic Free Press* asserted that the Whigs had had a full share in the passage of the free banking law and had organized most of the banks under it. The paper argued, "the Whig party headed by their wild cat whig bank presidents, directors, and stockholders have the audacity and hardihood to endeavor to throw upon the democratic party the responsibility of the irredeemable issue of wild cat banks." It also began to reprint demands from other antibank Democratic organs such as the *Indiana Democrat,* the *Ohio Statesman,* and the *Chicago Democrat.* The failure of the Michigan State Bank late in the year came not as a blow to the Democrats but as a kind of emancipation that allowed them to be consistently antibank. The *Democratic Free Press* charged the failure to Detroit Mayor DeJarmo Jones and his "Whig friends," and printed a letter from the popular Jacksonian senator John Norvell minimizing the amount owed the bank by Democratic politicians.[9]

The suspension of specie payments finally pushed the Democrats into an antibank stand. It occasioned the blatantly antibank article "Bank Currency," published in the *Democratic Free Press,* which argued,

> Better be poor than the panderers to vice; better reduce our currency to *commodities,* than ourselves to be fleeced of our hard earnings by faithless banks and banking institutions. . . . Will the people tacitly permit a bank clique and party to ruthlessly en[t]ail these miseries upon them again in continuous succession, while every other state is restraining, restricting and guarding its bank issue?

In his valedictory Governor Mason chastised suspension as the result of a "false and pernicious system of banking." The banking system must be changed to protect the public by personal liability, a stricter criminal code, and private banking. "Take from them to this extent the corporate veil, which now encourages, and at the same time conceals and protects their frauds and villanies." Mason assured his audience that these simple reforms would insure adequate capital and responsible management. All of these evils could be traced to the free banking law.[10]

Revelations of fraud and unbusinesslike activities added to the distrust of banks. In Illinois this turned members of both parties against the state bank. The Whig press had moderately defended the state bank, charging that the Democrats desired to establish a new bank under their own control. Individual Whigs, however, seemed willing to let the state bank die. Abraham Lincoln wrote John T. Stuart in December 1839 that the legislature had "suffered the Bank to forfeit its charter without *Benefit* of *Clergy.* There seems to be but very little disposition to resuscitate it."[11]

The report of the Illinois legislative committee investigating the state bank confirmed most Democratic charges and silenced Whig defenders, who had been at best moderate. It showed that the Chicago branch of the state bank was involved in pork speculation, and that the branch in Alton was deeply involved in the attempt to make that city the center of the lead trade on the upper Mississippi. The state bank also lent too freely to directors and members of the legislature. Other violations of the law were revealed, as were generally unsound management practices. An even more critical minority report argued that the bank held an excessively large amount of Illinois state stocks in its portfolio.[12]

The Democrats made as much political capital as possible out of the disclosures and the suspension, but they shied away from killing the bank. The *Illinois State Register* continued to urge moderation. The legislature, which was dominated by Democrats, sanctioned suspension until the close of the next session of the legislature in the interests of the state. A number of Whigs, such as Lincoln, were disgusted by the way the Democrats used the bank issue for partisan purposes, "detaching a fragment from their party to help the Whigs pass a measure and then turn around and kick and cuff us for it. . . ." The *Chicago American* believed that the Democrats were adopting a "rule or ruin" policy against the state bank. Since it would not become their "political engine," the Democrats had "in a most unnatural manner turned against their own bantling, because it had more honesty than its fathers."[13]

Table 1. Percentage Antibank Sentiment in the Illinois State Legislature, 1837-1841*

| Session | Senate (%) | Assembly (%) |
|---|---|---|
| Tenth Assembly | | |
| Regular Session 1836–37 | 45 | 45 |
| Special Session 1837 | 36 | 48 |
| Eleventh Assembly | | |
| Regular Session 1838–39 | 85 | 86 |
| Special Session 1839–40 | 85 | 55 |
| Twelfth Assembly 1840–41 | 81 | 67 |

* Reproduced from Rodney O. Davis, "Illinois Legislators and Jacksonian Democracy" (Ph.D. diss., Univ. of Iowa, 1966): 189, and is based on extensive and sophisticated roll call analysis. It is reprinted here with Professor Davis's permission.

During 1840 general economic conditions improved slightly; but the reputation of the Illinois State Bank had been harmed immeasurably by the hostile report of the investigating committee, and the financial condition of the state government deteriorated. Carlin again attacked the banks for suspending. Such "usurpations," for whatever seemingly good purpose, led to "political slavery." "The idea that the people should look up to [government] for assistance in time of pecuniary distress, is most revolutionary in its tendency . . . ," especially when the effect of government intervention was to aid private interests, thus to destroy equality. "In the pure republican days of the Revolution, merit and demerit, virtue and vice, alone drew the line of separation between one man and another: now the pampered fed monopolist scorns an association with honest poverty."[14]

The Democrats chose to interpret the end of the special session called to deal with financial problems as the termination of legalized suspension. They were thus able to force the banks to resume over the protests of the Whigs. This compulsory resumption months before the other banks of the country had begun to pay specie had the expected result. The state bank was drained of $455,000 in specie and forced to curtail its business drastically, increasing the pressure on debtors and causing a fall in the price level. The policy of curtailment covered loans to the state. This, combined with the bank's refusal to cash the salary warrants the state had issued to its employees in the emergency, caused a minority of Democrats to vote with the Whigs to legalize suspension. Again, similar provisions restricting the bank's activities were part of the bill. This time the bank was allowed to issue bills in denominations of $1, $2, and $3 to ease the currency shortage. In exchange for this, the bank was forced to take $50,000 of 6% Illinois bonds at par every six months for the next two years.[15]

# 2

Whig action in Illinois was generally in line with the policy of currency expansion that was urged by Whigs in other states in 1840 and 1841. In 1839 the Whig victory in Michigan had been complete, giving them control of both houses of the legislature and the governor's chair. It was obvious that one question with which the new administration would have to deal was that of currency and banking. During the fall, the *Daily Advertiser* contented itself with attacks on the Michigan State Bank and assertions that the Democrats could only view banks as political machines run by party men. In October the Whig paper attacked the Bank of the United States for suspending and argued that the suspension represented further failure of loco-foco Democratic policy.

> The suspension of the U.S. Bank is the climax of the assertion, that every financial scheme of the present administration is sure to fail. *The* pet Bank system was the first. That failed. The Pennsylvania U.S. Bank scheme was next. *That* has failed.—If even the Sub-treasury goes into operation, that will fail. Equally unsuccessful have been all the fiscal schemes of the loco focos of this State.

They gave us the wild cat system. *That's* gone, *They* took the State Bank to their bosom and that sleeps. You can't make current jelly out of calves' heads.[16]

In December 1839 newly elected Governor Woodbridge received advice from several Whigs. Robert Stuart, a shrewd politician from western Michigan, saw the main problem as one of adequate currency. He favored a state bank, but feared it either would become a "political engine" or would fall into the hands of men who would misuse it. Private banks, he believed, were less likely to fail and less open to fraud. Like other Whig correspondents of Woodbridge, he believed that a state bank could not be organized quickly enough to give adequate relief. Perhaps the state should take advantage of the Detroit banks, therefore, by diverting internal improvement funds. He emphasized that "the Banks [must] be enabled to extend that relief that is so much needed." He was not particular about how it was done. There was not enough currency even to pay taxes, let alone move crops. The threat of necessity to resume specie payments seemed to Stuart the reason that banks could not provide needed currency. He recommended that Woodbridge should sanction suspension, but should do so covertly by demanding resumption at some future date. Stuart expressed the dynamic view of the function of money held by many Whigs who believed that only adequate currency could revive the economy. He had no use for retrenchment. He was glad to hear Woodbridge agreed that more than "digging in the earth" was needed.[17]

Other letters to Woodbridge also reflected the view that the legitimate function of banks was to encourage industry and facilitate trade by supplying a sufficient and sound currency. One correspondent who agreed basically with Stuart suggested the state buy the already existing banks, reform them, and make state officers their directors. He also suggested that the banks lend money to farmers on produce deposited at accessible points. The proceeds of the sale minus shipping would go to the farmer.[18]

Many of these ideas appeared in Woodbridge's inaugural message in January. While he laid the blame for the evils of the currency at the door of the recent Democratic administrations, he analyzed the problem as had Stuart:

> The melancholy truth is now brought home to us all, that for the want of [sound currency], the ample products of our soil—the richest fruits of the toil of the husbandman, are in imminent danger of remaining a mass of useless rubbish in his yard and granaries, *because a safe and convenient currency can alone* furnish the avenue through which an appropriate market can be found.

Obviously the state was limited and Congress must act. Until then a temporary solution must be found. Because experience had shown there was not sufficient capital for a state bank, the existing banks had to be used. They should give the relief the people demanded by increasing bank issues to facilitate the movement of crops. Woodbridge concluded by suggesting that if city banks were used, they should first be thoroughly investigated.[19]

During the session the Whig press advised that a state bank like Indiana's was probably the best way to supply the additional $2 million dollars needed to move crops.

> Hundreds of thousands of dollars worth of wheat are heaped up in counties where absolutely, there is not a sufficient circulating medium if it were all scraped into one pile, to meet the town, county and state taxes. This state of things is intolerable, and must be remedied.[20]

The *Daily Advertiser* was favorably disposed to a plan presented to the senate by a select committee headed by Democrat Samuel Etheridge to which the Whigs on the committee agreed. This report examined banking in various foreign countries and concluded that none offered a completely safe precedent and in general such examples of banking systems were "not in accordance with the genius of our political institutions." A banking system had to be designed that fit Michigan's problems and aided in restoring prosperity. The paper suggested a state bank like that of Indiana, where the officers of the state were the bank directors. It was hoped that such a system could provide adequate facilities to all parts of the state and investment opportunities to capi-

talists without the multiplication of weak institutions, as under
the free banking law, and without the costs of the charter system.
The committee also wished to avoid the corruption of the charter
system, and the political domination seen under the New York
Safety-Fund. By the committee's admission, their plan was an
attempt to gain the advantages of free banking without its draw-
backs. The plan for such a state bank never got out of the senate,
where it was opposed by those Whigs who still showed distrust
of a politically controlled institution.[21]

In general the Whigs followed Woodbridge's suggestion to
make use of the Detroit banks—the Bank of Michigan and the
Farmers' and Mechanics' Bank. The two Whigs comprising the
majority of the committee considering this possibility blamed the
poor state of the currency on the policies of Jackson and Van
Buren, as did Woodbridge. Now "the states are compelled to re-
sort to the most available means in their power to sustain their
own credit, and mitigate, if possible, the embarrassments of the
people." Michigan *"should not reject"* the use of existing banks
for relief. To force them to resume and wind up affairs would only
further accentuate the effects of the depression. Instead of minis-
tering to perverted "party madness" and "the clamors of hireling
partizans," the recommended measures, the committee hoped,
would secure the "best circulating medium within the power of
the legislature to obtain, and to our citizens the most ample reward for the products of their labor and industry." It was a choice
between this or leaving "the country wholly destitute of the means
of liquidating balances between our citizens."[22]

Throughout March the *Daily Advertiser* defended the Currency Bill, as the impending Whig legislation was called. Everyone would be hurt by a *"no-currency"* policy. The Currency Bill
was the best way to augment the currency and to "enable the
farmer to sell his produce at a fair price—the mechanic and laborer to find employment at living wages—and the merchant to
sell his merchandise to pay his debts."[23]

On March 20 the legislature passed the Currency Bill, authorizing the sale of the drafts for the installment of Michigan's internal improvements loan. These future drafts would serve as the

95

basis for a loan to the state. In this way the banks were to supply the state with currency to pay its contractors. In exchange for this the banks were allowed to legally suspend until February 1, 1841, and to increase their issue to the amount of their paid-in capital. A number of other restrictions were added to safeguard the public. In an unusual vote, the measure was carried through the senate, with every Whig favoring and every Democrat opposing it. In the house one Democrat joined the 29 Whigs who favored the bill, and one Whig joined the 12 Democrats who opposed it. The Currency Bill was clearly a party measure. The Whig Legislative Address took full credit:

> Not only will it enable the state to pay off its debts, promptly, to its contractors on public works—and thus enable the contractor to pay off his laborers—and thus enable the laborer to feed and clothe his children—and thus enable the merchant to pay off his debts; but will create a circulation for the purchase of the farmers produce—give life to trade and commerce—labor to the mechanic —credit to the state abroad—and business energy and spirit to everyone. It will not only do all this, but will give us, what is indispensable to the successful prosecution of business, a sound, healthy, redeemable currency.[24]

While Whig confidence in mid-1840 turned out to be no more justified than that of the Democrats the previous year, their program reveals the kind of solution Whigs were likely to propose and their underlying attitude toward banks. They tended toward a corporatist view of the economy that emphasized cooperation between government and business and the interdependence of the various elements of the economy. They favored an expansion of the currency supply to spur economic development and bring relief to the entire population. Fearing an irredeemable currency, they chose to base this expansion on bank currency, so they sponsored the banks they believed to be strongest. When the Bank of Michigan finally went under after Whig attempts to support it had proved futile, the *Daily Advertiser* was as bitter in its criticism as any loco-foco Democratic organ. The paper violently attacked the bank as having "proved itself treacherous and rotten —a marble-encased mass of fiscal putridity—unprincipled and selfish—willing, if it may but escape itself, to smother a whole People with its rags." Throughout the state the Whig press echoed the charge that "the bank had played the people false." The Whigs favored a convertible currency and specie-paying banks, Whig newspapers argued. It was "no part of the Whig creed to sustain rotten banks or irredeemable currency." The Democrats were the ones who favored wildcat banks, the suspension of specie payments, and "shinplasters."[25]

Privately most Whig leaders agreed with the substance of the newspaper charges. Yet they generally condemned their tone, especially that of the *Daily Advertiser*, the state's Whig organ. Its personal attacks on Trowbridge were resented by his friends, and the general stance of the paper endangered party unity. With his usual candor Stuart wrote Woodbridge, "unless you give us a more *comely 'monster,'* than I anticipate, from the present shuffling in your ranks, we had better 'give up the ship.' "[26]

The Whigs' reactions to defeat as well as to success help clarify their position. They had made Stuart's "choice of evils" in a situation most of them believed would only have been aggravated by liquidation. The banks had insisted that they could sustain themselves if given time, and this seemed the only alternative to a disastrous curtailment. Whigs were naturally embittered when the Bank of Michigan failed. To most of them this offered only further proof that a national bank was necessary to attain their goal of a convertible bank currency, and they generally viewed President John Tyler's veto of the Whig bank bill in August 1841 as "a gross outrage against the expressed will of the People."[27]

# 3

Indiana Whigs revealed similar attitudes as they attempted to bring relief to their state. Governor David Wallace urged legislation that would provide as much uniformity as possible between specie and paper. In late 1840 he criticized banks that did not have proper capital and praised the Scottish system for its frequent settlements. His successor, Samuel Bigger, made the Whig position very clear in his inaugural address. He urged legislators to watch the banks "with a jealous eye," but assured them that "properly regulated banks" exercise a "beneficial influence on labor and enterprise." A convertible paper currency was "essential to our progressive improvement" because

> In it is laid the foundation of the true credit system, which is our surest protection against actual monopolies of capitalists. Credit constitutes the capital of the poor man, bestowed upon him as the reward of his enterprise and integrity. With it he can compete successfully with wealth in all its forms. Without it, labor and property would be brought entirely within the heartless grasp of individual wealth, whose operations can never be under the control of legislation.

Bigger concluded by criticizing those who would set interest against interest. The various branches of business are mutually dependent, he argued, and it is the duty of government to protect each from the undue encroachment of the others. Here the Whig position was clearly delineated.[28]

Whigs generally defended the Indiana state bank and backed the legislation increasing its stock and authorizing it to issue small bills. At the same time, they favored legislation prohibiting the issue of irredeemable currency by both the state and private entrepreneurs. Whig legislator Charles Test charged the Democrats with being in favor of irredeemable currency so that the public would eventually revolt and demand a specie currency. "Our object," he asserted, "should be to give all proper encouragement to good banking institutions, and thrust aside the miserable trash with which the community is threatened." Like most Whigs, he favored the issue of small notes by the state bank in the expectation that these would drive out the worthless "shinplasters" Whigs associated with the Democratic party.[29]

## 4

Although some Democrats agreed with these views, the official party response to Whig policies reveals a contrasting set of attitudes. In general, their view of economic society was atomistic; they tended to see the various elements of the economy in beneficial competition. To Democrats, Whig attempts to use the banking system or other corporations smacked of special legislation and a violation of the principle of equality in economic affairs. Unlike the Whigs, they feared price rises and believed that relief would only come with retrenchment. They did not trust bank money, and many turned to demands for a specie currency. Most of them distrusted government, particularly legislative interference in the economy. As the depression grew worse the party moved toward deflation, hard money, and laissez-faire.

The attack on the Currency Bill by Michigan Democrats clearly reflected these attitudes. According to the hostile minority report on suspension and the Whigs' relief proposals, suspension struck at "the basis of civil liberty" and was a "corporate infringement of individual right." What the people wanted was relief from banks and bank frauds. Only by reinstituting the only "constitutional currency," gold and silver, could the state return to prosperity. The Democratic press asserted that the bill would provide relief only to the bankers. All the Whigs were doing was using public funds to save the tottering Bank of Michigan. Antibank articles charging the Whigs with being the party of speculators, monopolists, and suspensionists were printed in the various Democratic papers. These two themes dominated: the Whigs favored an irredeemable currency ("Whig wild cat currency"), and the Whig legislation was a triumph of the "money power." The only alternative offered was a return to "constitutional currency." To the Democrats the idea that an increase in currency, credit, and prices could spur economic recovery was absurd. Currency only represented wealth; it could not create it and therefore could not have a dynamic function. The only answer was economy and retrenchment.[30]

In the Michigan election of 1841, Democrat John Barry, a Kalamazoo merchant with a moderately antibank record who opposed continued suspension in 1841, won the governorship by playing on antibank sentiments in both parties and advocating a return to economy in government. (Legend has it that he had the cuttings from the capitol lawn baled and sold to augment government revenues.) His nomination was a victory of the "conservative" faction of the Democrats. It was believed that his wide popularity, based on his success as a businessman and his reputation for personal honesty, would unify the Democrats and draw many Whigs to his support.[31]

This was obviously a clever political strategy, for Barry won easily in a bitter campaign despite Whigs castigating him as "the great patron of the 'irredeemables'" and insinuating that he was the puppet of the southern politician John Forsyth, who had been Van Buren's secretary of state. Barry and the Democratic press took the broad Jeffersonian position that he would "protect the interest of the people of Michigan irrespective of party." He attacked the "evils of irredeemable bank note circulation," but emphasized the Democratic program of the Independent Treasury.[32]

While historian Floyd Streeter in his *Political Parties in Michigan* has called Barry a "conservative," his actions as governor must be designated "radical" in relation to the bank question. On his recommendation in 1842, the legislature enacted a law making refusal to redeem notes in specie the test of insolvency. The same legislature abolished the corporate rights of the banks established under the free banking law and repealed the charters of those banks not then redeeming their notes. They also made it unlawful for municipalities to issue currency and repealed the act creating the state bank. In his annual messages of 1843 and 1845, Barry bitterly attacked the banks and suspension and praised the legislature for the reforms enacted. Fearing "most disastrous consequences to the public," he attempted in 1845 to suppress the revival of the Bank of Michigan. Barry's antibank ideas were written into the state Democratic platform, which stated that the party was "entirely opposed to the further incorporation of banks of issue in the state." Barry's successor, Alpheus Felch, an early and consistent opponent of banks, and the Democratic press would join in this antibank stance, espousing it throughout the remainder of the decade.[33]

Antibank sentiment flared up momentarily in the early 1840s in Indiana and then abated when the Democrats captured the statehouse in 1843. Opponents of the state bank admitted its importance to the state, but hoped to limit its power and lay the foundation for its eventual destruction. In 1842 they bitterly opposed legislation investing various state revenues and school and college funds in stock of the state bank. Public interest would be sacrificed by throwing these important funds into "the harlot lap of the Bank." Although most Democrats in the house did support the bill, the *Sentinel* attacked it as the product of "bank influence." One opponent bemoaned, "[the bank] has shot its roots so deep, and in so many branches, that it is not only difficult to eradicate it, but even to prune it. . . ." Following the Democratic victory in 1843, the new governor, James Whitcomb, took typical Democratic positions on the causes of the depression, the nature of money, and the desire to "again seek the ancient land marks of frugality and republican simplicity from which too many have unwittingly strayed." After he replaced Samuel Merrill with a Democrat as president of the state bank, little was heard about the bank question in Indiana.[34]

In Illinois both parties became increasingly antibank after the failure of the state bank in February 1842. This resembled the pattern in Michigan, where many Whigs turned antibank when the Bank of Michigan closed. In the election of that year, ex-Governor Joseph Duncan was attacked as "a British Bank Whig." His constant reply was that he had been hostile to banks as governor. The question that remained was how to wind up the affairs of the state bank. The new Democratic governor, Thomas Ford, urged moderation and was opposed only by a small minority of "ultra," hard money Democrats.[35]

From 1843 to 1851, Michigan and Illinois were antibank and Democratically controlled. Jacksonian governors there argued that the economic revival in each state resulted from the policies of retrenchment urged by their party and followed a consistently antibank line. Antibank "ultras" seem to have been predominant, writing their ideas into the state platforms. Throughout the decade John Wentworth's *Chicago Democrat* kept up its antibank barrage, while even the more moderate *Illinois State Register* was forced to insist that it was unequivocally opposed to banks. The

Indiana governors had similar leanings but refused to attack the state bank, which remained under Democratic control.

# 5

Only in Ohio did the Whigs retain control during these years. In that state the bank issue played a key role, and an intensive examination reveals the contrasting partisan attitudes toward the issue. By 1840, Dawson's Democratic *Cincinnati Advertiser* was vehemently against nearly all banks and opposed to the "bank reform" views of Democratic Governor Shannon. Although Medary defended the governor in the *Ohio Statesman,* his paper was also violently antibank. This was true of the Ohio congressional delegation as well, particularly Senators Benjamin Tappan and William Allen, and most of the Democratic politicians in Columbus. But a sizable minority still supported "bank reform," and the party was dangerously split on the eve of the presidential election. Party moderates, most of whom generally opposed banks, moved quickly to heal the breach in the party. Generally they did not wish to dump Shannon, who was extremely popular (particularly with the Germans of the state) and who privately admitted that his message had been a mistake. Emphasizing the need for party harmony, these broker politicians secured the renomination of Shannon on a platform that guaranteed a zealous pursuit of bank reform "until all the rottenness of the present system has been fully exposed, and effectual measures adopted to secure the people against future fraud and impositions." In the legislature the Democrats revived the law prohibiting small notes and also banned circulation of "post notes" and notes not redeemable in specie. This was hardly satisfying to the most violent opponents of banks, but the split in the party was, for the moment, breached.[36]

The Ohio Whigs opposed Van Buren's Independent Treasury and tended to defend the banks as in the other states, but they were not opponents of bank reform. Governor Shannon's 1839 message may have caused consternation in his own ranks, but it

102

was widely applauded by the Whigs. They even considered nominating Shannon as a Whig if he were dropped by the Democrats. Whig county conventions called for a properly restricted banking system affording a convertible currency. These demands were incorporated into the party's platform in 1840. During the campaign of that year, the *Ohio State Journal* pictured the Democrats' "War on Credit" as a direct attack on the poor, who without the benefit of credit were at the mercy of the wealthy. There, and in other sympathetic papers, Whigs were portrayed as the friends of the common man. They denied that the party of Van Buren had any right to the name Democrat.[37]

Veteran politicians believed the campaign of 1840 the most vigorous they had ever witnessed. An unprecedented turnout swept Whig Thomas Corwin into the governor's chair. The new governor suggested two possible solutions to the state's banking problems: either a state bank or the rechartering of the present banks under the direction of a state board of control, which would issue all bank notes and examine the banks. The majority of the Whigs favored the latter plan which also included a safety-fund provision modeled on that of New York, but neither proposal could be carried through the legislature because of Democratic opposition in the state senate. The Democrats insisted on unlimited liability. The Whigs countered that it would restrict stock ownership to the most wealthy, whereas small denominations of bank stock would open good investments to the "little man," for whom the risks of unlimited liability would be too great.[38]

Conditions worsened during 1841. The amount of specie in Ohio banks declined to almost half what it had been a year earlier, and many banks failed. Their defeat of 1840 was widely interpreted by Democrats as the result of the corrupting influence of banks. With antibank sentiment rising, the more radical elements gained control of the Democratic party to redeem Ohio "from the thralldom of the paper money discredit party." County meetings took violently antibank stands. When the Democrats regained the legislature in 1841, requests from banks for renewal of their expiring charters were rejected. Bank riots (probably initiated by the Democrats) broke out in Cincinnati in January 1842.

The *Ohio Statesman* responded by denouncing bankers as thieves. The paper expressed sympathy for the rioters, but hoped that "the people—a robbed, swindled, and ruined people—will restrain their feelings under the outrages of these shin-plaster gamblers."[39]

When Whig plans for a revived national bank were squelched by President Tyler's vetoes, Governor Corwin again suggested the adoption of either a state bank or the safety-fund system he had earlier recommended to solve the state's problems. Some sort of action was imperative since the federal government could not be counted on and the charters of most of the state's banks were due to expire at the end of 1842. Corwin favored the establishment of a state bank, but a Whig bill to create one was killed by the Democratic legislature. Most Democrats had come to agree with Moses Dawson that "the next greatest evil to a United States bank . . . is a State Bank and branches."[40]

The majority of the Democrats were "hards"—that is, adamantly antibank—but there were differences of opinion on how to deal with the probank "softs," and the popular Shannon was again nominated as a compromise candidate. Although there were fears that the newly elected legislature was a "bank legislature instead of a *Democratic* one," it was nevertheless guided by the "hards." Under their aegis it passed a law rescinding the charters of all banks that did not redeem their notes in specie. It also established a general banking law sponsored by Democrat Bela Latham that placed restrictions on future banks of issue: capital had to be paid in specie before opening, loans to directors and stockholders were limited, stockholders and directors were liable for the notes of the bank, and a safety fund was established. Banks not complying with the law were prohibited from issuing notes.[41]

The Latham law should not be confused with later free banking laws. It did not embody the principle of a bond-secured (or even a mortgage-secured) currency, and the banks created were to be "joint stock partnerships" rather than corporations. The intention of the Democrats who supported the law was not to create opportunities in the banking business and expand the supply of credit and currency. Quite the contrary. Although the bill was amended in 1843 to placate the "softs," who threatened to revolt after the "hards" had defeated an attempt to extend charters of existing banks, the Latham law, even with its later amendments, represented a political compromise designed to be acceptable to all factions of the Democracy except the most implacable "softs." Some of the "hardest of the hards" readily admitted that it was a scheme by which banks could be completely eliminated while they were ostensibly being reformed. Hard money advocate and Democratic state legislator Edwin Stanton was unhappy that his "friends instead of maintaining the true position of hostility to the whole system, have again begun to temporize"; but he added, "no banking will be done under it, [the Latham law] and if adopted, it cannot bring along with it the power the old system possesses."[42]

The Whigs voted solidly against both the original Latham law and the 1843 amendment. They attacked the Democrats for playing politics with the currency and suggested that there could be no sound currency until the Democrats were voted out of office. The laws of 1842 and 1843 were "humbug" designed to destroy the banks. They failed to regulate the banks in existence, they did not provide adequate security, and they created no new banks. The currency question had been "narrowed down to the smallest objects of party success, leaving the great interests connected with a sound currency to take care of themselves."[43]

Whigs generally agreed with this analysis and expressed support for an expanded sound currency, but they disagreed on the importance of the currency question in relation to other issues. Some believed that it was much less important than moral reform; others, that it was hurting the party and should be dropped or reformulated; and still others, that it was beneficial because the issue would split the Democrats. Corwin wanted to settle the issue in any way practicable and compatible with Whig principles, so the Democrats would be forced to oppose the Whigs' popular stand on the tariff issue. Yet the people of Ohio were dissatisfied with the Democratic failure to provide a sound currency, and the Whigs capitalized on this discontent by making "banks or no banks" the main issue in 1843. The *Ohio State Journal* asserted that "it devolves upon the Whigs to repair the destruction" left by the Democrats. When the Whigs carried the election in 1843, they interpreted their victory as a popular rejection of Democratic bank ideas.[44]

The Democrats continued to bicker among themselves over the banking issue, which figured in the party split over the nominee for the coming presidential race. The antibank radicals, who backed Van Buren, seemed to have control; but there were certainly enough supporters of Lewis Cass for the nomination to make that control unsure. Shannon complicated matters by continuing to advocate "a well guarded, well restricted system of local banks." In January the Democrats met and decided on David Tod as their gubernatorial candidate and a strongly antibank platform. Tod was not an opponent of all banks but an advocate of bank reform in terms of the Latham bill and its amendment. When he attempted to unite the party on these principles, his public statement left both factions unhappy. Open warfare broke out when a group of "softs" joined with the Whigs in 1844 to extend the charters of five banks, including the Wooster Bank, which was in the hands of Cass Democrats. This conflict within the party and the public "cry for banks" shifted the political scales again in favor of the Whigs; their candidate, Mordecai Bartley, was elevated to the governor's chair in 1844.[45]

By an extremely odd coincidence, Bartley replaced his own son, Democrat Thomas W. Bartley, who had become acting governor when Shannon received a diplomatic post. The younger Bartley had been responsible for the 1843 amendment to the Latham law. In his annual message in 1844, he had defended his party's action, vigorously attacking special legislation and praising the Latham law. He had expressed faith in "the laws of trade, which regulate and control prices and currency . . . [and] are as searching, as all pervading and as irresistible as the law of nature." While he had favored general laws, he had been opposed to a bond-secured currency as "the most objectionable and dangerous . . . to the independence and purity of the government, and the liberties of the people." It would be "a union of bank and State . . . an incestuous and unholy coalition" like the Bank of England, a danger to liberty. Only "punctual conversion" and the use of short-term loans "on strictly commercial paper" could secure paper money and prevent its depreciation.[46]

While the younger Bartley had espoused the Democratic idea of free banking, his father advocated the Whig conception of free banking, which provided for incorporation and a bond-secured currency. Mordecai Bartley's inaugural address carefully considered the banking question. Of the current systems of banking, he believed that state banks had shown themselves to be little better than local banks, which gave rise to curruption and special privileges. The existing general law was impracticable. The New York system was probably best, but it was liable to the objection that it was controlled by Wall Street. Thus, he suggested a tightly restricted free banking system with currency secured by Ohio bonds or Ohio real estate. Security was to be protected by the maintenance of a 33 1/3% specie reserve against circulation as well as by these stocks. He assured his constituents that fate of the free banking law would not be the same as Michigan's, because the Ohio land that would be used as security was cultivated and salable.[47]

In the state senate the Standing Committee on Currency, under the direction of Alfred Kelley, quickly introduced a banking bill. Kelley was a long-time Whig who had played a major role in the state's canal policies and would later be important in the fight over taxation. The Kelley bank bill bore the stamp of a pragmatic political broker and of the type of western developer Daniel Boorstin has termed the "booster"—that is, someone who thought primarily in terms of community development.[48]

It was clear that Kelley believed the purpose of the bill to be the establishment of "a safe and convenient currency" and aid in providing capital for "commercial and manufacturing operations." The committee found that a system of associated banks similar to the state banks was most popular in areas where there was local capital and that in capital-shy areas free banking was favored. "To reconcile these conflicting opinions and to extend to the different sections of the State that relief which the people so generally demand at the hands of the General Assembly," the

107

Kelley bank bill proposed to establish a state bank of Ohio and to provide for free or, as they were called, "independent" banks. In this way security for the billholder would be guaranteed, while proper inducements would be offered capitalists. The proposed state bank was not to be a central bank, but rather an association of twelve branches, with capital between $100,000 and $500,000 and supervised by a board of control. The branch banks would be required to redeem their notes at all times, and the amount of notes would be limited in ratio to specie. As added security each branch was to contribute 10% of its notes to a safety fund invested in Ohio stocks, United States stocks, or Ohio real estate. The independent or free banks could be smaller, with capital of $50,000. Stocks of either Ohio or the United States equal to each bank's capital were deposited with the state treasurer to secure the note issue. There were also to be yearly examinations.[49]

Although the Kelley bill included a free banking provision, its intention was to meet the demand for well-secured banking facilities in capital-poor areas rather than to oppose monopoly or to give free rein to the "natural laws of trade." Kelley warned that the idea that banks should be free like any other business was a false analogy. A well-restricted but open system, rather than free competition, was the only way that the community could have the benefits of banks without the dangers of a debased currency.

The Kelley bill was a Whig measure carried through the legislature by a strict party vote, but this unanimity was the product of compromise between the factions of the party. The majority of Whigs, particularly those in the northern part of the state, preferred a free banking system patterned on that of New York, and many disliked the monopoly aspects of the state bank proposal. Most Whig politicians and editors agreed that "the people—the farmers and mechanics of both parties desire good banks." Compromise was necessary if any bill was to pass in the face of Democratic opposition to all banks. The *Ohio State Journal*, which leaned toward a free banking system, supported the compromise and acclaimed the bill as a move toward a true system of banking open to all. In his annual message of 1845, Governor Bartley praised the new system and credited the rising prosperity to it. Truly a credit system was essential to a free and enterprising people. "In those countries where despotism prevails to the greatest extent, and where the laboring classes of people are most oppressed, banks of issue are not known." Because of this, the governor argued, "the man who is indigent in early life, whatever may be his native ability and energy of character, ends a tedious existence as he commenced it." By providing credit to all men of good character, regardless of their status, banks served as the key to economic opportunity.[50]

Democrats, both in the legislature and outside, had expected the Whigs would "curse" the state with "bank rags" and lost no time in attacking the "Monster Bank Bill." Bartley vowed to expose the "deformities of Kelley's Sea Serpent," which he believed "the most dangerous political engine" ever created in the state. "The prevailing disposition among Democrats," he wrote Benjamin Tappan, "is to give the new banking system no quarter." The *Ohio Statesman* demanded the law's repeal, but an attempt at repeal led in the house by the radical Cincinnati Democrat, Charles Reemelin, was defeated by the Whig majority. The *Statesman* feared that with the bill's passage "a few old hunker nabobs" would rule. The Hamilton County Democratic meeting saw it as "a monstrous and dangerous system of paper." The *Cadiz Sentinel* equated Kelley with the eighteenth-century financier John Law and the

> mistaken idea that a flood of bank paper will add to the prosperity and happiness of the people. Idleness and vice, speculation and rascality, are necessary attendants upon the excessive emission of paper money.

In the senate, David T. Disney, an ex-director of the Ohio Life Insurance and Trust Company, now seemed to see the true Jacksonian light. He believed the bill much too complex for the people to understand. "No wise, no pure, no sound legislation" requires the combination of these two different systems. By flooding the country with paper money, it could only lead to the rule of the wealthy and the "ruin of a free and independent people."[51]

When repeal efforts failed, the Democrats carried the issue to

109

the people. With federal patronage and, to a degree, because the Kelley bill was a Whig measure, the "hards" were able to control the party and dedicate it to a hard money course. Charles P. Wolcott, a vigorous opponent of banks, wrote Benjamin Tappan,

> Is it not about time for the Democratic Party *throughout the State,* to abandon the humbug deceptive unmeaning cant about "Bank Reform" and speak out plainly for "Bank Destruction"? Let that be made one of the tests, a *sine qua non,* of the true and only Democracy.

Many Democrats believed that conciliation of the "softs" had been disastrous to the party, for it had lost the votes of "honest men." No longer would the "truckling of professed democrats on the currency question" be tolerated. In July the state convention denounced the Kelley bank bill as "a corrupt, irresponsible, and swindling system of monopolies" and demanded its immediate repeal. County conventions repeated this demand. The vociferous Democrats of Hamilton County resolved:

> that metallic currency has been tested by the experience of the ages. On the contrary, all systems of paper currency ever yet contrived have failed, and in their inevitable overthrow have entailed more distress and loss, and perpetuated more robbery and fraud than would colonize a continent with convicts and paupers. Nor have we seen in the Whig legislature of last year any symptoms of a wisdom superior to the paper-mongers who have gone before them—but a compound rather of all shallow schemes of their predecessors.[52]

The Whigs countered that credit was necessary to the progress of civilization, while hard money was monarchical, savage, and a detriment to the laboring classes. For the time being, the people agreed. The Whigs were successful at the polls throughout the remainder of the decade.[53]

# 6

In each of the states of the Old Northwest a similar pattern appeared in the decade following the Panic of 1837. Gradually the Democrats moved from acceptance of banks to "bank reform" and then to the opposition of all banks of issue. Their outlook was constantly regressive, searching for purity, simplicity, and virtue. They feared debt and desired to simplify and purify the governmental process. When they advocated free banking, it was generally out of faith that the "natural laws of trade" would easily assure honesty if corporate privileges were removed and small notes eliminated.

The Whigs' position was not antithetical to the Democrats'. Rather, its emphasis was different, stressing what is today called economic development. Banks and bank credit could serve a dynamic function in the developmental process. The Whig outlook tended to be progressive in that it looked to the opportunity offered by an expanding economy. Gradually Whigs came to accept free banking under general incorporation laws with notes based on government stocks. Such a system would provide a safe currency and adequate accommodations for business enterprise and would draw capital into developing areas.

The contrasting attitudes of the two parties toward banking revealed slightly different views of the good society. These were more fully developed in the constitutional debates of the midnineteenth century.

# CHAPTER 5

## THE DIALOG OF PARTIES: FREE BANKING IN THE CONSTITUTIONAL CONVENTIONS, 1846-1851

### 1

In July 1851 the *Democratic Review* noted that

> During the last ten years the attention of the people of the United States has been powerfully drawn to the subject of their constitutions, and within the last five years eleven State Conventions have been held, for the formation of eleven constitutions, for eleven of the old independent states, while many other states are still agitating the question; and seven conventions in new states have provided as many new constitutions for an equal number of new independent sovereignties. In all these constitutions many improvements, suggested by the working of the old ones have been made upon the instruments; and the constitutions of the new states, having the advantage of the experience of the old ones, contain all the "latest improvements" adapted to the new state of things.

Certainly these years represent one of the most important periods of constitutional reform in American history, as Americans strove to write into the fundamental law of their states the lessons of experience and the teachings of "the modern science of government."[1]

The *Democratic Review* went on to acclaim the basic alterations embodied in these new charters. The judiciary was general-

112

ly remodeled and made elective as were all executive offices. "Reform . . . also extended to the law-making branch, and the powers and influence of those bodies [were] restrained." Biennial sessions often replaced annual meetings of the legislature and both the length of the sessions and the legislator's pay were limited. Constraining the legislative branch's role in financial affairs was a major objective. Legislative power to lend and borrow money and to grant "special privileges to corporate bodies" was strictly circumscribed. Restraints on the power to create corporations were

> particularly pointed at banking institutions. . . . The evils which the public suffered from the excessive debt and inordinate bank-expansion, were a lesson of experience which has not now been lost. Its effects upon the public mind are recorded in all the constitutions, and at this moment, when the losses have been recovered and general prosperity tempts to a renewal of the paper schemes of former years those restraints are beneficially felt.[2]

Among the states referred to by the *Democratic Review* were those of the Old Northwest. There the banking issue was debated at length in the constitutional conventions meeting in Wisconsin in 1846 and again in 1847–48, in Illinois in 1847, in Indiana in 1850, in Michigan in 1850, and in Ohio in 1850–51. These debates reveal crucial differences between the parties on this issue, differences that were rooted in contrasting conceptions of the proper economic base for democratic government. The "radical" faction dominated the Democratic party, advocating return to specie, in accordance with their desire to regain purity and simplicity in government. The Whigs continued to argue that an "adequate, well secured" currency was necessary to stimulate economic growth. To this end, Whigs generally advocated free banking. In each convention the Whigs, along with a faction of the Democratic party that was unwilling to give up the benefits of bank facilities, combined to defeat hard money proposals. The heated debate over the banking question gives a unique insight into the differences between the parties and the way in which this crucial issue functioned within the persuasion of each party.

113

## 2

Nearly everywhere in the country the Democrats led the movement for constitutional change. Throughout the 1840s the *Democratic Review*, which was widely read by Democratic politicians in the Old Northwest, agitated for reform and reported its progress. Ohio Democrat Clement L. Vallandigham listed constitutional revision among the basic principles of the "radical progressive Democracy."[3]

The initial attempts to call constitutional conventions in the early 1840s, however, met with little success. Wisconsin voters, who by and large feared increased taxes and government interference with their pursuits, rejected statehood proposals four times before 1846. In the 1830s the Democratic governor, Henry Dodge, had been an advocate of statehood, but during the next decade the Whigs and Governor James Doty led the campaign. By 1846, when the issue was finally decided, the Democrats had swung behind the movement. They dominated the convention of that year and produced a constitution in line with "radical" Democratic doctrine. After it was defeated at the polls, a second convention met and drew up a new constitution, which was accepted in 1848.[4]

Voters in Indiana and Illinois showed a similar hesitancy about revising their constitutions. There was a series of unsuccessful attempts to call a convention to revise the Indiana constitution, then only narrow acceptance of the idea in 1846. Fewer than half of the Hoosiers who voted for the governor registered an opinion on the convention referendum. Illinois voters defeated a proposed convention in 1842 but finally sanctioned it four years later.[5]

While the Illinois convention met in 1847, the Indiana convention was delayed for nearly five years by constitutional problems and politics. Revision had not been a party issue in 1845, but the support given revision by the Democratic *Indiana State Sentinel* associated constitutional change with the Democrats, automatically drawing opposition from the Whigs. In 1846 the Whig legislature refused to summon a convention on the grounds that legitimate doubt existed as to the will of the people and the constitutionality of such a convention. During the next two years the Democrats continued to push the issue. Twice in 1848, Governor James Whitcomb advised calling a convention to rid the state of the evils of special legislation, thereby to cut the expenses of government. The Democratic State Convention, which met in early 1849, echoed this demand. The opposition from the Whigs was moderate. Generally, they argued that there seemed no indication the people wanted change although a sizable number of Whigs seem to have feared that the convention might permit slavery in the southern counties. Finally, in early 1849 the legislature sanctioned a convention; it was accepted by the people and convened in 1850.[6]

While the Indiana convention met, similar bodies assembled to alter the fundamental law of Ohio and Michigan. The Democratic governor of Michigan, Alpheus Felch, demanded reform of the constitution; but the question of a convention was never a party issue there. In the election of 1849, which returned the tightfisted Democrat John Barry to the governor's chair, the voters favored a convention by a large margin. What opposition there was came from Whigs, but it appears that more Whigs voted for the convention than against it.[7]

The fight over constitutional revision in Ohio was more clearly a party contest, with the Democrats again leading the drive for revision. In 1843, Governor Wilson Shannon suggested the calling of a convention. After the passage of the Kelley law in 1845, Democrats increased efforts to have the legislature convene on constitutional revision. The Whigs, who feared Democratic hard money "ultraism" and the destruction of the banking system, were able to block such attempts in 1847 and 1848. Democratic demand for revision was relentless, however. Both the Democratic and Free-Soil platforms in 1848 endorsed the idea of a convention. Throughout the year Samuel Medary's *Ohio Statesman* and a weekly special, the *New Constitution*, kept up the demand. The following year the Whigs gave up their opposition, and the voters of the state approved the calling of a convention.[8]

## 3

Within five years, six conventions met and revised the constitutions of the five states of the Old Northwest. The "radicals" or the "progressives", as they called themselves, within the Democracy led the battle for reform. Most Whigs took a "conservative" position on the question of change, and agreed with the *Indiana State Journal* that

> A change in the fundamental law should not be made for trivial causes. It ought to be made only to abrogate some great wrong resulting from its provisions. Frequent changes impair the respect in which a constitution to be valuable ought to be held by the people.[9]

The dichotomy of "progressive" Democrats and "conservative" Whigs is almost universal in the historical literature on the period. Too often these labels have been allowed to take on twentieth century connotations, while their content in the context of the 1840s has been ignored. The Democrats who took the initiative in the movement for constitutional revision had a fairly well-defined program in which banking reform played a central role. This set of reforms made up the content of "progressivism" in its antebellum form. Medary's *Ohio Statesman* carried on its masthead the basic principles of the "progressive" Democracy: "The Sovereignty of the People—The Rights of the States, and a Light and Simple Government." The general principle that "the best government is that which governs least" was accepted as the only sure guard against encroachments on individual liberty. In the mid-1840s the Ohio Democrat Clement L. Vallandigham asserted that the "progressive" Democracy

> will contend to the utmost, for the largest wholesome *individual freedom* of action in all things, and oppose with our whole heart, that pernicious and anti-democratic intermeddling of government with those private affairs and relations between man and man, which of right and upon policy ought to be left to the individual citizen himself.

116

The central conflict within the country was "a war between man and money." To alleviate this condition the "progressive" Democracy advocated "the right of revolution, of universal suffrage, of freedom of trade, of overthrow of banks, of the establishment of a constitutional currency."[10]

In this argument there was a moral imperative. Essentially, it represented a secularized version of the conflict between Christ and the anti-Christ in its equation of money with power, and power with corruption. All virtue emanated from the people; all corruption, from the "money power." The *Milwaukee Courier* asserted that men were "able to trace the artificial inequality of wealth, much pauperism and crime, the low state of public morals, and many of the other evils of society directly to this [paper money] system." Broken banks, a debased currency, and the struggles to repay the huge internal improvements debts seemed implicitly to argue for simplicity and economy as the only viable course. Indiana's governor, James Whitcomb, warned against swelling prosperity that might induce another "orgy" of speculation. "The sure and only sure remedy against this threatening evil, is, the observance of economy and industry, and above all, *to resist the allurements of credit.*"[11]

This outlook dictated a certain number of reforms that Democrats advanced in all of these western states. Although there was some deviation, particularly among the conservative "Old Hunker" faction in Wisconsin, on the whole the party advocated the election of all state officials including judges. On the question of suffrage, the "progressive" Democracy stood for universal *white* manhood suffrage, a right they were willing to extend to resident aliens. With these reforms the branches of government would be effectively separated so the influence of the executive would be lessened and the government would more truly represent the people.[12]

In addition to making the government more representative, Jacksonian "progressives" wished to check corruption and governmental intrusion on individual rights. The target of this agitation was the legislature, which was held responsible for the evils of debt, banking, and "special privileges." In most cases Democrats favored a strong veto. The executive was the representative of the will of the people; but his functions were thought to be purely negative, as the emphasis on the veto indicates. His duty was to protect the people's rights from violation by the legislature.[13]

Democrats looked upon the legislature as a center of corruption rather than as a representative body. It was the arena in which the power of money and special interests held sway. It was responsible for the ruinous internal improvements projects and the depreciated currency. It saddled the people with a complex and confusing body of "unnecessary laws" and fostered "special privilege." All this was done at a tremendous expense to the taxpayer. In order to make the legislative process cheaper and rid the states of the inequities of special legislation, the Democracy advocated general laws. If this reform were implemented, the legislature would be able to conduct its necessary business in much shorter time, making possible biennial or even triennial sessions. This would mean a tremendous saving to the taxpayers. By substituting general laws for the numerous instances of special legislation, equality, simplicity, and economy could be achieved.

Even with this reform, the tendencies toward corruption had to be blocked in certain instances. Constitutions should protect the people from the excesses of legislatures, particularly by limiting the size and nature of the public debt and by eliminating banks of issue. The *Cleveland Plain Dealer* spoke for the "progressive" Democracy when it said,

> It must not be left to the corrupt cupidity or caprice of future Legislatures to say whether this State shall be dotted over with Bank Corporations or cut up with Plank and Rail Road Corporations, with such tyrannical and exclusive privileges as shall make them masters, we their slaves.[14]

While some Democrats seemed willing to support a well-guarded banking system, everywhere the party as such stood solidly opposed to all banks. Hard money advocates were assured that the "currency question so long a rock on which many have foundered . . . no longer distracts our friends," that "*the voice of the Democracy says no Banks."* By the mid-1840s the Democracy of every state in the Old Northwest except Indiana had written into the party platform a demand for the elimination of banks of issue and a speedy return to the "constitutional currency" of gold and silver. The Democratic governors of Michigan and Illinois echoed these demands in addresses to their legislatures.[15]

In Indiana all of the standard demands for biennial sessions, general laws, and limitations on the state debt were aired by the governors and the state Democratic convention, but the banking issue was sidestepped. However, by the late 1840s the hard money element had considerably increased its power. A lengthy list of Democratic demands urged by the *Goshen Democrat* in late 1848 included the revision of the banking system. By 1850 the *Indiana State Sentinel* listed the abolition of banks of issue and a return to "constitutional currency" as basic principles of the Democracy. The majority of the party favored the complete abolition of banks of issue and the use of an exclusive specie currency, or at least one with no bills under $20. This was the view put forth in the party's platforms, adhered to by Democratic governors in their addresses to the legislature, and championed as the "true test of Democracy" by the leading party organs in every state.[16]

If the Democrats favored general laws in most cases, their stance on banks should not be confused with an advocacy of free banking. They vehemently opposed any type of inflation, and their program was, in fact, harshly deflationary. Democrats opposed banks of all kinds, not merely those created by special charters. Party leaders like John Barry of Michigan and Augustus French of Illinois made it clear that free banking was no better than any other paper money system. Barry believed that the argument for a stock-secured currency was "as indefensible as others that have preceded it." French's 1846 message was at the time misinterpreted by some people as favoring free banking, yet in his later messages he was unmistakably clear that he advocated the complete prohibition of banks. In 1849 he saw nothing to "recommend the new system [free banking] over the old chartered institutions." Two years later he told the legislature that the seemingly anti-monopolistic features of free banking were only a way to cover up the "odious features" all banking systems possessed. Democrats generally agreed with the *Ohio Press* that the Democracy would "reform banking by the entire abolition of all chartered and special privileges and by a return to the constitutional currency of gold and silver."[17]

Because of the two-party nature of American politics, it is common to conceive of one party as the antithesis of the other. This dangerous tendency is encouraged by party rhetoric, which attempts to picture the opposition as antithetical to the interests of "the people," which each party claims to represent. In the argument over constitutional revision the Democrats charged that the Whigs opposed the interests of the people by resisting universal suffrage, advocating an irredeemable paper currency, and generally defending the interests of the privileged monopolies. Since the Whigs were after all a political party contending for power and would hardly admit to these charges, the Democrats generally charged that the Whig denials of Democratic accusations were insincere; the Whigs were trying to fool the people. "In relation to the great subject of constitutional reform, there appears to be a studied effort to deceive," charged the *Daily Lafayette Courier*.[18]

While Whigs were on the defensive in the fight over constitutional revision and spent a great deal of time denying Democratic charges, they did present a program for reform. It is this program that makes up the content of Whig "conservatism." When examined in detail, it hardly proves to be the converse of Democratic "progressivism."

On most of the major questions concerning democratic government, the Whigs and their opponents agreed. Both parties advocated electing state officials, including judges. Both parties favored universal white manhood suffrage.* The only real difference on the question of suffrage was that the Whigs usually wished to limit suffrage to native and naturalized citizens. They also tended to be more amenable to the establishment of common schools.

---

* A minority of the Whigs wished to extend suffrage to the black population, and there were probably as many Whigs as Democrats who favored female suffrage. In any case the number was very small in both parties.

But generally the parties agreed on other social issues like the elimination of imprisonment for debt and the exemption of homesteads and tools in bankruptcy proceedings. It goes without saying that each was willing to gerrymander its state under the guise of reform.[19]

In contrast to the Democrats, the Whigs opposed executive veto power. They saw the legislature as the truly democratic element of the government. This does not mean that the Whigs advocated unrestricted legislative power. They usually joined their Democratic opponents on curbing the state's ability to incur debt, on the substitution of general laws for special legislation, and on the necessity of biennial sessions to save the taxpayer money.

The two parties came into direct conflict on the question of banking. Whigs took a positive stand that was clearly at odds with Democratic antibank, hard money positions. Here was an issue that defined the character of the parties.

By the mid-1840s the free banking element dominated the Whig party. To Whigs of every state free banking meant expansion of credit and the establishment of a secure currency. A typical editorial reported,

> We voted for a Constitutional convention because we wanted the following changes: Biennial sessions; electing of judges and all other officers; a general [free] banking law; a homestead exemption law; fines to go to the school funds of the township.[20]

State conditions caused some variations in the arguments. Where there were no banks, as in Michigan and Illinois, Whigs were clearly and almost unanimously in favor of free banking. Ohio Whigs stood for retention of the Kelley Law, which combined free banking with a state bank. In Indiana the party split between groups wishing to retain the state bank, which had performed so well, and those wishing credit expansion through free banking. As the Indiana convention showed, these factions of the Whig party were not entirely at odds and both eventually supported free banks.

The situation in Wisconsin was complicated by the fact that the Whigs in powerful Dane County—the county in which Madison, the state capital, was located—passed a resolution in favor of

a direct and positive prohibition against the granting by legislature of any charter for banking purposes, or the passage of any
law whereby any monopoly or any special exclusive rights and
privileges may be conferred for private purposes.

Several days later the Whig paper the *Madison Express* avowed
its support for the position of the majority of Whigs—namely, that
a mixed currency of specie and paper money was essential to national prosperity. However, the time was not yet ripe for state
banking in Wisconsin. The paper argued that Wisconsin's situation was comparable to Michigan's in the 1830s and urged the
postponement of banking until the public could be secured against
a similar failure.[21]

Other Wisconsin Whigs took a more positive attitude toward
free banking. In particular, the dynamic young Whig John Tweedy
pressed in the convention for the adoption of a free banking system like New York's. The *Milwaukee Sentinel and Gazette* supported his proposal. Its editor, Rufus King, encouraged Tweedy
to amend "the absurd provision about banks and banking" so that
it would not block passage of the constitution. In the 1846 convention, Whigs were unsuccessful in their effort to have free banking principles written into the constitution. The following year
they organized the opposition to the proposed antibank constitution and, with the aid of a faction of the Democratic party, were
able to defeat it.[22]

Whigs generally believed that the majority of the state's people
opposed the banking article. Contemporary politicians reported
that in the eastern part of the state and especially in Milwaukee
this provision was unpopular and that the Whigs were openly
"declaring and preaching for banks." Edward Ryan, the Racine
Democrat responsible for the stringent article against banks, wrote
his fellow "radical" Democrat Moses Strong, who lived in the
western part of the state: "The opposition may *talk* about mar-
ried women and exemption, but here along the Lake Shore at all
events, the real opposition is to the restrictions against Banks, internal improvement, and State debt." Everywhere in the state it
was conceded that the only real issue was the article eliminating

banks. Because of the generalized opposition to this measure, the coalition of "Whigs and pseudo Democrats" were able to defeat the constitution and force the calling of a second convention. While Democrats mourned the defeat of "the best Constitution ever formed by any of the Union," the Whigs rejoiced. By the second constitutional convention, the Whig influence had increased. A free banking provision was accepted in the new constitution, which in other ways did not alter the 1846 document.[23]

# 4

In the course of these convention debates, the strength of the various factions within the parties was exposed, and the appeals of the two parties fully developed. The Democrats had majorities in all the conventions and nearly complete control in Wisconsin and Michigan. Consequently, most of the oratory came from the Jacksonians. Not a little of this was directed as much to their constituents as to their fellow convention members. While there may have been consensus on the banking issue, there was still no unanimity. The issue incited such intraparty feuding as to cause John Palmer, an Illinois Democrat, to praise the Whigs for having "shown so much judgement and discretion as to keep silent, and leave this war entirely in the hands of the 'harmonious' democracy. . . ."[24]

Regardless of the intraparty strife the debate engendered, it did clarify the ideas of the Democracy on banking. Probably the single document most representative of Democratic views was the Majority Report from the Committee on Banks and Currency presented to the Ohio convention. It was written by John Larwell, a merchant from Wayne County and an avowed hard money Democrat, and signed by the other three Democratic members of the committee, while the Whigs on the committee dissented. This report suggested that the constitution prohibit the formation of any new banks of issue and forbid the "circulation [of] any bank notes or paper of any description" by any corporation or associations then in existence.[25]

In defending this total prohibition of banks and paper, the Ohio majority report offered several arguments that had already been advanced by Democrats in the other states. "The great objection to the policy of the paper money banking system," the Ohio report maintained, "consists in its corrupting and dangerous political tendency and the stupendous frauds, and the occasional extensive disasters to [sic] which invariably, sooner or later, result from it." In establishing the moral case against banks of issue, the Democrats invoked and built upon the arguments and rhetoric that had evolved since the 1830s. To the fiery editor of the *Detroit Free Press*, John S. Bagg, the issue was clear. He told the Michigan convention,

> Our government is based upon equal rights—banks upon fraud and corruption; and no man dare deny that they are unequal in their practices; a bundle of absurdities, of hypocrisy and incongruity, from their commencement to their death; and in justice to equal rights let us have no banks.

By the destruction of equal rights, the banking system permitted the growth of a monied aristocracy with no productive, economic function. Most Democrats would have agreed with Bagg that "All wealth is the result of labor, yet, strange enough the man who does the labor never has the wealth." This was in part because "the whole system of paper money is a tax upon labor, produce and commerce." Through it the wealth created by the producing classes was transferred "to a class who produces nothing," the monied aristocracy.[26]

This monied aristocracy was not simply destructive of republican equality. It represented the source of corruption of the entire political system. In every convention the Democrats argued that the constitution had to prohibit banks and paper money in order to protect the people from the reckless actions of legislatures, so easily corrupted by the "money power." In Wisconsin Edward Ryan, the leading hard money Democrat, declared,

> Constitutions are made to restrict and restrain legislatures, as well as to protect the citizen . . . who can tell when there will be a

'soft' legislature? . . . I fear the 'softs.' They cannot be killed.
The hundred heads of the hydra might be lopped off, but the
'softs' have no heads. They spring up at every hand; they sway
and govern legislatures.

Zadoc Casey, a leader of the Illinois Democracy and president of
his state's convention, defended his demands for a smaller legislature that would hold biennial sessions limited to 60 days on the
grounds that all the evils of the state could be traced to the legislative branch. "If we had no Legislature for the last Twelve years
we would now be a happy and prosperous state."[27]

The most obvious example of corruption was in the chartering
of banks in opposition to the interest of the people. The legislatures were the instruments by which the bank frauds were perpetrated. A Michigan Democrat sarcastically remarked that the
people could not trust the legislature because, while its members
were opposed to banks when "fresh from the people," they underwent "some unaccountable changes" in the course of the session.
In this way banks and paper money became the source of all political, social, and personal corruption, "a gangrene on the body
politic" that must be exorcised.[28]

The Democrats denounced banks for constitutional as well
as for moral reasons. Many Democrats asserted that state banks
of issue were unconstitutional. Here the main argument was, as
the Ohio report stated, that "Gold and silver coin, the constitutional currency, has been thrown out of circulation by the paper
medium." Ohio Democrats, like those of Illinois and Indiana, assumed bank notes to be bills of credit and, as such, within the
scope of the constitutional prohibition of states issuing bills of
credit (art. 1, sec. 10). If the states themselves could not emit
bills of credit, agencies created by the states could hardly have
this power. Thus, the creation of banks of issue by the states was
"a derogation of the true intent" of the constitutional proscrip-
tions of creating bills of credit and making something other than
gold and silver legal tender. This argument forced the Democrats
into some unusual positions for a party opposed to centralization,
for the argument had nationalistic overtones. To defend the Dem-

ocratic position, one Cincinnati lawyer even appealed to "the opinion of [the] eminent whig judges" John Marshall, Joseph Story, and John McLean; and a leading Ohio Democrat, Charles Reemelin, declared, "the power over the standard value, belongs to the General Government, and no other authority." This was not a call for paper money inflation, but rather a demand for a return to exclusive use of the only "constitutional currency," gold and silver. Reemelin, who went further than most Democrats in his willingness to acknowledge Congress as the arbiter of the value of gold and silver, was first and foremost a hard money man.[29]

Aside from being unconstitutional and morally dangerous, "The policy of a system of paper money," the Ohio report declared, "is condemned alike by sound principles of political economy, and by the history of paper money banking in every country in which it has been in use." Certainly the argument from history and experience was one of the most powerful arguments put forth by the Democracy. To the states of the Old Northwest, it was an especially cogent one. In every convention Democratic "historians" detailed the long train of bank frauds and failures. Their bias found the periods devoid of banks to be those of great prosperity and those in which banks of issue had multiplied to be the periods of social chaos and economic distress. Most concurred with the Illinois Democrat who said he "had often heard of well regulated banks, but he never knew one of that character." His own state's experience with banks had been "fraught with ruin and disorder."[30]

These historical arguments applied both to state and national banks. In nearly every convention Democrats referred to the Bank of the United States to bolster the argument from experience. They likened "Whig paper money" to the *assignats* issued during the French Revolution and the "Continentals" that depreciated during the Confederation period. More historical parallels were suggested in the Michigan convention. "All systems of banking," it was argued, "are but modifications of the gigantic schemes for swindling, . . . the South Sea bubble, . . . John Law's Mississippi banking scheme, and the old bank of the United States." Reemelin, a native of Germany who had returned to Europe several times since his migration to America, declared that in Europe republicanism and hard money went hand in hand as the example of Switzerland proved. From his own personal experience as a "merchant on two continents" he concluded that "those of our merchants who acted upon the hard money principles have been the most successful." "I know that our trade, our business, our wealth, our prosperity, our happiness and [that] of the generation after us," he continued, "are jeopardized by the creation and use of paper money."[31]

Often Democrats cited the "standard authors on political economy" to vilify bank monopoly and condemn all relations between government and banking. These authors were also sometimes invoked to attack paper money inflation on the grounds that paper, lacking intrinsic value, did not have the stability and uniformity necessary for a sound currency. In fact, it tended to drive sound currency out of circulation. Democrats generally used these authorities to "explode" the "fallacies" that paper currency was convenient, that banks created capital, that increased circulation stimulated productivity, and that there were inadequate supplies of gold and silver for this enlarged circulation. This mode of argumentation appeared less dogmatic and more scientific. The *Wisconsin Argus* clearly enunciated the Democratic defense of total prohibition of bank currency:

> But, says the advocate of bank paper, if you drive these ones and threes and fives from circulation, there will be just so much less money in circulation, and farmers cannot sell their wheat, nor merchants their goods. Well, all we can at present say to this is that the objection betrays a most lamentable ignorance of the laws which regulate trade and currency. Drive paper money or any portion of it from circulation in Wisconsin, and an equal amount of specie would as certainly take its place as that water will seek its level; and a political economist would as soon think of objecting to the navigation of the ocean on the ground that water displaced by a ship on its course would never close up as to raise such an objection against the rejection of paper money.[32]

Since it was clear to the Democrats that the "standard authorities" counseled the prohibition of banks of issue, they believed

127

that those who advocated banks and paper money were either "blinded by interest or prejudice, or . . . superficial observers who looked only upon the surface of things, and never examine into the philosophical principles by which they are governed." Reemelin summed up the argument against the alleged value of banks:

> "Regulate the currency" should read "disorder the currency," "create capital" means destroy it, "bank facilities" should be bank difficulties, in facts short, banks should bring about results directly the reverse of what is claimed for them. . . .[33]

Just who these "standard authorities" were is not always clear. At various times Democrats referred by name to Albert Gallatin, William Gouge, William Cobbett, J. R. McCulloch, Jean Baptiste Say, Henry Wayland, Thomas Macaulay, and Adam Smith. No wonder, then, that the opposition to banks should have been cast in laissez-faire terms. Everywhere banks were seen as a "monopoly" repugnant to the teachings of classical economics. State chartering of banks and ownership of bank stock were just the kind of governmental interference that prevented the true functioning of the "natural laws of trade." An Illinois Democrat insisted, "The regulation of currency and the regulation of credit are both affairs of trade. Men want no laws except such as are necessary for the protection of equal rights." To him this meant the complete prohibition of all banks of issue and paper currency.[34]

Because of the existence of the state bank in Indiana, its convention debated at length the wisdom of the bank's affiliation with the state government. The most "radical" Democrats stigmatized the relationship as analogous to the "union of Church and State" and therefore as a threat to republican society. But more important, as one Indiana Democrat put it,

> All the evils that have heretofore flowed from the business of banking may be traced to one source: that of governments interfering with the natural laws of trade, by selecting this business out from the ordinary occupations of mankind, and by charters placing it above competition with exclusive rights and immunities not allowed to any other business, and of becoming stock jobbers themselves.[35]

Laissez-faire, antimonopoly biases caused a few Democrats to advocate merely the destruction of special charters and the implementation of general laws. Some conceived the laws to be a radical application to business of the principles of laissez-faire, the only checks on issue being unlimited liability. One plan would have made banking free under general laws, but would have allowed the banks to issue notes equivalent in value to the specie in their vaults. In Ohio and Indiana some Democrats joined with the Whigs in advocating free banking on the model of New York. The arguments defending these plans were antimonopoly arguments that emphasized equal rights rather than economic growth and development.[36]

The most important aspect of these proposals was the violent denunciation they received from most Democrats. Almost unanimously these Democrats agreed that the true policy of their party was the elimination of all banks of issue, be they established by special charter or general law. After G. Volney Dorsey, an Ohio Democrat from a Whig district, proposed that the constitution incorporate the free banking principle, the representative from the strongly antibank Knox County "rose to add a remark by way of protestation on behalf of the Democracy, against the insidious and deceptive theory here put forth in the shape of a democratic theory." He did not think it was necessary for Mr. Dorsey to sustain the argument for "the gentlemen on the opposite side of the House." He later presented a petition signed by 62 of his constituents that warned,

> We are aware that certain members of your body, elected under the hard money issue, are about to prove recreant to their constituents, or to their duty. We beg leave respectfully to remind those members of the fate of Judas, and the doom of Arnold.

In Illinois a Chicago mechanic's proposal for free banking met similar abuse from his fellow Democrats. His plan was chastised as "wild, ambiguous, and dangerous" and "the most consummate system for swindling purposes that the ingenuity of the Convention could devise." Several Democrats believed that it would be better to keep the old system of special charters than to allow

129

"the creation of these monsters all over the state, leaving its impress on the prosperity of the people forever." In Michigan free banking elements were also suppressed. Faced with a defection to free banking from the Democratic ranks during the convention, one party leader attacked the New York free banking system as the worst and most dangerous system ever attempted and predicted that it would end by "beggaring the people." Similarly, in the Indiana Convention Horace Carter told his Democratic colleagues, "The main difference between free banking and any other system is that it only opens the door to let the 'stealings,' become general, to fifty or one hundred monopolies instead of fifteen or twenty." In making this rather common argument, Carter revealed why a significant number of his party in Indiana defended the state bank. The conservative policies of the state bank—particularly, its general policy of lending to farmers and agricultural wholesalers instead of to "merchants and speculators" and its limited expansion of note issue—appealed to many Democrats who feared the inflationary tendencies of free banking.[37]

# 5

The Democracy was split on the banking issue, but the overwhelming majority stood solidly opposed to banks in any form. In every convention the Democrats proposed the complete abolition of banks and paper money. Everywhere they charged that banks violated the basic republican principle of equal rights, corrupted the legislative process, were unconstitutional, and were invalidated by historical experience and "true philosophical principles."

On many issues in these conventions the Whig position was close to the Democratic one, but on the money question Whigs and Democrats were widely divergent. Most Whigs defended paper money and banks. Outnumbered in every convention, they were much less vocal than the Democrats, but they were also much more unified on this question. A portion of Whig arguments in favor of banks and paper money was a defensive rebuttal of

Democratic arguments; in the Ohio convention, for example, a Whig lawyer made a point-by-point refutation of the Democratic case in a lengthy discussion of the constitutionality of banks of issue. At the same time the Whigs could be more aggressive. They denied Democratic charges that they were the "bank party" and turned these same charges on their opponents. Whigs also argued against the feasibility of eliminating paper currency. Experience showed, they contended, that in the course of trade specie moved to eastern financial centers, leaving the western areas without any currency to carry on day-to-day affairs. Since some sort of currency was necessary, spurious "foreign" notes and private issues like "George Smith's money" ultimately would be used. Prohibition could not work. In fact, it constituted an abdication of the government responsibility to protect its citizens.[38]

This complaint about the possible consequences of Democratic policy signaled a difference between the parties concerning the proper function of the state. The Democrats tended to fear the state as a danger to individual freedom and to take a negative view of its functions. This was exemplified in their emphasis on the gubernatorial veto and the strict circumscription of legislative power. The liberalism of the day leaned toward anarchism, conceiving the state as a necessary evil at best. In political economy this led to a rabid laissez-faire position that set itself against public education and even government ownership of the post office. The Democrats veered in this direction.

In general, Whigs subscribed to a moderate form of liberalism that, without rejecting the main elements of liberal thought, questioned an absolute faith in laissez-faire, as had in fact Adam Smith and many of the early classical economists. Whigs did not deny that governmental power constituted a threat to liberty. The centralization of power over the currency could be dangerous, an Indiana Whig argued, but all "useful powers" were dangerous in proportion to their usefulness. Decisions on the extent of power invested in government must be left up to the people acting through the legislature, otherwise the constitution would "deprive them of the exercise of their free will." Most Whigs agreed that they "must delegate power to guarantee individual rights and to

131

protect public liberty." State government was instituted to protect the rights and privileges of the citizens through the passage of a few "direct and wholesome laws." Beyond these few laws individual enterprise would monitor social activity. One of the leading Whig advocates of free banking in Indiana, John Niles, maintained that while men usually should be permitted to follow their own interests, "the business of issuing paper to circulate as money is of a widely different character, and must be governed by stringent rules." Such laws as would insure security to the billholder were the "indispensable prerequisite to free competition." In spirit this argument varied little from that of Adam Smith, and one of the few Whig arguments from authority noted that free banking was "demonstrated as the only true system of banking by Adam Smith, who was the first expounder of the true doctrines of political economy." Within the bounds of liberal thought, the Whigs nevertheless emphasized the more positive functions of the state as an aid to social action where they thought individual effort would have been futile. To view them as Burkean conservatives or neomercantilists—or, for that matter, as advocates of the modern welfare state—is to misunderstand them.[39]

Whigs were as opposed to monopoly as their opponents, but they did not agree with the Democrats that banks were necessarily monopolistic. Whigs defended free banking as a republican system resting on "our notions of free government and equal rights." Like the Democrats they saw monopoly as a source of fraud and oppression, but, as one Indiana Whig asserted,

> By making the system general and extending to all the same rights under it, we not only obviate this obvious odious feature, but we invite into the field the same salutary and wholesome competition in banking which now exists in all the other departments of trade and occupations of life.

John Niles explained that he opposed the State Bank of Indiana solely because

> It does give to a few citizens exclusive privileges which are denied to others. Such monopolies should be created only on the ground of absolute necessity for they are inconsistent with the doctrine of equal rights. And if it can be shown that another sys-

tem may combine the principle of free competition and equality of
rights with safety and usefulness, that circumstance alone will be
a strong argument in its favor.[40]

Accepting the need for a paper currency and the responsibility
of the government to protect the rights of the citizens, Whigs were
faced with the decision of how to best provide a safe and adequate
currency. For most Whigs the price of monopoly was too high to
pay for security if any alternative existed. They desired "to see
[a system] established which [would] combine the principles of
free competition and of security to the bill holder." Whigs generally thought that free banking with stock collateral to secure
the billholder was such a system and that the example of New
York showed such a system might work. Only in Indiana did any
sizable group of Whigs argue for the maintenance of a single
institution, and then on the grounds that this was the only way to
provide a secure currency and control the "money power" in the
public interest. One such Whig asserted, "I have no objection to
allowing men of capital to associate their wealth for banking purposes but I do not want them to acquire a power paramount to
the State."[41]

Whigs warned that Democratic policy would result in domination of the state by the rich. Under unmitigated laissez-faire the
power of money would rule unchecked. Prohibition of banks
"would make the rich man more wealthy and the poor man poorer,
and the debtor class would be entirely ruined." Hard money would
mean low prices for the farmer and an economy in which the poor
man, lacking the facilities of credit, could only look forward to
his continued existence in the lower strata of society. "Money
power" uncontrolled by the state would enslave the people, making them "serfs and tillers of the ground for the profit of others."
To the Whigs free banking seemed the best way to supply the currency and credit necessary for continued commercial growth
while at the same time assuring the billholders against loss.[42]

# 6

The votes on various issues in these conventions yield some idea
of the relative size and location of factions in the two parties and

clarify the position of the parties on the banking question. It is clear from the voting in the Wisconsin, Illinois, and Ohio conventions that in these states nearly every Whig favored free banking, while a majority of the Democrats stood true to the party's hard money position.

Wisconsin's Democrats supported a constitution that would "secure the safety and welfare of those for whom it is made" and supported the hard money doctrines expressed in the 1846 constitution. The Democracy broke ranks only after the defeat of the first constitution at the polls. As it was, the bank article in the 1848 constitution, which opened the way for free banking, passed by a slim margin of five votes. The majority of Democrats continued to oppose banks of any sort. The voting of the representatives in the convention and the popular vote show slightly different patterns that may signify differences between the more established settlers and the new migrants to the state. About half the convention votes against free banking, including all of the opposing Whig votes, came from the western counties; but only one of the votes for free banking came from this area, although the representatives of Columbia County, directly north of Dane, and those of Green to the south supported the bill. The popular vote on the 1846 constitution also showed opposition to banks in the western counties of Iowa, Lafayette, Richland, and St. Croix. But eastern Democratic strongholds like Washington, Brown, and Mantowac also favored the hard money policy.[43]

The pattern of the vote was not clearly sectional. Crawford and Grant in the west turned in three-to-one majorities against the constitution, while Dodge, Fond du Lac, Racine, Walworth, and Waukesha in the east all registered large minorities for the constitution. One sectional element opposed to free banking was the southwestern counties, located in the oldest part of the state. These were settled by upland southerners from Kentucky and Tennessee, many of whom had moved from Illinois into this area. In these counties the farm land was not as good as it was further to the east; and the mining industry that gave the "Lead Region" its name was already beginning to decline. Free banking gained its strongest support in the more populous eastern half of the

134

state, although even in these counties the majority of Democrats opposed all banks. This portion of the state was emerging economically, and businessmen in the growing Lake Michigan ports demanded banking facilities. The area was populated by the newer immigrants to the state who had come either with the Yankee migration from New York through the northern half of the Old Northwest or from Europe. Immigrants such as the Irish (led by men like the volatile Edward Ryan) and the Germans gave solid support to hard money, even in eastern cities. It was the Yankee Whigs who most strongly supported banks, aided by the few Democrats who deserted their party to vote with the Whigs for free banking.[44]

To the south in Illinois a similar pattern emerged. The "hards" in the Illinois convention were known as the "fifty-eight." Fifty-three of these were Democrats, accounting for a little less than 60% of the total party membership attending the convention. Of the remaining 40% of the Democracy, all but an insignificant number of the delegates were opposed to free banking. By the end of the convention an additional 27% of the Democracy were willing to join the "fifty-eight" original prohibitionists to send a hard money article separately to the voters. If they had held their ranks together and maintained normal attendance, they could

Table 2. Occupation and Party in the Illinois
Constitutional Convention, 1847*

| Occupation | | | Party | | | |
|---|---|---|---|---|---|---|
| | | | Democrats | | Whigs | |
| | No. | (%) | No. | (%) | No. | (%) |
| Farmers | 76 | 46.9 | 48 | 52.7 | 28 | 39.4 |
| Lawyers | 53 | 32.7 | 26 | 28.5 | 27 | 38.1 |
| Merchants | 9 | 5.5 | 4 | 4.4 | 5 | 7.0 |
| Other | 24 | 14.8 | 13 | 14.3 | 11 | 15.5 |
| Total | 162 | 99.9† | 91 | 99.9† | 71 | 100.0 |

* Based on biographical data presented in Charles Arthur Cole, ed., *The Constitutional Debates of 1847* (Springfield: Illinois State Historical Library, 1919): 949-83.
† Rounding error.

135

have carried the issue. But this is just what they failed to do. The final attempt at prohibition was defeated by one vote, 68 to 69. On the day of the vote ten of the "fifty-eight" were absent, including some of the most vociferous antibank men in the convention. Probank Whigs carried the day by holding their troops together and getting out the vote. Among the Whigs 75% voted for free banking, another 17.5% favored the old system of individual charters, and a very small group, about 7.5%, opposed all banks. A handful of Democrats who either favored free banking or wished to retain the special charter system aided the Whigs in defeating prohibition.[45]

The data in tables 2, 3, and 4 on delegates in the 1847 convention show place of origin as far more important than occupation in affecting delegate response to the bank issue. The one occupational group solidly supporting banks was the merchants; each other group split. Farmers born in slave states and living in southern counties formed the core of opposition to banks; farmers born in free states and living in northern counties tended to favor free banking. Northern-born physicians supported banks; those from the South opposed them. Four of the five delegates born outside the United States voted with the hard money forces while only four of 22 New Englanders opposed banks and 17 took the most probank position. The most significant thing about the Illinois vote was the degree to which hard money sentiment was concentrated in the southern and west-central sections of the state (map 1). This was the oldest part of the state, originally settled by upland southerners migrating from Virginia through Kentucky and Tennessee. Concentrations of Germans dotted this area. The northern counties were populated by the Yankee migrations; as in Wisconsin, some of these Yankee Democrats in Illinois broke with their party and voted against prohibiting banks.

The geographic pattern in Ohio is less clear. Again, a large majority of the Democrats in the convention stood for prohibition and were beaten by a combination of Whigs and "bank Democrats." Over 80% of the party voted to prohibit chartering banks

136

# MAP 1. Bank Vote in the Illinois Constitutional Convention, 1847

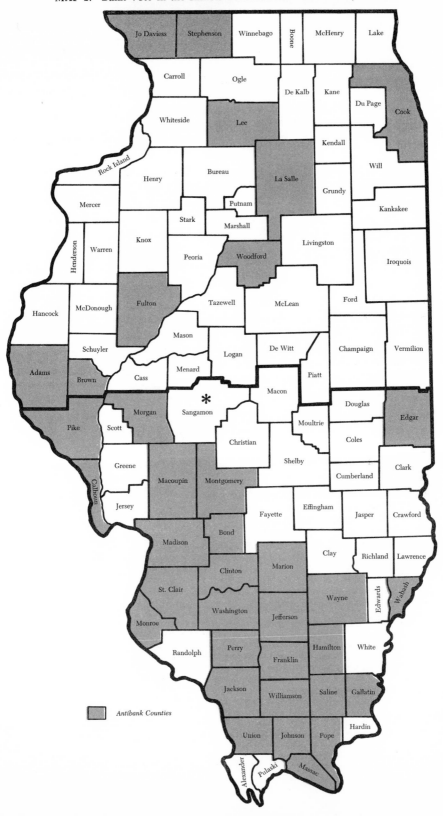

Table 3. Party, Occupation, and the Bank Issue in the
Illinois Constitutional Convention, 1847*

| | | Party | | | |
|---|---|---|---|---|---|
| | | Democrats | | Whigs | |
| Bank Stance | Scale Type | No. | (%) | No. | (%) |
| The "Fifty-eight" | 0 | 53 | 61.6 | 5 | 7.1 |
| Moderate prohibitionists | 1 | 16 | 18.6 | 1 | 1.4 |
| Chartered bank advocates | 2 | 9 | 10.5 | 12 | 17.1 |
| Free bank advocates | 3 | 8 | 9.3 | 52 | 74.3 |
| Total | | 86 | 100.0 | 70 | 99.9† |

| | | Occupation | | | | | | | |
|---|---|---|---|---|---|---|---|---|---|
| | | Farmers | | Lawyers | | Merchants | | Other‡ | |
| Bank Stance | Scale Type | No. | (%) | No. | (%) | No. | (%) | No. | (%) |
| The "Fifty-eight" | 0 | 30 | 40.0 | 20 | 40.0 | 0 | 0.0 | 8 | 34.8 |
| Moderate prohibitionists | 1 | 9 | 12.0 | 4 | 8.0 | 0 | 0.0 | 4 | 17.4 |
| Chartered bank advocates | 2 | 10 | 13.3 | 4 | 8.0 | 2 | 25.0 | 5 | 21.7 |
| Free bank advocates | 3 | 26 | 34.7 | 22 | 44.0 | 6 | 75.0 | 6 | 26.0 |
| Total | | 75 | 100.0 | 50 | 100.0 | 8 | 100.0 | 23 | 99.9† |

| | | Occupation and Party | | | | | | | |
|---|---|---|---|---|---|---|---|---|---|
| | | Farmers | | | | Lawyers | | | |
| | | Democrats | | Whigs | | Democrats | | Whigs | |
| Bank Stance | Scale Type | No. | (%) | No. | (%) | No. | (%) | No. | (%) |
| The "Fifty-eight" | 0 | 30 | 63.9 | 0 | 0 | 17 | 74.2 | 3 | 11.1 |
| Moderate prohibitionists | 1 | 9 | 19.1 | 0 | 0 | 3 | 12.9 | 1 | 3.8 |
| Chartered bank advocates | 2 | 5 | 10.6 | 5 | 17.8 | 1 | 4.3 | 3 | 11.1 |
| Free bank advocates | 3 | 3 | 6.4 | 23 | 82.2 | 2 | 8.6 | 20 | 74.0 |
| Total | | 47 | 100.0 | 28 | 100.0 | 23 | 100.0 | 27 | 100.0 |

* Based on a Guttman scale (0-3) derived from three roll calls given in Cole, ed., *Debates of 1847*: 101-03, 808. One delegate did not vote on any of the roll calls and five of those who voted on only two could have been in in either scale type 1 or 2. These six delegates were excluded from the anal-

of any kind. Whigs voted solidly (94%) for a proposal to allow the voters to choose between free banking and "no banks." They were unanimously opposed to the Democratic version of a free banking proposal that proscribed bank notes of a denomination less than the most valuable coin issued by the federal government and that also failed to provide any security other than unlimited liability.[47]

The southern element of the Ohio population was smaller than that of either Indiana or Illinois, but it gave solid support to the demands for the elimination of banks. So did the strongly Democratic Irish Catholics and the sizable German enclave concentrated around Cincinnati, Reemelin's home, and in the tier of counties in the north-central part of the state. The Yankee counties of the Western Reserve and along Lake Erie formed a stronghold of support for free banking.[48]

The situation in Indiana, where the success of the state bank confused the party alignments, was the most complex. Both parties were split on the banking issue. With one exception Whigs stood for banking of some kind. The division between free banks and a state bank was fairly even. Slightly more than half the Whigs preferred a state bank, while a sizable minority (47%) advocated free banking. The Democrats were divided into three factions. At the outset about half opposed all banks, and a smaller group, perhaps one-fourth, favored a state bank. As the convention progressed, the free banking element grew to number slightly less than a majority of the party. When it became evident that no one faction could carry its principles, a compromise was worked out by Whig banker Alan Hamilton permitting both free banking and a state bank with branches autonomous from the state govern-

---

ysis. The coefficient of reproducibility is .96. A convenient summary of this technique can be found in Lee F. Anderson, *et al., Legislative Roll Call Analysis* (Evanston, Ill.: Northwestern Univ. Press, 1966): 89-121.

† Rounding error.

‡ Among this category the only group large enough for analysis was physicians, who are treated in the text. Although some historians have associated mechanics with "hard money," the four mechanics in the convention split, with two favoring and two opposing banks. The two delegates who were ministers voted Whig and favored banks.

Table 4. Yule's $Q$ Association of Party, Occupation, Residence,
Birthplace, and the Bank Vote in the Illinois
Constitutional Convention, 1847*

|  | Antibank (Scale types 0, 1) | Probank (Scale types 2, 3) |
|---|---|---|
| *Party* | | |
| Democrats | 69 | 17 |
| Whigs | 6 | 64 |
|  | | $Q = .95$ |
| *Place of Birth* | | |
| Slave states or foreign countries | 45 | 35 |
| Free states | 30 | 46 |
|  | | $Q = .33$ |
| *Residence* | | |
| Southern counties† | 43 | 35 |
| Northern counties | 32 | 46 |
|  | | $Q = .28$ |
| *Occupation* | | |
| Farmers | 39 | 36 |
| Nonfarmers | 36 | 45 |
|  | | $Q = .15$ |
| *Farmers by Residence* | | |
| Southern counties | 23 | 12 |
| Northern counties | 16 | 24 |
|  | | $Q = .48$ |
| *Farmers by Birthplace* | | |
| Slave states or foreign countries· | 28 | 15 |
| Free states | 11 | 21 |
|  | | $Q = .56$ |

* Based on data presented in Cole, ed., *Debates of 1847*: 944-83. The derivation and interpretation of this statistic appears in John H. Mueller, Karl F. Schuessler, and Herbert L. Costner, *Statistical Reasoning in Sociology*, 2d ed. (Boston: Houghton Mifflin Company, 1970): 290-92.

† An arbitrary line following the northern boundaries of the tier of central counties from Pike on the Mississippi to Edgar on the Indiana border was used as the dividing point (see map 1).

ment. The only opposition to the compromise came from two hard money Democrats and twelve Whig advocates of a state-owned bank. While the desire to produce a constitution eventuated in a compromising of Jacksonian dogma, the early votes revealed a sectional split like that in Illinois. The area from the National Road south—the oldest part of the state, having the poorest soil, settled mainly by southerners, and with a larger foreign immigrant population than the rest of the state—produced 80% of the total Democratic hard money votes.[49]

# 7

The positions taken by the parties on the banking question are usually explained as appeals to the class interests represented in the parties' constituencies. The Democrats were "the party of the ordinary run of citizen." In the West they received support from "the frontiersmen and small farmers." Whigs, on the other hand, "tended to be townspeople of substance—bankers, lawyers and businessmen." Some variant of this division of the parties along class and occupational lines is accepted by practically every historian who has written on the period and is used to explain the Whig adherence to banks and paper money and the Democratic antipathy to them.[50]

On an occupational rather than a class basis, there is some evidence in support of this thesis. Most well-off businessmen were probably Whigs, particularly merchants; so also, but to a lesser degree, were manufacturers and other entrepreneurs. Lawyers divided nearly equally between the parties.[51]

The party affiliation of bankers, however, has yet to be determined. The standard contention, a hypothesis originally advanced by New York Democrats in the late 1830s but almost universally adopted by historians, is that the growing antibank sentiment in the Democracy drove bankers from the party, accounting for Whig successes in 1840. Floyd Streeter in his *Political Parties in Michigan* argues, for example, that the growing radicalism of the Michigan Democracy after 1837 alienated a large number of the state's well-to-do men. His sole evidence is a letter from John R. Williams to William Woodbridge giving the impression that bankers and other wealthy men trooped en masse into the Whig party, accounting in part for the 1840 Whig success in Michigan.[52]

Banker Williams was not one of the defectors, however. He remained loyal to the Democracy throughout his life. While no systematic study of partisanship among bankers has been made, the only quantitative monograph dealing with banker affiliation tends to contradict the traditional hypothesis. Alexandra McCoy reports in her Michigan study, "Political Affiliations of American Economic Elites," that there were more bankers among the Dem-

141

ocrats than among the Whigs, and also that in 1844 there was a higher percentage of bankers among the Democrats than among the Whigs in Wayne County's economic elite. At that time the Michigan Democracy was unequivocally antibank. The appeal the Democracy had for its banker constituents was apparently not an economic one.[53]

This traditional interpretation has lacked perspective. On the one hand, there were not very many bankers in the Old Northwest in the 1840s. On the other hand, there is no good reason to suspect that the Whig party was controlled by the bankers, even if it could be shown that all bankers were Whigs. Among the party leadership, there was little class and occupational difference between Democrats and Whigs. While the Whigs were less successful at the polls than their opponents, the base of their electoral strength was sufficiently broad and pluralistic to preclude domination by a single occupational group, especially an unpopular one like the bankers. Ronald P. Formisano's study of voting behavior in Michigan has shown the simple class interpretation of party support to be totally unfounded and has demonstrated the appeal of both parties to the broad spectrum of class groupings in the society.[54]

In the conventions Democrats and Whigs courted the same economic groups. The Democrats echoed the old Jacksonian appeal to the "producing classes," who, they argued, were the most hurt by the depreciation of bank notes. But Democrats made explicit appeals to the merchants and businessmen on the grounds that only a specie currency could create a sound economy. They violently opposed any kind of inflation and assured the farmer that his interests were best served by his own honest labor and the beneficial effects of free enterprise. The Whigs' appeal was also broad-gauged. They promised both farmers and merchants higher prices and economic expansion. By providing adequate currency and cheap and easy credit, the banking system would assist the farmer and the laborer as well as the businessman. A typical editorial from the *Milwaukee Sentinel and Gazette* argued that the "agricultural interest," most important to the state, would be stifled by the high interest rates and low prices that would result from the hard money policy. Inadequate credit and currency also hurt mechanics and workingmen by keeping wages low, while the wheat merchant and the moneylender profited. "Is it the master builder, the manufacturer, the merchant, or the forwarder that suffers most from this circumstance?" the Whig journal asked. No,

> Not they; for whatever the rate they must pay for the money which they must borrow . . . a proportionate reduction is made in the remuneration allowed to the men in their employ. Can it be necessary to multiply these illustrations to show that this pretended war against capital and currency is in fact a war upon labor?

Hard money was a policy injurious to the mechanic, the farmer, and the laborer. It was "legislating for the rich, at the expense and to the detriment of the poor." It was neither a fair nor a democratic policy.[55]

Although the parties vied for the support of the same occupational groups, they clearly differed on economic policies, particularly the bank issue. At the same time, available studies of voting behavior indicate that ethnoreligious factors rather than class or occupation were the prime determinants of party affiliation. This conclusion seems anomalous only because of the tendency to view political behavior in terms of a rather narrow economic determinism. A less restrictive social interpretation of the role of the bank issue in western politics can explain partisanship in the Old Northwest.

While the parties did not represent different economic classes, they did represent different economic *attitudes* and different *styles* of economic activity. Glyndon Van Deusen had economic style in mind when he characterized the midwestern Whigs as "the pushing, ambitious, go-ahead bankers and businessmen, canal promoters . . . lawyers with an eye to the main chance, and farmers anxious for internal improvements." The party was future-oriented and appealed to those men, *regardless of class*, who put their faith in economic progress. By progress the Whigs meant the commercialization of the society. Ohio senator Thomas Corwin, who generally expressed typical Whig views, believed that commerce

143

was "the most efficient civilizer of our Barbarous race." Whigs envisioned an expanding commercial economy, in which agriculture, labor, and business alike were benefited, as the proper basis for American society.[56]

These "commercial-minded" Whigs viewed the legislature as potentially a positive force in structuring the society of the future. Since the Whig party in this area was built upon a Yankee-Protestant social base, it is likely that the Whigs' willingness to have government play a positive developmental role in the economy may be traced to the Puritan willingness to use the government actively in religious and moral affairs. Throughout the North, Whigs attempted to legislate moral reform and showed little fear of using political power to extend Yankee culture and mores across the face of the land. Whigs conceived of government as a tool the people could use to create the necessary conditions for commercial as well as moral progress. For the Whigs the bank issue was tied to the economic and moral development of the society. Banks were an economic necessity. They lubricated the wheels of commercial progress. At the state level free banking was the key to progress toward a commercial society.[57]

As Marvin Meyers has argued in *The Jacksonian Persuasion,* Democrats tended to be "agrarian-minded." They "wanted to preserve the virtues of a simple agrarian republic without sacrificing the rewards and conveniences of modern capitalism." To these "agrarian-minded" Democrats, the state was dangerous and therefore best limited to a minimum of police functions in order that society might develop "naturally." To this way of thinking commercial and urban society was by its very nature corrupt. The bank issue had social and psychological import that exceeded simple economic interest. Banks symbolized the fact that commercial development had corrupted the "virtuous agrarian republic." Opposition to banks became the focal point for resistance to the commercialization of American life. In a period of swift economic and social change, those groups least able or willing to adapt— thus, most threatened by change—could direct their animus toward banks as an institutional symbol of the new society that jeopardized their status.[58]

144

# CHAPTER 6

## FREE BANKING TRIUMPHANT, 1851-1852

### 1

In the early 1850s four of the states of the Old Northwest passed free banking laws. Economic expansion required credit and currency, and free banking was the way in which certain elements of the community attempted to answer these needs. The "revulsion against banks" of the 1840s left these states without adequate legal sources of currency and credit. Maurice Ross has compiled indices for Indiana of the growth of capital stock, discounts, and note issues during these years and has compared these with the growth of population, property evaluation, and improved acreage. His data clearly show that the legal circulating medium did not keep pace with Indiana's population growth and economic expansion. These conclusions apply to the other states of the Old Northwest as well. In 1850, Michigan's four banks had paid-in capital of $392,530 or about $.98 per capita for the state. At the same time the per-capita share of bank capital in the whole nation was $9.37. The same is true of both circulation and deposits. The per-capital share of notes in Michigan was $1.57; of deposits, $.67. Both figures were only fractions of the national averages. Illinois had no banks of issue. A variety of unauthorized and extralegal issues filled the currency vacuum. Some of these were sound, such as "George Smith's money," which circulated throughout Illinois and Wisconsin on a par with specie; but others were of dubious value.

These conditions spurred demands in all of the states of the Old Northwest for increased banking facilities that were legally controlled and for the prohibition of unauthorized and foreign issues.[1]

Throughout these years the Democratic party in the Old Northwest continued to stand solidly against banks, paper currency, and inflation. Democratic platforms, though varying slightly from state to state, were uncompromisingly hostile to all banks "authorized by either general or special laws." Banks violated the republican concept of equal rights and the sound principles of political economy. Hard money was the only just currency and the only currency recognized by the Constitution. There were to be no more "special privileges" for "swindling corporations," but a "gradual return from the paper system," which defrauded the farmer and the laborer. In their addresses to the state legislatures, Democratic governors warned against the establishment of banks as dangerous to the public interest and unnecessary for economic advancement.[2]

The intractable John Barry, who had led the fight against banks in the early 1840s, was again governor of Michigan, and his attitudes regarding banks had not changed. He praised the new constitution for eliminating the monopoly aspects of banking by establishing a free banking system and found favor with its attempt to insure bank issues. However, he basically distrusted free banking as a conspiracy of the bankers. Like many other Democrats, Barry scorned free banking because it perpetuated public debt. If banks had to be based on "the evidence of public misfortunes," there was "at least presumptive evidence that the evils of the banking system are so far inherent and inseparable, that little hope can be entertained for results more favorable in the future."[3]

While the governors of Indiana and Ohio only attacked banks as they then existed, Governor Augustus French of Illinois and Governor Nelson Dewey of Wisconsin joined Barry in categorically opposing free banking. Experience, argued French, had shown that all banks were "wrong in principle" and led only to disastrous fluctuations. French concluded in typically turgid Jacksonian fashion,

146

A currency resting upon credit, upon mere promises to pay, while it is the most seductive, as holding out inducements to the idle, the cunning, and the profligate to enrich themselves without labor, is likewise the most uncertain fluctuating and fallacious ever devised to cheat the toiling industrious mass of mankind out of the fruits of their labor, and, next to the immediate interposition of Providence, to thwart the expectations of industry, the most to be shunned and deplored.[4]

Each governor echoed the theme that banks and paper money only aided bankers and other nonproducers in their struggle to secure wealth without labor and that any state that was "mainly agricultural" did not need a paper currency based on credit. "The great body of the people are producers," wrote Governor Dewey, "their prosperity consists in honest industry, and they look to a different source than banks for their real wealth." Joseph Wright, the antibank governor of Indiana, believed that paper money and inflation most hurt the laboring man, who mainly wanted "uniformity and regularity in prices."[5]

The leading Democratic newspapers in each of these states strongly supported these ideas. The *Kalamazoo Gazette* professed that Governor Barry's "remarks on banks and banking find a full response in our inmost soul." In Wisconsin the *Madison Daily Democrat* praised Governor Dewey, as a representative of the "Young Democracy" and asserted unequivocally, "That Banks are an evil—though by some considered a necessary evil—is uncontroverted."[6]

"Long" John Wentworth, the volatile editor of the *Chicago Democrat*, exemplified the moralistic tone of the antibank argument. Between 1846 and 1851, Wentworth led the antimonopoly and antibank agitation in Illinois. Aside from banks he attacked "grain monopolists" and steamboat combinations. Like most Democrats he exalted agricultural and "producing" classes. In 1848, Wentworth retrospectively praised the Specie Circular: ". . . it broke up the speculators, the land mongers, and drove them out of the country. Banks are made for speculators, and not for the industrial classes." An intense partisan, he identified these "industrial classes" with the Democracy and the bankers and land specu-

147

lators with the Whigs. His attacks on bankers, monopolists, speculators, and businessmen as parasites and robbers were reminiscent
of William Cobbett's vilification of industrialism in England. This
style of thought revealed a romantic neo-Jeffersonian sensibility
in its assault on the developing industrial and commercial world.
His condemnation of the rising cities, the "creation of Whig policy," was especially acrimonious. They were the centers of all de-
gradation, "festering in corruption," peopled by starving "opera-
tives" or shopworkers, degraded loafers, and fallen females.
"And as long as we multiply commercial agents, by banks and
tariffs, and privileged monopolies, we necessarily multiply cities
which are supported entirely at the expense of the country." Although Wentworth was a political chameleon and his career a
maze of contradictions—a land monopolist who attacked land
monopoly, an urban booster who disliked cities—the language of
the *Chicago Democrat* in this period typified party attitudes.[7]

While the Democratic party generally stood for equal rights
and against exclusive legislation, for "constitutional currency"
and against paper money, it was willing to countenance a "free"
banking system made up of banks that were unincorporated partnerships, with unlimited liability, and prohibited from issuing
notes less than $20. It was part of the Democratic creed to oppose
all incorporated banks as monopolies inimical to the interests of
the "producing classes." Banks and corporations symbolized the
commercialization of American life, which gathered men into the
corrupt and corrupting cities, where "the pampered aristocracy—
the men of silk who neither toil nor labor, but yet are clothed in
purple and fine linen"—profited at the expense of the hard-working
rural classes.[8]

Still, significant numbers of midwesterners, including some
Democrats, were at odds with this reactionary view. They believed
that expanding currency and credit resources were necessary and
regretted that their states were being "overrun" with "foreign"
issues of dubious quality. In Illinois private currency was supple-
mented by Ohio "red backs" and Indiana "shinplasters." Nearly
half a million dollars issued by St. Louis banks circulated throughout Illinois in 1850. George Smith's far-flung interests led to the

148

circulation of notes in Illinois issued by his Georgia banks. While Illinois was an extreme case, every state in the Northwest was plagued by shoddy "foreign" currency. To some men it seemed that economic progress was being sacrificed to outdated "scruples about banking."[9]

Demands for extended banking facilities had been heard in the constitutional conventions, giving impetus to the establishment of free banking systems in each of these states. These demands had generally originated in urban and commercial areas and had been to a degree nonpartisan. Businessmen in Cincinnati and Cleveland had held meetings calling for more banks. As soon as the Illinois constitution instituting free banking had been ratified by the people, a committee of the Chicago Board of Trade drafted a free banking act in line with the requirements of the new constitution. At the same time a group of Chicago's leading businessmen petitioned the legislature for sound banking legislation. Meetings of "businessmen and other citizens" were held at Indianapolis and at Logansport in the northern part of Indiana to demand the establishment of a free banking system because the state was being flooded with unsound "foreign" paper and lacked adequate sound currency. It was felt that many areas of the state were being commercially inhibited. A free banking system would drive out spurious notes, extend credit facilities throughout the state, and draw active businessmen and capital to Indiana.[10]

This entrepreneurial thrust for credit, rather than the traditional Jacksonian moralistic censureship of monopoly, led to the passage of the free banking laws. While enough Democrats supported these laws to give them a nonpartisan cast, free banking was still basically a Whig measure, gaining its strongest support from Whig newspapers and politicians. In every state the Whigs took the initiative in establishing these laws and solidly supported them. The main body of the Democracy fought them. A small body of Democrats broke with party orthodoxy and joined the Whigs, creating the majorities necessary for passage of the free banking laws. These Democrats generally came from rapidly developing areas inhabited by settlers from New England and New York, whose economic views conformed closely to those of the Whigs.

149

## 2

Michigan had forced its few banks to supply bond security as collateral for their issue in the 1840s, but the earlier experience with free banking made Michigan legislators reluctant to reenact similar legislation. In 1851, however, a free banking bill was brought before the house against the wishes of Governor Barry, indicating the strain that the need for credit facilities placed on Democratic orthodoxy, even in the home of the "wildcats."

The Whig press took a moderately favorable stand toward the bill, but obviously sought to avoid making it a partisan issue. The Democrats, particularly in the urban areas, found themselves in the uncomfortable position of not wishing to attack Barry, yet not wanting the Whigs to have the credit for satisfying the growing demand for more banks. The *Free Press* opened the year by attacking the "Whig suspension policy" and associating the Democrats with the idea of a stock-based currency. As the debate on the bill raged, the paper reported its course but avoided taking any position. The correspondent of the *Free Press*, "H. W.," seemed to take both sides, praising the idea of the bill but also opposing the specific structure it proposed.[11]

The legislature bitterly debated the bill. Men of traditional Jacksonian persuasion were staunchly hostile to it. Those who argued for the bill emphasized that it would give the businessmen of the state a home currency in which they could have confidence. This argument seems to have influenced a number of men in both parties, because the bill was defeated by only a single vote. A sizable majority of the Whigs favored the bill, while 60% of the Democrats opposed it. Yet free banking was not simply a partisan measure. Local needs often overrode party affiliation. Although all but one of the representatives from Detroit's Wayne County voted against the bill, contemporaries noticed a tendency for those from other cities and towns to favor the bill and for farmers to oppose it.[12]

The old Jacksonians were fighting a holding action. In Michigan they held off "progress," but in the other states of the Old Northwest they were unsuccessful. During the first two years of the decade, Ohio, Illinois, Indiana, and Wisconsin established free banking systems.

While the Ohio constitutional convention met, fear that it would outlaw banks encouraged the proposal of a free banking law in the legislature. In every other way a typical free banking bill, it included an unusual provision for a 30% specie reserve and a unique compromise on the question of liability. If there were fewer than six stockholders, they would be individually liable. Otherwise, liability would be limited to the amount of stock held.[13]

Ohio Whigs had consistently advocated bank expansion and defended the idea of free banking against antibank Democrats. In the legislature the Whigs voted nearly unanimously for the free banking bill; and although the Jacksonians dominated both houses, enough members of the Democracy voted with the Whig minority to secure passage of the bill in March 1851.[14]

In their own party "bank Democrats" were a minority. Most of the Democratic papers in the state opposed the law and denounced it in typical Jacksonian terms once it had passed. Those Democrats who had not insisted on the "constitutional currency" were chastised along with the Whigs. The Stark County Democratic Convention meeting in March reaffirmed opposition to any kind of bank currency, and the state convention in July again included opposition to banks in the party platform. The leading organ of the Democracy, the *Ohio Statesman*, attacked the free banking law and assured its readers that if the people had voted on the law, "they would have knocked it into a cocked hat."[15]

The people of Illinois did have the chance to vote on free banking. The struggle for a free banking law there clearly shows the Whig leadership of the movement and the nature of the coalition of Whigs and Democrats that brought success. Opposition to banks was strongest in the area below Sangamon County, which had been settled early by upland southerners. In contrast, the northern half of the state which had been populated by the westward migration from New England and New York demanded free banking.

A free banking bill was introduced on January 9, 1849, but was defeated in the house. The vote revealed the same sort of split in the Democratic ranks that had appeared in the constitutional convention, a split that would widen in the next few years. Early backing for the law came from the *Chicago Daily Journal* and portions of Chicago's business community, although many conservative businessmen feared stock security and individual liability. When the bill was defeated, the *Daily Journal* charged that the Democrats were obstructing a popular referendum on the bank issue. Public sentiment in favor of some kind of banking law in the northern half of the state worried Democratic leaders, who feared that the issue would split their party. One northerner tried to explain the predicament of the northern Democrats to Governor French. He claimed that it was harder to sustain party orthodoxy in the north of the state than in the south because the largest part of the northern population was from states such as New York "where Banking is tolerated." He believed that for strategic reasons the Democrats should at least allow a referendum on free banking:

> There is the Whig party in a body for Banks—the Abolitionists
> mostly and about one fourth of the Democrats and if the Whigs
> up here could place us as opposed to even permitting a vote to be
> taken on the bank question, I am sure we would be defeated. . . .[16]

Most Democrats heedlessly continued to oppose banks. Throughout 1850 the *Illinois State Register* and the *Chicago Daily Democrat* attacked all banking plans as unsuited to agricultural communities and fraught with danger. Individuals petitioned the legislature, opposing banks as "a curse to the Mechanic, the Farmer, and the Labouring Man."[17]

At the same time the Whigs mounted an effective campaign for a free banking law. Petitions favoring the proposed measure greatly outnumbered those opposing it. The leading Whig papers in the state pushed for a free banking law during 1850 as the state election approached. The *Rock Island Advertiser* complained,

> the present system has driven capitalists from the state to invest
> their wealth elsewhere, and domestic enterprise hobbles about
> on crutches, being forced to pay the unlicensed usurer twenty

and twenty-five per cent interest, for the poor privilege of moving at a snail's pace.

The *Tazewell Mirror* and the *Illinois State Journal* joined in the demand that Illinois be allowed to control circulation within its boundaries and that local capitalists be permitted to profit from it. The Whig convention to choose a candidate for state senator from Kane, Dekalb, Lee, and Ogle Counties in the northwest adopted a resolution favoring a free banking law. A similar Whig meeting for McHenry, Boone, and Winnebago Counties opposed "the wild destructive course" of the Democrats that had "cramped the energies of our industrious population, and driven capital into neighboring states." The convention supported free banking in order to aid the "rapid growth and permanent welfare of our State" while providing adequate security to the billholders. In calling for the election of legislators who favored a banking law, the Free-Soil *Chicago Tribune* summed up the argument for a free banking law:

> It is a matter of deep regret, that while the Eastern cities have a good currency, and business men are supplied with temporary loans at a fair interest, to meet extraordinary emergencies, our city and State labor under the most biting stringency, have a currency composed of rags and shinplasters, from every part of the Union and Canada. We have heretofore averred to this and pointed out the remedy in the organization of a Free Banking system in our State based on our State Stocks.[18]

Nevertheless, Democrats dominated the new legislature. Governor French greeted them with a standard antibank speech, charging that the use of bonds to secure the note issue was merely "show" to cover up the "odious features" of the system.

> No good can follow the application of ill timed and unnatural stimulants which may serve to infuse into the spirit of trade a temporary, feverish impulse to be succeeded by a corresponding depression.

French favored general laws in most cases, but his opinion of banks remained unchanged.[19]

153

Although the legislature had Democratic majorities in both houses, there were indications that those from the northern part of the state would yield to the demands for banks. The *Peoria Democratic Press*, for example, came out in late December in favor of free banking as the only "way to regulate the currency." The paper mainly emphasized the need for sound currency rather than an expansion of credit. Both the *Illinois State Journal* and the *Peoria Democratic Press* attacked the governor's message. Even John Wentworth's usually orthodox *Daily Democrat* acquiesced that if a banking law had to be passed, it would be best to base it on the New York free banking act. An Elgin Democrat wrote French that the Democrats were being "assailed at every corner" by people demanding a free banking law. He recommended allowing a referendum on the issue so the Whigs could not charge that French was "interposing" himself between the people and the ballot box.[20]

The *Illinois State Journal* argued that the initiative lay with the Democrats since they controlled both houses, and, indeed, it was a group of Democrats who steered the free banking bill through the legislature. Early in the winter 1850–51 session, Thomas Dyer engineered the election of Sidney Breese as speaker of the house and received the chairmanship of the Committee on Banks and Incorporations as a reward. On January 14, 1851, he reported the bill from committee. It was passed by the house on February 8 and by the senate five days later. Governor French, however, vetoed the measure and returned it to the lawmakers on February 15.[21]

French offered five reasons for opposing the bill: (1) the absence of a specific specie reserve meant that gold and silver were "virtually dispensed with"; (2) it lacked adequate stockholder liability; (3) it offered no safeguard against speculation; (4) it placed no check on foreign circulation; and (5) it could not comply with the constitution because no general election would be held in November 1851. Again he insisted that free banking was a dangerous experiment and had still to be proven in New York.[22]

With little change in the vote, the measure was passed over the governor's veto. The bill enacted was a broad free banking law allowing the use of any state or federal bonds except those of Illinois and providing no personal liability and no specific specie reserve. There was a bank commission, and the banks were to publish quarterly statements. A provision that later created some problems limited interest rates banks might charge to 7%.[23]

An analysis of the house vote shows that the Whigs backed the bill and that its greatest support came from legislators representing districts north of Sangamon County. When the bill was before the legislature, the Democratic *Illinois State Register* attacked the law and the Whig *Illinois State Journal* supported it. The parties split rather evenly in the senate. In the house the Whigs supplied a majority of the votes in favor of the law when more than 80% of the Whigs voted for free banking. The law passed because a large minority of the Democrats in the house and a slight majority in the senate voted for it. Looked at sectionally, over 80% of the representatives from northern Illinois favored the bill, while nearly 70% of those from the southern part of the state opposed it. Even avowed antibank representatives from the northern counties supported the bill because of their constituents' demands and their belief that it was politically more expedient to set the question before the people than to allow it to divide the party.[24]

The bill could not become law until voted on by the people. As French had pointed out, however, there was to be no general election in 1851. To meet this objection a bill was forced through the legislature that removed all county treasurers, thus necessitating a November election to fill the vacancies. During the summer and fall the partisan press zealously debated the banking question, with Whig papers for and Democratic papers against the bill. Yet sectional division was apparent as well as partisanship. The *Chicago Daily Democrat* remained discreetly neutral. Wentworth explained, "There is a perfect mania in this area for banks and the man who says a word against this is bound to be run over." On the other hand, southern Whigs supported the law less ardently than their northern counterparts. The usually partisan *Alton Telegraph* remained silent, and one of French's admittedly prejudiced correspondents claimed that in Belleville both parties opposed the bill. Eleven southern, staunchly Democratic counties held rallies damning the bill. Opposition to the bill was still basically partisan, coming from "radical" Democrats in the north and south. Party leaders such as Gustave Koerner and James Shields spoke against free banking. Only the *Peoria Democratic Press* supported it. The other leading Democratic papers, including the party organ, the *Illinois State Journal*, presented a solid front against the measure. A group of Democrats in the western part of the state established the *Rock Island Weekly Republican* to advocate a return to "a constitutional currency as the circulating medium."[25]

In general these Democratic papers echoed the governor's veto and the traditional antibank arguments, asserting that all bank "schemes" inevitably led to "disastrous contractions." As usual, the Democrats argued that the passage of the bill was accomplished by fraud and engineered by the "Chicago money oligarchy." Uri Manly, a southern Democrat and partner in Governor French's land speculations, chastised the Democrats of the northern part of the state for devoting "themselves entirely to the service of the Mammon God." The *Benton Standard* added a new twist to the old arguments by connecting the free banking law with Free-Soilism. It believed that the Democratic party should be divested of

> those Bank Mongers who have so far been a curse to it, and . . . those who would destroy this glorious Union, for the purpose of severing the relation of master and servant in the Southern States, and we declare our increasing hostility to banks—to freesoilism and freesoil men, wherever and whenever they present themselves.[26]

Most Democratic party commentators, however, followed old and familiar lines. Banks were wrong in principle. They hurt the interest of the many while favoring the few who live without labor. Aside from being aristocratic and antirepublican, banks added nothing to "the productive industry of the country" but led instead to disastrous expansions and contractions. The *Galena Jeffersonian* held that all forms of banking, including free banking, were

156

a curse—a legacy that the aristocratic tendencies of a bygone age has left, as a means to fill the place of baronial usurpation and feudal exactions. They are the engine of the new form of oppression.

Democrats were cautioned to see that the evils of all banks were implicit in the free banking law.[27]

Democratic advocates of the free banking bill tried to picture the question as a nonpartisan one. Whigs such as Judge William Thomas, who wrote to the *Morgan Journal* that the bill involved no test of Whig principle and the question was thus up to the Democrats, corroborated their point. The *Chicago Daily Journal* reminded its readers that a committee dominated by Democrats introduced the bill and a Democratic legislature passed it. The *Illinois State Journal* referred to the law as the "Democratic Bank Law."[28]

There was even some vocal Whig opposition. The *Chicago Commercial Advertiser* revealed a strain of Whig antagonism to free banking similar to that of the Indiana Whigs who supported the state bank. This view, which was not widely accepted, represented conservative distrust of a bond-secured currency and the desire for a return to the old system of banking on capital with adequate checks against fraud.[29]

Yet, for all this, it is clear that the Whigs predominantly favored the bill. Judge Thomas, an old-line Whig, was defending the bill when he insisted the Democrats would decide the question. If the *Alton Telegraph* remained neutral, the most important Whig papers in the central and northern parts of the state, the *Illinois State Journal* and the *Chicago Daily Journal,* ardently supported the bill.[30]

Proponents of the law leveled the usual recriminations and charges of misrepresentation against the opposition. Whigs rebutted French's veto message, attacked the *State Register* for being unwilling to trust "the honest judgement of the people," and emphasized the superior security of the bill and the fact that it gave local control over the currency. Illinois suffered all the disadvantages of banks but had none of the advantages. A familiar

Whig theme appeared in the *Illinois State Journal*. A free banking law would lower interest rates by extending the supply of
credit, thus enabling mechanics to compete with wealthy men in
business. Free banking would make "the poor man equal to the
rich, by putting the credit and enterprise of the one on par with
the money bags of the man of wealth, (true democracy that)."
Expanded credit and a reasonably sufficient money supply aided
all classes by providing for increased business and "healthy and
rapid growth." A series of articles signed by "Mechanic" pointed
out the evil effects of an inadequate currency and high interest
rates, which the writer believed would be alleviated by the free
banking law. This led to an exchange with the editor of the *Illinois State Register* in which "Mechanic" argued that by stimulat-
ing the economy and making credit available, banks extended
opportunity. Each of these articles eulogized the self-made man
rising from his position as a poor but industrious laborer.[31]

Although a number of Democrats predicted the bill's defeat
and some northern politicians assured their southern compa-
triots that they personally would vote against it, the free banking
act carried by a vote of 37,573 to 31,321. The northern Democrats
who had broken with party orthodoxy seem to have represented
the wishes of their constituents. Only four counties north of Sangamon turned in antibank majorities, while in the southern part
of the state the law was overwhelmingly opposed in all except
traditionally Whig strongholds. French's correspondent in Chicago who had assured him that hardly anyone favored the "bank
project" had indulged in wishful thinking, for that area turned
in majorities from 85% to 95% in favor of the law.[32]

The most rabid opposition to banks came from "Egypt," the
southernmost part of the state, while probank and particularly
free banking sentiment was concentrated in the northern part of
the state. Rather than indicating simply a sectional conflict rooted
in economic differences, this breakdown reflects settlement patterns and the conflict of subcultures. The hostility between the
upland southerners, who originally settled the state and remained
in the southern counties, and the Yankees, who moved into the
northern half of the state after 1830, has been detailed by a num-

ber of historians, who have also noted the contrasting life styles of the two groups. Differences in economic behavior and attitudes, or, more simply, economic styles, were clearly one aspect of this conflict. In their own day the enterprising northerners were often contrasted with the slow-moving inhabitants of the southern counties, whom ex-Governor Ford described as "unambitious of wealth and great lovers of ease." The *Alton Telegraph* acknowledged the relationship between the bank issue and these contrasting economic styles. It attributed the stand of the southern counties to their sparse farm population and its "little relish or aptitide for speculation." They did not feel the need "for banking facilities experienced by those men imbued with the spirit of 'go-aheaditiveness.' " A Democratic editor from the central part of the state made an even more explicit and revealing observation. He charged that "rag money" principles

> might be entertained with some favor in New England—as the idea of enriching a people by issue of paper money is not much more absurd than the burning of indefensive old women on the charge of witchcraft—but, rude as the descendants of the much vaunted "Pilgrim fathers" may consider the intelligence of the western farmers to be they have too much common sense to believe that they can gain wealth through any other medium than honest industry.

He advised anyone "anxious to cultivate" banks to return "to the land of witchcraft where he could no doubt by invoking the spirits of the 'Pilgrim fathers' achieve more popularity for his rag money doctrines."[33]

This impressionistic evidence and the sharp sectional division of the votes in Illinois's constitutional convention in 1848 and again in the legislature in 1851 indicate that the bank issue must be understood in relation to the bitter social conflict in Illinois between the original settlers and the incoming Yankees. The ten banner probank counties in 1851 were in the area most heavily settled by New Englanders, while their hard money counterparts were in "darkest Egypt," untouched by the Yankee invasion (see map 2).[34]

# MAP 2. Bank Vote in the Illinois Assembly and the Banner Counties in the Illinois Referendum, 1851

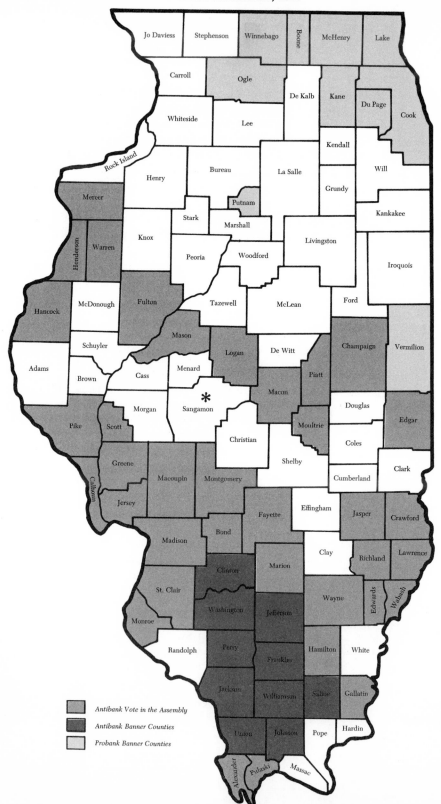

A clearer picture of the differences of areas opposing banks in contrast to those favoring banks can be obtained by correlating political, social, and ecological variables drawn from the 1850 federal census with the opposition to banks expressed in the 1851 referendum (see table 5).* The clearest correlate and probably

Table 5. Pearsonian *r* Correlation of Selected Variables and the
Percentage Opposition to Banks by County in the
Illinois Referendum, 1851

| Variable | Correlation Coefficient r |
|---|---|
| % Democratic, 1852 | .815 |
| % Antitemperance, 1855 | .702 |
| % Free Democratic, 1852 | −.538 |
| % Whig, 1852 | −.537 |
| % For Negro prohibition, 1848 | .506 |
| "Southerness" scale | .730 |
| Native illiterates per 1,000 population | .639 |
| Age of county | .460 |
| Population growth rate | −.417 |
| Towns | −.350 |
| Number of students | −.335 |
| Number of schools | −.275 |
| Farm value per acre | −.633 |
| Sweet potato production | .615 |
| Wheat production | −.487 |
| Total farm value | −.393 |
| Cheese production | −.378 |
| Wool production | −.360 |
| Improved land (ratio) | −.343 |
| Value of farm machinery | −.325 |
| Number of Congregational accommodations | −.390 |
| Number of Episcopal accommodations | −.236 |
| Number of Baptist accommodations | .232 |

* Tables 5 and 6 were made up from a correlation matrix that at its most extensive included 99 variables taken from *Compendium of the Enumeration of the Inhabitants and Statistics of the United States as Obtained at the Department of State from the Returns of the Sixth Census* (Washington, D. C.: Thomas Allen, 1841); J. D. B. DeBow, ed., *The Seventh Census of the United States* (Washington, D. C.: Robert Armstrong, 1853); *Springfield Illinois Journal*; *Springfield Daily Register*; Theodore Calvin Pease, ed., *Illinois Election Returns, 1818-1848* (Springfield: Illinois State Historical Library, 1923); W. Dean Burnham, *Presidential Ballots, 1836-1892* (Baltimore: John Hopkins Univ. Press, 1955); and Thomas J. Pressly and William H. Scofield, eds., *Farm Real Estate Values in the United States by Counties,*

the most important determinant of the antibank vote was partisan affiliation. Regular Democratic counties most strongly supported hard money, while Whig and Free-Soil areas were heavily pro-

---

*1850-1959* (Seattle: Univ. of Washington Press, 1965). The computations were made using the program "BMDO3D Correlation with Item Deletion— Version of Nov. 13, 1964, Health Sciences Computing Facility, U.C.L.A."

Several of the variables listed require further explanation. The "souther- ness" scale is a subjective ordinal scale grouping the counties of the state into eight categories from those having the smallest to those having the largest population of southern origin. The basic source was William V. Pooley, *The Settlement of Illinois from 1830 to 1850* (Madison: Univ. of Wisconsin, 1908). The variable called towns was a scale made up of the number of towns over 200 in population in each county as given in the *Seventh Census*. This is related to both style of migration of the county's pop- ulation and its political, social, and economic structures and outlooks. (See the brilliant development of these relationships in Stanley Elkins and Eric McKitrick, "A Meaning for Turner's Frontier, Part I: Democracy in the Old Northwest," *Political Science Quarterly* 69 [Sept. 1954]: 321-53, and "A Meaning for Turner's Frontier, Part II: The Southwest Frontier and New England," *ibid.* [Dec. 1954]: 565-602.) The figures available on farmers are from the *Sixth Census* and are thus of limited usefulness. The correlation be- tween the number of farmers per 1,000 population and the percentage of antibank vote, however, is insignificant (.187).

* There has been a great deal of debate among social scientists over the value of ecological analysis. This has often taken the form of a conflict be- tween advocates of survey research and those using the more easily available aggregate data. [See the differing views expressed in William S. Robinson, "Ecological Correlations and the Behavior of Individuals," *American Socio- logical Review*, 15 (June 1950): 351-57; Rudolf Heberle, *Social Movements* (New York: Appleton-Century-Crofts, 1951), pp. 197-265; Austin Ranney, "The Utility and Limitations of Aggregate Data in the Study of Electoral Behavior," in *Essays in the Behavioral Study of Politics*, ed. Austin Ranney (Urbana: Univ. of Illinois Press, 1962), pp. 91-102; and Mattei Dogan and Stein Rokkan, eds., *Quantitative Ecological Analysis in the Social Sciences* (Cambridge, Mass.: M.I.T. Press, 1969).] Two practicing historians have followed Robinson, at least to a degree, and have suggested the limitations of using county data. [See Thomas B. Alexander et al., "The Basis of Ala- bama's Ante-Bellum Two-Party System," *Alabama Review* (Oct. 1966): 255; and Ronald P. Formisano, "Analyzing American Voting, 1830-1860: Methods," *Historical Methods Newsletter* 2 (Mar. 1969): 1-11.] However, Hayward Alker shows in his article in *Quantitative Ecological Analysis* that other "fallacies" may result from the study of individuals or homogeneous townships, wards, or beats. It is more important to have a sufficient number of cases (here counties) to gain statistical reliability than to sacrifice reli- ability in trying to avoid the problems Robinson has discussed. While his- torians must be aware of these problems, it seems unlikely that such a valu- able tool as ecological analysis should be given up. Rather, it should be used with care and in combination with all other traditional tools of analysis.

bank. The counties favoring banks contained more productive land and were economically much better off than those opposing banks. The value of farms per acre correlates highly with pro-bank sentiment; moreover, the evidence indicates that probank views were strongest in areas dominated by wheat production and having large farms, high ratios of improved land, and high investment in farm machinery. Such were the newer and more rapidly developing counties into which the Yankees, who often brought capital with them, had moved. Various cultural indices such as the production of cheese and wool (products associated with New England), numerous small towns, Congregational churches, and low rates of illiteracy, combined with large numbers of schools and students, indicate the relation between the New England element and the drive for banks. Further correlations with two other referenda show these areas also strongly supported temperance and mustered what opposition there was to the prohibition of free blacks.

Southward, in areas opposing banks, was a markedly different society, economically less well off and growing less rapidly than the north. It was a land of small-scale diversified farming that was less oriented toward the market than the northern probank regions. The landscape was dotted with fewer small towns and schools. It was an area dominated by the southern migration. The cultural characteristics historians have associated with this southern element—high rates of illiteracy and the production and consumption of sweet potatoes—correlate very highly with the advocacy of hard money. The religious affiliation of these areas tended to be Baptist or Methodist, but the evidence of a relation of these sects to the antibank vote is less clear than it is with other indicators (see table 6). Finally, the most avidly antibank counties led the resistance to temperance, public schools, and antislavery, and most strongly supported the successful movement to prohibit free blacks from the state.[35]

While these correlations tend to confirm the hypothesis of subcultural conflict on the bank issue, the number of variables remains large and none of the variables functions by itself as an adequate index of the subcultures involved. Multiple factor analysis repre-

Table 6. Pearsonian *r* Correlation of the Number of Protestant Churches by Denomination and the Raw Bank Vote in the Illinois Referendum, 1851

| Denomination | Probank | Antibank |
|---|---|---|
| Congregationalist | .537 | −.039 |
| Episcopal | .502 | .048 |
| Presbyterian | .346 | .185 |
| Methodist | .285 | .408 |
| Lutheran | .132 | .243 |
| Baptist | .040 | .323 |

sents a way of statistically clustering related social indices in order to approach multivariate indicators of the presence of the social groups discussed in the impressionistic literature. The five factors used are denoted "Yankee subculture," "southern

Table 7. Pearsonian *r* Correlation of Five Factors with the Percentage Antibank Vote in the Illinois Referendum, 1851 by County*

| Factor | Percentage Antibank |
|---|---|
| Factor 1—Yankee Subculture | −.454 |
| Factor 2—Southern Subculture | .415 |
| Factor 3—Foreign-born | −.207 |
| Factor 4—General farming | −.043 |
| Factor 5—Population | −.199 |

* Computed using program BMDO3D.

subculture," "foreign-born," "general farming," and "population" (see appendix A). The first and second factors are especially useful because of the degree to which they include indices of the contrasting subcultures both impressionistic evidence and the correlational analysis indicate to have been at odds on the bank issue. The fourth factor should allow us to ascertain better the response of Illinois farmers to the bank issue.

Of these five factors only the first and the second clearly and significantly correlate with the percentage antibank vote in the referendum. The factor reflecting the Yankee subculture correlates highly and negatively, while "southern subculture," representing upland southerners, correlates nearly as highly and positively with the opposition to banks. There would seem to be no relationship at all between farming and response to the bank issue.

The related techniques of partial correlation and multiple regression analysis can further clarify the relative importance of each factor in relation to the probank and antibank votes. The partials given in table 8 reveal once again the sharp contrast be-

Table 8. Partial Correlation of Four Factors and the Bank Vote
in the Illinois Referendum, 1851, Holding Population
Constant*

| Factor | Antibank | Probank |
|---|---|---|
| Factor 1—Yankee subculture | −.311 | .471 |
| Factor 2—Southern subculture | .523 | −.374 |
| Factor 3—Foreign-born | −.217 | .138 |
| Factor 4—General farming | .287 | .018 |

* Computed using BMDO2R.

tween the areas of Yankee and southern dominance. Here, factor four, "general farming," approaches significance on the antibank vote; but, interestingly, when both factors five and two are controlled for, the partial is close to zero (.09). The five factors taken together account for 79% of the variance in the probank vote and 45% of the variance in the antibank vote (see table 9), with the "southern subculture" factor, rather than "population," surprisingly accounting for the majority of the latter variance.

The picture needs to be sketched with greater precision through similar analysis at the township and ward levels, where other strong Democratic groups, such as the Lutheran Germans and the Irish Catholics, would undoubtedly be found resisting banks and the Whigs of non-Yankee origin supporting them. Focusing only on the religious variables clarifies this situation (see appendix B). Both "Congregational accommodations" and "Episcopal ac-

Table 9. Percentage Variance in the Bank Vote Accounted for by
Five Factors, Illinois Referendum, 1851*

| *Factor by Bank Stance* | Variance (%) | F Value When Entered |
|---|---|---|
| *Probank* | | |
| Factor 5—Population | 66 | 188.3 |
| Factor 1—Yankee subculture | 8 | 27.3 |
| Factor 3—Foreign-born | 3 | 13.2 |
| Factor 4—General farming | 1 | 4.0 |
| Factor 2—Southern subculture | 1 | 8.3 |
| *Antibank* | | |
| Factor 5—Population | 17 | 20.5 |
| Factor 2—Southern subculture | 22 | 35.9 |
| Factor 3—Foreign-born | 2 | 3.3 |
| Factor 1—Yankee subculture | 4 | 7.3 |
| Factor 4—General farming | 0 | .2 |

* Computed using computer program "BMDO2R—Stepwise Regression—Version of April 13, 1965, Health Sciences Computing Facility, U.C.L.A." F values exceeding 3.95 are significant at .05 level of probability.

commodations" account for significant percentages of variance in the probank vote, while "Roman Catholic accommodations," "Baptist accommodations," "Methodist accommodations," and "Lutheran accommodations" all significantly affect the variance on the antibank vote.

This would suggest that the foreign-born may have split along ethnoreligious lines on the bank issue as on other political matters and that opposition to banks was part of a pattern of political behavior rooted in ethnoreligious group consciousness. Those areas in which German Lutherans were strong tended to be antibank. Similarly, the existence of large numbers of Irish Catholics tends to correlate positively with a county's opposition to banks. On the other side of the issue, the existence of Episcopalians, many of whom were undoubtedly "New British," signaled a probank tendency in the referendum vote. This latter group often shared Yankee cultural perceptions and economic mores, and very likely cooperated with the Yankees in their crusade for banks and the increased commercialization of society.[36]

Consequently, most leading Democrats, including Stephen A. Douglas, opposed the law; but there seems to have been a consensus among those from the northern part of the state that politically it was best that the question was out of the way. They warned French that the Democracy had to be careful not to be defeated in Illinois "purely by the cursed bank question" as they had been in Missouri and Wisconsin. Douglas reflected that since the combination of Whigs and "bank-Democrats" could pass any measure, it was politically inexpedient to "carry the question into the next general election [and] enable the combination to carry not only that measure but the Legislature and the state Government."[37]

# 3

A similar pattern to that found in Illinois can be seen in Wisconsin, where a coalition of Whigs, Free-Soilers, and Democrats created a free banking system that was accepted by the state's voters in 1852. Because of restrictions in the Wisconsin constitution, bank advocates had first to place the question of "banks or no banks" on the ballot. If the people were found to favor "banks," they then had to construct a banking law, guide it through the legislature, and again place it before the voters.

In the fall election of 1850 an attempt was made to set the question of "banks or no banks" before the people. The assembly passed the referendum, but antibank Democrats blocked it in the senate. The most violent opponent of the bill was Moses Strong, who maintained that all banks were evil, undemocratic, and unwanted by the people. Antibank papers like the *Waukesha Democrat* and the *Milwaukee Commercial Advertiser* defended the action of the senators and bitterly denounced as traitors those Democrats who had voted for the bill. Those papers advocating banks, particularly the Whig *Milwaukee Daily Sentinel and Gazette*, insisted that the people should be allowed to vote and suggested that the Democrats who blocked the bill lacked faith in the judgment of the people.[38]

The following year the legislature succeeded in passing a similar bill and set the issue before the voters in the 1851 election. Again Whig papers favored submitting the issue to the public while Democratic papers opposed it. Much of the argument revealed the cultural antagonisms that were such a crucial part of Wisconsin's early politics. Strong argued that the bill would undermine the intent of the recently ratified constitution and equated free banking with *extending the vote to blacks* and *restricting foreigners from the polls.* Another Democratic opponent of submission argued that all banks should be opposed because their whole effect was "towards crushing and enslaving the poor"; only the aristocracy, living on the toil of others, benefited. The *Daily Sentinel and Gazette* countered that banks were needed, particularly in the Lake Michigan ports, where businessmen, mechanics, and farmers all favored banks. At least the question should be submitted to the people.[39]

In the fall election the Whigs came out openly for a new bank law and associated the referendum on "banks or no banks" with their gubernatorial candidate, Leonard J. Farwell, and those Whigs running for the legislature. They reasoned that even if the people favored banks, a Democratic legislature would hesitate to pass a law creating them. Democrats who, like Moses Strong, urged the legislature not to act regardless of how the people voted verified their point.[40]

The Democratic candidate for governor, Daniel A. J. Upham, found his situation extremely precarious. He avoided the bank issue, assuring only that he would respect the wishes of the people. The *Waukesha Democrat*, which had argued early in the year that it was the duty of every voter to oppose banks, had moderated its stand by the time of the election. The paper contended that the referendum was not a partisan matter and that it would accept banks if a sound system could be established. The voters must have been impressed by the Whig arguments, because they overwhelmingly favored banks, elected Farwell, and gave the state a Whig legislature.[41]

Farwell's inaugural address to the new legislature recommended a free banking law with a stock-based currency. The Democratic papers expectably heaped scorn upon his suggestions. The *Daily Argus* characterized his message as "tinctured with the fallacies of Whiggery." While the bill was before the legislature, the Democratic press relentlessly attacked it, calling for unlimited liability and the prohibition of notes under $20. When it became obvious that the bill would pass, the *Daily Argus* supported Strong's amendment, which allowed the banks to use railroad securities as collateral as well as state stocks. The *Daily Argus* believed that only in this way might some good result.[42]

The vote in the legislature revealed intraparty division. Free-Soilers supported the bill, as did 70% of the Whigs and slightly more than 50% of the Democrats. Much of the Whig opposition to the law came from men who opposed the use of railroad securities as collateral. Democrats favoring the law were clearly representing the opinion of their constituencies.[43]

The Democratic papers continued their opposition, but less vehemently, trying to play down the issue, while Whig papers defended the bill. In November 1852 free banking was overwhelmingly accepted by the voters. Both in the legislature and at the polls, the counties along Lake Michigan and in the northern and central parts of the state most strongly desired free banking. Hard money sentiment was greatest in the older areas, particularly in the economically declining Lead Region, which had originally been settled by upland southerners who had migrated up the Mississippi River. However, even in the eastern counties traditionally Democratic ethnic groups, such as the Irish Catholics and the Milwaukee Germans, maintained a staunchly antibank stance. The pattern of support for free banking paralleled that of Illinois.[44]

# 4

In Indiana several free banking bills were introduced into the legislature during the 1851–52 session. While the state bank had performed quite admirably, its expansion had clearly not kept pace with the growing needs of the state's economy. Moreover,

the mutual liability principle had made the bank directors hesitant to open branches in the newer parts of the state. The constitutional convention in 1850 had revealed the degree to which
such demands for added facilities had taken hold of the Whig
party and shattered the solid front of the Democracy on the bank
question. It is not surprising that a free banking proposal drew
bipartisan support in 1852. Alexander F. Morison, a Democratic
merchant from Marion in the northern Grant County, chaired an
Indianapolis meeting of "businessmen and other citizens" demanding a free banking law. John Defrees, the politician-editor of
most important Whig paper in the state, the *Indiana Journal*, was
its secretary.[45]

The bill was introduced by a northern Democrat and was reported favorably out of a committee including ten Democrats and
four Whigs. Based on the earlier New York law, it was designed
to provide adequate new facilities in the safest possible manner.
The lack of such facilities, it was argued, forced down prices and
acted as a check on "growth and prosperity." A large number of
Democrats voted for it in both houses; and a Democratic governor, Joseph Wright, signed it into law.[46]

Although a bit more complex, the Indiana situation was comparable to that of the other states. The Democrats were generally silent on the bank question, preferring not to widen the rift
in their own ranks. The party clearly favored a general law but
split on its nature. Those Democrats who accepted banking had to
violate well-established tenets of party doctrine. Whereas party
orthodoxy opposed state debt and "swindling corporations" and
advocated a "gradual return from the paper credit system," free
banking created fiscal corporations that issued paper currency
based on government debt. In the opposition's camp, Governor
Wright distrusted paper money and feared inflation. He was
never happy with the bill and only signed it because his advisers
convinced him of the need for the bill and because he believed
that his party supported it. With some encouragement from his
friends, however, Wright quickly became the system's adversary
once it was instituted. A similar course was taken by the *Sentinel,*
the organ of the Indiana Democracy. While the bill was under

170

consideration, it generally reserved judgment on the issue, but opposed the system immediately upon its creation. (The editor later insisted that he had been an opponent of the law all along.)[47]

The vote on this measure clearly revealed the division in Democratic ranks. Of the 34 senate Democrats, 20 favored the bill, while of the 46 house Democrats, 24 opposed it. This split in the Indiana Democracy followed geographic divisions that, like Illinois and Wisconsin, reflected settlement patterns as well as economic areas. The Democrats who supported free banking tended to come from the northern and central counties of the state, which had been settled by the Yankee migration and which were emerging as the economically most dynamic sections of the state.[48]

The position of the Whigs was more sharply defined. The party stood for the extension of credit and currency facilities and divided on the question of the efficacy of a state bank versus a free banking system. A majority favored free banking. John Defrees was the first to introduce a free banking bill in the 1851–52 session, and his paper constantly backed free banking. In the legislature R. N. Hudson, a Whig lawyer from Terre Haute, was one of the most forceful supporters of the new law. The vote on the bill revealed strong Whig commitment to free banking. In the senate, where the Whigs were badly outnumbered, six of the nine who voted favored the bill. The percentage of Whig support in the house was even higher. There 86% of the party supported the bill and provided the largest block of votes for free banking.[49]

## 5

By the end of 1852, Ohio, Indiana, Illinois, and Wisconsin had implemented free banking laws, and a similar measure was defeated in the Michigan house by only a single vote. In each case the bill was backed by a coalition of Whigs and Democrats. While historians have generally noted this, they have either ignored or misunderstood the role of the Whigs and have overemphasized the degree to which these laws were a product of antimonopoly sentiment or "agrarian radicalism" among the Democrats.[50]

The crusade for free banking was led by the Whig press and Whig representatives, who accounted for a plurality of votes for the laws. But the bank question cleaved their ranks also. Historians have generally reasoned that the Whigs, since they opposed the antimonopoly Democrats, must have favored "monopoly." This was hardly the case. There was a conservative minority in the Whig party that opposed free banking as a danger to economic stability and preferred to establish some kind of state bank or return to the old system of legislative charters. This made them "monopolists" in the parlance of the day. Yet this group was a small, minority segment of the Whigs. While there is no reliable way to judge its size among the rank and file, the votes in the state legislatures show that it accounted for fewer than 20% of the Whig representatives. This percentage was probably smaller among the rank and file, for the vast majority of the Whig party and the leading party organs in every state stood solidly opposed to "monopoly" and in favor of free banking. The views of this majority group were modernist: they were in tune with the economic changes taking place at the time. These Whigs conceived of the economy in dynamic, expansionist terms. They cast their appeal to the electorate in terms of the benefits all groups would derive from this expansion. The keynote of their policy was equality of economic opportunity. While they were not pure and simple inflationists and emphasized the idea of convertability of paper into specie, it was this faction of the Whig party that advocated attempting to increase general economic activity and boost agricultural prices by expanding the money supply. On the question of interest this group usually recommended the establishment of legal limits, and one powerful argument for free banking was that the competition of new banks would hold interest rates down. Most important, at the base of Whig policy was a positive conception of the role of government that in spirit was antithetical to that of their Democratic opponents.

In contrast, the Democrats held a negative conception of governmental powers. No faction within the Democratic party in 1850 was demanding inflation to aid the "debtor" interests, as historians have generally argued. The party and its leading spokesmen stood for quite the opposite and warned of the dangers of rising prices induced by inflated currency. The debtor was looked upon as morally suspect and a social consequence of banks and paper money. In their policy toward interest rates, the Democrats opposed usury laws that purported to set a legal rate of interest as vehemently as they opposed inflation and thought the Whigs remiss for advocating these policies, which interfered with the "natural laws of trade."

The Democrats were split into two factions on the bank question. The majority of the party rehashed Jacksonian objections to banks and paper money. Their traditional fear of government debt further caused them to oppose free banking laws at the same time they favored general laws in other areas. Yet a minority broke with the Democratic majority to support free banking laws as the safest way of obtaining a sound, well-secured currency. In general, these Democrats represented the more newly settled areas of their respective states and those with the greatest economic potential. In contrast to the older sections, these areas harbored populations primarily from New England and New York. Their legislative representatives found it politically necessary to eschew Jacksonian fiscal dogma. Neither Democratic group, however, embraced a Whig-like dynamic view of the economy. A large number of the "no bank" group were rural reactionaries opposed to the industrialization and commercialization of American life. This antipathy was basically a simple, reflexive perpetuation of traditional Jacksonian rhetoric by older areas that resented being economically and culturally dominated by the newer areas.

The clash between the "commercial-minded" Whigs and the "agrarian-minded" Democrats over banks was an aspect of the conflict of subcultures within the region that structured the political battles of the period. The Irish Catholic, the German, and the upland southerner were all threatened, not only by commercialization of the economy, but also by the energetic attempts of the Yankee-Protestants to make society over in their own image. Commercialization was but one of a complex of Yankee-Protestant attitudes against which the Democratic coalition struggled. The bank issue played an important symbolic role in this conflict highlighting the contrasting economic styles of these groups.

As the political and social dominance of the upland southerners in the older sections of the region became increasingly threatened by the influx of Yankees, they clung more tightly to their economic and social morality. They were constantly sensitive to Yankee self-righteousness and the disapproval of their manners and customs implied by it. Banks symbolized the commercialization of economic life that the southerner saw as an aspect of the growing domination of the society and culture by the transplanted Yankees. It is hardly surprising that the upland southerners fought Free-Soilism, temperance, and common schools with a vigor equal to their opposition to banks. Each symbolized their declining status and threatened the maintenance of their way of life.[51]

Yankee-Protestant domination of the society also threatened the Irish Catholics and the Germans (many of whom were Catholics), who equaled the upland southerners in their vehement oppositon to banks. Both of these groups were overwhelmingly Democratic during these years because of the Democracy's acceptance of cultural pluralism in contrast to the Whigs' insistence upon what contemporary sociologist Milton M. Gordon has termed Anglo-conformity. Irish and German economic attitudes and behavior also conflicted with the entrepreneurial spirit of the Whigs and coincided with the Democratic insistence upon frugality and simplicity.[52]

Throughout the Old Northwest the bank issue became intertwined with these cultural conflicts. It was a symbolic as well as a "real" issue inasmuch as decisions on banks revealed the status of subcultural groups. The acceptance of banks signaled the dominance of the economic style of the Yankee-Protestants and, with it, the ascendancy of their moral and social outlooks. Those threatened by Yankee-Protestant control of the government and the society banded together in the Democratic party, ignoring their mutual differences, to resist the extension of Yankee hegemony and to maintain familiar life styles.

# CHAPTER 7

## POLITICAL AND ECONOMIC ADJUSTMENTS, 1852-1857

### 1

The passage of the free banking laws brought neither the financial utopia their advocates had envisioned nor the disaster their enemies had foretold. There were both successes and failures; the dominant note of the period between 1852 and 1857 was experimentation, as each state modified and altered its banking laws to meet its needs for credit and sound currency. The Panic of 1854 spurred the advocates of free banking to attempt to reform these systems to alleviate the problems that crisis had disclosed. At the same time the disappearance of the Whigs, the splintering of the Democrats, and the emergence of the Republican party and its achievement of dominance in the Old Northwest altered the political situation. The efforts of Republicans to reform the banking laws reveal a continuity between them and the Whigs on the money question. Like the Whigs, the new party strove to supply adequate credit and currency through the use of free banking. Like the Whigs also, the Republicans emphasized the creation of opportunity through economic development. Although the political situation increasingly eclipsed the bank issue, the Democracy still, if less vociferously, maintained its traditional hostility toward banks of any kind and its conservative attitude toward economic change.

The period between the end of the severe depression of the late

1830s and early 1840s and the onset of economic troubles in 1857 was one of spectacular growth and expansion. With the exception of two temporary setbacks in 1847–48 and 1854, each year witnessed increased production and trade. Although such rapid growth, particularly in the cities, created new social problems, the standard of living in the country measured by per-capita real income rose. The boom was sparked by growing population, an improved transportation and communications network, and a jerry-built credit system.[1]

In the Old Northwest free banking became the predominant credit and currency arrangement. The American people of the mid-nineteenth century chose to place certain limitations on the banks' development in this area. Within these limits, they struggled to establish institutions to answer the needs created by economic change. Despite its faults, free banking facilitated an unprecedented boom.

Nationally this period was one of extensive railroad building. By 1850 there were about 8,500 miles of track in the United States. In only 7 years this grew to nearly 24,000, and investment in railroads rose from $372 million to approximately $1 billion. The Old Northwest benefited most from this expansion. Although in 1860 the less-developed states in the area, Michigan and Wisconsin, ranked fourteenth and eleventh, respectively, in miles of track, the older states, Ohio, Illinois, and Indiana, stood first, second, and fifth in the nation. In all cases the growth rate was phenomenal. Ohio had 39 miles of track in 1840 and nearly 3,000 by 1860.[2]

The population growth of the Old Northwest was also phenomenal. During the decade of the 1850s, its demographic dimensions jumped from 4½ to nearly 7 million people. Illinois, already a relatively large state by 1850, more than doubled its population to become the fourth most populous state in the Union by 1860. At the same time agricultural production leaped forward. By the end of the decade, Illinois, Ohio, and Indiana were 3 of the top 4 corn-producing states in the country. Illinois led this expansion also. Its output increased from 22,634,000 bushels in 1839 to 115,174,000 bushels in 1859. Even Michigan, a relatively backward state, made advances. Its population grew from 212,267 in 1840 to 397,654 by

1850 and 749,113 by 1860. During the decade of the 1850s its railroad mileage increased from 349 to 779 miles. At mid-century Michigan farmers produced 5½ million bushels of corn and slightly less than 5 million bushels of wheat. The state exported oats, wool, potatoes, butter, and cheese in large quantities. During the next decade a copper mining boom, the fishing industry, and the beginnings of the lumber business led Michigan "Out of the Wilderness."[3]

Entrepreneurs moved quickly to organize free banks under the newly established free banking laws. Twelve new banks appeared in Ohio during 1851 and another was organized early in 1852 before the attorney general ruled that further banks would be of doubtful legality under the new constitution. Ninety-four free banks were organized in Indiana in the three years following the passage of the new law. In Illinois the prospective bankers were slow to organize, hoping that their state's law would be liberalized and the discrimination against Illinois bonds removed; but by the end of 1852 there were seventeen new banks in the state. Within two years this number had grown to thirty-one, ten banks being located in Chicago alone. With Wisconsin undergoing a similar expansion, it is not surprising that in the years between 1852 and 1854 economic activity increased in the Old Northwest. In a single year, between 1853 and 1854, loans and discounts in the West increased 37%. A careful student of economic trends during this period believes "that capital was more abundant than any time on record."[4]

## 2

Following the passage of the free banking laws, the Whigs defended the new system, while the Democrats were either silent or sharply critical. Democrats from northern Illinois were generally happy to have the issue that had divided their ranks settled, but an active effort was still made to revive the no-bank issue and repeal the free banking law. Joel Matteson received the Democratic nomination for governor in 1852 only after assurances that he was really opposed to banks. The following year the antibank Democrats pushed a repeal bill through the senate, but it died in committee in the house.[5]

Indiana's Democrats were skeptical about free banking. Governor Joseph Wright, one of the state's leading opponents of banks, predicted the law contained insufficient restrictions against abuse. He warned of the problems of inflation and of business fluctuations, which aided speculators but hurt the "producing classes." Unless the law was modified, a sound currency could not be provided. He would limit the denominations to less than "five or ten dollars," create a bank commission and a special office to control currency, limit the security to Indiana stocks or real estate, and require directors to be residents.[6]

Ohio Democrats continued their opposition to banks, although this sometimes took new forms. Even though the hard money forces in the Ohio Democracy had been unable to insert prohibition of banks into the new constitution and had failed to block the passage of a free banking law in 1851, in practice their policy was implemented, for the restrictions in the constitution made expansion of the old banking system impossible. Moreover, the state's Democratic attorney general undermined the free banking law just one year after its passage by ruling the law unconstitutional.[7]

The main technique of the opponents of banks in Ohio during these years was severe bank taxation, a strategy designed more for its political appeal than for its economic feasibility. In the 1840s Democrats had shown themselves sensitive to the problem of bank taxation. In 1846 over Democratic opposition, the Whigs revised the state's tax system so that, in Alfred Kelley's words, "every citizen [would pay] an equal share of the public burden in proportion to his ability to sustain it. . . ." At that time revenues were totally inadequate (the state had operated in the red for ten years) and favoritism was rife (horses and cattle were taxed, sheep and hogs were not). Kelley, who had fathered the state's banking system, was responsible also for the revenue law of 1846. It is clear from his report to the senate at that time that the sponsors of the bill had intended to provide adequate revenues by more fairly distributing the tax burden, and the Whigs had defended the law on these grounds. Although the law had given no new advantages to banks, which continued to be taxed for 6% of their profits, state stocks had been exempted from taxation. The Democrats ignored the need for a new tax system and the many equities the Kelley law would institute, attacking it as a measure designed simply to aid those banks based on state stocks. One Democrat asserted that state stocks should be allowed to depreciate *"because the banks are based upon those stocks, and if the State stocks go down so must the banks."*[8]

Throughout the next decade the Democrats continued to argue that banks were being favored over other forms of property. In its 1850 convention the party proposed taxing banks in the same way "the people" were taxed. In 1851 and 1852, Democratic tax laws were passed extending bank taxes to all forms of bank "property": notes issued, bills discounted or purchased at a profit, and average amounts of money loaned. The institutions were not allowed to deduct their debts from their assets. The banks took the issue to the courts, where they were upheld and the laws of 1851 and 1852 were eventually declared unconstitutional. While this litigation was in progress, a final Democratic measure called the "Crow Bar Law" was enacted, permitting county treasurers to break into the vaults of protesting banks and seize unpaid taxes plus penalties and costs incurred.[9]

Whigs, Free-Soilers, and a few bank Democrats resisted these laws. They tended to view them as an attack on the banks rather than as a system of "equal taxation." While they were not opposed to taxing the banks, they were against what they considered the unconstitutional and overly harsh taxes imposed by the Democrats. In 1850 the Whigs and Free-Soilers strengthened the provisions of the 1846 law and provided for taxing banks' capital and surplus. The Republican administration in 1856 enacted a new law taxing banks. Like the 1846 revenue law and the 1845 bank law, this, too, was written by Alfred Kelley, who had recently joined the new party. The new law imposed taxes on capital, surplus, contingent fund, and undivided profits. In the party press the Democrats condemned the earlier courts' decisions on banks

179

and this new law, while the Republicans supported Kelley and his law against political "demagogues" and the "absurd and unconstitutional" laws of the Democrats. The *Ohio State Journal* argued that the harsh tax laws retarded the economic development of the state. They helped only lawyers, sheriffs, and officeholders, and the people were tired of such a "specimen of Locofoco legislation."[10]

# 3

The free banking systems received their first trial during the brief economic downturn of 1854. The upswing of the early years of the decade had featured an increased investment in railroad construction along with a general rise in prices spurred by European crop failures and the outbreak of the Crimean War in 1853. The war, however, injured foreign investments, and the sale of both railroad and state securities declined. Since the railroads badly needed construction capital, they entered the midwestern market. As a result interest rates climbed and the money stringency dampened business. A continual rise in the rates of New York exchange from 1853 to November 1854 precipitated a run on the Ohio free banks in May, which soon spread to Indiana and Illinois. At the same time eastern bank notes, which still composed a large percentage of western currency, were being withdrawn, leaving only the local notes, themselves undermined by declining stock prices and a drain on the banks' specie. In August the Cincinnati banks refused to take Indiana free bank notes, and confidence in the free banks was shattered. Indiana was severely hit and most of her new institutions failed. Ten of Ohio's banks and eight of Illinois's new banks also fell, although the systems of these two states withstood the shock reasonably well.[11]

The Panic of 1854 was mainly financial and quickly gave way to a renewed boom from 1855 to 1857. This boom was particularly felt in the West, and demands for currency increased amid a mild revival of antibank attitudes. In all the states credit facilities had to be provided; and in the light of the experience of 1854, alterations in the free banking systems seemed essential.

180

The year 1854 brought not only a break in economic expansion, but also a disruption of the party system and a realignment of political groups and interests. The new Republican party emerged to replace the Whig party, which soon disappeared. At the same time the Democratic coalition was altered. The process of party realignment was not immediate but ongoing throughout the mid-1850s. Some early leaders quickly fell from the public eye; others, later to become leaders, were still unheard from.

The two issues most responsible for this political upheaval were the rise of nativism, with its corollary the temperance movement, and the question of the expansion of slavery revived by the passage of the Kansas-Nebraska Act. Traditionally the Whigs had been the party of native Protestants, and the strange combination of political reform and anti-Catholicism that arose in the early 1850s appealed to many members of the older party. This spirit strengthened once the votes of immigrants appeared to have been responsible for Pierce's victory of 1852.[12]

In the Old Northwest nativism was strongest in Indiana and weakest in Michigan and Wisconsin. A struggle developed within the movement between the "Jonathans," who were anti-Catholic and antislavery, and the "Sams," who tended to avoid the slavery issue and emphasized the Union and opposition to immigration. While conclusive evidence is not yet at hand, it would seem that most "Jonathans" eventually went into the moderately nativist Republican party. The numerically less important "Sams," who were financed and exploited, in Illinois at least, by the Democrats, served as a refuge for conservative Whigs, who eventually either joined their former opponents or dropped from the scene. The temperance movement, which was closely related to nativism, served to draw native Protestants from the Democracy and was a symbolic outlet for moderate nativists. Temperance advocates, who were often also opposed to the expansion of slavery or were outright abolitionists, swelled the ranks of the new Republican party.[13]

Slavery was also a divisive issue. The Whig party in the North had been losing steadily to antislavery third parties, which bit less deeply into the Democratic electorate; and the rank and file of the party were more sympathetic to antislavery views than

181

most Democrats. However, the Nebraska question caused a small but significant group of Democrats to split with their traditional party. A few genuinely deplored the inhumanity of slavery, but the majority of these Democrats were racist Negrophobes alarmed by the growing prosouthern orientation of the Democracy, which manifested itself in the Kansas-Nebraska Act. Either they believed that the "Doughface" Democracy had sacrificed their economic interests on issue of land and improvement legislation, or they merely resented the personal power and arrogance of the southern politicians in their party. A similar spectrum of thought could be found among the large majority of northern Whigs, who were developing antislavery and antisouthern attitudes. The Nebraska issue served as a rallying point for antisouthernism in both parties.[14]

The connection between these issues and the bank question is not immediately obvious. Historians have generally assumed that the antibank radicalism of the ex-Democrats who joined the new party contributed markedly to Republican ideology. Certainly, during the period 1854 to 1857, neither party talked much about the issue. Both sides wished to play down old, divisive issues. The first Republican platform of Michigan favored "postponing and suspending all differences with regard to political economy." According to the *Ohio State Journal*, it was "no more a question of Tariff or Bank. No more a question of economy or policy in regard to matters of finance, that is to be decided at this election [1856], but it is the great question of HUMAN LIBERTY." Similar sentiments were expressed in the other states as the Republicans attempted to attract antislavery Democrats; and the party of Pierce, Douglas, and Buchanan tried to lure the more conservative elements of their former opponents. This strategy seems to have confused the situation as anti-Nebraska Democrats, many of whom were also antibank "radicals," were given positions of power so as to draw additional support from their former followers. It would seem that any party that included such adamant opponents of banks as Salmon Chase, Lyman Trumbull, John Wentworth, and Kinsley Bingham in major leadership positions would also embody their opposition to banks. Yet this was not the

182

case. The new party took over the economic views of the more progressive Whigs, including advocacy of free banking. The state legislatures' attempts to cope with banking problems in the period of party transition clearly reveal the continuity between Whig and Republican economic policy.[15]

## 4

In Indiana the nearly complete collapse of the free banking system combined with the expiration of the charter of the state bank in 1857 to make action imperative. One contemporary colloquially wrote, "Our money matters is in a most Deplorable condition and all eyes is turned to the legislature." This necessity eventually resulted in the chartering of a new, privately owned Bank of the State of Indiana and a reformation of the state's free banking system. While these actions were confused even more than usual by personal cupidity, they reveal a continuity of opposition to banks among Democrats and an extension of Whig attitudes through the transitional Fusion movement, which captured the legislature in 1854, to its successor, the Republican party.[16]

Indiana's new constitution prohibited rechartering the state bank. Its directors determined to wind up the bank's affairs in accordance with the constitution, but a "syndicate" of politicians formed to obtain a charter for a new institution similar to the old state bank. If Hugh McCulloch's memory can be relied upon, this syndicate began its campaign in 1854 before the panic undermined the free banking system. According to McCulloch's account in *Men and Measures of a Half Century*, the syndicate was made up of "a number of active and influential politicians of both parties." While there were a few important Whigs in this group, Democrats dominated, with Judge Thomas L. Smith as its moving spirit. Lieutenant Governor Ashbel Willard was also deeply involved. Of the seven members of the syndicate serving in the legislature, five were Democrats. The "syndicate" apparently made careful use of the political situation and a few well-placed "bribes." Austin Puett was promised 100 shares of stock in the new bank to influence his brother-in-law, the governor; and the editor of the *State Sentinel* receive 500 shares to assure a favorable press. Very little effort was wasted on Fusionists, who would probably have voted for an extension of currency and credit in any case. Of the thirteen bribes reported by historian Logan Esarey, ten were offered to Democrats, which may account in part for the six representatives and one senator who opposed free banks but favored the Bank of the State of Indiana.[17]

The bank was clearly a straight business deal entered into by the members of the syndicate, who allowed neither ideology nor ethics to interfere with their course. The politicians cashed in by selling their newly acquired stock to the stockholders and the former directors of the old state bank, who assumed the management of the new institution. All in all, the incident is a curious example of the workings of American politics and shows the degree to which nineteenth-century politics could itself be a business. The members of the syndicate had never intended to become bankers. Their actions were not entirely reprehensible. Actually, they had defrauded no one; they had only "bent" the law to their own profit. In the long run their actions would be justified, because the new bank continued the sound policies of its predecessor.[18]

Even though Democrats predominated in the syndicate, the vote on the bill demonstrates the continuing antibank sentiment among most Democrats. The bill was opposed entirely by Democrats and supported almost to a man by Fusionists. Nearly all of the state's Democratic papers assailed the new bank, with the exception of the *State Sentinel*, much to the consternation of most of the party. It seemed impossible "that at this late day *any* Democratic paper should be willing to repudiate the Democratic doctrine in relation to paper money." The bill had created "a monopoly [which] should be nipped in the bud before its immense powers can be brought to bear upon political affairs." Democratic Governor Wright, who was extremely embarrassed by the participation of his friends and political allies in the creation of the Bank of the State of Indiana, vetoed the bill on the grounds that it was dangerous and unnecessary as well as unconstitutional; but it was passed over his veto.[19]

The Fusionists' enthusiasm for a state bank, shown by their wholesale support of it in the legislature, was paralleled by efforts to maintain and reform the free banking system. A revision of the old law was carried through the same Fusionist legislature that created the Bank of the State of Indiana.

The panic seriously shook confidence in free banking, so much so that even the *Indiana Journal* joined the *State Sentinel* in opposing the system. After the onset of the panic, the state auditor called for reform of the system. He favored enforcing a permanent location for each bank and uniform banking hours. He explained that

> it is suggested, as to location, to prevent the practice of selecting remote and unknown situations, that no bank should be located at any point which does not contain from two to three thousand permanent citizens.

He also suggested a specie reserve of 20% to 25% and a universal redemption center at the state capital.[20]

Most Democrats took the opportunity to express their opposition to free banking in principle and to pay homage to traditional Democratic antibank rhetoric. The editor of the *State Sentinel* reaffirmed that as "a democrat of the radical stripe we have always opposed Banking on any basis whatever." He reminded his readers that the *State Sentinel* had stood against free banking since the constitutional convention and had worked against the passage of the law. Governor Wright had never supported the free banking system, and his present attacks on these banks only worsened the situation. According to his biographer, Wright "cheered from the sidelines as bank after bank went under" in 1854, believing that the "rotten" banks would be eliminated and inflation would be checked. He warned in his message late that year, "We shall always have revulsions, expansions, contractions, and derangement in the whole business of the country, so long as we foster any system that makes promises to pay, money, instead of gold and silver." Wright shared the common Democratic faith that if

185

the "inferior" paper circulation were withdrawn, "we should find a sufficient amount of constitutional currency among our people for all ordinary purposes." Yet Democratic opponents of free banking, including the governor, generally restricted their demands to the enactment of reforms similar to those suggested by the state auditor.[21]

Although banking was not the primary issue in the 1854 election, the Peoples or Fusion party generally supported the free banking system against Democratic attacks and called for cooperation between the free banks and the state bank. In the legislature the new party carried the fight for a feasible reform of the free banking system. An ex-Whig advocate of free banking introduced a new version of the free banking law that provided for regular hours, a central redemption center at Indianapolis, and the establishment of banks only in towns of 1,000 or more inhabitants to eliminate wildcats. It was easily carried through both houses of the legislature, although there was opposition from the Democrats and a small group of Fusionists who preferred a state bank.[22]

The *State Sentinel* opposed the bill, which the paper believed would not have passed had there been more Democrats in the legislature. Governor Wright decided that the bill did not conform to his suggestions, and he vetoed it. To his old criticisms of the law he added that free banking currency was less valuable than gold or silver and that such systems in general had lost the confidence of the people. It is difficult to see how a free banking system in any form would have satisfied the governor.[23]

Although Wright's arguments moved seven Democratic senators to change their votes, the legislature passed the bill over his veto. Both this vote and the initial vote on the bill were bipartisan, and there can be no doubt that many Democrats were willing to accept a reformed free banking law. Late in the session an attempt to repeal the free banking law failed. This vote reveals much more clearly than the earlier votes the tendencies of the Democrats to maintain their traditional opposition to banks and of the Fusionists to carry on the Whig position. Seventeen Fusionists (80%) and nine Democrats (40%) favored free banking with four

Fusionists and thirteen Democrats opposed. Democratic aversion to banks, encouraged as it was by the governor's veto, undoubtedly had the chance to express itself during the period between the initial vote on the bill and the attempt at repeal.[24]

Once the 1855 revision of the free banking law was passed, most Democrats accepted it. At least discussion of the bank issue was minimized in the Democrats' struggle to maintain control of the state. Even Wright moderated his opposition to banks during the 1856 election campaign, in which he supported Ashbel Willard, the Democratic candidate for governor. In 1857, Wright told the legislature he was convinced that the changes in the free banking law amply secured the currency and that the bill merited the people's confidence. Typically he found the freedom from monopoly the most noteworthy feature of the law.[25]

# 5

To the last, Ohio Democrats held tenaciously to their antibank stand in the face of demands for increased banking facilities. Charles Reemelin, who earlier had led the fight against banks in the constitutional convention, reported to the governor on "The Condition of the Ohio Stock Banks." This report was basically a hard money, antibank document. Although it accepted the existence of the state's banks, it took a strong stand against all paper currency as "one of the two great social and political evils of the republic" and chastised the banks for failing to provide a sound currency. Reemelin opposed free banking and praised the attorney general's opinion on the unconstitutionality of the 1851 law. He saw no need for more bank capital and attributed the scarcity of currency to bank paper, which drove specie out of the country. The report concluded with 12 recommendations to patch the laws. They included the traditional Democratic demand for prohibition of all notes under $20 and a recommendation that the interest laws be made realistic. Governor William Medill praised the Reemelin report in his message to the legislature in 1856 and warned that "the opinion was fast obtaining ground that neither commerce or credit is benefited by legislative interference." The *Cincinnati Enquirer* featured a lengthy letter on "Banking and Finance," which argued similarly:

> Banks, tariffs, paper money, restrictions upon the movement of commodities and enfranchisement from liability of ones conduct mark and disgrace every step of commercial progress to this hour. The law making power has always been perverted.

Such interferences with the "commercial and mercantile system" sacrificed its natural development. But the main trouble arose from banks, which destroyed credit and drove up interest rates. More banks would only cause more trouble. The Democrats also ridiculed Republican promises to provide a sound currency and extend credit.[26]

Hidden beneath more volatile issues in the Ohio gubernatorial campaign of 1855 were Republican promises for better banking facilities. The new Republican governor, Salmon P. Chase, was a marginal politician who did not firmly identify with either party until the mid-1850s and even then was more popular with the voters than the politicians. Chase was particularly anathema to the ex-Whigs, who believed he had been unethical in his maneuvering with the Democrats to gain his election to the senate in 1849. Nevertheless, there is evidence that he was nominated to the gubernatorial candidacy as part of a deal enabling the ex-Whigs to implement "a liberal commercial policy and banking system."[27]

Chase's early attitude on the currency question had fluctuated between a hard money stance and a limited acceptance of banking. He had been partially responsible for the adoption of Democratic economic views by the Free-Soil party of Ohio and had been able to convince both Democratic regulars and Free-Soil Democrats of his monetary orthodoxy. In 1850, Chase had asserted that he favored "free principles, in land, currency, trade and men," but his exact meaning remained obscure. In his inaugural in 1856, Chase made it clear that his position now was closer to that of the former Whigs than that of the Democrats; and he insisted that he did not object to a convertible currency, only to "mere paper money systems." He believed that the best

188

currency would be one of coin and large bills, but that the variety of state laws made such a currency available only through congressional action. To answer the public demand for increased facilities, he proposed a free banking law to provide for a convertible currency, to guard abuses of power, and to extend its benefits to "all who will give the ample securities and guarantees which you will doubtless require." Hopefully such a law would lead to a lowering of interest rates.[28]

The new Republican legislature responded by proposing a law similar to the Kelley law of 1845. Although it was modified to meet some Democratic criticisms, it was clearly designed to increase the number of banks. The opposition to the bill came mainly from Democrats, but the Democratic press was more restrained than in previous battles with similar "monsters." The *Cincinnati Enquirer*, which was making open appeals to the "Old Line" conservative Whigs, generally avoided the issue. Although it did praise the new clauses in the law concerning liability and amendment, the *Enquirer* criticized the Republican's whole financial program and thought the most notable feature of the bank bill was that no one would organize under it. If expediency caused the paper to moderate its hard line, it still was fundamentally opposed to banks and paper money as unnecessary evils.[29]

Although some Republicans legislators voted against the new bank law, its supporters came from the new party. In contrast to the Democratic press, the Republican papers said a great deal about the currency question and possible alternative solutions to Ohio's problems. The *Massillon News* called for an increase in banking capital and attacked the limitations of the "onerous constitution." The paper hoped that Republicans could inspire confidence in the state and bring back capital that had been driven from the state by the Democrats' "unwholesome legislation" and "executive tyranny." The paper further called on the farmers of Ohio to invest in bank stock to encourage the growth of towns and business, which would in turn provide farmers with a larger market, increase prices, and enhance the value of their property. Also in contrast to the Democratic papers, the Republican organs printed numerous suggestions for extending credit facilities. The *Ohio State Journal* encouraged the legislature to construct a system that would draw "*bona fide* capital," not the capital of the "Wall Street operator . . . whose cunning [would] enable him to slip the noose from his own neck and transfer it to that of the people." At the same time the paper emphasized that the bill-holder must be protected and the law "guard the interest of capital and labor alike." The *State Journal* backed the bank bill and regretted its defeat when it failed to receive the necessary support in the fall election.[30]

The constitution required that any new bank law receive a majority of the whole number of votes cast at the fall election. While there were over twice as many votes for as against the charter, a large number of people voting in the election did not vote on the issue and the necessary majority was not obtained. It is clear from the returns that the bill received its strongest support in heavily Republican counties, including four that had switched from their earlier Democratic allegiance.[31]

The following year another Republican attempt to establish a state bank was similarly defeated. Nevertheless, the problem of added banking facilities was alleviated by the state supreme court, which ruled in 1856 that, contrary to the earlier opinion of the attorney general, the new constitution did not abrogate the free banking law of 1851. Chase was encouraged to recommend the use of the 1851 act rather than the passage of a new law. Again he argued that federal action was necessary and insisted that any banking law should offer the "most liberal extension of the franchise, with such restrictions upon its exercise as will effectively protect the community against a mere paper money currency." Some Republicans believed that experience had proved the necessity of a state bank as well as free banks, but all accepted the free banking system. The Democratic press attacked the court's decision and defended the attorney general's opinion. In Ohio the Democracy continued to be the party of the financial status quo.[32]

# 6

The need and desire for banking facilities in Michigan finally led to the passage of a new law in the original home of the wildcats. The dearth of currency had led to a variety of unauthorized banks and a resuscitation of a number of dormant institutions. An 1853 law limited unauthorized banking, but the problem of a currency composed largely of the issue of "foreign" banks, over which Michigan had no control, still plagued the state. The governor reported in 1853 that of the $4 million in circulation in the state, $3 million was supplied by banks outside the state's jurisdiction. During these years Michigan Republicans led a growing movement for a new free banking law.[33]

Early in the 1850s a number of Democratic newspapers also favored free banking; and Democratic governor Robert McClelland, amid appeals to the antibank wing of his party, noted that the constitution provided for a well-secured general law. Perhaps such a law would be better than the "flood" of dubious "foreign" currency; and if the local banks were established, the state could at least tax them.[34]

After the Panic of 1854 and the party crisis of that year, the Democracy, led by the *Detroit Free Press* under the editorship of Wilbur F. Storey, returned to Jacksonian monetary orthodoxy. Andrew Parsons, the acting governor in 1855, gave notice that antibank sentiment still dominated the party. Using traditional Jacksonian rhetoric, he warned experience showed that even stock-secured currency was not entirely safe. The best suggestion he could offer to solve the state's problems was a prohibition of all notes under $5 so that such "trash" would not drive specie "beyond the reach of our producing classes." If all the states adopted such a provision,

> over bank issues, expansions and contractions in the money market, would to a great extent be checked, and the raging and dangerous spirit of speculation so common to the people of our country, be much guarded against.[35]

Many of the same sentiments were expressed in the inaugural of the new Republican governor, Kinsley S. Bingham, who had been a leading loco-foco. Both past and present history, argued Bingham, proved that banks were responsible for depreciation of the currency and wild fluctuations that bore most heavily on the laboring classes. Thusfar Michigan had luckily escaped the free banking mania that had grasped Ohio, Indiana, Illinois, and Wisconsin and that had produced such disastrous results in Indiana. He, too, believed that specie would spread throughout the country if small notes were prohibited. Yet, the idea of a free banking law was not completely rejected by Bingham; and there were indications that a properly secured law would receive his approval.[36]

Evidently the law passed by the 1855 legislature did not meet the governor's standards, for he vetoed it. At the time he did not write a veto message; but in his message to the legislature in 1855, he explained he still worried that the establishment of banks in remote places and the possibilities of failure and fraud endangered a sound currency. He suggested that banks be forced to pay out only their notes so that quick redemption would be assured and circulation limited to the local area. He also advocated the prohibition of small notes. California gold, he believed, would make this feasible. Under such a system the "poorer classes" would be protected from losses because of depreciated paper money, and the business classes would secure the benefits of banks.[37]

The *Daily Advertiser* defended Bingham's veto on the grounds that he truly hoped for a law that would provide better security. The paper assured its readers that Bingham was not, like the Democratic *Free Press*, opposed to any bank bill. At the same time the *Advertiser* pushed constantly for a free banking law to boost the state's financial condition. The paper made it clear that only a well-guarded system would be acceptable, but also suggested that the system should not be so rigid that it would "scare" capital away from the state. The *Monroe Commercial* also supported free banking as an inducement to development, but at the same time stressed the need of proper security to avoid another plague of wildcats. These Republican papers applauded the security and antimonopoly aspects of free banking. The *Advertiser* asked a Democratic paper that accepted the idea of a stock-based currency but not free banking, "Why should [banking] be a close[d] monopoly which only certain favored parties might enjoy." Later, defending the free banking bill to the legislature in early 1857, the Republican paper stated its position clearly:

> We are decidedly opposed to granting special privileges to any
> association or corporation and the sooner the old bank charters
> are permitted to run out the better for the people, and for the
> financial credit of the state.[38]

Besides pressure from the Republican press, the new legislature
was met with two probank petitions from Berrien County signed
by 79 people and a "monster" petition sponsored by Detroit Republicans that contained 346 signatures.[39]

The main opposition to the free banking law came from the
Democratic press. The *Free Press* praised Bingham's veto as being in line with his earlier "sensible" notions about banking. Mis-
takenly, "We were of the impression that when he went over to
fusion and confusion he left his banking views behind him in the
same manner he left behind him other Democratic principles. . . ."
The *Free Press* prophesied that if Bingham adhered to his principles, no further bank issues would be authorized. Its article en-
titled "A Metallic vs. a Paper Currency" argued that the increased
gold output from California mines made it possible to dispense
with paper currency altogether. The paper called for abolition
of all notes under $10 and then the swift transition to "a hard
money currency."[40]

It was the contention of Democratic papers generally that more
banks were unnecessary and that the free banking law would
bring only the dangers of inflation. According to the *Jackson Patriot*, "the farmer needs no bank to help him cultivate his fields."
Nor do mechanics, artisans, or merchants: ". . . it is only the speculator, the gambler in stocks that wants more banks, the people
do not. . . ." The *Free Press* pointed out that no petitions demanding a free banking law were coming from the rural districts. It
was only the people in the cities and villages that wanted the bill.
The *Ann Arbor Argus* asserted that free banking was purely a
party measure, but one that never appeared in the Republican
platform. "The Republicans are in power and the mask is thrown
off."[41]

Democratic orators, as well as editors, warned of the dangerously inflationary nature of the bill and recalled the recent experience of Indiana and Illinois with such a system. One invoked

193

the spirit of Andrew Jackson, arguing that the bill should be defeated for the same reason that Jackson had annihilated the Bank of the United States.

> The democratic party, in their pure design of protecting the welfare of the poorer classes and commercial enterprise of the merchants, has always opposed the establishment of *scheming* banking associations and therefore you must not be surprised to see the democratic members of this House take a negative position on the question.[42]

In 1857 the Michigan legislature enacted a Republican-sponsored free banking law. The house votes show that 75% of the Republicans favored the bill while a majority of Democrats opposed it. Four of the six Democrats in the senate voted with the Republicans for free banking. Governor Bingham signed this bill and later praised it as one of the important measures of his administration, even though it included neither a prohibition of small notes nor a provision forcing banks to pay out only their own notes. While the *Advertiser* applauded the measure and supported the governor's action, the *Free Press* called the bill the "most pernicious measure spawned by the present legislature" and chastised the governor for not vetoing it.[43]

The people approved the new bill by a vote of 41,006 to 19,865 in an unspirited contest. Although the vote does not lend itself easily to a partisan interpretation, heavily Republican counties such as Branch, Calhoun, Hillsdale, Kalamazoo, Kent, Lenawe, St. Joseph, and Washtenaw gave the bill its strongest support.[44]

# 7

Although Illinois's free banking system survived the Panic of 1854, it was altered and perfected during these years by the Republicans. Following the panic the bank commissioner had suggested the abolition of the 7% ceiling on interest to draw more capital to the free banks and to discourage the unregulated brokerage houses that the provision had spawned. He also suggested that a specified specie reserve be required. Democratic governor Joel Matteson, busy organizing the largest banking chain in the state, praised the system and suggested that the legislature consider the commissioner's recommendations. Although two minor bills were passed during the 1855 session, there was no major revision of the system. In the following year the system was expanded to include 61 banks with a total circulation nearly twice what it had been two years earlier.[45]

The election of 1856 brought the new Republican party to power in the state. William Bissell, the new governor, had been an anti-Nebraska Democrat who had opposed the free banking law when it was first passed. His new association had moderated his views, and his inaugural praised the law. At the same time he argued that amendment of the bill could strengthen the system and add to the security of the billholders. The Republican legislature complied with Bissell's request by a major revision of the law. To eliminate true wildcats, the law provided that business could only be transacted at the office specified in the certificate of incorporation and that the office had to be in a community of over 200 people. The act made more stringent provisions concerning capital and the redemption of notes and removed the prejudice against Illinois bonds. Finally, the maximum legal interest rate was raised to 10%. Each of these changes, which mirrored solutions proposed in other states, helped stabilize the free banking system. Further defects, however, would be revealed in the years of economic chaos that preceded the Civil War.[46]

# 8

To discern any simple pattern in the confused politics of the 1850s, particularly on a secondary issue such as banking, is nearly impossible, and any generalization would have innumerable exceptions. Yet, it is clear that the party transformation of this decade did not basically alter the contrasting partisan positions in relation to the monetary conflict. Democratic opposition to banks and paper money was moderated by the political situation, but hostility to banks remained basic. Republican emphasis on credit and currency expansion and, in particular, its advocacy of free banking differed little from the earlier Whig position.

Although the nature of the monetary conflict is complex, the reasons for this continuity are easily explained. In the first place most Republican party leaders were ex-Whigs. In the formative years of the party the old Whigs took backstage roles, strategically pushing into the forefront Democrats who joined the new organization so as to draw voters from the old party of Jackson. They consciously avoided public statements on controversial issues, but, as the party grew, they played an increasingly dominant role in policy-making. The economic policies instituted by the new party, particularly in its 1860 platform, were clearly an extension of the policies of the more progressive elements of the Whig party.[47]

Among the voters most people who had been Whigs became Republicans. Lincoln's belief that "nine tenths of the anti-Nebraska votes have to come from old Whigs" was undoubtedly an overestimate, particularly for 1856. But when one looks at the entire period from the late 1840s to 1860 and considers the Old Northwest as a whole, Lincoln's estimate is not far from the truth. It is also clear that by 1860 well over 90% of the Whig electorate had joined the new party.[48]

Further, it appears that the most conservative members of the older party avoided the new organization unless their religious and ethnic background determined an interest in reform. Lincoln saw this tendency in Illinois; and contemporary studies of Illinois, Indiana, and Ohio find that the most conservative Whigs clung tightly to the Native American party in 1856 and either became politically inactive or joined their former opponents at the end of the decade. Alexandra McCoy's systematic study of the economic elite of Wayne County, Michigan, "Political Affiliations of American Economic Elites," shows an increase in nonparticipation among this group. When her findings are compared with general voting shifts, it is clear that the percentage of "elite" Whigs who became Republicans was somewhat lower than the percentage of all Whigs who joined the new party.[49]

In its policies, its leadership, and its support, the Republican party was much more a continuation of the Whig party than historians have been willing to admit. It found its greatest strength in economically dynamic areas and among groups of Yankee origin who were also Congregationalist, Quaker, or Presbyterian. To an even greater extent than the Whigs, the Republicans were the party of Yankee-Protestantism, and their opponents bitterly attacked the intrusion of "Puritanism in Politics." Nearly every county in Illinois, Indiana, and Ohio that shifted from Democratic to Republican allegiance could be distinguished by its economic dynamism and the Yankee rather than southern origins of its population. As has been argued, the partisan conflict of these years was essentially a cultural one based on ethnic and religious differences. This cultural conflict expressed itself in the major issues of the day: the veiled nativism of temperance and the antisouthernism implicit in opposition to slavery and slavery extension.[50]

This basic cultural conflict encompassed differences on economic policy. In the contests over free banking and the expansion of credit facilities, it was in the Yankee-Protestant areas, such as northern Illinois and central Indiana, that Democrats were forced to support these laws by their probank constituents. The Yankee-Protestant element of these areas gave them an acceptance of commercialism and a quest for "improvement" that was less prevalent in the older areas dominated by southern migrants. The *Indiana State Journal* contrasted the "active, industrious, enterprising and intelligent population" of northern Indiana and Illinois with the "slow, lazy, thriftless and ignorant population" of the southern parts of those states, and lamented the fact that the latter gave "such heavy Locofoco majorities as to control the politics of both states." The *Ohio State Journal* believed that "the most enlightened and enterprising portion of the state backed the Republicans. Samuel Brimblecom of Ogle County in northern Illinois wrote the Illinois congressman Elihu Washburne,

> When we move into a territory and find people there from Penna., Indiana, Ohio, or New York, we find a class which joins us in making all the improvements of those states. We build school

197

houses & churches, educate our children, build railroads and in a thousand things consult the comfort of all people, and soon draw around us society congenial to our habits and tastes.[51]

The contrast in the interest in "improvement" can be seen in the literacy rates for Indiana and Illinois, which show these skills more widespread in Yankee areas. Similarly, the fastest growing counties in these states were Republican. Throughout the Old Northwest agriculture in Republican areas was more commercially oriented and the ratio of improved to unimproved land was greater. It seems that these were the areas of "go-aheaditiveness."[52]

The new Republican party was the party of reform and "improvement." The Republicans took over the economic attitudes of the most progressive Whigs, which were based upon a dynamic conception of the economy that at its core valued highly the expansion of economic opportunity and the promise of success. Their symbolic hero was not the pastoral yeoman farmer but the man who worked his way up from lowly origins to a position of power in the new commercial-industrial world. Henry Clay had originated the term "self-made man," and his disciple, Abraham Lincoln, exploited it to draw the laboring man and the market-oriented farmer into the Republican coalition. The idea of free banking was congenial to this general frame of reference.[53]

# CHAPTER 8

## CRISIS, 1857-1862

### 1

Following the Panic of 1857 a writer in *Hunt's Merchants' Magazine* predicted that the question of "Banks or No Banks," which had been "in past times so often and so obstinately discussed in our country," would again become a "prominent topic." While this issue did not regain the importance it had held in the 1840s, it was never far from the surface during these years. The period between 1857 and 1862 was one of emotional upheaval and trial for the American people. Amid the many aspects of the chaos preceding the Civil War were two economic crises, which forced further revision of the free banking laws in the Old Northwest. The first, in 1857, was strictly financial in origin, although it had deep political implications. The political situation of 1860 and the issue of secession precipitated the second. The free banking systems weathered the storm of 1857 much better than most historians have supposed, but they collapsed during the 1860–61 crisis. The Democrats, who had been losing ground in the North since 1854, attempted to use these crises, particularly that of 1860–61, to reconstruct their party around the traditional Jacksonian issues. They blamed the economic problems of the nation on irresponsible banking and paper currency while reasserting their belief in the economic wisdom of hard money. The Republicans tried to unify the party nationally on the tariff, placing the blame for the nation's economic ills on the Democrats' free trade policy. In the states they continued to try to provide a sound and adequate currency through the reform of the free banking laws and, after 1860, through the establishment of state institutions like that of Indiana.[1]

**2**

By 1857 the confused situation of the mid-1850s seemed to be stabilizing. Although Michigan's law still had to be ratified by the people, all of the states of the Old Northwest had accepted free banking as the solution to money and credit problems. The experience of 1854 had pointed out to Illinois and Indiana legislators the needs for certain restrictions, and they altered their laws to eliminate the wildcat element from free banking. The political situation was also becoming clear. The Republicans had emerged from the confusion of the mid-1850s as the opponents of the Democrats for state and national power. In the economic sphere the new party increasingly perpetuated the Whig tradition of support for free banking, while the Democrats remained split on the issue. However, the impression of stability that early 1857 seemed to convey proved illusory; and the period from 1857 to 1862 was one of continued economic and political crisis.

The tremendous boom of the 1850s had been an international phenomenon spurred by railroad speculation and the output of California mines after 1849. These weaknesses were compounded by the international situation. The Crimean War had debilitated the French economy, which was suffering at the same time from the twin evils of overpopulation and low agricultural production. The situation forced the Bank of France to draw specie from the Bank of England, which resulted in a high bank rate in London and, in turn, adversely affected British investment in American securities. Frauds in railroad management and the failure of many roads to produce hoped for returns combined with the rising bank rate to bring about a reversal in the flow of British capital and a subsequent decline in the market for American stocks and bonds in 1856 and 1857. This decline reduced the assets of many American banks and financial institutions, weakening their ability to withstand any strong shock. The entire banking system lacked

200

overall policy and even primitive cooperation between banks. The dominant position of New York as the money market caused "country banks" to keep deposits in New York. These deposits represented the "country banks'" reserves in case of emergency, while the New York banks used this money in the call loan market. In good times this was advantageous for all involved, but during the crisis of 1857 it proved extremely dangerous.[2]

The seasonal drain of funds from New York precipitated the crisis. Without warning, one of the nation's leading financial concerns, the Ohio Life Insurance and Trust Company, closed its doors on August 24. As the banks scrambled to fortify their position and securities, prices plummeted and other bank failures followed. Continual runs on the banks resulted in the suspension of specie payments in October. By this time commerce and industry were at a standstill and unemployment mounted.

The financial crisis passed quickly, but the depression hung on. During this slump, lasting in some areas until 1860, the Old Northwest was particularly hard hit. The suspension of navigation during the winter of 1856–57 had led to a rise in the rate on eastern exchange. Throughout 1857 the money market remained tight, and a continuous stream of specie flowed eastward. The flow of capital into the West, which had supported the boom of the mid-1850s, was reversed. According to historian Thomas S. Berry, "The backbone of speculation was broken in 1857, judging from the fact that prices of commodities and securities failed to respond fully to the prevailing easiness of money and credit [after 1857]." The downturn of that year was preceded by extensive land speculation geared to the expansion of the supply of money and credit. With the drain of funds, the land bubble burst. A western correspondent of the *New York Herald* wrote, "Nine-tenths of our people owe, and have no immediate way to pay. Everything in the shape of property is low."[3]

The farmers faced a combination of bad crops and extensive debt. In 1856 crops had been poor in Michigan, and the severe winter of 1856–57 had ravished the livestock. The three seasons from 1857 to 1859 brought crop failures throughout the whole Northwest. The weather oscillated between extremes.

Overabundant rainfall and rot in 1858, drouth and burning in
1859, winter killing and frost, blight and the army-worm, each
made their contribution toward low yields which farmers experienced at the close of the decade.[4]

The depression hung on. There were many more business failures in Wisconsin in 1858 than during the previous year. In 1859
an Illinois paper commented that there was "not grain enough
in the country to pay debts contracted before the hard times
commenced." Horace Greeley, who was traveling through the
area, wrote back to his paper, the *New York Tribune*, in early
1860, "The West is poor. The collapse of the railroad bubble . . .
has spread desolation over the land." Many farmers had over-
bought land, and tax sales increased during these years. Many
others had speculated in railroad securities. The *Washington
County* (Wis.) *Democrat* reported,

> It is said that from 2,000 to 3,000 farms are thus mortgaged to
> railroads in Wisconsin, that the railroads cannot pay, and to re-
> lease their farms will strip nine-tenths of them of the hard earn-
> ings of many years.[5]

Unemployment struck laborers as businesses failed and factories shut down. Lumberjacks in Michigan and Wisconsin found
themselves suddenly without pay and driven to the verge of star-
vation. In the cities unemployment was widespread. The *Grand
Rapids* (Mich.) *Enquirer and Herald* reported that in Detroit

> Most of the larger establishments have discharged their em-
> ployees, by which a larger number of persons are thrown out of
> employment than at any former time . . . the smaller mechanics
> have been compelled to reduce their force of operatives, and their
> mechants have cut down their force of clerks to the lowest pos-
> sible number. At a low estimate there are five thousand persons
> out of employment in the city at the present time.

In Chicago alone 204 business failures were reported. While
Cincinnati escaped most of the ravages of the depression, about
half of the city's 2,500 employees in clothing establishments were
discharged.[6]

In the face of this, the performance of the banking system was better than might have been expected or than historians have often believed it was. Bray Hammond's statement in *Banks and Politics* that the Indiana free banks were "choked off" by the Panic of 1857 is contradicted by the evidence of Indiana's governor Ashbel P. Willard, who in 1859 praised the 1855 amendment to the free banking law because it had permitted only one failure in four years. The Bank of the State of Indiana, of course, proved itself one of the nation's strongest banks during the crisis and was one of the few not to suspend specie payments.[7]

A similar situation existed in Ohio, where the failure of the Ohio Life Insurance and Trust Company had its greatest impact. That institution was so intimately connected with the state government and the state bank that George W. Van Vleck in his *Panic of 1857* called it "The nursing mother to all the financial institutions of Ohio." The collapse, precipitated by the embezzlement of nearly its entire assets by its New York cashier, staggered the Ohio State Bank. Although the state bank's condition was shaky in late 1857, it soon stabilized itself; and throughout the crisis of 1857 the banks of Ohio, along with those of Indiana, did not formally suspend specie payments. Only seven of Ohio's authorized banks, including the Ohio Life Insurance and Trust Company, closed their doors; of these, two had failed before the panic and two had not been active since 1854. Governor Chase noted in his message of January 4, 1858, that Ohio had 54 functioning banks.[8]

Although there were many defects in the Wisconsin free banking system, the Panic of 1857 and the depression that followed did not interrupt its steady growth. The number of banks in the state increased from 32 to 50 during 1857, and 25 new banks opened the following year. The panic severely set back the state, and numerous businesses failed; but Wisconsin's banks successfully weathered the economic storm.[9]

Similarly, Illinois banks suspended specie payments to all but a few favored customers in late August 1857, but the free banks of that state came through the crisis reasonably well. Six banks out of fifty-four failed, and of these all but one fully redeemed their notes. The crisis was brief and recovery nearly complete by the opening of 1858. In January 1859 the bank commissioners praised the free banking system for its performance during two years of financial crisis and depression. Governor Bissell joined in the praise of the system that had limited losses to a "mere trifle."[10]

The free banking systems of the Old Northwest stood up fairly well during the Panic of 1857, and most of the failures were unauthorized private banks or old banks such as those of Michigan and the Ohio Life Insurance and Trust Company, whose special charters were passed before the free banking era.

# 3

If the crisis caused the failure of only a few banks, it did reveal a serious weakness in the system's inability to maintain currency at par. In mid-1857 the notes of Indiana's free banks began to go at a discount, and the crisis accentuated their depreciation. Illinois and Wisconsin experienced similar difficulties. The fundamental problem was the quality of securities. Nearly half of Illinois currency was secured by the bonds of the state of Missouri, which declined after early 1857. The Wisconsin bank comptroller explained the predicament faced by the bankers that accounted for large holdings of the less safe securities:

> It is obvious that the safest bonds, viz: of states that are in the most prosperous financial condition, and relatively the least encumbered with debt, do not secure the highest rate of interest, and if liberal interest is paid on them they can not be bought at low prices. No banker, therefore, buys U.S., New England or New York bonds as security for his circulation, but mainly such as are in fact more or less depreciated, confiding in his own good luck and in the future development of the resources of the States of which he has become the creditor. . . . As the law stands we effectually encourage the bankers to buy as security the least safe class of bonds or stocks, and put obstacles in the way of purchasing the best.

This problem went unsolved in the period following the Panic of 1857; it remained the greatest weakness of the free banking systems of the Old Northwest.[11]

The year 1860 was a very good year for the farmers of the Old Northwest, and the economic situation began to right itself. The last years of the 1850s had witnessed an increase in the number of banks, and credit was easily available in most states. While Michigan's free banking law produced only one new bank, the West as a whole increased its banking facilities by 20%. In 1860, Wisconsin had 104 banks. Its southern neighbor, Illinois, had gone from 39 banks in 1858 to 74 by 1860 and 104 by 1861. In the period between the Panic of 1857 and the economic crisis of 1861, the total circulation of Illinois doubled.[12]

In the states of the Old Northwest, particularly Illinois and Wisconsin, free banking made possible this increase in credit and circulation. The situation however, was a dangerous one because inadequate reform measures had been instituted concerning the quality of stocks backing this currency.

The uneasy political situation paralyzed business and precipitated a decline in the value of southern securities, which struck at the basis of free bank currency. Between July and December 1860, the price of the bonds of several southern states declined from 20% to 25%. Missouri bonds fell from 80% to 61%. During October the securities of Virginia, North Carolina, and Tennessee averaged an 8% drop. The bonds of these states were widely used in the Old Northwest, particularly in Illinois, to secure free bank currency, and the decline in their value precipitated a banking crisis.[13]

In general, Ohio and Indiana suffered less than either Wisconsin or Illinois. Most of Ohio's banks were branches of the state bank rather than free banks. The free banks of Indiana were forced to make good the loss through the Missouri and Louisiana bonds; as a result, a small number were forced to suspend, while 16 withdrew their circulation entirely. The situation in Illinois and Wisconsin was one of utter collapse. Two-thirds of the bonds used by Illinois's banks to secure their currency were obligations of southern states. As prices began to sag, the bank commissioners called on the banks to deposit additional securities to support their note issues. In November a similar demand resulted in the liquidation of 17 banks. Chicago bankers began to refuse the notes of "country banks" based on southern bonds. By 1861 faith in Illinois bank currency had dissipated, and the notes of only 23 banks were accepted at par. The hoarding of good notes made the situation intolerable. In April 1861 the Chicago banks refused to accept the notes of any "country banks," precipitating a sectional fight among the bankers and merchants of the state. A month later Chicago merchants attempted to stabilize the situation by agreeing to accept at par all notes of banks on the list drawn up by Chicago bankers. This and several other attempts failed. By the summer of 1861 the bank commissioner declared all but 17 banks insolvent, and the situation worsened with the failure of J. Young Scammon's Marine Bank. The circulation of Illinois banks had fallen from approximately $12 million to $3 million by October 1861 and finally to $566,163 by the end of 1862. The collapse of free banking in Illinois was complete, and the state was left with hardly any currency.[14]

Wisconsin faced many of the same problems. Of the $5,133,565 of securities supporting the currency of Wisconsin's free banks, $3,658,000 were in the bonds of Missouri, Virginia, Tennessee, North Carolina, and Louisiana. Most of these were obligations of Missouri. As in Illinois, the bank comptroller had to forbid further deposit of these bonds as their prices fell in 1860. As the bonds depreciated the banks were forced to add new securities. By April 1861 three such levies had been made, and at that time thirteen banks were unable to comply. The value of Wisconsin currency was further hurt by the action in April of the Chicago bankers, who refused to receive the notes of 40 Wisconsin banks. Milwaukee soon followed suit, resulting in the discrediting of a million dollars of paper currency. The state Bankers' Association, which had been formed in 1857 to stabilize the free banking system, then dropped support of 18 additional banks and discredited another million dollars of currency. For a time the action of the Bankers' Association in support of 70 of the state's banks forestalled a further decline; but 18 banks were unable to meet a second levy to replace the stocks that continued to depreciate. By midsummer the situation had so degenerated that Milwaukee became the scene of a bank riot by German laborers, who were being paid in depreciated notes. Free banking in the Old Northwest had reached its nadir.[15]

# 4

No one could argue that during these years the banking question again attained the prominent spot in the political arena it had held in the 1840s. More fundamental and important issues formed the main concern of the parties on the eve of the Civil War. Yet the economic situation forced consideration of banking problems, and the parties responded with distinctly different attitudes on the issue.

The Panic of 1857 and the subsequent depression produced renewed criticism of banks and a reiteration by the Democrats of the Jacksonian stand. This return to the faith had perhaps more political than economic overtones. It began in the late 1850s and gained momentum following the debacle of 1861. A small minority of Republicans, the most prominent of whom was the old foe of banks John Wentworth, joined in the renewed attack on all banks; and many others, like the Whigs of the late 1830s, criticized the actions of the banks. Even the more moderate *Chicago Tribune* said, in August 1861,

> We wash our hands of the whole business. If the farmer will sell a dollar's worth of his produce for the pictures of any bank whatsoever which does not redeem its issues at some convenient place in the State *at par*, he loses his share of his just earnings . . . all banks of issue are a curse to the community.[16]

Still the main thrust against banks came from the Democrats. While they had won the presidency in 1856, it was clear that in the Old Northwest the party of Jackson was in danger of losing its majority status. The new Republican coalition drew away enough votes to shift the scales in this traditional Democratic stronghold. The Lecompton question and the economic policy of the Buchanan Administration further complicated the problems of the Democrats. It was hoped that a return to the old issue could pull the feuding factions together and draw recent converts to Republicanism back into the fold. Attempts to pacify the South were mixed with appeals to the conservative business interests. The widely read *New York Herald* told its readers to forget "Nigger Agitation" and rally the government to the relief of business. Once the war came, antibank agitation increased and was tied with the highly emotional peace issue.[17]

Unfortunately for the student of the period, the Democratic position was neither universally held nor without ambiguity, and can best be described as a "central tendency." Buchanan's message to Congress in late 1857 clearly reveals the ambiguity of the Democrats' position. The president opened that message with a lengthy discussion of the banking question. The passage begins, ends, and is dominated by Jacksonian orthodoxy. Jackson's interpretation of the nature of economic "revulsions" had not been altered in two decades:

> It is apparent that our existing misfortunes have proceeded solely from our extravagant and vicious system of paper currency and bank credits, exciting the people to wild speculations and gambling in stocks.

Buchanan also attacked paper-inflated prices that varied from "true values" and extravagant importations; and there were intimations of the neoorthodoxy of Senator Thomas Hart Benton and Secretary of the Treasury James Guthrie, who had advocated in the mid-1850s that Congress tax all state bank notes out of existence to bring the currency of the country to a true specie basis. Buchanan believed that

> If experience shall prove it to be impossible to enjoy the facilities which well-regulated banks might afford without at the same time suffering the calamities which the excesses of the banks have hitherto inflicted upon the country, it would then be far the lesser evil to deprive them altogether of the power to issue paper currency and confine them to the functions of banks of deposit and discount.[18]

Yet 1857 was not 1837, and Buchanan's message showed a tinge of heresy. He himself accepted

> the existence of banks and the circulation of bank paper . . . [as] so identified with the habits of our people that they can not at

this day be suddenly abolished without much immediate injury
to the country.

He seemed to condone specie-paying banks and even endorsed,
albeit with qualifications, stock-backed currency: it was "doubtless wise . . . [but] there was no adequate security against over-
issues . . . [and] it may be perverted to inflate the currency."[19]

Democratic newspapers like the *New York Herald* took the
same position as the president and lamented the "expansion of
the currency" as the major economic problem of the nation. Democratic intellectuals writing in the important business journals
*Hunt's Merchants' Magazine* and the *Bankers' Magazine* attacked
banks and paper money and laid the blame for the financial panic
on the deranged state of the currency. Amasa Walker, who had
given staunch support to Jackson's financial policy and the Independent Treasury plan, bitterly attacked a mixed currency and
called for a bank currency with 100% specie reserve. In a series
of articles and books, Walker provided the fullest intellectual defense of the hard money position. That venerable Jacksonian,
William Gouge, contributed to this new attack on excess bank issues and "paper money manufacturers." Daniel Hundley and
Richard Sully dealt specifically with the West and gave further
support to the view that the banking system and paper currency
were responsible for the crisis. They were joined by Peter Cooper,
the loco-foco ironmaster and later prominent Greenbacker, who
reiterated most of the traditional Jacksonian diagnoses and remedies. Not only was paper money the cause of the country's economic ills, but it bespoke a disregard for the sage advice of the
Founding Fathers and the higher wisdom of the philosopher
Emanuel Swedenborg. Paper money led to debt and overindul-
gence in luxuries, which in turn undermined the morals of the
country. It made prices unstable, hurting the farmer and mechanic
while helping only the debtor.

> If we desire to give stability in the future to the operations of
> trade and commerce, and to lessen the amount of poverty and
> crime, we must avoid all acts of special legislation, that favor the
> few at the expense of the many.

209

Like Buchanan, Cooper preferred a specie currency but realized that at the time it was unwise; consequently, his main suggestion was to eliminate all bills under $10.[20]

The revival of antibank sentiment, of which the Buchanan speech and these articles were a part, was injected into the politics of Ohio and Illinois in late 1857 as demands for control of state issues by the federal government spread. Stephen A. Douglas's correspondents assured him that he was supported by the "hards" and that they looked to him for "a bold and radical measure in regard to the currency question." Democrats were generally ready "to throw these state banks overboard." Senator Benton's plan to tax state bank notes out of existence and thus return to an exclusively "constitutional currency" gained popularity, but even this distinctly negative use of federal power smacked too much of centralism and led most "radicals" in the Old Northwest to continue to advocate state action.[21]

Only in Ohio did the opposition to banks immediately produce tangible results. In 1857 the *Ohio Statesman* again led the fight against banks and paper money and drew the traditional Jacksonian moral lessons from the panic. Referring to the law prohibiting the circulation of "foreign" notes under $10, the *Statesman* wrote,

> While the law was in force, there was specie enough in use to answer every demand. But the Black Republicans repealed this law, and in less than thirty days, the State was flooded with petty rags, many of them on banks the location of which it was impossible to trace out on any map yet published.

In line with the suggestions of Howell Cobb, Buchanan's secretary of the treasury, the Democrats also called for a state independent treasury plan that would create depositories other than banks for state monies. The failure of the Ohio Trust and Life Insurance Company, a state depository, made this idea popular; and the state treasury scandal gave substance to Democratic connection of free banking and moral laxity. To complicate the situation and add to the Democratic advantage, the Republicans

210

sponsored a bill to extend banking facilities. Both the bank proposal and its sponsors were defeated; and the legislature fell into the hands of the Democrats, although Chase managed to retain the governor's chair.[22]

With the tacit agreement of Chase, who did not want to alienate the ex-Democrats in his party, this legislature enacted a state subtreasury law and displayed its antibank leanings by reviving the severe tax measures of the early 1850s, which had been declared unconstitutional. The following year it revived the old "Crow Bar Law." According to the *Statesman*, the Democrats hoped in this way to seek a reversal of the earlier decisions. The state independent treasury and bank taxation were both featured parts of the Democratic platform.[23]

The Indiana Democracy, which controlled the government in the Hoosier State, and which had aided in establishing the free banking system, chose not to rock the boat with an antibank attack that might alienate some of the conservative ex-Whigs who had been drawn into their party. In 1859, Governor Willard praised both the free banking system and the Bank of the State of Indiana as "highly beneficial" to the interests of the state. But with a nod toward Jacksonian orthodoxy he qualified his remarks to the legislature:

> If the rule could be uniform throughout the United States it would perhaps be better that no paper currency was circulated. But, inasmuch as that uniformity is practically impossible, I think Indiana has established as safe systems of banking as any other State in the Union, giving her people as high security for redemption of the notes of the banks as any other State.[24]

During the campaign of 1860, the Democracy warned against adopting the views of the "fanatical abolitionized, canting, hypocritical New England States" on banking and the tariff. Following the political defeat and the commercial crisis, Abram Hammond, who served out Willard's term, attacked the free banking system and called on the state to establish an independent treasury system and to deal only in specie.[25]

# 5

The most extensive revival of antibank thought took place in Illinois, where these sentiments culminated in the proposed constitutional prohibition of banks in 1862. Following the Panic of 1857, demands in Illinois for the prohibition of all banks or for implementation of the Benton-Guthrie plan increased. When "radical" Democrats of the state refused to countenance the centralizing tendencies of the latter plan, reform proposals took the form of local prohibition. The Republican opposition had by no means been stabilized when the economic crisis of 1857 hit; and Illinois Democrats hoped to increase their declining popularity by reverting to orthodox, hard-line positions on banks, tariffs, and corporations in order to take advantage of disunity among Republicans. The Democrats thought that if Republicans were forced to deal with these questions, the dominant ex-Whig element would force on the new party protariff and probank views that would alienate the ex-Democrats in their ranks.

In this fight the Democrats received aid from one of the most outspoken opponents of banks, John Wentworth, now a Republican. He and a number of ex-Democrats resented the dominance of former Whigs in the new party and feared they might introduce their economic views into the Republican platform. Wentworth wrote in the *Daily Democrat* in mid-1860 that he saw great efforts being made

> to turn this Republican party which is founded altogether on opposition to slavery, into a second edition of old blue-light federalism and Whiggery. We see efforts made to lug high protective doctrines into it; to ring in a lot of old fossil know-nothings and old whigs into it by bribery of good fat officers, and influential positions, while old free soilers are left shivering out in the cold. Bye and bye, we may expect to see efforts made to have a national bank plank added to the platform, and then the party will have emerged from its chrysalis condition into a full grown federal, whig party.

About six months later, immediately after the reform of the free banking system passed through the legislature, Wentworth complained, "Men who were sound on the banking question were rotten on the negro question, and men who were sound on the negro position were rotten on the banking question."[26]

Wentworth's attacks on the banks increased with the crisis of 1860–61. In traditional Jacksonian rhetoric he called on the laboring classes to "arouse" against the "Wild Cat aristocracy of Chicago." While Wentworth led the way, most other Democratic papers, including the two major party organs, the *Illinois State Register* and the *Chicago Times*, took up the old Jacksonian stand. As 1861 wore on and the eventual collapse of the free banking system became clear, the Jacksonian position came to be widely held. The leading student of antibank thought in Illinois, Stanley Jones, has concluded that "by 1862 a majority of the Democratic party was again pledged to a program to wipe out the banking system of Illinois and to drive paper money of all kinds from the state."[27]

The Democrats gained the opportunity to implement their views on the currency question in the constitutional convention that convened early in 1862. The growth of the state had rendered the 1848 constitution obsolete. In the election of 1860 the voters had decided in favor of calling a convention, with the northern sections of the state yielding the largest majorities. While the movement for a new constitution was originally nonpartisan, by 1861 the Democrats saw the convention as an opportunity for reviving their party by building on discontent with the war and the economic crisis. The *Urbana Weekly Democrat* advised its readers, "Unless we revive our party on the issue as far as regards state and local elections, it may be expected that we will have to witness in silence the overthrow . . . of Democratic principles." Throughout the summer the *Illinois State Register* made clear that a revival of "Democratic principles" meant a return to orthodox Jacksonian dogma, including a "constitutional currency."[28]

While the leading Republican papers agreed that there should be reform to eliminate wildcats, they generally paid little attention to the election but called for the election of nonpartisan candidates. In a light turnout the Democrats won an overwhelming victory, completely controlling the convention. Forty-five of the candidates were Democrats and ten were prowar Union Democrats, who voted with the Democrats on economic questions. Of the twenty Republicans, John Wentworth and Alexander Campbell were ardent opponents of banks.[29]

With the aid of the Republican Wentworth, the Democrats wrote a thoroughly Jacksonian document. In its banking provisions it prohibited the creation of any banks in the state and provided for the complete elimination of paper circulation. In this, as in other questions, the Democrats voted solidly as a party and defended their actions on Jacksonian grounds.[30]

The partisanship of the convention, in particular the apportionment arrangement, and the quasi-legislative function it attempted to perform led to a bitter attack on the new constitution by the Republicans. The *Illinois State Journal*, although initially it had praised the delegates as "able" men, described the convention as "revolutionary" and "a mere machine for resuscitating and re-organizing the Democratic party of the State." From this latter, basically accurate appraisal the Republicans went on to attack it as the "Copper Head Convention" and to charge its members with disloyalty to the Union. Governor Richard Yates, who was the target of Democratic animus, wrote Senator Lyman Trumbull, "Secession is deeper and stronger than you have any idea—its advocates are numerous, powerful, and respectable." He believed it was the intention of the Democrats "to disarm the State Government."[31]

Most of the Republican attacks on the constitution took this form and emphasized apportionment, which Republicans easily related to economic questions. Before the convention a reporter for the *Chicago Tribune* had worried that the ideal of the Democrats was the "social life and civilization" of the southern part of the state, known as "Egypt," which showed "a natural prejudice toward all modern forms of progress: particularly banks, corporations and even railroads." The *Tribune* had called on the convention to reform rather than assault the banks, because the paper believed good banks were necessary to modern society and were "the means by which labor can avail itself of the immense assistance of accumulated capital." After the convention the

*Aurora Beacon* pointedly asked, "Shall the manufacturing, agricultural and commercial interests of northern Illinois be put into Egyptian bondage?" The whole of the state's economic progress seemed to Republicans to be challenged by the new document. "We are a great commercial State," said the *Chicago Post*.

> This Constitution fetters commerce; cuts off the avenues of trade; blocks up the channels of communication with other states; discourages the investment of capital; drives away manufacturing; stops internal improvements; paralyzes enterprise, turns away from us the tide of immigration, and scandalizes us before the world.[32]

While this was hardly the case, the banking provisions were impractical and reactionary. Some Democratic papers recognized this, but most of them chose to "play on new frustrations with old formulas." In this, Wentworth took the lead in the northern part of the state, contributing articles to the *Chicago Times* and attacking the banking system at Democratic mass meetings. The *Peoria Union* argued that the new constitution was truly a "poor man's constitution" because "it protects him against chartered monopolies and monied aristocracies, chartered privileges and special legislation, peculations and plundering; it puts all men on an equal footing." Further south, the state's most important Democratic paper, the *Illinois State Register*, defended the constitution as the product of a "People's Convention" and a bulwark in the defense of the people's interest against the intrusion of corporate privilege.[33]

This was old Jacksonian fare, but it still had appeal. While the banking provision, which was voted on separately, was defeated, it was by a narrow margin. The voting pattern was not nearly so sectional as it had been earlier. In Cook County, which had strongly been for free banking, businessmen, farmers, and laborers combined to vote against depreciated or, as they put it, "stumptail" currency. Elsewhere it is probable, as one of Trumbull's correspondents reported, that "the Bell and Breckenridge vote went with the democracy for its adoption." But by 1862 the issue of Greenbacks by the federal government completely altered the currency question.[34]

215

# 6

In the four years after 1856 the Republicans in the Old Northwest gained strength; but, as the state elections of 1858 showed, they were still a minority party. What victories they had were attributable to the Democratic element of their party, and they depended on this element for success in the future. Yet during these years the old Whigs openly took control of the new party, as can be seen by comparing the former affiliations of the governors nominated in 1860 with those of 1856, when Republican governors were all former Democrats. By 1860 all gubernatorial nominees were former Whigs, and their presidential candidate was a long-time Whig politician. In some areas this increasing Whig bias meant a slightly more conservative outlook; everywhere there was an open reversion to Whig economic ideas. In the lake districts and the northern parts of the Old Northwest, this stance on economic questions served to draw into the Republican fold a few Democrats who were disgusted with Buchanan's prosouthern economic policies and eager for government protection of their interests.

Banking remained a highly emotional issue, and the new party had to handle it gingerly. Basically, Republicans moved in the direction of reform of the free banking systems. But the crisis of 1860–61 forced them to act more vigorously and the position they assumed was not unlike that of the Whigs during the post-Jackson economic crisis. Their main goals seem to have been a safe currency and adequate credit. Their first attempts were to try to secure these through a reform of all free banking systems.

Immediately following the Panic of 1857, Ohio's Republican governor Chase called upon a Democratic legislature to reform the free banking system "to secure the interests of the masses of the people." He praised the general working of the system but believed that specie reserve requirements should be raised, the proportions of securities to circulation should be increased, and only Ohio and United States bonds should be accepted as collateral. These reforms seem to have been dictated by the western experience with free banking, and were typical of the direction in which Republican thought was moving. Each of these would have been a constructive alteration of the law, but none was enacted by the succeeding Democratic legislatures.[35]

Wisconsin's Republican governor Alexander Randall was somewhat more successful in obtaining his suggested reforms. In 1858 he complained of the lax requirements concerning paid-in capital and the establishment of banks in often remote and inaccessible places. Since banks located in large cities were apt to have their notes presented constantly for redemption, the major cities often found their bank facilities languishing at the same time that the overall number of banks was rising. While the banks of Eau Clair, Wisconsin, isolated in the lumber regions, had a total circulation of $536,764, for example, the circulation of Milwaukee banks was only $86,521. An association of the state's bankers was formed to help implement the governor's suggestions for redemption centers in Milwaukee and Madison. The legislature forbade the establishment of banks in towns of fewer than 200 voters and proscribed railroad bonds as security.[36]

The governor was generally satisfied with these changes, which were accepted overwhelmingly by the voters; but the problems of redemption and the quality of the securities used as collateral remained. In 1860 both the governor and the bank comptroller called for further reform to meet these problems. Finally, under the strain of the secession crisis, Wisconsin's Republican legislature adequately reformed the law in April 1861. These new amendments to the free banking law limited securities to those of Wisconsin and the United States, insisted on a bona fide cash capital of $15,000, restricted note issue to three times the paid-in capital, and required every bank to maintain a central redemption office in Milwaukee or Madison.[37]

A similar pattern of reform evolved in Illinois. The reform of 1857 had made the free banking law in that state one of the best, but there were still major flaws in the system. The slump of 1857 revealed that some attention should be paid to the quality of bonds on which the currency was based. While the earlier reform had tried to eliminate banks in inaccessible places, nearly all the banks created in the expansion after 1857 were in small towns and none was in Chicago. Finally, the specie reserves of Illinois banks were lower than any others in the state. As a consequence Illinois currency circulated at a discount outside the state. In 1859, Governor Bissell praised the system but spotlighted some of these problems and suggested the legislature consider reforming the system. The only specific recommendation he made was that some central redemption center be established. The bank commissioners further asked that Illinois bonds be given preference to other securities and that their power to enforce small note provisions be increased. The legislature, which was dominated by Democrats, refused to act on these proposals.[38]

Pressure to reform the system came from the *Chicago Tribune* early in 1860, before the secession crisis occurred. Chicago had only one commercial bank, and the paper felt reform was necessary to obtain satisfactory currency. As bond prices slackened and the threat of secession increased, the *Tribune*'s demands, and the demands of Chicago business leaders for reform multiplied. John Wood, a staunch Republican who served out Bissell's term, called for reform in early 1861. He suggested a limitation of security to stocks of Illinois and the United States. In this way he believed the legislature could best implement the system favored by the people.[39]

The elections of 1860 resulted in a resounding Republican triumph that carried Richard Yates to the governorship with a solidly Republican legislature to support him. While the banking crisis was not the most important problem before the new governor, he faced it squarely and called vigorously for reform of the system. He saw it as a "troublesome question" and showed a general disgust for "speculators, stock brokers, and panic makers." In general, he favored the free banking system, which he thought had performed well, and cautioned against radical change that would do more harm than good. He did, however, make five specific suggestions: (1) stabilization of the system through a central redemption agency, (2) limitation of security to the stocks of Illinois and the United States, (3) quarterly or semiannual examinations of the quality of securities, (4) tighter restrictions on transfers and removals of bonds, and (5) personal liability.[40]

Under pressure from Chicago businessmen to reform the free

banking system, the legislature acted quickly on the governor's request. An old Whig advocate of free banking from a strongly Republican county introduced the bill and wrote a special report to the legislature that followed Yates's suggestions. The result was an excellent bill, which met little opposition in either house. It limited securities to those of Illinois or the United States; established redemption centers in Springfield and Chicago; limited circulation to three times the paid-in capital, giving the state auditor authority to check the actual paid-in capital; and prohibited the establishment of banks in towns of less than 1,000 inhabitants. The only major reform recommendation not included concerned a minimum on specie reserves. Unfortunately, reform in Illinois came too late, for the banking situation deteriorated before the new legislation could be implemented.[41]

# 7

The crisis of 1860–61 had made some sort of banking reform necessary, but not all Republicans were convinced that reform of free banking would be adequate. At the same time that these reforms were being implemented, other alternatives were being considered. During the crisis of 1860–61, while the free banking systems of Indiana, Illinois, and Wisconsin were crumbling, the Bank of the State of Indiana had stood solidly as an example of sound, conservative banking. This example was not lost on the other states of the Old Northwest.

The Ohio State Bank had shown itself to be strong during the crisis, and had been one of the last banks to suspend specie payments. Efforts had been made in the mid-1850s to increase the capital of the state bank and extend its corporate life. In January 1861, Republican governor William Dennison praised the state bank and renewed suggestions that its capital be increased and its charter (which was to expire in 1865) be renewed. Banking capital in the state, he believed, was insufficient; and

> so long as the supply of circulating notes issued by our banks,
> is insufficient for the transaction of business of the State, it will

. . . be in vain to attempt, by legislative enactment, to expel the issues of foreign banks.

The following year Dennison again brought the state bank before the legislature. The crisis had shown the weakness of free banking and the use of state bonds as security for note issue. To his mind the Ohio system, which provided that branches of the state bank be mutually liable for all issues and accept the notes of all other branches at par, had proved the best way to secure the value of paper currency. Dennison was leaving office, however, and a new governor, David Tod, the old antibank Jacksonian, counseled the legislature to wait on the question until the federal government had acted on Chase's suggestions for a national banking system.[42]

In Michigan desperation as much as anything else led to the attempt to establish a state bank. The free banking law had not succeeded in the hoped for expansion of credit and currency. Believing that the liability provisions established by the constitution held back banking development, the 1859 Republican legislature had proposed an amendment to the constitution limiting liability to the extent of the individual's stockholding. The amendment had been accepted by the voters in the election of 1860. Although the Republicans had continued to try to reform the free banking system to assure a safe, abundant currency, they had not limited themselves to any single method to achieve this goal. The onset of the war dampened the impact of these changes, and early in 1861 a movement to relieve the state's financial problems through the establishment of a state bank similar to those in Indiana and Ohio was begun by the *Detroit Daily Advertiser.* This required an alteration in the state constitution, which at the time limited the legislature to the creation of banks only by general laws. In the senate the Committee on Banks and Incorporations reported favorably on the establishment of a state bank, and the legislature asked the people to amend the constitution accordingly in the election of 1862. Although the amendment passed, a state bank never became a reality because of the creation of the national banking system.[43]

The same session of the Illinois legislature that reformed the free banking law in 1861 proposed the Union Bank of Illinois, which was to be a state bank of 30 branches with a total capital of $10 million. Only in the senate did this receive much opposition. There the opposition was predominantly from Democrats, some of whom had voted for reform of the free banking system. According to the 1847 constitution the proposal for the Union Bank of Illinois had to be ratified by the people at the November 1861 election. By that time the complete collapse of the free banking system had increased antibank feeling. At the same time the constitutional convention was about to meet. Under these conditions the Union Bank bill was defeated by a large majority.[44]

While a state bank, as such, was not established in Wisconsin, the government of that state became thoroughly embroiled in its banking system after the crisis of 1860–61. In the summer of 1861 the Wisconsin banking system was in a chaotic state. The constructive reform of the free banking system passed by the Republican legislature in April would not go into effect until it was acted upon by the voters in the November election. It seemed like the Illinois reform: too little too late. The crisis had revived sagging antibank feeling. Mass antibank meetings were held, and agitation for the repeal of the free banking law increased. The situation was complicated by the state's inability to float a war loan in the New York money market. The congruence of the two problems suggested a single solution. In mid-May, Alexander Mitchell, a Milwaukee financier, proposed just such a solution to Governor Randall. Over the opposition of the Democrats, arrangements were made between the state and the bankers. The bankers would purchase $800,000 of Wisconsin bonds and deposit these with the comptroller to take the place of the depreciated bonds he held. The bankers were also to work to keep Wisconsin money at par and redeem the notes of a number of discredited banks. This connection with the state, the reform of the free banking law, which was accepted by the people at the election in 1861, and the responsible action of the Wisconsin Bankers' Association combined to give the state a sound banking system throughout the war years.[45]

## 8

By 1862 all of the states in the Old Northwest were troubled, in varying degrees, by inadequate credit facilities and a fluctuating, unstable currency. Wisconsin had made good progress in solving her problems, and the state banks in Indiana and Ohio were basically sound institutions; but the situation in Illinois and Michigan was chaotic.

The period from 1857 through the crisis of 1860–61 witnessed a general tendency on the part of the Democrats to revert to the old Jacksonian formula of no banks and a "constitutional currency." The Republicans were responsible for the alterations of the free banking laws limiting banks to towns of a certain size, tightening capital requirements, restricting the quality of securities, and insisting on accessible redemption centers to avoid the excesses of the wildcats. Experience had taught that these limitations on freedom of action might be necessary to insure security under an open system. Basically, the Republicans were searching for ways to provide a sound and adequate currency and to expand the supply of money and credit; they were not tied wholly to the free banking idea. The same Republican legislatures that attempted to reform the free banking laws often encouraged the establishment of state banks similar to that of Indiana. There is no good reason to believe that most Republicans differed from Governor Dennison of Ohio when he told his legislature in 1861,

> The subjects of banking and currency, address themselves with equal force and directness to the people of the State. Whatever theories we may entertain on these subjects; whatever ingenious and beautiful visions of a people without banks and gold and silver their only currency, the political realities are before us:— We have banks; we have paper money.[46]

The real question was what system would best provide adequate credit and a sound, secure currency. Given the depreciation of stock in the crisis of 1860–61, one might wonder not why proposals to follow the successful model of Indiana were entertained, but why Republicans continued to advocate free banking laws and why reform was attempted in the face of the Democratic demand for complete abolition of the banking systems.

The attitudes on the banking question shown by the two contesting parties during these years indicate a continuation of views formed in the party struggles following the destruction of the Bank of the United States. As such, these were differences about state policy in the absence of federal action. The Democrats in 1862 held the same ground they had 20 years earlier, when they had fought for hard money, simple government, and constitutional purity. They still stood solidly against centralism and, even at the state level, feared positive government action. Growing out of the Whig tradition, the Republicans were committed to securing an adequate and sound currency. They feared neither banks nor government activity, and were willing to use both to secure their ends.

For over two decades the money question had been a local issue. The Civil War changed this, elevating it once again to the national stage. The violence of the debates and the way the issue had become woven into the fabric of party conflict dictated that the old arguments and attitudes would be carried into the new arena.

# CHAPTER 9

## THE WEST AND THE NATIONALIZATION OF FREE BANKING, 1861-1865

### 1

The Civil War made federal action on the money question necessary. On the one hand, secession precipitated an economic crisis that severely undermined the existing system. On the other hand, the expenses of war caused a financial crisis within the government itself. In 1862–63 the Thirty-seventh Congress authorized the issue of the legal tender notes called "Greenbacks" and took the first step toward the establishment of the national banking system. Western Republicans played key roles in the enactment of this legislation; and both the Greenbacks and the national banking system received their solid support. In contrast, the western Democracy unanimously opposed both measures. These Democrats continued to mouth Jacksonian rhetoric and to offer little in the way of constructive answers to the problems facing the government and the economy. The Republicans showed a willingness to employ the government in a positive fashion to solve these problems. The Greenbacks were an emergency measure, but the national banking system was conceived as a fundamental reform of the nation's currency. The plan was based on the models of the free banking systems that had been erected in New York and the western states, and embodied the types of restrictions westerners had found necessary in their experience with free banking at the state level. To implement this system, Secretary of the Treasury

Chase, western Republicans, and their allies had to overcome the opposition of the eastern bankers and conservatives as well as the western Democrats.

# 2

When the new Lincoln administration assumed office in 1861, it faced not only a rebellion but also a hopelessly garbled financial situation. Secession had disrupted the interregional balance of trade and had precipitated a wave of commercial failures in the East assuming greater proportions than in the Panic of 1857. Over $300 million owed by the people of the South to northern merchants was a total loss. In the West the currency based on the bonds of southern states depreciated rapidly, leaving the whole area of the Old Northwest with hardly any means of exchange. In addition, government credit was so shaky that Buchanan's last secretary of the treasury was forced to negotiate $15 million in loans at the rates of 10% and 12%.[1]

The magnitude of these problems dictated a radical shift in the nation's financial policy. Since the time of Jackson, currency and banking matters had been decentralized and the powers of the federal government limited. Faced with the necessities of war, a nationalistic administration reversed this policy. With the passage of the legal tender acts and the establishment of the national banking system, the process of nationalization was extended to the nation's currency.

The Old Northwest played a significant role in this legislation and one that can be misunderstood if studied in the light of the debates of the postwar decades. The conflict over this legislation is much clearer if viewed as the culmination of the monetary debate begun by Jackson's veto of the Bank of the United States.

The new secretary of the treasury, more responsible than any other man for these alterations, was a westerner, Salmon P. Chase. He was appointed to the cabinet because he was from the Democratic element of the Republican party. He had little experience in financial matters and was hesitant to take the job because he had already been elected as senator from Ohio. When he decided to accept the cabinet post, he explained to Governor Denison,

> the President has thought fit to call me to another sphere of duty, more laborious more arduous and fuller far of perplexing responsibilities. I sought to avoid it, and would gladly now decline it if I might. I find it impossible to do so, however, without seeming to shrink from cares and labors for the common good, which cannot be honorably shunned.[2]

Like most men at the time, Chase underestimated the cost and length of the war. At first he hoped that an increase in the tariff and an issue of treasury notes could finance suppression of the rebellion. He wrote to the Massachusetts antislavery Congressman Henry Wilson,

> It is clear that some measure must be adopted to revive the sinking credit of the nation; and this bill [the Morrill Tariff] will certainly contribute to that result. A Treasury note bill without a Tariff bill is a dangerous experiment. The two together may answer a good purpose.[3]

The Morrill bill was passed and included an authorization for the secretary of the treasury to issue $10 million in bonds and treasury notes. When revenues lagged behind Chase's expectations, he made use of this power and an earlier authorization to borrow the necessary money to finance the war. In July 1861, Chase requested the power to borrow an additional $240 million to cover the increasing expenses of the war. He still seemed to believe that tariff revenues would increase, and he was hesitant to institute an adequate program of taxation because of the "temporarily deranged" economic conditions.[4]

In July and August, Congress authorized the secretary to borrow $250 million through the use of various kinds of securities. The largest portion of this was in the form of treasury notes sold with the aid of the banks of Boston, New York, and Philadelphia. However, as the year continued, revenues lagged and expenses rapidly increased. At the same time, the currency situation in the West worsened. Senator James Doolittle of Wisconsin wrote to

Chase from Chicago in September 1861, "The Northwest is almost destitute of paper currency of their own." The *Bankers' Magazine* noted, "A radical change in the banking system is demanded . . . particularly in the Western States." It was becoming clear to Chase that some more permanent reform of the currency was necessary.[5]

# 3

Although the Jacksonian tradition was sanctioned by academic economic orthodoxy, it proved particularly unsuited to Chase's needs. Since the 1830s the Jacksonians had emphasized decentralization and states' rights, laissez-faire and a specie currency. Banks, like slavery, had been treated as "local institutions" beyond the reach of federal power, to be regulated by the states. The Independent Treasury had been designed to minimize the interaction of the government and the economy, and at the suggestion of Secretary of the Treasury Howell Cobb, several states had established their own independent treasury laws. The main thrust of the Democrats had been toward the elimination of bank notes and a "return" to hard money. In the mid-1850s, Secretary of the Treasury James Guthrie had suggested the possibility of federal taxation of the state bank issues to bring the country closer to a specie currency, but fear of centralization had prevented even this scheme. The monetary debate precipitated by the Panic of 1857, though interesting, had yielded little in the way of practical suggestions. The weight of orthodox opinion generally supported Jacksonian views; and Charles H. Carroll, a well-known authority on banking and currency, writing in *Hunt's Merchants' Magazine*, revived and urged upon Congress the idea of federal elimination of state bank issues and a national currency made up of certificates representing "dollar for dollar" coin held by the government.[6]

Short-term interest-bearing treasury notes in large denominations had been issued in emergencies by Democratic administrations before the Civil War, but the idea of a permanent national paper currency had no place in the Jacksonian tradition. Shortly before his death Jackson had written to his friend Moses Dawson, the editor of the *Cincinnati Enquirer*, bitterly denouncing any such proposal. The *Democratic Review* explained to its readers that treasury notes were not currency but a form of capitalist investment essentially like government stocks. "The issue of them is to be avoided as far as practicable on the general principle that the incurring of debts in any shape should be avoided, as far as possible, by a republic." It was believed that "any attempt of Government to furnish a paper medium for general commercial purposes must infallibly do harm."[7]

The Whig tradition, emphasizing nationalism, an expanding currency, and a more positive role for government in monetary affairs, proved more fruitful for Chase's needs. However, the main Whig idea, a national bank, had been generally discredited. Although demands for a national bank had been revived following the Panic of 1857, the New York banker who wrote Chase in 1861 that "A Government Bank is odious to our people" was undoubtedly correct.[8]

Two other plans for a national currency had been proposed by Whigs in the 1840s and revived after the Panic of 1857. The more radical proposal, advanced by New York merchant Edward Kellogg, had suggested a kind of national land bank. The government would create a national legal tender currency to be lent on real estate mortgages through branches of a national institution established in each state. The details of Kellogg's plan are less important than is his insistence on the idea that the interest charged by bankers and money-lenders robbed the laborer of his product and that this could be alleviated by a national currency issued on the credit of the nation.[9]

The plan that had stirred the most interest was that proposed by businessman and banker Laurent Bonnefoux and popularized by Millard Fillmore in his widely read report as New York State comptroller. Fillmore's report had suggested that if Congress would authorize the state bank notes

> secured by the stocks of the United States to be received for public dues to the national treasury, this would give such notes

a universal credit, coextensive with the United States, and leave
nothing further desired in the shape of a national currency.

In essence Bonnefoux and Fillmore had suggested a national free
banking scheme based upon the existing state banks.[10]

What popularity these plans for a national currency had had
was among Whigs; they had both received bitter condemnation
from Democrats. The organ of the Polk administration, the *Washington Union*, had blasted Fillmore's report; and in the West, the
*Illinois State Register* had called it a "Federalist scheme." Kellogg
was treated with contempt. Benjamin Tappan, the Ohio hard
money senator, had thought him "too ignorant to give instruction
in political economy." To Tappan the Constitution clearly gave
Congress "no power to make paper money or authorize a private
company to do it." Paper money in any form was a "curse." The
*Racine* (Wis.) *Advocate* had described Kellogg's "Currency: The
Evil and the Remedy" as an example of the "currency tinkering
[that] seems to be the besetting mania of a portion of the people
of this country." His plan was a wild idea that would do an "injustice somewhere and in the end everywhere."

> To us it seems evident that no panacea will ever again find favor
> in this country. The precious metals must soomer or later become
> the currency *and* exchanges be made by mercantile enterprise
> and depended upon mercantile credit for the credit of paper. . . .
> We still think that if the currency were once regulated by not be-
> ing regulated at all, the protection against usury would be much
> less needed if it were needed at all.

When Kellogg's major work *Labor and Other Capital* had appeared in 1849, it had been hostilely received by the *Democratic
Review*.[11]

The monetary debate after 1857 led to the revival of these ideas.
Although they were mainly concerned with the tariff, economic
observers Henry C. Carey, Stephen Colwell, and Henry Carey
Baird defended banks and credit against the hard money advocates, who were usually also free-traders. The Carey-Colwell
"school" emphasized economic nationalism and a concept of the
unity of interests within the nation that underlay the Whig-

229

Republican tradition of economic thought. In 1861, Laurent Bonnefoux published a lengthy article in the *Bankers' Magazine* advocating Fillmore's plan for a national currency to bind the nation together. In this article he republished his "Investigation of the True Principles that Paper Currency Ought to be based Upon" and the series of letters he had written the *New York Mirror* on the subject in 1849. The first year of war also saw a republication of Kellogg's *Labor and Other Capital* under the title *A New Monetary System*, and Kellogg's daughter pressed his proposals upon Republican Senator John Sherman, who would play a prominent role in the monetary legislation of the 1860s.[12]

# 4

Throughout 1861 recommendations poured into Secretary Chase's office. Carey suggested the annihilation of state bank notes and the substitution of a government currency. On the whole, westerners supported similar proposals. Alexander Campbell, the Whig-Republican mayor of La Salle, Illinois, was thinking along the lines of Kellogg, whose *Labor and Other Capital* he would later read and praise as an *"excellent work . . . the Gospel of Finance."* He believed that 90% of the "producing and Commercial classes" were in favor of further issues of treasury notes and that the only opposition to them came from those interested in "flooding the country with a worthless currency or the money worshipers of wall street and their satelites [*sic*] through the country." He suggested that the government issue non-interest-bearing treasury notes in denominations from $5 to $500 to replace the state bank currency, which had degenerated into "worthless trash." Wisconsin senator Doolittle and Joseph Medill, whose *Chicago Tribune* strongly favored a national bank currency, suggested taxing state bank notes so as to replace them with treasury notes and rid the West of "the rags of 1,000 'debt factories.' "[13]

As governor of Ohio, Chase had asked congress to regulate the currency. But he had not formulated any distinct plan; rather he had worked to reform the free banking system in his own state.

Mainly he had been opposed to bank monopolies and had supported a convertible currency; but he had not been, as is usually thought, a radical opponent of all paper money. His experience with free banking had been favorable, and he responded readily to the plan submitted to him in August 1861 by Orlando B. Potter, a New York businessman. Essentially a revival of Fillmore's earlier suggestion, the plan would

> Allow the banks, and bankers duly authorized in the loyal States, to secure their bills by depositing with a superintendent appointed by the Government United States stocks at their par value in the same way that the banks and bankers in New York secure their circulation by depositing New York State and United States stock with the State, thus making the stocks of the United States a basis of banking on which alone a national circulation can be secured.[14]

Chase's annual report, issued December 9 1861, considered the entire problem at length. After reporting his negotiations with the bankers concerning the loans and giving a dismal review of the revenues and expenses of the government, the secretary outlined the problems of the currency. He called on Congress to assert its authority in this area to rationalize the chaotic situation of more than 1,600 banks chartered under varying state laws:

> Under such a system, or rather lack of system, great fluctuations, and heavy losses in discounts and exchanges, are inevitable; and not infrequently through failures of the issuing institutions, considerable portions of the circulation become suddenly worthless in the hands of the people. The recent experience of several States in the valley of the Mississippi painfully illustrates the justice of these observations; and enforces with the most cogent practical arguments the duty of protecting commerce and industry against recurrence of such disorders.[15]

He offered two plans for the consideration of Congress. The first followed the Carey-Campbell suggestion to withdraw the bank issues of the nation and replace them with treasury notes. A tax on bank notes would insure their withdrawal. Chase believed that if a national currency were to be issued according to the "real needs of the people" and to remain at par with specie, the people would have the advantage of a uniform national currency that was also sound and the government would have a loan without the burden of interest. But he feared inflation and a depreciating currency; to his mind, "these possible disasters . . . far outweigh the probable benefits of the plan."[16]

The secretary much preferred a second plan, the one that had been suggested by Potter and Bonnefoux. The circulation of notes would be placed under a common authority holding United States stocks as security against notes issued. This plan would make use of the already existing state banks, which would also be required to hold specie reserves adequate for prompt redemption of their issue. In this way the people could be given a uniform national currency effectively safeguarded against depreciation and loss to the noteholder. This method would also help facilitate government loans and improve general business conditions by lowering interest charges "without risking the perils of a great money monopoly." Chase reminded his readers that the plan was one that had been tested in New York and other states "and has been found practical and useful."[17]

Designed to strengthen the Union by increasing the common interest in its preservation, this plan had nationalistic overtones. It was more than an emergency war measure. Chase argued that although the plan would aid the war effort, it was not just a relief measure; he was advocating a basic reform of the entire money and banking structure of the nation in such a way as to combine safe circulation and convenience.[18]

Chase's report received general acceptance among Republicans, but it was particularly praised by his western correspondents. Several believed it comparable to the reports of Alexander Hamilton. One saw in it a "great, lasting and beneficial revolution in our monetary system." To another it represented a "death blow to the whole mischievous system of private Banks of issue and paved the way for a full supply of Government notes to answer all the demands of a paper circulation for the entire country." A Saint Paul correspondent who had long supported a national currency believed that "the idea of a uniform currency will never be relinquished by the West," although it would be opposed in the East. "The subject is hopeless where it now rests," he wrote; "make it national, and a permanent and safe policy is possible." Alphonso Taft, father of the future president, wrote from Cincinnati,

> I am exceedingly glad to see that you have not hesitated to recommend that the government of the United States assume the function which was designed for it and which by its nature belongs to the government of providing the circulating medium of the country.[19]

The House referred Chase's report to a subcommittee of the Ways and Means Committee, chaired by Buffalo banker Elbridge Gerry Spaulding. When he discovered that Chase had not drawn up a bill effecting his recommendations, Spaulding drafted one based on the New York free banking law. While writing the bill he "came to the conclusion, that it could not be passed and made available quick enough to meet the crisis pressing upon the Government for money to sustain the Army and the Navy." As a consequence, he added to the bank bill a section providing for the "issuing [of] legal tender notes direct from the Treasury while the bank bill was put in operation throughout the country." Thus, as originally conceived, the Greenbacks and the national bank notes were to be complementary.[20]

# 5

The economic situation changed drastically in late December and forced an alteration of these plans. During the summer and fall the banks of the major seaboard cities had acted in essence as underwriters for $150 million in government loans. The bankers had hoped that Chase would make use of an adjustment in the Subtreasury Act to use their banks as government depositories, but the secretary chose to construe the act rigidly and demanded specie from the banks. While this was probably a blunder, the flow of specie was sufficient to enable the banks to handle the three payments to the government. This cycle of borrowing depended on continued confidence in the government; but this confidence was shaken in December by the secretary's gloomy report, which showed revenues lagging behind his July estimates and expenditures increasing at a more rapid pace than anticipated. At about the same time the Trent affair threatened to erupt into a war with Britain and specie went into hiding. With their reserves falling precipitously, the New York banks decided to suspend specie payments on December 28. The situation was grim. As Spaulding put it,

> No more gold could be loaned to the Government, except in small and wholly inadequate amounts, because it was not to be had. State bank bills could still be obtained, but the banks having suspended specie payments, this currency was depreciated, and had only a local character and credit—not being much known out of the States where the banks were located. Hesitancy and delay, with the expenses of the war running at an average of $2,000,000 per day, would be fatal.[21]

Since Spaulding had been warned that the bank bill would meet with opposition, he made the legal tender section into a separate bill to answer the needs of the crisis. With the only alternative for immediate financing being a plan, advocated by banker James Gallatin and supported by the leading bankers of New York, Boston, and Philadelphia that did not provide for any kind of national banking system, Chase reluctantly backed the legal tender measure. While prominent roles were played by Spaulding and Samuel Hooper of Massachusetts, congressmen from the Old Northwest took an active part in the debate. Among the westerners who spoke in the debate there was a division along party lines, with Democrats bitterly opposing the bill and Republicans generally advocating its passage.[22]

Although eastern Republicans like Roscoe Conkling and Justin Morrill opposed the legal tender bill, the main opposition came from those doyens of the western "progressive" Democracy, Ohioans Clement Vallandigham and George Hunt Pendleton. They made standard hard money arguments based on a strict construc-

234

tion of the Constitution. Pendleton argued the bill would impair the obligation of contracts. Vallandigham was willing to support an issue of short-term treasury notes but denied "the right of the Federal Government to provide a paper currency intended primarily to circulate as money. . . ." While he was willing to endorse such treasury notes, which were sanctioned by Jacksonian experience, he opposed making them legal tender, which he said would "banish gold and silver from circulation." If this were accepted, "there would be no end to the legion of paper devils which shall pour forth from the loins of the Secretary."[23]

In the House three western Republicans spoke against the bill, doubting its constitutionality and expressing fear over the danger of an inconvertible currency. However, the main body of western Republicans who spoke advocated the bill's passage. John Bingham of Ohio, William Kellogg of Illinois, Harrison Blake of Ohio, and Samuel Shellabarger of Ohio all spoke in favor of the bill. The debate in the Senate was dominated by westerners led by John Sherman of Ohio; to a man the Republicans urged passage of the legal tender provision.[24]

The basic argument was that of necessity. Sherman told his fellow senators,

> I am authorized—nay required—to vote for all laws necessary and proper for executing these high powers [to uphold the government]. . . . This is not the time when I would limit those powers. Rather than yield to revolutionary force, I would use revolutionary force.

These speeches also reflected a great deal of antibank sentiment that was being expressed in correspondence to western Republicans. Bingham protested that he could not

> keep silent when [he saw] efforts made . . . to lay the power of the American people to control their currency—a power essential to their interests—at the feet of brokers and of city bankers, who have not a title of authority, save by the assent or forbearance of the people, to deal in their paper issued as money.

He believed the Congress had to "assert the rightful authority of the American people, as a nationality, sovereignty, under and by

235

virtue of their Constitution." The speaker of the house, Kellogg, attacked those who would send 600,000 young men to war and then say "the great interests of capital, of currency, must not be touched." "We are not legislating for the money-shavers who oppose this bill," argued Harrison Blake, "but for the people, the soldiers, and the laboring classes." With the aid of Chase's endorsement, the bill was finally brought to a vote. The crucial legal tender provision narrowly passed the Senate 22 to 17 and passed by a wider margin in the House, 95 to 55.[25]

An analysis of the vote on the bill shows most Democrats voting against the Greenbacks and most Republicans favoring them, although a sizable segment of the latter joined the opposition. The votes of the congressmen of the Old Northwest show a greater unanimity. In the Senate, the only Democrat from the Northwest, Jesse Bright of Indiana, did not vote, nor did the two Republican Senators from Illinois. The other seven Republican Senators all voted for the bill. The House vote is even more revealing. Of the thirteen Democrats from the Old Northwest who voted, everyone opposed the legal tender act; while among the Republicans from this area, twenty-six favored the bill and three opposed it.[26]

# 6

While Chase was forced to ask for an additional issue of legal tenders, he did not give up his plan for permanent banking reform. Most western Republicans also continued to look toward a fundamental change in the banking structure. Most of them probably agreed with Congressman Samuel Hooper of Massachusetts, who, urging passage of the first legal tender act, admitted that "the proper inauguration of the new banking scheme . . . will require time." Certainly in the minds of men like Sherman and Zachariah Chandler of Michigan, the legal tenders were a stopgap measure until real reform could be completed.[27]

Throughout the debate on legal tenders, Chase had continued to urge action on a banking system. He had been upset that his allies were not pushing hard enough for it and had written Spaulding that he attached more importance to "the Banking bill as a measure of relief" than did the New Yorker. Later in the year he recorded in his diary his unhappiness with the use of legal tenders and the seeming refusal of "the President and his counsellors" to contemplate reform. In October he explained to John Bigelow in Paris that

> [the adoption] of this system will furnish all the money that is needed at reasonable rates, and insure an early return to specie payments without any serious business convulsion. Even should the war be unhappily protracted beyond the current financial year, the adoption of this system, by uniting the capital of the country with the credit of the government, will probably avert great disasters otherwise to be apprehended.[28]

In 1862, Hooper introduced a banking bill based on Spaulding's earlier bill embodying Chase's suggestions; but it became tied up in committee by Thaddeus Stevens, who supported the legal tender bill but wished stronger control over the state banks than Spaulding's bill provided. Chase saw this as a sign that "A majority of both House and Senate Financial Committees were incredulous or hostile," but he was encouraged by the support of Hooper and Robert J. Walker, ex-secretary of the treasury.[29]

In December, Chase received the backing of the nation's most powerful western Republican, the president. Lincoln praised the legal tender acts for answering "the long-felt want of an uniform circulating medium, saving thereby to the people immense sums in discounts and exchanges." However, he doubted that such a currency could "be permanently, usefully, and safely maintained." To secure "the great advantages of a safe and uniform currency," he suggested "the organization of banking associations under a general act of Congress, well guarded in its provisions." Such a system would offer numerous advantages to the government and "protect labor against the evils of a vicious currency."[30]

Several days later Chase reviewed the financial legislation of 1862 and again suggested a national banking system. It was his belief that the suspension of specie payments created an emergency situation that left the government a choice between state bank currency and legal tenders. He preferred the Greenbacks and on the whole thought they had performed well since its inception. He worried about inflation, which he ascribed to the increase of state bank issues; and he proposed a moderate tax on these notes. He also feared that the legal tenders would become the permanent currency of the nation; to avoid this, he urged a national banking system to establish "one sound uniform circulation, of equal values throughout the country, upon the foundation of national credit with private capital." He also assured the legislators that his was not a "mere paper money scheme," that it would facilitate the return to specie payments.[31]

Although Stevens still was hostile toward the Hooper bill, he reported it out of committee. When it hit rough sledding in the House, the initiative on a banking bill shifted to the Senate. On January 7, Chase appealed to the Finance Committee of the Senate.

> No measure, in my judgement, will meet the necessities of the occasion, and prove adequate to the provision of the great sums required for the suppression of the rebellion, which does not include a firm support to public credit through the establishment of a uniform national circulation, secured by bonds of the United States.

Ten days later Lincoln sent a special message to Congress urging a tax on state bank circulation to curb inflation and the establishment of a uniform currency through a national banking system.[32]

The man who took charge of the bill in the Senate, and to whom "more than any other person Mr. Chase owed successful passage of the bill," was John Sherman. Chase sent Henry Cooke, the brother of the well-known banker Jay Cooke, to influence Sherman to take up the bill; and Robert John Walker encouraged the senator to act on the measure. From his entrance into Congress, Sherman had desired a reform of the currency system; and he agreed with one of his constituents that it was a "fitting time to inaugurate a new system, and by so simple and popular a measure as that of a National Currency teach the people that we are a Nation." However, he wanted to alter Chase's plan by "restricting the charter (which at present is perpetual) to twenty years, [and] to prevent inflation [by] limiting the amount of circulation to be issued and apportion it among the States."[33]

On January 26, Sherman introduced the plan with modifications and stoutly defended it with what was reported as a "powerful and effective" speech. He presented arguments detailing the advantages to the government and the people. On the first count, he echoed Chase in maintaining that the bill would furnish a uniform currency, create a market for bonds, furnish depositories for public funds, and supply a means for payment of public dues. With much more vigor than the secretary, Sherman extolled the nationalistic aspects of the plan. Some years later he would write, "The policy of this country ought to be to make everything national as far as possible. If we were dependent upon the United States for a currency and a medium of exchange, we would have a broader more prosperous nationality." The want of such nationality, he believed, was responsible for the rebellion.[34]

Sherman directed the other half of his argument toward the advantages of a national currency over state bank issues. Like Chase he decried the system of 1,642 banks chartered by 28 different states whose "laws were as diverse . . . as the human countenance." This multiplicity of banks made a national currency impossible. He called for a common regulator to control them and harmonize their actions to secure a sound currency for all areas of the country. He also echoed some distinctly western complaints about the New England currency circulating in the West and the loss "of exchange from west to east on local currency." These arguments, along with the idea that the new currency would be less easily counterfeited, appealed to westerners; but they were less readily accepted in the eastern and middle states, "where their banking system had been so improved that bank failures were rare, and bank bills were protected by mutual guarantees." Michigan senator Chandler supported Sherman's appeal to the needs of the West. He told his colleagues,

In my judgement very little demand will arise in the eastern States for this circulating medium. It will be different in the West. In

239

the West, our circulation having been destroyed virtually, as it was based upon southern bonds, at the commencement of the war, there will be some demand.

The bill, he believed, would provide a better currency with better security than local banks. James Doolittle of Wisconsin added that the system would have none of the objections of earlier national banks since it did not create a monopoly.[35]

Two western Republicans who had voted for the legal tenders joined Justin Morrill and Jacob Collamer, the leading Republican opponents of the bill. John Gurley of Illinois defended the Greenbacks and cautioned against further experimentation, particularly with a type of banking that had failed in the West "most disastrously [for] all classes." Richard Harrison of Ohio feared that the new system would recreate the western wildcats.[36]

Democrats generally opposed the measure. Earlier Vallandigham had attacked Chase's proposal for a national banking system as a "magnificent National Paper Mill." While only one western Democrat spoke in the debate on the national banking act, he echoed Vallandigham and predicted that "like all great paper money schemes, it is fraught with many evils."[37]

The vote on Sherman's bill, which was very close in both houses, showed the bill to be a Republican measure; but many Republicans joined the Democrats in opposing the bill. However, the party division among westerners was much clearer than the debate would indicate. Lyman Trumbull, who also opposed the legal tenders, was the only western Republican senator to vote against Sherman's bill. In the House all 13 western Democrats opposed the bill; and Daniel Voorhees of Indiana, who was absent, noted later he would have voted with them. Of 27 western Republicans, 23 voted for the bill and it passed.[38]

Bearing out Chandler's prediction, the West showed a greater tendency to join the new system during its first year. In the first report of the comptroller of the currency, 73 of the 134 banks in the new system were reported as being located in the Old Northwest. Ohio, with 38 such banks, had almost twice as many as any other state in the Union. The comptroller, Indiana banker Hugh

McCulloch, who later became secretary of the treasury, commented that "The rapidity with which national banks are being organized in the western states, and the high character of most of the stockholders thereof, indicate the popularity of the system in that part of the Union."[39]

Certainly this popularity is not hard to explain. The free banking systems of Illinois and Indiana had been discredited, and the charter of the State Bank of Ohio was about to expire. The small number of new banks in Wisconsin and Michigan can be explained by the new state system in the former and a conflict concerning legal interest requirements in the latter. Of the 184 national banks reported for the Old Northwest in the comptroller's report of 1864, Michigan and Wisconsin each had only 15.[40]

At the end of 1863, Chase, Lincoln, and McCulloch all praised the new system; but the opposition from eastern bankers kept it from fulfilling expectations. McCulloch, who had gone to Washington as a state banker to oppose the system, had become convinced that a national currency was an absolute necessity and accepted the appointment as comptroller. McCulloch's first report had suggested an amendment of the law to make the banks, as well as the currency, truly national by bringing them all under federal charter. Chase incorporated this into his report, and a new national banking act, following McCulloch's suggestions and making it easier for banks to join the system, was passed by Congress on June 3, 1864. This added a large number of new banks to the system. Not until the prohibitive tax on state bank notes long urged by westerners was passed in March 1865, however, did the new national bank notes, along with the Greenbacks, give the United States a totally national currency.[41]

# 7

Support for the Republican financial program was a partisan rather than a sectional or class response. The nearly unanimous action of western Republicans in Congress was indicative of the widespread support of the party in the West. Correspondence from constituents ran heavily in favor of their legislators' action, and the leading party organs advocated and encouraged Chase's policies. In 1862 most western Republicans defended the legal tenders; and a year later, when the first national banking bill was passed, they gave it enthusiastic support. Although a tax on state bank notes was not enacted until 1865, this policy had been constantly agitated for, both in and out of Congress, by western Republicans.

The western Republican papers lauded the report of the secretary of the treasury and defended the legal tender bill as a measure necessary to the war effort. The *Detroit Daily Advertiser* supported the issue of treasury notes against the criticism of the *New York Post*:

> Here in the West we are suffering for currency. . . . Must we then make up the deficiency by using issues of irresponsible private institutions, liable to failure and depreciation, or shall we have a National currency in the safety of which the whole country is interested?

It seemed to the editor of the *Advertiser* that the government should not benefit individuals, particularly the "selfish . . . New York financiers with whom the interests of the people and especially of the Great West are entirely overlooked," but should safeguard the interests of all people. The *Cincinnati Gazette* and the *Milwaukee Daily Sentinel* defended the legal tender bill with similar arguments. The West needed a sound currency, and the people of the West favored a national currency from which the government rather than the selfish eastern bankers would profit. Although initially hesitant about the legal tender clause, the *Chicago Tribune* reversed itself, accepting it as necessary given the situation that faced the nation. Like the other western papers, it attacked the "money sharks" of the East who were trying to profit from the war debt.[42]

The legal tender law of 1862 received support from western Republicans of all economic groups. T. C. Day wrote Senator John Sherman from Cincinnati, "There is an unanimity of sentiment here on the Treasury note issue, especially on the 'legal tender clause.' " One of Senator Benjamin F. Wade's correspondents assured him that "all loyal men" favored the legal tender bill. "*The people* in a mass are in favor of it and praying for its passage." Reports from throughout the Old Northwest indicate particularly strong support for the legislation in the business community, but these usually added that the "great commercial interests of the Cities and the producing masses" also supported the legal tender act. The Chicago Board of Trade and the Cincinnati Chamber of Commerce encouraged similar organizations in the major cities of the Old Northwest to officially proclaim their support for the measure.[43]

Republican farmers also favored the legal tender act. "We have a hope that a better time for the western farmer is at hand," wrote one farmer from northern Illinois to Congressman Elihu B. Washburne. "The passage of the Treasury Note bill and the continued success of our armes [sic] gives encouragement to our people." He hoped that Congress would do more for farmers but, in typical Republican fashion, related farm prosperity to the growth of manufacturing and the development of a local market. These, he believed, would give Illinois "a permanent prosperity equal at least to that of the other states." How widespread this forward-looking optimism was remains unclear; but whatever their reasons, most Republican farmers in the West, like most urban Republicans, supported the party's national financial measures.[44]

While there is not a great deal of evidence on the attitudes of western bankers, it appears that Republican bankers encouraged the passage of the legal tender act for reasons similar to those advanced by other Republicans. J. Young Scammon, the Chicago banker-politician, urged passage of the legal tender act and a provision making the public debt payable in coin. These two enactments would give the West a sound circulating currency. "The only real ground of opposition to it," he believed, "comes from Eastern bankers that want a circulation in the West." James Mitchell, the president of the Stephenson County Bank in Freeport, Illinois, was more explicit. "I notice that there is a struggle going on between the Government and the [eastern] Banks," he wrote Washburne. "I am fearful that the Banks will win, but hope it may be otherwise." He believed that the bankers' plan to aid the financing of the war that had been presented by James Gallatin was "radically selfish" and that Congress should ignore "the whole selfish crew . . . and at once pass the Bill for the issue of Treasury notes."[45]

That western bankers exhibited seemingly antibank feelings only reveals the complexity of the situation. As in the debates in Congress, much opposition to Wall Street bankers and "rag factories" was expressed by western Republicans in their defense of the legal tender act, which it should be remembered was an alternative to the proposal of the New York bankers put forth by James Gallatin. Some of this sentiment came from old Jacksonians who had gone over to the new party. However, most western Republicans continued to approve of banks in principle and restricted their aspersions to eastern banks that to them seemed avaricious and unpatriotic in their dealings with the government and responsible, along with a few poorly run local banks, for the motley currency circulating in the West. Solomon Sturgis of Chicago wrote to Chase that "The people of the North West are with the Government and against the Banks." He supported the legal tenders and advocated taxing the state bank issues out of existence. So did Joseph Medill, editor of the *Chicago Tribune*: "The government and the country are in more danger . . . from debt factories than from the rebels." An Ohio farmer summarized the western Republican criticism of eastern bankers:

> The reported proposal of the Bankers and Brokers of N. York to farm out the public revenue is dangerous and inadmissable. This civil war was commenced by the Southern Rebels to continue the inordinate power of a class of men, the representatives of Slave Oligarchy; who were crushing Republicanism out in this country. And if another Class interest is to succeed them, the country will have gained but little. The Wall Street money changers would be if possible as exclusive as the dealers in men and as sordid and selfish in preferring the peculiar interests of their Class to those of the Republic.

Such views were widespread among western Republicans and were used to justify a general reform of the currency based on a national banking system.[46]

244

Although some members of the party, like the radical advocate of paper money Alexander Campbell, favored the issues of legal tenders but opposed Chase's plan for a national banking system, most western Republicans supported both measures. While praising the legal tender act as a blow to selfish bankers and those "like Vallandigham and Pendleton, who would be willing to see the institutions of the country destroyed," a Cincinnati Republican urged Chase to continue his attempt to have his banking proposal enacted. Many other western Republicans who had supported the legal tenders encouraged Chase to work to establish a national banking system and later congratulated him on its passage. G. Volney Dorsey, an old Whig supporter of the Ohio free banking law, favored Chase's bank plan because it would link the states more closely to the federal government. One man, who described himself as an "old Whig and a Republican," told Sherman that he approved of the bank plan because it would support the government rather than the banks and capitalists. Among Republicans it was widely believed that the creation of the national banking system was wanted by "a large majority of the union loving people," and would be one of the most popular laws ever passed by Congress.[47]

Western Republicans generally associated support for a national banking system with advocacy of the proposal to tax the state bank notes out of existence. The most vigorous exponent of this position was *Chicago Tribune* editor Joseph Medill, who had been urging such action since 1861. "If Chase's bill will arrest the frightful deterioration of the currency," he wrote Washburne, "why not pass it? Can this Congress afford [to] adjourn and leave the currency of the country to the devil under the double operation of continual Bank Expansion and the legal tender emissions." He was bitterly opposed to the eastern state banks and charged that the "untaxed, bloated banks . . . will surely wreck the vessel of State if left alone." Western Republicans saw themselves "flooded with Eastern Currency" of dubious value, which they hoped to see taxed out of existence and replaced with the national currency as Chase's plan proposed. "Let us have a uniform *Government Currency*," a supporter of the bank bill wrote Sherman, ". . . one that can only go down when our country does." The constitutionality of the proposals was never doubted, since it was believed that the government had "the exclusive right to form our currency."[48]

Western Republican bankers showed little of the extreme hostility displayed by eastern bankers toward Chase's plan. An article by Minnesota senator John Jay Knox appearing in *Hunt's Merchants' Magazine* in January 1863 probably typified their attitudes. He saw no reason why the proposal would fail if the administration would give it support. "We believe its adoption is demanded by the people, and that no time ever has or ever will again exist like the present to remedy the greatest financial evil of the times [a local currency]." The country needed a safe, convertible, uniform currency that was not easily counterfeited. Chase proposed permanent national currency could bring "a new era in the history of the country." He called on the legislators to "seek rather the good of the whole people than the interest of a few private corporations" and predicted that a national banking system would increase economic growth to such a degree that "a large part of the cost of the present rebellion will be returned to the people during the next half century." Other bankers offered suggestions based on western experience to make the plan more workable and successful, particularly the creation of central redemption agencies in each state, district boards of control, and the elimination of remote and inaccessible banks. A few worried about the tax structure and suggested it be changed to make their business more economically feasible. They probably favored inducements to draw the state banks into the national system rather than to eliminate them entirely through tax coercion. At least one banker confided that, while it was against his own interest, he supported the measure for "the sake of the cause." Another believed it the *"only feasible method"* of carrying on the war without inflation; and he assured Sherman "public feeling in this section is *universal* in its favor."[49]

In the state legislatures of Michigan, Ohio, and Indiana, Republicans solidly supported the banking scheme, and the Republican press in the West gave it continued encouragement. The *Chicago Tribune* had responded immediately to the secretary's report in 1861, calling for the establishment of a national currency through the creation of a banking system. The paper believed that reform of the currency could come only through national action and that the war presented an opportunity to rid the country of the "absurd" old system. The *Detroit Daily Advertiser* believed that the western states were suffering from the evils of a "foreign" currency and that the want of a "judicious" banking system retarded the economic development of the area. Even if the war were quickly ended, the good of the country demanded "establishing an enduring plan of finance." To the editor of the *Milwaukee Daily Sentinel* it seemed that the "impossibility of regulating the state currency" was clear and that the federal government must act. The Republican papers all underscored the national nature of the currency problem and the nationalistic aspects of the banking proposal. There was fear that "the 'rag money' clique" was "too strong for the friends of an improved currency" and that selfish interests would prevent passage of the bill. When the bill passed, the partisan press expressed relief. Although a truly national banking system would not be constructed until 1864 and the long-demanded tax on state bank issues would not be enacted until 1865, western Republicans were generally happy with the financial measures enacted by the Thirty-seventh Congress. Throughout the Old Northwest the Republican press praised this legislation as the basis for "the universal prosperity of all classes."[50]

These policies were in line with western economic needs, particularly the desire for a sound uniform currency, and with the economic traditions of the party. After the destruction of the Bank of the United States, the Whigs, and later the Republicans, had maintained the goal of a sound, convertible currency that would expand adequately to meet growing business needs. The nationalization of the currency seemed to enable them, at least momentarily, to achieve that goal. The legal tender acts and the national banking acts reasserted some degree of national control over the currency. As such this legislation was central to the process of transferring power from the states to the federal government. One Republican described the national bank bill as "more than a vic-

tory over the rebels. This is a victory over the disintegrating dog-
mas of State rights. It is a step forward—a grand step forward to
the goal of nationality." A Philadelphia Republican paper argued,

> State banking is really the most practical and efficient exemplifi-
> cation we now have of the heresy of state rights and in reorganiz-
> ing, strengthening and centralizing the government we must do
> away with many other obsolete and pernicious systems of a simi-
> lar character.

The Republican financial measures ushered in a new era of economic nationalism and a shift to a more positive conception of
federal power. David Wilder, Jr., praised Chase and hoped that
"at last we are to have some common sense on the subject of currency and that the *infamous* doctrine that the government is not
to care what the people suffer is to be exploded."[51]

# 8

In keeping with their arguments of three decades, western
Democrats were solidly against such centralizing tendencies and
monetary "heresies." Even before the first legal tender bill was
enacted, the *Chicago Times* had charged that the Republicans
were failing in their single duty, to preserve the credit of the nation. The same paper had predicted that Republicans would "sub-
stantially fail in the performance of this duty" and that they would
"aggravate the failure by legislation . . . as wicked as [it is] injurious." Subsequently, as each new measure was enacted Democratic organs like the *Times*, the *Illinois State Register*, the *Indianapolis State Sentinel*, the *Detroit Free Press*, and Samuel
Medary's the *Crisis* detailed its wickedness and prophesied ir-
reparable injury to the republic.[52]

Although the report of the secretary of the treasury in December 1861 had generally been looked upon as an able document, its
proposals had been questioned as revolutionary and dangerous as
well as unconstitutional. The legal tender bill met with Democratic hostility. It was seen as a revolutionary measure that sub-

verted the Constitution by tending to create "a CONSOLIDATED Government with powers as full as Monarchies have." The *Detroit Free Press* believed the Greenbacks would be worse than the wildcat currency and predicted that they would "embarrass [t]he government and . . . beggar the people." According to the *Chicago Times*, "all financial experience the world over, condemns [the law] as uncertain as a measure of temporary relief to the government and as eventually disastrous to the credit of the government and to the business relations." Ohio senator George Hunt Pendleton's speech against the legal tender bill was reprinted by the *Daily Milwaukee News*, which commented that "the Northwest has a no more trustworthy and able representative in Congress." The *Indianapolis State Sentinel* attacked the legal tenders as "An Irredeemable Paper Currency—The High Road to Financial Ruin." Aside from the usual arguments that irredeemable paper would bring a wave of speculation followed by a depression, the *Sentinel* charged that creditors would be injured by inflation. Democratic judge Samuel E. Perkins ruled that legal tender legislation should be invalidated because it "operated as a fraud on the public creditors" and amounted to confiscation of private property without compensation.[53]

Democrats charged that the Greenbacks would act as a tax "upon labor and upon the agricultural states for the benefit of the capitalists and manufacturing states." Editor Wilbur F. Storey explained in the *Chicago Times* that currency like Greenbacks was always evil because of

> the stimulating influence on the prices of all the productions of labor, but not of labor itself; [and] the relative increase in the value of real money, and its rapid exportation abroad, until this unnatural condition of affairs breaks down of its own weight, bringing ruin and destruction in its train.

Such a paper money system would nullify all the Jacksonian Democrats had struggled to maintain in the preceding quarter-century.[54]

If the legal tenders seemed a departure from the tested ways of sound finance, the national banking system became "a symbol

249

of the complete abandonment of Democratic doctrines." The *Cincinnati Daily Enquirer* told its readers, "The enormity of this bill is sufficient to make General Jackson who killed the old Bank of the United States, turn in his coffin . . . the design is to destroy the fixed institutions of the States, and build up a central moneyed despotism."[55]

The new system was seen as nothing more than a return of the old "money monopoly"; it would give rise to an aristocracy ten times worse than the "slavocracy" that would "domineer over white men." The *Chicago Times* argued that it constituted "simply the multiplying of agencies for corruption and bribery" and was open to all the objections "urged against the old bank of the United States." In the *Crisis*, Samuel Medary emphasized that the "monstrous Bank Bill" subverted the interests of the western farmer to the profit of those of the New England capitalist. He called for "a return to the constitutional standard of gold and silver" and the election of Democrats "of the bold and daring school of Jackson" to do it.[56]

To Democrats who had begun their political careers in opposition to the "Biddle centralizers," this new nationalism in monetary affairs clearly undermined the purity of the Constitution by altering the traditional relation between the states and the federal government and by investing the latter with dangerous powers. Democrats predicted that the financial program of the Republicans would lead to "a centralization of power more dangerous than monarchy." The *Illinois State Register* viewed this legislation as

> part of a stupendous and wicked whole, involving the subversion of the existing form of government and erecting in its stead a central consolidated government 'blessed' with a stupendous debt, held by the 'rich and wellborn' against the toiling millions who by the payment of annual interest shall support a privileged class of masters.

The *Daily Milwaukee News* urged the people to turn back from this revolutionary "absorption of power" by the federal government. "The hopes of the future lie in the salient energy and unfailing resources of the states! There we find law, order, treasure, men—all that is necessary to construct a government—all that is necessary to avert revolution." The *Indianapolis State Sentinel* feared that once subverted, the "old standard orthodoxy" of the Constitution might never be regained. Not only did the Lincoln administration promote the "absorption of all functions of the States by the Federal authorities," but it also falsely believed *"that this federal government was created to do about everything, instead of little or nothing."* The *Daily Milwaukee News* expressed the traditional Democratic belief that the Founding Fathers wisely withheld

> from the government all power of interference, not only with matters of a local nature, but with the business pursuits of the country. It was assumed as a fundamental principle, that the just province of government did not comprehend, the control and dictation of the people, or the regulation of their affairs in any particular, except so far as it was necessary to *protect* them, individually and collectively, in the enjoyment of the largest possible freedom.

Clearly, the paper insisted, the federal government had never been "invested with positive powers" to force education upon the people, undertake internal improvements, encourage industry, control religion and morals, or to "dictate commercial and financial relations." [57]

While there were sectional overtones to the argument of the western Democrats against the Republican financial legislation, it was basically partisan and similar to that of their eastern counterparts. Much of it was reprinted directly from the eastern press, particularly the New York City papers the *Express*, the *Journal of Commerce*, and the *Herald*. New York Democrat Horatio Seymour was looked upon in the West as the Jefferson of his time; and his January 1863 speech attacking corruption, the extension of governmental power, and consolidation was widely praised by western Democrats. What have been viewed as antieastern sentiments in the Democratic papers were in fact cultural rather than sectional, directed against "Yankee shrewdness," the "oligarchs of New England privilege," the "roundheads," and the "Puritan

251

patriots who are fattening on the spoils of war." The "New England abolitionists" had brought on the war through their "fanatical prejudice"; now the financial program of the "abolition Congress" would subordinate the interests of the laboring masses to the desires of the New England manufacturers. The Greenbacks were the currency that "abolition misrule has forced upon the country." The *Illinois State Register* reprinted an article from the *New York Express* that argued that the inflation connected with the Republican financial policies was "the cost of Abolition to the White Laboring Man." It represented "a tax on white labor to support the negroes." The *Daily Milwaukee News* attacked the legal tenders and the national banking system as products of "the puritan element," which ruled the country through the Thirty-seventh Congress.[58]

"New Englander," "Puritan," and "Abolitionist" were synonymous and part of the general attack on "Puritanism in Politics," which was designed to appeal to the diverse anti-Yankee-Protestant coalition that made up the Democratic party. Democrats viewed centralizaton of the economy and the growth of federal power as part of a program of cultural domination by the "ever meddling" descendants of the Puritans, who wished "to make government a moral reform society." The nationalization of the nation's financial system marked the onslaught of an "era of New England terrorism under Lincoln," whose trend would be toward the amalgamation of all "climates, habits, and social organizations." Emotional power was added to this argument by equating cultural homegeneity under "Puritan" domination with a racial policy designed to "reduce" whites and blacks "to a common level —until our heretofore proud white Republic shall become a disgusting mass of mongrels and hybrids until indeed we adopt and practice amalgamation!"[59]

# 9

The Civil War laid bare the cultural conflict that formed the basis of mid-nineteenth century politics in the Old Northwest.

This conflict between the Yankee-Protestants in the Whig and Republican parties and the heterogeneous Democratic coalition touched all matters of governmental organization and policy. The banking question was no exception.

The Republicans, and the Whigs before them, represented the "Puritan party in politics" and showed a desire to shape the culture in terms of Yankee-Protestant values. They were willing to use the coercive power of both the state and federal governments to enforce moral behavior and supply the needs of a developing economy. Free banking was designed to provide credit facilities and an adequate currency to meet these needs while insuring safety to the billholder. Such a policy would avoid the odium of monopoly and promote equality of economic opportunity within the context of a commercial economy.

Being composed of an ethnically and religiously diverse constituency, the Democratic party combined enthusiasm for cultural pluralism with vicious antiblack racism. They defined liberty for white men in terms of the freedom of individuals from interference by the government. They emphasized states' rights and respect for local institutions; but even in the states, they feared the misuse of legislative power: a "light and simple" government was deemed best. In relation to banks, they moved to simplify the governmental process and destroy governmentally created privilege through the relatively simple formula of hard money. Yet the choice of target and the moralistic tone of the crusade against banks revealed a deeper fear of commercialization, an economic indicator of cultural domination by Yankee-Protestant values and habits.

The Civil War brought to a close the debate over banking begun in the wake of the Panic of 1837. The necessities of war forced the Republicans to innovate on a wide scale in matters of finance. To solve the pressing needs of the government, the Greenbacks were issued as an emergency measure in 1862. The following year the national banking system was created on the model of the state free banking systems and embodying restrictions dictated by the lessons of experience. In the course of the war there were further issues of Greenbacks and a strengthening of the national banking system. While these changes bore a distinct relationship to the past, the institutional structures that grew out of the war ushered in a new era of monetary debate in the Old Northwest and the nation as a whole. The old issues concerning state banking and hard money that had occupied the political arena for 30 years were themselves no longer relevant. The concepts and clichés developed by the parties in the antebellum years had to be transformed to deal with new economic and political situations following the war. The deeper cultural conflict they reflected remained.

# APPENDICES

## Appendix A
### Factor Analysis of Thirty-nine Variables From the 1850 Illinois Census

Factor analysis is a technique of multivariate analysis developed primarily by L. L. Thurstone and his associates for use in interpreting social-psychological tests and questionaires. It has had wide use in this field since the 1930's and more recently has been applied in other areas of the social sciences. Brief introductions to the technique can be found in Herbert M. Blalock, Jr., *Social Statistics* (New York: McGraw-Hill Book Company, 1960), pp. 383-91; and Fred N. Kerlinger, *Foundations of Behavioral Research* (New York: Holt, Rinehart and Winston, 1964), pp. 650-87. The technical aspects of the method are surveyed in Harry Harman, *Modern Factor Analysis* (Chicago: Univ. of Chicago Press, 1960). Historians will find of much more use the essays in Mattei Dogan and Stein Rokkan, eds., *Quantitative Ecological Analysis in the Social Sciences* (Cambridge, Mass.: M.I.T. Press, 1969), pp. 299-456, 487–506, especially that of Carl-Gunnar Janson, "Some Problems of Ecological Factor Analysis," which reviews recent literature applying factor analysis to ecological variables. Several studies of aspects of American history have attempted to use the technique in a variety of ways with varying success: Harold F. Gosnell, *Machine Politics* (Chicago: Univ. of Chicago Press, 1937); Duncan MacRae, Jr., and James A. Meldrum, "Critical Elections in Illinois, 1888–1958," *American Political Science Review* 54 (Sept. 1960): 669–83; Michael Rogan, *The Intellectuals and McCarthy: The Radical Specter* (Cambridge, Mass.: M.I.T. Press, 1967); and Michael B. Katz, *The Irony of Early School Re-*

*form– Educational Innovation in Mid-Nineteenth Century Massa-chusetts* (Cambridge, Mass.: Harvard Univ. Press, 1968). A con-temporary article that uses factor analysis in a way similar to this study is Glen Gordon and Philip Coulter, "The Sociological Bases of Party Competition: The Case of Massachusetts," *Socio-logical Quarterly* 10 (Jan. 1969): 84-105.

Using the computer program "BMDO3M–Factor Analysis–Version of January 1, 1966, Health Sciences Computing Facility, U.C.L.A.," a four factor matrix was created according to varimax criteria. This solution was chosen for this study because the factors thus generated seemed to best represent multivariate indica-tors of the presence of social groups discussed in the traditional historical literature (cited in chapters five and six). Each factor is made up of those variables which loaded most highly on it. The loadings express the correlation of the variable and the factor. So that population might be controlled in the partial correlation analysis presented in the text (See table 8), a fifth factor was constructed out of the variables "population," "white adult males," "births," and "deaths." The final five factors were named "Yankee subculture," "southern subculture," "foreign-born," "general farm-ing," and "population."

| *Factors* | *Loading* |
|---|---|
| 1.  Yankee subculture | |
|         Wheat production | .88 |
|         Number of schools | .84 |
|         Total Farm value | .83 |
|         Number of students | .82 |
|         Value of farm machinery | .82 |
|         Improved land (ratio) | .79 |
|         Number of towns over 200 population | .71 |
|         Number of marriages | .63 |
|         Cheese production | .62 |
|         Farm value per acre in 1860* | .59 |
|         Number of Congregational accommodations | .58 |
|         Farm value per acre in 1850* | .52 |
| 2.  Southern subculture | |
|         Sweet potato Production | .81 |
|         Native illiterates | .79 |

* Data is from Pressly and Scofield, eds., *Farm Real Estate Values.*

|  | |
|---|---|
| Total illiterates | .76 |
| "Southerness" scale† | .64 |
| Age of county | .60 |
| Population growth scale (inverse) | .53 |
| Number of Baptist accommodations | .40 |

3. Foreign-born

|  | |
|---|---|
| Number of Episcopal accommodations | .90 |
| Foreign-born | .90 |
| Foreign-born white adult males | .88 |
| Total church accommodations 1860 | .82 |
| Number of Roman Catholic accommodations | .82 |
| Total church accommodations 1850 | .80 |
| Number of Presbyterian accommodations | .68 |
| Number of Lutheran accommodations | .57 |
| Other Protestant accommodations | .43 |

4. General farming

|  | |
|---|---|
| Corn production | .80 |
| Orchard products | .67 |
| Wool production | .62 |
| Number of Methodist accommodations | .61 |
| Number of Christian accommodations | .58 |
| Home manufactures | .57 |
| Number of farmers in 1840 | .55 |

5. Population

| | |
|---|---|
| Population | (had loaded .69 on factor 1) |
| White adult males | (had loaded .93 on factor 3) |
| Births | (had loaded .64 on factor 1) |
| Deaths | (had loaded .60 on factor 1) |

Unweighted factor scores were computed for each county simply by summing the component variables. These new scores were then correlated with the percent of antibank votes in the 1851 Illinois referendum using computer program BMD03D to give the simple correlation coefficients and with the raw probank and antibank votes in that referendum, using program BMD02R to give the partial correlation coefficients, holding population constant.

† The construction of this scale is explained in the note on table 5. It should not be confused with the "southern subculture" factor, of which it is only one element.

# Appendix B
# Religious Groups and the Vote on the 1851
# Bank Referendum in Illinois

If the hypothesis presented in the text is valid, there should be at least some correlation between religious indicators and responses on the bank referendum, since ethnic background *and* religion were the main distinguishing social characteristics of the conflicting subcultures. Counties dominated by religious groups such as Congregationalists should have tended to support banks, while those in which Baptists predominated should have opposed them.

The techniques of partial correlation and multiple regression were used to judge the relationship between the existence of certain religious groups and the vote on banks. Hubert M. Blalock, Jr., *Social Statistics* (New York: McGraw-Hill Book Company, 1960), pp. 326-58, offers a brief introduction to these techniques. Using computer program "BMD02R—Stepwise Regression—Version of April 13, 1965, Health Sciences Computing Facility, U.C.L.A.," the following results were obtained.

When size of the religious population as measured by total accommodations is held constant, the significant partial correlations between accommodations and the probank vote are: Congregationalists, .41; Episcopalians, .27; and Methodists, −.26. The partial correlation between Baptist accommodations and the probank vote is −.18, which conforms to the hypothesis inasmuch as it is negative, but only approaches statistical significance.

When a similar operation is performed on the antibank vote, the significant partials are: Episcopalians, −.38; Baptists, .32; Methodists, .28; and other Protestants, −.24. The last variable is made up of the minor sects. Important for the hypothesis presented in the text is the fact that higher order partials for "Roman Catholic accommodations" and "Lutheran accommodations" become significant.

The ten religious variables explain 62% of the total variance in the probank vote. As one would expect, "total accommodations" accounts for 42% of the variance; but more surprisingly "Congregational accommodations" accounts for 10% more of the variance, and "Episcopal accommodations" accounts for an additional 6%. Only these two variables have significant F values at .01 level of probability. In the case of the antibank vote the ten variables explain 40% of the variance. However, of this 40% "Total accommodations" accounts for only 12% while "Episcopalian accommodations" accounts for 13%. "Roman Catholic accommodations" accounts for 5%; "Baptist accommodations," for 4%; "Methodist accommodations," for 4%; and "Lutheran accommodations," for 3%. All have F values significant at .01 level of probability. (It should be recalled that the correlation between "Episcopal accommodations" and the antibank vote was negative.)

These findings also give support to the contention in the text that counties containing contrasting proportions of the religious groups loading on factor 3 acted in conflicting ways on the bank issue. Here, as above, the analysis is hampered by the problem of multicollinearity discussed by Hubert M. Blalock, Jr., in *Social Forces*, 62 (Dec. 1963): 233-38; thus, any conclusions must be considered tentative. Nevertheless, if one focuses on the five religious groups loading on that factor, there seems to be a clear split between those counties with a large number of Episcopalians, and to a lesser extent Presbyterians, which tended to be probank, and those counties with a large number of Roman Catholics, and to a lesser extent Lutherans, which tended to be antibank.

# NOTES

## Abbreviations

| | |
|---|---|
| *AHR* | *American Historical Review* |
| *Banks and Politics* | Hammond, Bray. *Banks and Politics in America from the Revolution to the Civil War.* Princeton, N. J.: Princeton Univ. Press, 1957. |
| *Chicago Banks* | James, F. Cyril. *The Growth of Chicago Banks.* 2 vols. New York: Harper and Brothers, 1938. |
| *Cong. Globe* | U.S., Congress, Senate. *Congressional Globe,* 37th Cong. |
| *Debates of 1847* | Cole, Arthur Charles, ed. *The Constitutional Debates of 1847.* Springfield: Ill. State Historical Library, 1919. |
| *Debates of Ind.* | *Report of the Debates and Proceedings of the Convention for the Revision of the Constitution of the State of Indiana, 1850.* Reported by H. Fowler. Indianapolis: A. H. Brown Printer, 1850. |
| *Debates of Mich.* | *Report of the Proceedings and Debates in the Convention to Revise the Constitution of the State of Michigan, 1850.* Lansing, Mich.: R. W. Ingals State Printer, 1850. |
| *Debates of Ohio* | *Report of the Debates and Proceedings of the Convention for the Revision of the Constitution of the State of Ohio, 1850-51.* Columbus: S. Medary, Printer to the Convention, 1851. |
| *Frontier State* | The Centennial History of Illinois. Vol. 2, Pease, Theodore Calvin. *The Frontier State, 1818-1848.* Springfield: Ill. Centennial Commission, 1918. |
| *Governors' Messages* | Fuller, George N., ed. *Messages of the Governors.* Lansing: Mich. Historical Commission, 1925-26. |
| *Ill. Governor* | *Illinois Governor* |
| *Ill. House Journal* | *Illinois Legislature. House Journal.* |

| | |
|---|---|
| *Ill. Senate Journal* | *Illinois Legislature. Senate Journal.* |
| *Ind. Doc. Journal* | *Indiana Legislature. Documentary Journal.* |
| *Ind. House Journal* | *Indiana Legislature. House Journal.* |
| *Ind. Senate Journal* | *Indiana Legislature. Senate Journal.* |
| *Jacksonians Versus the Banks* | Sharp, James Roger. *The Jacksonians Versus the Banks: Politics in the States After 1837.* New York: Columbia Univ. Press, 1970. |
| *JEH* | *Journal of Economic History* |
| *JPE* | *Journal of Political Economy* |
| *MA* | *Mid-America* |
| *Mass Political Parties* | Formisano, Ronald P. *The Birth of Mass Political Parties: Michigan 1827-1861.* Princeton, N. J.: Princeton Univ. Press, 1971. |
| *Mich. House Doc.* | *Michigan Legislature. House Documents Accompanying Journal.* |
| *Mich. House Journal* | *Michigan Legislature. House Journal.* |
| *Mich. Political Parties* | Streeter, Floyd Benjamin. *Political Parties in Michigan, 1837-1860.* Lansing: Mich. Historical Commission, 1918. |
| *Mich. Senate Doc.* | *Michigan Legislature. Senate Documents Accompanying Journal.* |
| *Mich. Senate Journal* | *Michigan Legislature. Senate Journal.* |
| *MVHR* | *Mississippi Valley Historical Review* |
| *OAHP* | *Ohio Archaeological and Historical Publications* |
| *OAHQ* | *Ohio Archaeological and Historical Quarterly* |
| *Ohio Doc.* | *Ohio Legislature. Documents . . . of the State of Ohio.* |
| *Ohio House Journal* | *Ohio Legislature. House Journal.* |
| *Ohio Senate Journal* | *Ohio Legislature. Senate Journal.* |
| *Passing of the Frontier* | Whittke, Carl, ed. *The History of the State of Ohio.* Vol. 3, Weisenburger, Francis P. *The Passing of the Frontier, 1825-1850.* Columbus: Ohio State Archaeological and Historical Society, 1941. |
| *TISHS* | *Transactions of the Illinois State Historical Society for the Year* |
| *UISSS* | *University of Illinois Studies in the Social Sciences* |
| *Western Prices* | Berry, Thomas Senior. *Western Prices Before 1861.* Cambridge, Mass.: Harvard Univ. Press, 1943. |
| *Wis. Assembly Journal* | *Wisconsin Legislature. Assembly Journal.* |
| *Wis. Senate Journal* | *Wisconsin Legislature. Senate Journal.* |

# Introduction

1. On the "Bank War," see Arthur M. Schlesinger, Jr., *The Age of Jackson* (Boston: Little, Brown and Co., 1945); Marvin Meyers, *The Jacksonian Persuasion: Politics and Belief* (Stanford: Stanford Univ. Press, 1957); *Banks and Politics*; Robert V. Remini, *Andrew Jackson and the Bank War: A Study in the Growth of Presidential Power* (New York: W. W. Norton and Company, 1967). On monetary controversies during the Civil War and Reconstruction, see: Robert P. Sharkey, *Money, Class, and Party: An Economic Study of the Civil War and Reconstruction* (Baltimore: Johns Hopkins Press, 1959); Irwin Unger, *The Greenback Era: A Social and Political History of American Finance, 1865-1879* (Princeton: Princeton Univ. Press, 1964); Richard Hofstadter, "Free Silver and the Mind of 'Coin' Harvery," in *The Paranoid Style in American Politics and Other Essays* (New York: Alfred A. Knopf, 1965): 238-314; Walter T. K. Nugent, *The Money Question During Reconstruction* (New York: W. W. Norton and Company, 1967); idem, *Money and American Society, 1865-1880* (New York: Free Press, 1968); Allen Weinstein, *Prelude to Populism: Origins of the Silver Issue, 1867-1878* (New Haven: Yale Univ. Press, 1970). [The major works on the antebellum period by Avery O. Craven, Roy F. Nichols, and Allan Nevins totally ignore the bank issue. This neglect is a product of what Joel H. Silbey termed "The Civil War Synthesis in American Political History" in an article by that name in *Civil War History* 10 (June 1964): 130-40.]

2. For general reviews of the historiography of the Jacksonian period, see: Charles G. Sellers, Jr., "Andrew Jackson Versus the Historians," *MVHR* 44 (Mar. 1958): 615-34; Alfred A. Cave, *Jacksonian Democracy and the Historians* (Gainesville: Univ. of Florida Press, 1964); Edward Pessen, *Jacksonian America: Society, Personality and Politics* (Homewood: Dorsey Press, 1969): 352-93; Frank Otto Gatell, "Beyond Jacksonian Consensus," in Herbert J. Bass, ed., *The State of American History* (Chicago: Quadrangle Books, 1970): 349-61.

3. Frederick Jackson Turner, *The Frontier in American History* (New York: Henry Holt and Company, 1920), p. 32. *See also*: Charles Beard, *The Rise of American Civilization* (New York: Macmillan Company, 1930), I: 685. On the Progressive historians, see Richard Hofstadter, *The Progressive Historians* (New York: Alfred A. Knopf, 1969): 238-39.

4. Frederick Jackson Turner, *The United States,1830-1850* (New York: Henry Holt and Company, 1935): 318. Ibid.: 318. Ibid.: 124-27, 317-22; quotations: 126. [Turner's position at the time of his death was thus similar to that put forward by Chester McArthur Destler in *American Radicalism 1865-1901: Essays and Documents* (New York: Octagon Books, 1963), and differed only in emphasis from that of Schlesinger, *Age of Jackson*: 78-82, 208-9, 262-63.]

5. Bray Hammond, "Banking in the Early West: Monopoly, Prohibition, and Laissez Faire," *JEH* 8 (May 1948): 1-25; *Banks and Politics*: 605-

30. Hammond, "Banking in the Early West": 2. *Banks and Politics*: 624. Ibid.: 598. [Interestingly enough, Schlesinger, *Age of Jackson*: 336-37 and Gatell, "Beyond Jacksonian Consensus": 358, agree.]

6. *Jacksonians Versus the Banks*: 321. [Sharp develops an argument suggested earlier by William G. Carleton, "Political Aspects on the Van Buren Era," *South Atlantic Quarterly* 50 (Apr. 1951): 167-85. Donald B. Cole, *Jacksonian Democracy in New Hampshire, 1800-1851* (Cambridge, Mass.: Harvard Univ. Press, 1970): 136-215, presented quite a similar argument. In relation to Sharp's statement about the 1850's, Eric Foner has also argued that it was necessary to turn away from the financial issues of the 1840s in order to bring together the coalition of ex-Democrats and ex-Whigs that formed the Republican party in the 1850s (*Free Soil, Free Labor, Free Men: The Ideology of the Republican Party Before the Civil War* [New York: Oxford Univ. Press, 1970]: 168-72).]

7. Erling Arthur Erickson, "Banks and Politics Before the Civil War: The Case of Iowa, 1836-1865" (Ph.D. diss., Univ. of Iowa, 1967), shows a pattern similar to the one described here for the Old Northwest and concludes that party was the major determinant of attitudes on the bank issue. He does not attempt to go further in his analysis, but the evidence on Iowa voting behavior presented in William E. Dodd, "The Fight for the Northwest, 1860," *AHR* 16 (July 1911): 774-88, George H. Daniels, "Immigrant Vote in the 1860 Election: The Case of Iowa," *MA* 44 (July 1962): 146–62, Robert P. Swierenga, "The Ethnic Voter and the First Lincoln Election," *Civil War History* 11 (Mar. 1965): 27-43, and Robert R. Dykstra and Harlan Hahn, "Northern Voters and Negro Suffrage: The Case of Iowa, 1868," *Public Opinion Quarterly* 32 (summer 1968): 202-15, suggests the possibility of an analysis of the bank issue in Iowa politics similar to that presented here.

8. The assumptions of the historians' traditional model have been undermined by the work done in survey research since 1940. The relevant studies are Paul B. Lazarsfeld, Bernard Berelson, and Hazel Gaudet, *The Peoples Choice* (New York: Columbia Univ. Press, 1948); Bernard Berelson, Paul B. Lazarsfeld, and William McPhee, *Voting* (Chicago: Univ. of Chicago Press, 1954); Bernard Berelson, "Democratic Theory and Public Opinion," *Public Opinion Quarterly* 16 (fall 1952): 313-30; Herbert McClosky, Paul J. Hoffman, and Rosemary O'Hara, "Issue Conflict and Consensus Among Party Leaders and Followers," *American Political Science Review* 44 (June 1960): 406-27; Herbert McClosky, "Consensus and Ideology in American Politics," *American Political Science Review* 58 (June 1964): 361-79; Angus Campbell et al., *The American Voter* (New York: John Wiley and Sons, 1964); Angus Campbell et al., *Elections and the Political Order* (New York: John Wiley and Sons, 1966); Philip E. Converse, "The Nature of Belief Systems in Mass Publics," in David Apter, ed., *Ideology and Discontent* (Glencoe, Ill.: Free Press, 1964): 206-261.

9. Samuel P. Hays, "New Possibilities for American Political History: The

Social Analysis of Political Life" (Ann Arbor, Mich.: Inter-University Consortium for Political Research, 1964): 12. On symbolism in American politics, see: Joseph R. Gusfield, *Symbolic Crusade: Status Politics and the American Temperance Movement* (Urbana: Univ. of Ill. Press, 1963); Murray Edelman, *The Symbolic Uses of Politics* (Urbana: Univ. of Ill. Press, 1964); Robert J. Pranger, *Action, Symbolism and Order* (Nashville: Vanderbilt Univ. Press, 1968). [Professor Hays's critique of traditional political history and his formulation of the "social analysis" of political history have immeasurably influenced this study. See his essays: "History as Human Behavior," *Iowa Journal of History* 58 (July 1960): 193-206; "The Social Analysis of Political History, 1880-1920," *Political Science Quarterly* 80 (Sept. 1965): 373-94; "The Politics of Reform in Municipal Government in the Progressive Era," *Pacific Northwest Quarterly* 55 (Oct. 1964): 157-69; "Shame of the Cities Revisited: The Case of Pittsburgh," in Herbert Shapiro, ed., *The Muckrakers and American Society* (Boston: D. C. Heath, 1968): 75-81; "Political Parties and the Community-Society Continuum," in William Nesbit Chambers and Walter Dean Burnham, eds., *The American Party Systems* (New York: Oxford Univ. Press, 1967): 152-81; "A Systematic Social History," in George Athan Billias and Gerald N. Grob, eds., *American History: Retrospect and Prospect* (New York: Free Press, 1971): 315-66. This study was also deeply influenced by Lee Benson, particularly his chapter "Party Programs, Character, and Images," in *The Concept of Jacksonian Democracy: New York As a Test Case* (Princeton: Princeton Univ. Press, 1961): 216-53. Gene Wise has emphasized the difference between Benson's approach and that of the Progressive historians in "Political 'Reality' in Recent American scholarship: Progressives versus Symbolists," *American Quarterly* 19 (summer 1967): 303-28.]

10. On migration see: Ray Allen Billington, *Westward Expansion: A History of the American Frontier* (New York: Macmillan Company, 1967): 290-309; Avery O. Craven, *The Coming of the Civil War* (Chicago: Univ. of Chicago Press, 1966): 313-24. On the German vote in 1860, see: Joseph Schafer, "Who Elected Lincoln?" *AHR* 47 (Oct. 1941): 51-63, quotation: 58; Lee Benson, "Research Problems in American Political Historiography," in Mirra Komarovsky, ed., *Common Frontiers of the Social Sciences* (Glencoe, Ill.: Free Press, 1957): 172-81; Silbey, "Civil War Synthesis": 135-40; James H. Bergquist, "The Political Attitudes of the German Immigrant in Illinois, 1848-1860" (Ph.D. diss., Northwestern Univ., 1966); Paul J. Kleppner, "Lincoln and the Immigrant Vote: A Case of Religious Polarization," *MA* 48 (July 1966): 176-95.

11. *Mass Political Parties*: 10. [Formisano extends to the antebellum Midwest the pioneering approach presented by Benson in *Concept of Jacksonian Democracy*. Cf. Michael Fitzgibbon Holt, *Forging a Majority: The Formation of the Republican Party in Pittsburgh, 1848-1860* (New Haven: Yale Univ. Press, 1969); Paul J. Kleppner, *The Cross of Culture: A Social Analysis of Midwestern Politics, 1850-1900* (New York:

Free Press, 1970); Richard Jensen, "The Religious and Occupational Roots of Party Identification: Illinois and Indiana in the 1870's," *Civil War History* 16 (Dec. 1970): 325–43; idem, *The Winning of the Midwest: Social and Political Conflict, 1888-1896* (Chicago: Univ. of Chicago Press, 1971).]

12. Representative of the growing literature on religion and political behavior are: James S. Coleman, "Social Cleavage and Religious Conflict," *Journal of Social Issues* 12 (July 1956): 44-56; Gerhard Lenski, *The Religious Factor: A Sociological Study of Religious Impact on Politics, Economics, and Family Life* (Garden City, N. Y.: Doubleday and Company, 1961); Scott Greer, "Catholic Voters and the Democratic Party," *Public Opinion Quarterly* 25 (winter 1961): 611–25; Benton Johnson, "Ascetic Protestantism and Political Preference," *Public Opinion Quarterly* 26 (spring 1962): 35-46; Milton Gordon, *Assimilation in American Life* (New York: Oxford Univ. Press, 1964); Seymour Martin Lipset, "Religion and Politics in America Past and Present," in *Revolution and Counter-Revolution* (Garden City, N. Y.: Doubleday and Company, 1970): 305-73; Angus Campbell et al., *The American Voter* (New York: John Wiley and Sons, 1964); Lawrence H. Fuchs, ed., *American Ethnic Politics* (New York: Harper and Row Publishers, 1968); Michael Parenti, "Ethnic Politics and the Persistence of Ethnic Identification," *American Political Science Review* 61 (Sept. 1967): 717-26; Edgar Litt, *Ethnic Politics in America* (Glenview, Ill.: Scott, Foresman, and Company, 1970). [Lenski's book has had particular influence on this study.] On the effects of "social mobilization," see: Karl W. Deutsch, "Social Mobilization and Political Development," *American Political Science Review* 55 (Sept. 1961): 493-502; and Samuel P. Huntington, *Political Order in Changing Societies* (New Haven: Yale Univ. Press, 1968).

13. A brilliant study of the way cultural stereotypes filled psychological functions during this "Age of Anxiety," as he calls it, is William R. Taylor, *Cavalier and Yankee* (London, W. H. Allan, 1963). *See also:* David Brion Davis, "Some Themes of Counter-Subversion: An Analysis of Anti-Masonic, Anti-Catholic, and Anti-Mormon Literature," *MVHR* 47 (Sept. 1960): 205-24; idem, "Some Ideological Functions of Prejudice in Ante-Bellum America," *American Quarterly* 15 (summer 1963): 115-25; idem, *The Slave Power Conspiracy and the Paranoid Style* (Baton Rouge: Louisiana State Univ. 1969).

# Chapter 1

1. R. Carlyle Buley, *The Old Northwest: The Pioneer Period, 1815-1840* (Bloomington: Ind. Univ. Press, 1962), 1: 562-632, a fine discussion of most of the aspects of early banking in the Old Northwest, serves as a basis for this entire chapter. *See also:* Francis P. Weisenburger, "Charles Hammond, the First Great Journalist of the Old Northwest," *OAHQ* 43 (1934): 352-72; C. C. Huntington, "A History of Banking

and Currency in Ohio Before the Civil War," *OAHP* 24 (1915): 253-343; Harry Stevens, "Henry Clay, the Bank and the West in 1824," *AHR* 60 (July 1955): 843-48; Logan Esarey, "State Banking in Indiana, 1814-1873," *Ind. Univ. Studies* 10 (Apr. 1912): 221-42; George William Dowrie, "The Development of Banking in Illinois, 1817-1863," *UISSS* 2 (Dec. 1913): 22-48; Harlan Scott White, "Western Banking Ideas and Practices Before 1840," (A.M. thesis, Univ. of Ind. 1942): passim; *Chicago Banks*, 1: 70-117; Ralph C. H. Catterall, *The Second Bank of the United States* (Chicago: Univ. of Chicago Press, 1903): 132-63; *Western Prices*: 410-17; Rodney Owen Davis, "Illinois Legislators and Jacksonian Democracy" (Ph.D. diss., Univ. of Iowa, 1966): 78-96, 188.

2. U.S., Bureau of the Census, *Historical Statistics of the United States: Colonial Times to 1957* (Washington, D. C.: U.S. Government Printing Office, 1960): 13; Robert W. Johannsen, ed., *The Letters of Stephen A. Douglas* (Urbana: Univ. of Ill. Press, 1961): 35-36.

3. The most recent discussion of the "pets" is in Frank Otto Gatell, "Spoils of the Bank War: Political Bias in the Selection of Pet Banks," *AHR* 70 (Oct. 1964): 35-58.

4. The state of party development is treated in Homer J. Webster, "History of the Democratic Party Organization in the Northwest, 1824-1840." *OAHP* 24 (1915): 1-120, and Richard P. McCormick, *The Second American Party System: Party Formation in the Jacksonian Era* (Chapel Hill: Univ. of N. C. Press, 1966): 255-87, 320-26. Buley, *Old Northwest*, 2: 160-259, covers political developments during these years.

5. There were also "savings banks" and private banks, which were unincorporated partnerships usually lending money and sometimes issuing illegal currency. This study is concerned with only those banks that were corporations whose functions included the issuance of currency: chartered banks, state banks, and free banks. Chartered banks and free banks were sometimes called local banks in contrast to the centralized state banks.

6. *Western Prices*: 406-31; Richard C. Wade, *The Urban Frontier: The Rise of Western Cities, 1790-1830* (Cambridge, Mass.: Harvard Univ. Press, 1959): 195-97; *Passing of the Frontier*: 1-33; J. S. Buckingham, *Eastern and Western States of America*, quoted in *Passing of the Frontier*: 29.

7. *Ohio House Journal*, 1832: 8-13. [The following discussion of politics and banking in Ohio is based on Huntington, "Banking and Currency in Ohio": 343-63; Harold E. Davis, "Economic Basis of Ohio Politics, 1820-1840," *OAHQ* 47 (Oct. 1938): 311-14; and *Passing of the Frontier*: 277-85.]

8. *Cincinnati Advertiser and Ohio Phoenix*, Dec. 15 and 22, 1832, Jan. 2 and 19, 1833. [This paper is referred to in the text and below as the *Cincinnati Advertiser*.]

9. *Cincinnati Gazette*, in *Cincinnati Advertiser*, Dec. 22, 1832. *Cleveland Herald*, Jan. 12, 1833, in *Annals of Cleveland* 15: 49. *Ohio State Jour-*

*nal and Columbus Gazette,* Jan. 26, Feb. 6, 1833. *See also:* ibid., Dec. 29, 1832, Jan. 9 and 16, Feb. 2, Mar. 2, 1833. [The latter paper is referred to in the text and below as the *Ohio State Journal.*]

10. *Cleveland Herald,* Nov. 9, 1833, in *Annals of Cleveland* 15: 51. *Cincinnati Republican,* in *Ind. Democrat,* Dec. 4, 1833.

11. *Ohio House Journal,* 1833: 10.

12. Creed to Ewing, Feb. 4, 1834, quoted in John Michael McFaul, "The Politics of Jacksonian Finance" (Ph.D. diss., Univ. of Calif. at Berkeley, 1963): 95; *Passing of the Frontier:* 283; *Ind. Democrat,* Feb. 16, 1834. [Interestingly, Dawson's *Cincinnati Advertiser* remained ardent on this question.]

13. *Ohio House Journal,* 1833: 490; *Ohio Senate Journal,* 1833: 466-67.

14. *Ohio State Journal,* Jan. 15, Feb. 5 and 12 (quotation), 1834.

15. *Ohio House Journal,* 1833: 253, 503, 509, 517, 534, 559, 646-47, 666, 681, 684, 685, 688, 689. *Ohio Senate Journal,* 1833: 252, 454, 553, 684-85, 709, 710, 722, 751. [At least two of the banks voted on had a significant number of Democratic politicians as directors: the Ohio Life Insurance and Trust Company and the Bank of Columbus. For a defense of local banks by a young Ohio Jacksonian who was later a hard money man, see Thurman to Hough, Feb. 9, 1836, Thurman MSS.]

16. *Cleveland Herald,* Mar. 15 and 25, Apr. 12, 1834, *Cleveland Whig,* Dec. 31, 1834, in *Annals of Cleveland* 16: 151-53. [The analysis is based on roll calls listed in n. 15.]

17. *Ohio State Journal,* Feb. 6 and Mar. 2, 1833, Jan. 15 and Feb. 12, 1834. *Cincinnati Gazette,* Apr. 14, 1834, quoted in *Western Prices:* 422, n. 39. *Ohio House Journal,* 1834: 617.

18. *Passing of the Frontier:* 308-13; Harry N. Scheiber, "Entrepreneurship and Western Development: The Case of Micajah T. Williams," *Business History Review* 37 (winter 1963): 356-61; Davis, "Ohio Politics": 315. [The vote in a Jacksonian legislature was 40–27 to postpone, with the Democrats split, 17–25 (*Ohio House Journal,* 1835: 363). The eastern stockholders were connected with Martin Van Buren's Albany Regency. In 1837 the Ohio Life Insurance and Trust Company was made a federal depository.]

19. James D. Richardson, comp., *A Compilation of the Messages and Papers of the Presidents* (Washington, D. C.: By Authority of Congress, 1900), 3: 166. Davis, "Ohio Politics": 313. [The 1836 vote shows a distinct shift from the 1833-34 session, when both the parties split on the question of small notes (*Ohio House Journal,* 1833: 480).]

20. Linton to Tipton, June 14, 1832, in Nellie Armstrong Robertson and Dorothy Riker, eds., *The John Tipton Papers* (Indianapolis: Ind. Historical Bureau, 1942), 2: 327-28. "Message to the General Assembly, December 4, 1832," in Dorothy Riker and Gayle Thornbrough, eds., *Messages and Papers relating to the Administration of Noah Noble, Governor of Indiana, 1831-1837* (Indianapolis: Ind. Historical Bureau, 1958): 152. *Ind. Journal,* Jan. 2, 1833. *Ind. Democrat,* Jan. 30, 1833. *See also:* ibid., Jan. 5, 16, 19, 23, and 26, 1833. [The discussion of the establishment of the State Bank of Indiana, unless otherwise noted, is

from Esarey, "State Banking in Indiana": 242-43; William F. Harding, "The State Bank of Indiana," *JPE* 4 (Dec. 1895): 1-10; Fritz Redlich, *The Molding of American Banking: Men and Ideas* (New York: Hafner Publishing Company, 1947), 2: 22-25; and Philip M. Crane, "Governor Jo Wright: Hoosier Conservative" (Ph.D. diss., Ind. Univ., 1963): 27-31.]

21. Adams to Judah, Oct. 7, 1833, Judah MSS. *Ind. Journal*, Feb. 23, 1933. *Ind. Democrat*, Mar. 2 and 23, June 15, Sept. 28, Dec. 7, 1833. "Message to the General Assembly, December 3, 1833," in Riker and Thornbrough, *Noble Messages and Papers*: 210-11. Hugh McCulloch, *Men and Measures of Half a Century* (New York: Scribners and Sons, 1888): 113-23.

22. Ewing to Noble, Jan. 18, 1834, Noble MSS. "Message to the General Assembly, December 5, 1837," in Riker and Thornbrough, *Noble Messages and Papers*: 589. *Ind. Democrat*, Jan. 11, 1834. Ibid., Jan. 8, 15, and 18, 1834; *Ind. Journal*, Jan. 15, 1834.

23. *Ind. Democrat*, June 15, 1833, Jan. 8 and 11, 1834. *Ind. Journal*, Jan. 15, 1834. *See also*: ibid., Jan. 1, 1834.

24. For sample Whig opinion see: Hendricks to Smith, Jan. 31, 1834, Hendricks MSS; I'Anson to Judah, July 7, 1835, Judah MSS; *Ind. Democrat*, Jan. 11, 1834. Quote from Ewing to Noble, Jan. 18, 1834, Noble MSS. *Ind. Journal*, Jan. 1, 8, 15, 18, and 25, 1834.

25. *Ind. Senate Journal*, 1833: 268; *Ind. House Journal*, 1833: 352. Crane, "Governor Jo Wright": 30.

26. The following discussion of politics and banking in Illinois, unless otherwise noted, is based on Dowrie, "Banking in Illinois": 59-63, and *Frontier State*: 114-49, 303-6.

27. *Ill. Advocate and State Register*, Nov. 30, 1833, Jan. 11, Mar. 8, May 10, 1834. *Sangamo Journal*, Dec. 7, 1833, Jan. 11 and 25, 1834. *Alton American*, in ibid., Jan. 25, 1834. [The *Vandalia Whig* opposed a state bank at this time, in *Ill. Advocate and State Register*, Feb. 15 and 27, 1834. This paper is referred to in the text and below as the *Ill(inois) State Register*.]

28. *Chicago Democrat*, July 16 and 23, 1834; *Ill. State Register*, June 14, July 5, 12, and 26, 1834; *Sangamo Journal*, July 26, Aug. 30, 1834.

29. *Ill. State Register*, Nov. 26, Dec. 13, 1834, Jan. 21 and 31, Feb. 18, 1835; *Alton Spectator*, in ibid., Feb. 4, 1835. *Sangamo Journal*, Dec. 13, 1834, Jan. 10, 1835. Ewing and Duncan messages are in the *Ill. State Register* and *Sangamo Journal*, Dec. 13, 1834. [The *Chicago Democrat* did not at first take a stand on either the state bank or the extension of the charter of the Bank of Illinois at Shaweetown (Jan. 21, 1835, issue). But on June 10, 1835, the paper reprinted an article from the *Hartford Times*, saying, "Now is the time to take a stand against Banks and corporations generally."]

30. Duncan's message to the legislature, Dec. 9, 1836, in *Ill. State Register*, Dec. 16, 1836. [Elizabeth Duncan Putnam, "The Life and Services of Joseph Duncan, Governor of Illinois, 1834-1838," *TISHS, 1919* (n.d.): 107-87, is a pedestrian discussion of Duncan's career, but includes some interesting letters and segments from his diary.]

31. *Ill. Senate Journal*, 1835: 354, 360; *Ill. House Journal*, 1835: 504, 508, 512. Charles Manfred Thompson, "The Illinois Whigs Before 1846," *UISSS* 4 (Mar. 1915): 50; Davis, "Illinois Legislators": 117-24; John Francis Snyder, *Adam W. Snyder and His Period in Illinois History, 1817-1842* (Virginia, Ill.: E. Needham, 1906): 176-77. Johannsen, *Douglas Letters*: 13-14.

32. Bela Hubbard, *Memorials of a Half-Century* (New York: G. P. Putnam's Sons, 1887): 93-105. Thomas McIntyre Cooley, *Michigan: A History of Governments* (Boston: Houghton, Mifflin and Company, 1885): 254-56. [Rapid expansion is also emphasized in the standard accounts of early Michigan banking: idem, "State Bank Issues in Michigan: A Retrospect of Legislation," *Mich. Political Science Association Publications* 1 (n.d.): 1-20; Alpheus Felch, "Early Banks and Banking in Michigan," *Pioneer Collections: Report of the Pioneer Society of the State of Michigan* 2 (1880): 111-24. All subsequent writers have depended on these accounts, written by two extremely important Democrats.]

33. Clarence M. Burton, ed., *The City of Detroit, Michigan, 1701-1922* (Detroit: S. J. Clarke Publishing Company, 1922), 1: 227-35.

34. Burton, *Detroit*, 1: 633-34; Harry N. Scheiber, "George Bancroft and the Bank of Michigan, 1837-41," *Mich. History* 44 (Mar. 1960): 82-90; all stockholders are listed in *Mich. House Doc.*, 1841: nos. 61, 219-20. [Among those listed as stockholders in this "Whig Bank," along with Cass, are Robert A. Forsyth, A. T. McReynolds, Eraphroditus Ransom, T. C. Sheldon, and Justus Burdick, all Democrats.]

35. Burton, *Detroit*, 1: 636-40; *Mich. Senate Doc.*, 1841: nos. 42, 165-75, list stockholders and borrowers; *Daily Advertiser*, Oct. 7, 1839, contains a typical Whig attack on the Michigan State Bank. [On the political affiliation of Olcott and Corning, see: Lee Benson, *The Concept of Jacksonian Democracy: New York As a Test Case* (Princeton: Princeton Univ. Press, 1961): 91; Frank Otto Gatell, "Sober Second Thoughts on Van Buren, the Albany Regency, and the Wall Street Conspiracy," *Journal of American History* 53 (June 1966): 24-26, 36.]

36. Harold M. Dorr, ed., *The Michigan Constitutional Conventions of 1835-36: Debates and Proceedings* (Ann Arbor: Univ. of Mich. Press, 1940): 392, 390, 336, 391. [The roll call votes are listed in app. A.]

37. The designations "radical" and "conservative" used by Streeter in *Mich. Political Parties* have been followed by Dorr and most other historians. The narrative should reveal some of the problems in applying these terms, which are derived from factional positions on suffrage in the 1835 convention, to factional positions on banking.

38. *Mich. Political Parties*: 5. *Governors' Messages*, 1: 140-42, 174-75. Cooley, "State Bank Issues": 6-7; Felch, "Banking in Michigan": 113-14.

39. *Mich. Senate Journal*, 1836: 171, 232-33; *Mich. Senate Doc.*, 1835-36: no. 9. *Mich. Senate Journal*, 1836: 243; *Banks and Politics*: 600. See also: Robert E. Chaddock, *The Safety Fund Banking System in New York, 1829-1866* (Washington, D.C.: National Monetary Commission, 1910).

40. *Detroit Democratic Free Press*, Aug. 21, Dec. 14, 1836, Jan. 19 and 25,

1837, in particular; quotation is from the *New York Evening Star*, in ibid., Dec. 14, 1837. [On the controversy in New York, see: Redlich, *Molding of American Banking*, 1: 187-204; *Banks and Politics*: 572-600; and Benson, *Jacksonian Democracy*: 89-104.]

41. *Detroit Daily Advertiser*, Jan. 13, 1837.
42. Quoted in Felch, "Banking in Michigan": 115. *Mich. House Journal*, 1837: 30, 39, 41, 45, 55, 58, 61, 65, 67, 73, 77, 86, 87, 108, 137.
43. *Daily Advertiser*, Mar. 2, 1937.
44. *Michigan Political Parties*: 9. *Mich. House Journal*, 1837: 217; *Mich. Senate Journal*, 1837: 245. *See also*: Lawton T. Hemans, *Life and Times of Stevens Thomson Mason, the Boy Governor of Michigan* (Lansing: Mich. Historical Commission, 1920): 274; Felch, "Banking in Michigan": 115. *Daily Advertiser*, Mar. 15, 1837. *Democratic Free Press*, Mar. 14 and 29, Apr. 5, 1837.

# Chapter 2

1. Jackson's message relative to the Bank of the United States can be found in James D. Richardson, comp., *A Compilation of the Messages and Papers of the Presidents* (Washington, D.C.: By Authority of Congress, 1900), 2: 462, 528-29, 558, 576-91; 3: 5-19. On the background of the veto, see: Ralph C. H. Catterall, *The Second Bank of the United States* (Chicago: Univ. of Chicago Press, 1903): 164-332; Arthur M. Schlesinger, Jr., *The Age of Jackson* (Boston: Little, Brown and Co., 1945): 74-114; Fritz Redlich, *The Molding of American Banking* (New York: Hafner Publishing Company, 1947), 1: 162-78; Charles G. Sellers, "Banking and Politics in Jackson's Tennessee, 1817-1827," *MVHR* 41 (June 1954): 61-84; *Banks and Politics*: 326-450; Thomas Payne Govan, *Nicholas Biddle: Nationalist and Public Banker, 1786-1844* (Chicago: Univ. of Chicago Press, 1959): 112-246; Robert V. Remini, *Andrew Jackson and the Bank War* (New York: W. W. Norton and Company, 1967): 15-153.
2. Lynn L. Marshall, "The Authorship of Jackson's Bank Veto Message," *MVHR* 50 (Dec. 1963): 466-77; Marvin Meyers, *The Jacksonian Persuasion: Politics and Belief* (Stanford: Stanford Univ. Press, 1957): 3-32, passim. Richardson, *Presidential Messages* 2: 590.
3. On Jacksonian financial policy see: Frank Otto Gatell, "Spoils of the Bank War," *AHR* 70 (Oct. 1964): 35-58; idem and John M. McFaul, "The Outcast Insider: Reuben M. Whitney and the Bank War," *Pa. Magazine of History and Biography* 91 (Apr. 1967): 115-44; Govan, *Nicholas Biddle*: 223-375; *Banks and Politics*: 405-99; John Michael McFaul, "The Politics of Jacksonian Finance," (Ph.D. diss., Univ. of Calif. at Berkeley, 1963); Paul M. O'Leary, "The Coinage Legislation of 1834," *JPE* 45 (Feb. 1937): 80-94; Remini, *Andrew Jackson*: 109-75; and Harry N. Scheiber, "The Pet Banks in Jacksonian Politics and Finance, 1833-1841," *JEH* 23 (June 1963): 196-214; Peter Temin, *The Jacksonian Economy* (New York: W. W. Norton and Company,

1969): and Hugh Rockoff, "Money, Prices and Banks in the Jacksonian Era," in Robert William Fogel and Stanley L. Engerman, eds., *The Reinterpretation of American Economic History* (New York: Harper and Row Publishers, 1971): 448-58.

4. Richardson, *Presidential Messages*, 3: 236-60; quotation: 248.

5. Ibid., 249. [The Specie Circular is reprinted in Henry Steele Commager, ed., *Documents of American History*, 5th ed. (New York: Appleton-Century-Crofts, 1949): 283.]

6. Temin, *Jacksonian Economy*, is the most recent study; quotation: 127. On the panic *see also*: Reginald Charles McGrane, *The Panic of 1837* (Chicago: Univ. of Chicago Press, 1924); Henry David et al., eds., *The Economic History of the United States*, (New York: Holt, Rinehart and Winston, 1945– ), vol. 4, George Rogers Taylor, *The Transportation Revolution, 1815-1860*: 338-45; George Macesich, "Sources of Monetary Disturbances in the United States, 1834-1845," *JEH* 20 (Sept. 1960): 407-26; Jeffrey G. Williamson, "International Trade and United States Economic Development: 1827-1834," *JEH* 21 (Sept. 1961): 372-83; and Macesich, "International Trade and United States Economic Development Revisited," ibid.: 384-85. [Like most historians McGrane and Taylor acknowledge the importance of the Specie Circular. Richard H. Timberlake, Jr., in "The Specie Circular and the Distribution of the Surplus," *JPE* 68 (Apr. 1960): 111, and "The Specie Circular and the Sale of Public Lands: A Comment," *JEH* 25 (Sept. 1965): 414-16, reveals some of the weaknesses of the traditional view, but he has not disposed of the arguments presented by Hammond in *Banks and Politics*: 455-57, Scheiber in "Pet Banks": 206-8, and Carter H. Golembe in "State Banks and the Economic Development of the West" (Ph.D. diss., Columbia Univ., 1951): 207-9.]

7. Temin, *Jacksonian Economy*: 128-36; Timberlake, "Specie Circular": 114-16. *See also*: Golembe, "State Banks": 207-9.

8. Taney to Jackson, Oct. 27, 1836, in John Spencer Bassett, ed., *Correspondence of Andrew Jackson* (Washington, D.C.: Carnegie Institution of Washington, 1931), 5: 431-32; Johnson to Jackson, June 21, 1836, in ibid., indicates there were many Democrats who favored the act. *See also*: Thomas Hart Benton, Thirty Years' View (New York: D. Appleton and Co., 1854), 1: 658. [The problems created by the Distribution Act have been overemphasized, as Temin shows. Yet even he admits that Michigan and New York, which were closely related financially to all the midwestern states, did suffer from its effects.]

9. *Western Courier and Piqua Enquirer*, May 6, 1837, quoted in R. Carlyle Buley, *The Old Northwest* (Indianapolis: Ind. Historical Society, 1950), 2: 270.

10. Leonard C. Helderman, *National and State Banks: A Study of Their Origins* (Boston: Houghton Mifflin Company, 1931): 2-8. Charles Francis Adams, *Further Reflections Upon the State of the Currency of the United States* (Boston: William D. Ticknor, 1837): 5. [Martin B. Duberman, *Charles Francis Adams, 1807-1886* (Boston: Houghton Mifflin Company, 1961): 56-61, argues that Adams was connected with

neither party and that his comments on the crisis "countered" partisan assessments of Jackson. While the basic argument of Adams's pamphlet shows him to have held economic views that would have been more comfortable among Whigs in the 1840s, Duberman is essentially correct. The tone of *Further Reflections* differs greatly from contemporary partisan pieces.]

11. Meyers, *Jacksonian Persuasion*: 195-205. *Sangamo Journal*, Apr. 29, 1837. Woodbridge to Woodbridge, May 19, 1837, Woodbridge MSS.

12. Thomas Hart Benton, ed., *Abridgement of the Debates of Congress from 1789 to 1856* (New York: D. Appleton and Co., 1859), 13: 404-5.

13. Jackson to Taney, Oct. 13, 1836, in Bassett, *Jackson Correspondence*, 5: 430. Taney to Jackson, Oct. 27, 1836, in ibid., 5: 431-43. Richardson, *Presidental Messages*, 3: 236-60, 292-308; quotation: 248. On general theories concerning banking and the business cycle at this time, see: Harry E. Miller, *Banking Theories in the United States Before 1860* (Cambridge, Mass.: Harvard Univ. Press, 1927): 55-70, 187-208.

14. Jackson to Dawson, Aug. 31, 1837, in John J. Whealen, ed., "The Jackson-Dawson Correspondence," *Bulletin of the Historical and Philosophical Society of Ohio* 16 (Jan. 1958): 9-10. [Other Jacksonian editors had similar exchanges with Jackson; see, for example, the letters to and from Francis P. Blair in Bassett, *Jackson Correspondence*, 5: 474-79.]

15. Richardson, *Presidential Messages*, 3: 325-26.

16. "The Moral of the Crisis," *U.S. Magazine and Democratic Review* 1 (Oct.-Dec. 1837): 111, 108, 117. [This is referred to in the text and below as the *Democratic Review.*]

17. Paul A. Randall, ed., "Gubernatorial Platforms for the Political Parties of Michigan (1834-1864)" (A.M. thesis, Wayne State Univ., 1937): 10-11. *Governors' Messages*, 1: 209.

18. *Democratic Free Press*, May 10, 1837. Ibid., June 14, 1837. Ibid., July 5, 1837. *Constantine Republican*, in ibid., July 26, 1837. For the development of the argument, *see also*: *Democratic Free Press*, Dec. 14, 1836, Jan. 25, May 24 and 31, June 7 and 25, July 5, 1837.

19. *Ohio Statesman*, Jan. 3, 1838. *Washington Globe*, in *Ohio Statesman*, Mar. 14, 1838. *Ohio Doc.*, 1839; no. 1. Ibid., 1841: no. 1. Ibid., 1845: no. 1.

20. *Newark Advocate*, in *Ohio Statesman*, Oct. 24, 1837. *Ohio Statesman*, Oct. 27, 1837. Ibid., Aug. 9, 16, and 27, 1837.

21. Wentworth's course can be followed in Don E. Fehrenbacher, *Chicago Giant: A Biography of "Long John" Wentworth* (Madison: American History Research Center, 1957): 27-28. Governor Carlin's message of Dec. 11, 1839, in *Ill. Governor*, 1838-42. [Charles Manfred Thompson, "The Illinois Whigs Before 1846," *UISSS* 4 (Mar. 1915): 52, 83, asserts that Illinois bankers were Whigs, but he offers no systematically collected quantitative evidence.]

22. "Minority Report of the Select Committee of the Senate on the Governor's Message," in Dorothy Riker, ed., *Messages and Papers Relating to the Administration of David Wallace, Governor of Indiana, 1837-*

*1840* (Indianapolis: Ind. Historical Bureau, 1963): 376-81; quotations: 377, 378.

23. Ibid.: 380. Ibid.: 381.
24. *Indianapolis Ind. Democrat,* May 3, June 7 and 21, July 12 and 26, Sept. 6, 1837. [The *Charleston Indianan* did attack the state bank when it suspended: "We do not believe the people desire a bank longer. Let Indiana be first in the noble work . . ." (*Ohio Statesman,* Nov. 1, 1837).]
25. *Governors' Message,* 1: 371-72. *Ohio Doc.* 1838: no. 1. *Ill. Governor,* 1834-38. *Ind. Doc. Journal,* 1839, pt. 2: no. 9. "Minority Report . . . on the Governor's Message," and "Report of the Select Committee of the House on the Governor's Message," in Riker, *David Wallace Messages:* 376-81, 393-99. *Ind. Journal,* Jan. 14, Feb. 3 and 10, 1840.
26. Buley, *Old Northwest,* 2: 271. Thompson, "Illinois Whigs": 66. *Ind. Doc. Journal,* 1838: no. 1. *Ohio Doc.,* 1841: no. 76.
27. *Detroit Daily Advertiser,* Jan. 27, 1837. *Ann Arbor State Journal,* in ibid., May 23, 1837.
28. *Detroit Daily Advertiser,* Aug. 12, 1837, Mar. 5, 1838. [The list of bank presidents and cashiers is given in ibid., Aug. 11, 1838.]
29. Randall, "Gubernatorial Platforms": 20-28.
30. Gouge is quoted in the Dutchess County, N. Y., *Anti-Bank Democrat,* no. 4 (Apr. 1842): 61. *See also:* Meyers, *Jacksonian Persuasion.*
31. Richardson, *Presidential Messages,* 3: 344. *See also:* "The Moral of the Crisis," *Democratic Review* 1 (Oct.-Dec. 1837): 110-19.
32. Webster is quoted in Glyndon G. Van Deusen, *The Jacksonian Era, 1828-1848* (New York: Harper and Row, 1959): 122.
33. Richardson, *Presidential Messages,* 3: 342. [On the response of western Democrats to the Independent Treasury plan, see Schlesinger, *Age of Jackson:* 217-41, 250-66; Evarts B. Greene, ed., "Letters to Gustav Koerner, 1837-1863," *TISHS, 1907* (1908): 224-26; Tipton to Noble, Jan. 14, 1838, Noble MSS. [That the Democrats in the state legislatures did move strongly behind the administration's proposal after initial ambiguity is clear from Rodney Owen Davis, "Illinois Legislators and Jacksonian Democracy" (Ph.D. diss., Univ. of Iowa, 1966): 168-69.]

# Chapter 3

1. Lyon to Trowbridge, May 1, 1837, Trowbridge MSS.
2. Numerous letters boosting Michigan are in "Letters of Lucius Lyon," *Pioneer Collections* 27 (1897): 412-604. Smith to Portz, May 27, 1938, in "Letters from Ogle and Carrol Counties, 1837-1857," *TISHS, 1907* (1908): 247-61.
3. Carter H. Golembe, "State Banks and the Economic Development of the West" (Ph.D., diss., Columbia Univ., 1952).
4. *Ohio Statesman,* Dec. 2, 1837. *Dayton Herald,* in ibid., Dec. 4, 1837. *See also: Ohio Statesman,* Aug. 9, 16, and 23, Oct. 27, Nov. 20 and 26, Dec. 12, 1837, March 13, July 3, 1838; *Ind. Democrat,* June 7, Sept. 6,

Nov. 1, 15, and 22, 1837; *Charleston Indianan,* in *Ohio Statesman,* Nov. 1, 1837; *Ill. State Register,* June 3, Aug. 4, 1837; *Detroit Democratic Free Press,* July 9 and 12, Aug. 9, 1837, May 9, Sept. 18, Nov. 24, 1838.

5. This shift in the national Democratic party can be followed in the pages of the *Democratic Review* and is the subject of *Jacksonians Versus the Banks.* Rodney Owen Davis, "Illinois Legislators and Jacksonian Democracy" (Ph.D. diss., Univ. of Iowa, 1966): 140, 164, 166, 177, 186, 189, presents tables revealing the magnitude and timing of the shift within the Illinois Democratic party.

6. Butler to Trowbridge and Farnsworth, Dec. 19, 1836, and Lyon to Trowbridge, May 1, 1837, Trowbridge MSS; Lawton T. Hemans, *Life of Stevens Thomson Mason, The Boy Governor of Michigan* (Lansing: Mich. Historical Commission, 1920): 287; *Democratic Free Press,* May 24, 1837.

7. *Governors' Messages,* 1: 208-12.

8. *Mich. House Journal,* extra sess., 1837: 44, 455, 461. *Mich. Senate Journal,* special sess. 1837: 450. *Calhoun County Patriot,* in *Democratic Free Press,* June 28, 1837.

9. *Daily Advertiser,* Jan. 13 and 27, Feb. 28, Mar. 15 and 22, May 1, 1837. The Democratic Platform is reprinted in Paul A. Randall, ed., "Gubernatorial Platforms for the Political Parties of Michigan (1834-1864)" (A.M. thesis, Wayne State Univ., 1937): 10-13.

10. *Democratic Free Press,* Aug. 9, 1837.

11. *Daily Advertiser,* May 27, July 28, Aug. 12, 1837. The Whig platform is in ibid., Aug. 7, 1837, and is reprinted in Randall, "Gubernatorial Platforms": 8-10.

12. *Daily Advertiser,* July 28, 1837. *Ann Arbor Journal,* in ibid., Aug. 22, 1837. *Daily Advertiser,* Aug. 22, 1837. Ibid., Nov. 2, 1837. *See also:* ibid., Nov. 28, 1837.

13. *Democratic Free Press,* Sept. 6, 1837.

14. *Pontiac Balance,* in ibid., Sept. 20 and 27, 1837. *Grand River Times,* in *Democratic Free Press,* Oct. 11, 1837. *Ann Arbor Argus,* in *Democratic Free Press,* Dec. 20, 1837. *Constantine Republican* in *Democratic Free Press,* Jan. 17, 1838. *Tecumseh Democrat,* in *Democratic Free Press,* Nov. 8, 1837.

15. This material is based on many sources. The Williams MSS include an interesting letter from his cousin, Thomas Williams, concerning their uncle (probably Joseph Campau, a leading Democrat): "You undoubtedly recollect his maxim (d—n a poor man). Take heed nephews—incur not the displeasure of your uncle, make *money!* Make it honestly if you can but by all means make money!" (Williams to Williams, Oct. 17, 1836, William MSS).

16. Alpheus Felch, "Early Banks and Banking in Michigan," *Pioneer Collections* 2 (1880): 118; Joseph Gantz, "A History of Banking Legislation and Currency in Michigan, 1835-1865" (A.M. thesis, Wayne State Univ., 1936): 16-18: *Mich. House Journal,* adjourned sess., 1837: 82-83, 131; *Mich. Senate Journal,* adjourned sess., 1837: 178, 249.

17. Felch, "Banking in Michigan": 116. Campau to Eberts, Jan. 31, 1838,

Williams MSS. *Daily Advertiser*, Nov. 28, 1837. *See also*: ibid., Nov. 2, Dec. 5, 13, and 25, 1837, Jan. 30, 1838.

18. *Governors' Messages*, 1: 227-31.
19. *Daily Advertiser*, Jan. 13 and 30, 1838. Hastings to Woodbridge, Feb. 3, 1838, Woodbridge MSS.
20. *Daily Advertiser*, Feb. 5, Mar. 15, 16, and 19, 1838, reported the debates. Howard is quoted in Feb. 5, Mar. 15, 1838, issues.
21. *Democratic Free Press*, Mar. 28, Apr. 25, 1838. For Whig response see: *Daily Advertiser*, Mar. 12, 13, 14, 19, and 28, 1838; Hastings to Woodbridge, Feb. 3, 1838, and Trowbridge to Woodbridge, Mar. 5, 1838, Woodbridge MSS.
22. *Democratic Free Press*, Mar. 28, 1838. Ibid., Apr. 4, 1838. *See also*: *Calhoun County Patriot*, in ibid., Apr. 4, 1838; *Democratic Free Press*, Apr. 11, 18, and 25, Sept. 12, Oct. 17, 1838.
23. *Mich. House Doc.*, 1839: no. 29. *See also*: ibid., 1839: nos. 14, 26, 29; 1840: no. 4; Gantz, "Banking Legislation": 25-26.
24. *Kalamazoo Gazette*, in *Democratic Free Press*, Nov. 29, 1837. *Governors' Messages*, 1: 227-32.
25. *Democratic Free Press*, Feb. 7, Apr. 18, Sept. 12, 1838.
26. Trowbridge to Woodbridge, Mar. 5, 1838, Woodbridge MSS; Trowbridge to Moran, Mar. 27, 1838, Trowbridge MSS. [Hastings to Woodbridge, Feb. 3, 1838, Woodbridge MSS, opposed *any* new banks. The *Daily Advertiser*, Mar. 19, 1838, in another context, stated its belief that there were too many banks.]
27. Gantz, "Banking Legislation": 35-36. *Mich. House Journal*, 1838: 453. *Mich. Senate Journal*, 1838: 311.
28. *Democratic Free Press*, May 9 and 16, 1838. *See also*: ibid., Apr. 18 and 25, May 2, 1838; *Kalamazoo Gazette*, in ibid., May 2, 1838.
29. *Democratic Free Press*, Apr. 18 and 25, Sept. 5, 12, and 18, Oct. 17, Dec. 19, 1838. *Governors' Messages*, 1: 251-60. [The Michigan State Bank was a privately owned, chartered bank, not a state-owned institution, as the name might suggest; it was unrelated to the proposed 1838 state bank.]
30. *Daily Advertiser*, Aug.–Sept. 1838 issues nearly all attack the Independent Treasury plan; Aug. 18, Oct. 24, Dec. 27, 1838, Jan. 3, 1839, deal with the state bank plans. *Mich. House Doc.*, 1839: no. 29; *Democratic Free Press*, Mar. 27, 1839; *Mich. House Journal*, 1839: 286.
31. *Ind. Democrat*, May 31, July 26, 1837. William F. Harding, "The State Bank of Indiana," *JPE* 4 (Dec. 1895): 12. Merrill to Merrill, Dec. 11, 1837, and Jan. 5, 1838, Merrill MSS. Lanier to Noble, Sept 23, 1837, Noble MSS.
32. *Ind. Democrat*, June 7, 1837. *Charleston Indianan*, in *Ohio Statesman*, Nov. 1, 1837. *Ind. Democrat*, Nov. 1, 15, and 22, 1837.
33. *Ind. Democrat*, June 13, 1838. Hannegan to Tipton, Apr. 6, 1838, in Dorothy Riker and Nellie Armstrong Robertson eds., *The John Tipton Papers* (Indianapolis: Ind. Historical Bureau, 1942), 3: 589. *Ind. Democrat*, June 13, Nov. 21, Dec. 7, 1838, Feb. 28, 1839.
34. Paul L. Haworth, "Samuel Judah," in Dumas Malone, ed., *The Dic-*

*tionary of American Biography* (New York: Charles Scribners' Sons, 1946), 10: 227-28. [There are numerous hostile references in Riker and Robertson, *Tipton Papers*; e.g., Fitzgerald to Tipton, Nov. 21, 1832, 2: 716-18, which refers to "Sam the Jew."]

35. *Ind. Journal*, Jan. 20, 1838; *Ind. Doc. Journal*, 1837: nos. 30, 32. Milroy to Tipton, Jan. 19, Feb. 13, Mar. 23, 1838, in Riker and Robertson, *Tipton Papers*, 3: 509, 539-40, 576-77.

36. Gibson to Judah, Jan. 29, 1838, Judah MSS; *Ind. Senate Journal*, 1837-1838: 529-49; Dorothy Riker, ed., *Messages and Papers Relating to the Administration of David Wallace, Governor of Indiana, 1837-1840* (Indianapolis: Ind. Historical Bureau, 1963): 19. Blake to Tipton, Jan. 18, 1838, quoted in *Tipton Papers*, 3: 506-7.

37. *Ind. Doc. Journal*, 1838: no. 13. [Judah, of course, denied personal interest, but Hunt to Judah, Aug. 30, 1838, Judah MSS, indicated such motives.]

38. *Ind. Journal*, Feb. 15, 1839.

39. Ibid.

40. *Ind. Democrat*, Feb. 28, 1839. *Ind. Journal*, Feb. 15 and 19, 1839.

41. *Ind. House Journal*, 1838: 501-2.

42. *Ind. Doc. Journal*, 1838: nos. 1, 8. Riker, *Wallace Messages and Papers*: 25-26. *Ind. Journal*, Nov. 10, 1838, Feb. 15 and 19, 1839.

43. Davis, "Illinois Legislators": 125-34. *Ill. State Register*, Feb. 13, 1837. [Davis argues that these changes had little effect, but his data (140) reveal a shift toward the antibank position.]

44. *Frontier State*: 307-8. *Ill. State Register*, Aug. 14, Sept. 1 and 29, Oct. 6, Nov. 4, 1837. *Chicago Banks*, 1: 122-23; Davis, "Illinois Legislators": 168-69.

45. *Ill. State Register*, June 3, 1837. Ibid., June 24, 1837. Ibid., July 22 and 28, 1837. Ibid., Aug. 14, Sept. 8, Nov. 10, 1837. *Richmond Enquirer*, in ibid., July 28, 1837. [The confused situation in Virginia is the subject of Howard Braverman, "The Economic and Political Background of the Conservative Revolt in Virginia," *Va. Magazine of History and Biography* 60 (Apr. 1952): 266-87, and *Jacksonians Versus the Banks*: 215-73.]

46. *Sangamo Journal*, Jan. 2, May 21, 1836, Jan. 28, Feb. 11, 1837. Roy P. Basler, ed., *The Collected Works of Abraham Lincoln* (New Brunswick, N. J.: Rutgers Univ. Press, 1953), 1: 61-69. 240-41. *Ill. House Journal*, 1838-1839: 10-17. *See also: Chicago Banks*, 1: 126-27; Charles Manfred Thompson, "The Illinois Whigs Before 1846," *UTSSS* 4 (Mar. 1915): 66.

47. *Sangamo Journal*, May 6, 1837. Ibid., May 20, 1837. Ibid., June 24, 1837. Ibid., Aug. 26, 1837. *See also:* ibid., June 3, 10, and 17, 1837.

48. Ibid., Sept. 9, 1837.

49. Ibid., Oct. 28, Nov. 19, Dec. 16, 1837; *Belleville Representative*, in ibid., Nov. 19, 1837. *Ill. State Register*, Mar. 2, 1838. [Interestingly, each party termed the other loco-foco. See: *Sangamo Journal*, June 24, July 29, 1837; *Ill. State Register*, Aug. 4, 1837, Mar. 9, 1838.]

50. *Frontier State*: 136-49, 236-50; Thompson, "Illinois Whigs": 59-60.

51. *Ill. State Register*, Aug. 3, 1838. *Sangamo Journal*, Oct. 13, 1838. *See also*: ibid., June 2, Aug. 4 and 10, Oct. 28, 1838.
52. Carlin's speech of Dec. 7, 1838, in *Ill. Governors*, 1838-42.
53. *Biographical Dictionary of the American Congress, 1774-1961* (Washington, D.C.: U.S. Government Printing Office, 1961): 1745; John S. C. Abbott, *The History of the State of Ohio* (Detroit: R. D. S. Tyler and Co., 1875): 752-54.
54. *Ohio Doc.*, 1837-38: no. 1; 1838-39: no. 1. [The discussion of Vance's thought is based upon these two addresses.]
55. *Western Hemisphere* (Columbus, Ohio), May 17, 1837, quoted in *Passing of the Frontier*: 335. *Ohio Statesman*, Aug. 9, 16, and 23, 1837. *Newark Advocate*, in ibid., Oct. 24, 1837.
56. *Ohio Statesman*, Dec. 5, 1837. *Norwalk Experiment*, in ibid., Dec. 19, 1837. *Cleveland Advertiser*, in *Ohio Statesman*, May 9, 1838; *Ohio Statesman*, Nov. 22 and 23, 1837. Ibid., Nov. 13, 1837. Ibid., Feb. 6, 1839. *Cleveland Gazette*, in ibid., Feb. 6, 1839. *Ohio Doc.*, 1839-40: no. 1.
57. The Democratic position is clearly presented in *Ohio Statesman*, July 3 and 27, 1838; resolutions of Hamilton County Democrats in Dawson to Van Buren, Sept. 29, 1837, Van Buren MSS; Brough to Tappan, Nov. 8, 1838, Tappan MSS, Ohio Historical Society.
58. *Ohio Statesman*, July 3, 1838. Taylor to Thurman, Sept. 11, 1838, Thurman MSS. *Ohio Statesman*, July 31, 1838. Manuscript speech, Sept. 15, 1838, in Thurman MSS. *Ohio Statesman*, July 20, 1838. *See also: Passing of the Frontier*: 347-51; *Ohio Statesman*, July 27, 1838; Buchanan to Thurman, Sept. 25, 1838, Thurman MSS. [The official organ of the Democratic party, the *Washington Globe* (reprinted in *Ohio Statesman*, Aug. 14, 1838), praised Shannon's speech, and the *Ind. Democrat*, Dec. 28, 1838, showed agreement with his ideas as expressed in his inaugural.]
59. Vance to Sloan, Mar. 4, 1838, quoted in *Passing of the Frontier*: 348. *Ohio Doc.*, 1838-39: no. 1.
60. Brough to Tappan, Nov. 8, 1838, Tappan MSS, Ohio Historical Society. Shannon's inaugural is in the *Ohio Statesman*, Dec. 14, 1838. Osman Castle Hooper, "John Brough," *OAHP* 13 (1904): 44-50; quotation from Brough's report: 47.
61. "Banks and the Currency Question," *Democratic Review* 2 (Apr. 1838): 16. "Free Banking," ibid., 5 (Feb. 1839): 237-38. *See also*: "The True Principles of Commercial Banking," ibid., 2 (May 1838): 113-28; "The Resumption of Specie Payments," ibid., 2 (June 1838): 211-24; "The Credit System," ibid., 3 (Nov. 1838): 195-232, "The Credit System: Second Article," ibid., 5 (Feb. 1839): 147-76; "The General Banking Law of the State of New York," ibid., 5 (May 1839): 427-46.
62. The economic views of western Whigs like Judah, Vance, Lincoln, and Woodbridge were similar to those of William Seward. See his message on the New York free banking law in Charles Z. Lincoln, ed., *State of New York: Messages from the Governors* (Albany: J. B. Lyon Co.,

1909), 3: 727; and Glyndon G. Van Deusen, *William Henry Seward* (New York: Oxford Univ. Press, 1967): 55-71.

# Chapter 4

1. *Iowa Reporter,* in *Chicago Democrat,* May 11, 1837.
2. *Chicago Democrat,* May 1, 1839. *Cincinnati Advertiser and Journal,* July 31, Aug. 5, 1839.
3. For the county resolutions see: *Chicago Democrat,* Aug. 16, 1839; *Ill. State Register,* Nov. 23 and 30, Dec. 25, 1839. *Ind. Democrat,* Nov. 26, 1839; Oct. 23, 1839.
4. For Democratic responses to Shannon, see: Hough to Thurman, Dec. 8 and 15, 1839, Thurman MSS; Brough to Medill, Dec. 7, 1839, Thomas to Medill, Dec. 11, 1839, Barker to Medill, Dec. 13, 1839, and Cassell to Medill, Dec. 18, 1839, Medill MSS, opposed Shannon, while Ewing to Medill, Dec. 8, 1839 and Gaylord to Medill, Dec. 26, 1839, Medill MSS, praised him; Tappan to Stanton, Dec. 10, 1839, Tappan MSS, Ohio Historical Society.
5. Jackson to Dawson, Dec. 9, 1839, in John J. Whealen, ed., "The Jackson-Dawson Correspondence," *Bulletin of the Historical and Philosophical Society of Ohio* 16 (Jan. 1958): 17-18. *Cincinnati Advertiser and Journal,* Dec. 8, 10, 12, 13, 14, 16, and 18, 1839. *Springfield Republican,* in *Ohio State Journal,* Dec. 17, 1839. [The *Ohio Statesman* did defend Shannon on Dec. 25 and 28, 1839. Actually, Dawson's demands and those of the Cincinnati meeting were more strict than Jackson's as expressed in his December 9 letter to Dawson. Jackson suggested complete stockholder liability; limitation of issue to double the specie "in their vaults"; the revocation of charters of banks not redeeming notes and a bank commission to wind up those banks' affairs; gradual elimination of notes under $10; and making directors "liable to be prosecution [*sic*] for high misdemeanors and subject to fine and imprisonment to the state penitentiary."]
6. Carlin's message of Dec. 11, 1839, in *Ill. Governors,* 1838-42.
7. *Daily Advertiser,* Aug. and Sept. 1838 and Oct. 1839 issues. *Democratic Free Press,* Apr. 18, Sept. 5 and 12, 1838, Mar. 13, 1839. *Daily Advertiser,* Nov. 6, 1839.
8. *Michigan Political Parties:* 19-21, 35-37; Society of the State of Mich., "Letters of Lucius Lyon," *Pioneer Collections* 27 (1897): 525. [It is my contention that "conservatives" such as Berry were the opponents of banks, while the "radicals" associated with Mason were not.]
9. *Democratic Free Press,* Sept. 18 and 25, Oct. 16, 1838, Mar. 11, 1839. Norvell's letter, in ibid., Dec. 11, 1839. [DeJarmo Jones was the Whig mayor of Detroit and later a state senator.]
10. Ibid., quoted in *Governors' Messages,* 1: 287-89. [The valedictory was not delivered but was printed in the *Daily Free Press.*]
11. *Sangamo Journal,* Jan. 7, 1940. Roy P. Basler, ed., *The Collected Works of Abraham Lincoln* (New Brunswick, N. J.: Rutgers Univ. Press, 1953), 1: 159.

12. The majority report is in Basler, *Abraham Lincoln*, 1: 185-95. *See also*: George Williams Dowrie, "The Development of Banking in Illinois, 1817-1863," *Univ. of Ill. Studies in the Social Sciences* 2 (Dec. 1913): 90-94; *Chicago Banks*, 1: 136.

13. Dowrie, "Banking in Illinois": 94-95. *Ill. State Register*, Dec. 25, 1839. Basler, *Abraham Lincoln*, 1: 237-38. *Chicago American*, in *Detroit Daily Advertiser*, Jan. 31, 1840.

14. Dowrie, "Banking in Illinois": 95-100. Carlin's message is in *Ill. House Journal*, 1840: 18-30.

15. James, *Chicago Banks*, 1: 137-40; *Frontier State*: 311.

16. *Daily Advertiser*, Oct. 15, 1839. *See also*: ibid., Oct. 7 and 9, 1839.

17. Stuart to Woodbridge, Dec. 23, 1839, Woodbridge MSS.

18. Wells to Chapman, Dec. 30, 1839, ibid. *See also*: Dwight to Jones, Jan. 20, 1841, ibid. [Wells's plan was quite similar to the Populists' Sub-treasury plan.]

19. *Governors' Messages*, 1: 320-24.

20. *Daily Advertiser*, Jan. 17, 1840.

21. Ibid., Jan. 17, 1840. *Mich. Senate Doc.*, 1840: no. 49.

22. *Mich. Senate Doc.*, 1840: no. 50. *See also*: Rowland to Woodbridge, July 17, 1841, Woodbridge MSS.

23. *Daily Advertiser*, Mar. 7 and 9, 1840.

24. Joseph Gantz, "A History of Banking Legislation and Currency in Michigan, 1835-1865" (A.M. thesis, Wayne State Univ., 1936): 50-52. *Mich. Senate Journal*, 1840: 441. *Mich. House Journal*, 1840: 393. *Daily Advertiser*, Apr. 4, 1840.

25. *Daily Advertiser*, June-July, 1841; quotation, June 22 issue. *Genesee Northern Advocate*, in ibid., June 23, 1841; *Niles Republican*, in *Daily Advertiser*, June 23, July 1, 1841; *Flint Advocate*, in *Daily Advertiser*, June 29, 1841; *Ann Arbor State Journal*, in *Daily Advertiser*, June 30, 1841; *Jonesville Expositor*, in *Daily Advertiser*, July 1, 1841; *Mich. State Gazette*, in *Daily Advertiser*, July 5, 1841; *Marshall Statesman*, in *Daily Advertiser*, July 30, 1841; quotations are from the *Ann Arbor State Journal* article and a letter from "Old Guard" in *Daily Advertiser*, June 22, 1841. [The *Advertiser's* position on redeemable currency and a national bank was supported by the *Chicago American*, in *Daily Advertiser*, June 30, 1841.]

26. Butler to Woodbridge, July 9, 1841, Rowland to Woodbridge, June 25, July 17, 1841, Gates to Woodbridge, June 29, 1841, Trumbull to Woodbridge, July 5, 1841, and Stuart to Woodbridge, July 16, 1841, Woodbridge MSS.

27. *Daily Advertiser*, Aug. 23, 1841.

28. *Ind. Doc. Journal*, 1839, pt. 2: no. 9. *Ind. Doc. Journal*, 1840, pt. 1: no. 8. *Ind. Doc. Journal*, 1840, pt. 1: no. 9.

29. Test to editor of the *Richmond Palladium*, Jan. 19, 1841, in Gayle Thornbrough, ed., *Messages and Papers Relating to the Administration of Samuel Bigger, Governor of Indiana, 1840-1843* (Indianapolis: Ind. Historical Bureau, 1964): 193-95. For the opinions of other Whigs, see: "Introduction," Dorothy Riker, ed., *Messages and Papers Relating to*

*the Administration of David Wallace* (Indianapolis: Ind. Historical Bureau, 1963): 40-41. Judah to Noble, Oct. 26, 1839, in ibid.: 277-78. *See also*: Judah to editor of *Vincennes Saturday Gazette*, Jan. 24, 1841, in ibid.: 198-200; Judah to editor of *Vincennes Saturday Gazette*, Feb. 8, 1841, in ibid.: 226-28.

30. *Mich. Senate Doc.*, 1840; no. 51. *Democratic Free Press*, Jan. 29, Feb. 5 and 19, Mar. 11 and 18, Apr. 1, 1840; *Free Press . . . Extra*, Jan. 24, 1840. [It is significant that on March 11, 1840, the paper reprinted an *Ohio Statesman* article charging that *all* Whigs came from the "non-producing" groups in society: bankers, officeholders, lawyers, doctors, merchants, and speculators.]

31. E. Byron Thomas, "Political Ideas and Activities of John Stewart Barry, 1831-1851" (M.A. thesis, Northwestern Univ., 1935), covers Barry's political career. He voted for the free banking law and the first suspension of specie payments, but generally attempted to limit the powers of banks.

32. *Adrian Whig*, in *Daily Advertiser*, Oct. 25, 1841; *Detroit Daily Free Press*, Sept. 4 and 8, 1841. *See also*: *Detroit Daily Advertiser*, Sept. 8, 9, and 28, Oct. 6, 16, and 20, 1841; the Democratic platform is in Paul A. Randall, ed., "Gubernatorial Platforms for the Political Parties of Michigan (1834-1864)" (A.M. thesis, Wayne State Univ., 1937): 30-37.

33. Thomas, "John Stewart Barry": 81-84. *Governors' Messages*, 1: 448-54, 467-68, 489, 506-7; ibid., 2: 33, 81. Randall, "Gubernatorial Platforms": 64-70. *Daily Free Press*, Sept. 22, 1845; *Marshall Expounder*, in ibid., Sept. 11, 1845; *Pontiac Jacksonian*, in *Daily Free Press*, Feb. 6, 1846.

34. Chamberlain to the editor of *Goshen Democrat*, Dec. 11, 1841, in Thornbrough, *Bigger Administration Messages*: 395-98. *Ind. State Sentinel*, Jan. 17, 1842. Brown to Tappan, Jan. 31, 1842, Tappan MSS, Library of Congress. *Ind. Doc. Journal*, 1843, pt. 1: no. 8, 316. *See also*: Brown to Tappan, Nov. [?], 1841, Tappan MSS, Library of Congress; Chamberlain to the editor of *Goshen Democrat*, Dec. 11, 1841, in Thornbrough, *Bigger Administration Messages*: 349-54; William F. Harding, "The State Bank of Indiana," *JPE* 4 (Dec. 1895): 12; Logan Esarey, "State Banking in Indiana, 1814-1873," *Ind. Univ. Studies* 10 (Apr. 1912): 257. [Throughout the rest of the decade Whitcomb's speeches did not mention the state bank.]

35. *Frontier State*: 312; Dowrie, "Banking in Illinois": 113; Thomas Ford, *History of Illinois* (Chicago: S. C. Griggs and Co., 1854): 294-304. *Sangamo Journal*, May 13, 1842.

36. On Democratic views see: *Ohio Statesman*, July 30, 1839; *Cincinnati Advertiser and Journal*, Dec. 7, 1839; Hough to Thurman, Dec. 15, 1839, Thurman MSS; Baker to Medill, Dec. 13, 1839, Buchanan to Medill, Dec. 15, 1839, Brough to Medill, Dec. 25, 1839, Medill MSS; William Allen's speech of June 3, 1840, Allen MSS; Kaufman to Van Buren, Nov. 15, 1840, Van Buren MSS; Tappan to Stanton, Feb. 20, 1840, Tappan MSS, Ohio Historical Society. *Cincinnati Advertiser and Journal*, Jan. 11 and 14, 1840. [There are excellent discussions of Ohio

politics and banking questions in *Passing of the Frontier*: 387-440; *Jacksonian Versus the Banks*, 123-59; and Edgar A. Holt, "Party Politics in Ohio, 1840-1850," *OAHP* 37 (July 1928): 447-69. The following draws heavily on these accounts.]

37. Holt, "Party Politics in Ohio": 486-91, 510. *Ohio State Journal*, Oct. 23, Dec. 7, 1839, Jan. 4, Oct. 7, 1840.

38. *Ohio Doc.*, 1841-42: no. 76. Holt, "Party Politics in Ohio": 515-17. *Ohio State Journal*, Feb. 13, 1841.

39. Hastings to Van Buren, Oct. 23, 1841, Van Buren MSS; *Passing of the Frontier*: 406-7; Holt, "Party Politics in Ohio": 518-24; *Ohio Statesman*, Jan. 13, 1842. *See also*: Jackson to Van Buren, Nov. 12, 1840, and Kaufmann to Van Buren, Nov. 15, 1840, Van Buren MSS; Lumpkin to Tappan, Oct. 19, 1841, Tappan MSS, Library of Congress; *Ohio Statesman*, Dec. 14, 1841.

40. *Ohio Doc.*, 1841-42: no. 1. *Ohio State Journal*, Feb. 19, 1842. Dawson to Van Buren, Sept. 22, 1841, Van Buren MSS.

41. Stanton to Tappan, Jan. 30, 1842, Tappan MSS, Ohio Historical Society; *Passing of the Frontier*: 407-8; C. C. Huntington, "A History of Banking and Currency in Ohio Before the Civil War," *OAHS* 24 (1915): 405-6. Quote from Knapp to Tappan, Dec. 27, 1841, Tappan MSS, Library of Congress.

42. This distinction is made clearly by Democratic governor Thomas W. Bartley in *Ohio Doc.*, 1844-45: no. 1. *Cincinnati Enquirer*, Jan. 11 and 16, 1843. Stanton to Tappan, Dec. 27, 1842, Feb. 8, 1843, Tappan MSS, Ohio Historical Society.

43. Follett to Corwin, Nov. 18, 1842, in L. Belle Hamlin, ed., "Selections from the Follett Papers, II," *Quarterly Publications of the Historical and Philosophical Society of Ohio* 9 (July–Sept. 1914): 77-80. *See also*: Huntington, "Banking and Currency in Ohio": 406; Holt, "Party Politics in Ohio": 531-32, 539. *Ohio State Journal*, Feb. 26, 1842; Hans L. Trefousse, *Benjamin Franklin Wade* (N. Y.: Twayne Publishers, 1963): 48-51; Wade to his wife, Feb. 22, 1843, Wade MSS; Follett to Smith, Feb. 3, 1843, in L. Belle Hamlin, ed., "Selections from the Follett Papers, III," *Quarterly Publications of the Historical and Philosophical Society in Ohio* 10 (Jan.–Mar. 1915): 406.

44. For sample Whig opinion see: Fern to Corwin, Jan. 18, 1841, Ohio Governors' Papers; Wade to his wife, Dec. 4, 1842, Wade MSS; Follett to Corwin, Nov. 4 and 8, 1842, in Hamlin, "Follett Papers, II": 73-75, 77-80. Corwin to Follett, Nov. 12, 1842, in ibid.: 75-77. *Passing of the Frontier*: 411, 415. *Ohio State Journal*, Apr. 8, 1843. [In the November 12 letter Corwin explained to Follett, "Let it be at once understood that I have no childish egotism to be mortified by the rejection of 'my plan' of a State Bank; any system which is practicable and has in view the employment even of the present amt. of Bank capital in the State, and presents tolerable, even much less security to the public, than (as I conceive) a State Bank would, will be very cheerfully embraced by me." I take this to be a fairly typical Whig view in its emphasis on practicability, security, and sufficient resources.]

45. *Passing of the Frontier*: 415-18; Holt, "Party Politics in Ohio": 552-58. For sample Democratic opinion see: Stanton to Tappan, Jan. 8, Feb. 8, 1843, Tappan MSS, Ohio Historical Society; Medary to Van Buren, Apr. 27, 1843, Van Buren MSS; Medill to Tappan, Jan. 12, 1844, Morrison to Tappan, Mar. 19, 1844, Tappan MSS, Library of Congress; Whitman to Allen, Dec. 15, 1843, Medill to Allen, Jan. 11, 1844, Hough to Allen, Jan. 17, 1844, Faran to Allen, Feb. 13 and 25, 1844, Woodside to Allen, Feb. 14, 1844, Allen MSS. *Ohio Doc.*, 1843-44: no. 1. On Tod and his problems see: Whitman to Allen, Jan. 4, 1844, Tod to Allen, Mar. 22, 1844, Medill to Allen, Jan. 11, 1844, Allen MSS; Stanton to Tappan, Apr. 28, 1844, Tappan MSS, Ohio Historical Society; Parry to Van Buren, Mar. 29, 1844, Van Buren MSS; Birchard to Tappan, Mar. 20, 1844, Tappan MSS, Library of Congress.

46. *Ohio Doc.*, 1844-45: no. 1. [Thomas Bartley's views very much resembled those of Adam Smith, whom he referred to in this speech and later in the debate on the Kelley law.]

47. *Ohio Doc.*, 1844-45: no. 2.

48. Fritz Redlich, *The Molding of American Banking* (New York: Hafner Publishing Company, 1947) 2: 25-26; James L. Bates, *Alfred Kelley: His Life and Work* (Columbus: privately printed, 1888), passim. Daniel J. Boorstin, *The Americans: The National Experience* (New York: Random House, 1965): 113-68.

49. Bates, *Alfred Kelley*: 132-39. The committee report is in *Ohio Senate Journal*, 1845: app. 40-43. Huntington, "Banking and Currency in Ohio": 421-26.

50. *Ohio Senate Journal*, 1845: 399; *Ohio House Journal*, 1845: 534-36; *Huron Reflector*, in *Ohio State Journal*, Jan. 16, 1845; Clarke to Bartley, Mar. 12, 1845, Ohio Governors' Papers. *Canton Repository*, in *Ohio State Journal*, Jan. 23, 1845. *Ohio State Journal*, Jan. 7 and 20, Mar. 13, 1845. *Ohio Doc.*, 1845–46: no. 1. [These generalizations are based on editorials dealing with the bank issue from the *Lebanon Star*, *Circleville Herald*, *Cincinnati Gazette*, *Huron Reflector*, *Cincinnati Chronicle*, *Xenia Torch-Light*, *Zanesville Gazette*, *Newark Gazette*, *Buckeye Eagle*, *Piqua Register*, *Summit Beacon*, *Guernsey Times*, *Eaton Register*, *Athens Messenger*, *Steubenville Herald*, *Canton Repository*, *Buckeye Sentinel*, *Milan Tribune*, *Urbana Gazette and Citizen*, *Western Reserve Chronicle*, *Cincinnati Atlas*, *Fayette County Washingtonian*, *Harrison County Standard*, *Holmes County Whig*, *Gallipolis Journal*, *Mount Vernon Times*, *Clermont Courier*, *Tuscarawas Advocate*, *Belmont Chronicle*, *Conneaut Reporter*, *Ashtabula Sentinel*, *Lima Reporter*, *Geauga Republican and Whig*, *Morgan County Independent*, *Painesville Telegraph*, and *Lancaster Gazette and Express* that were reprinted in the *Ohio State Journal*, Jan. 13, 16–18, 20-25, and 29, Feb. 1, 1845.

51. Larwell to Allen, Dec. 26, 1844, Allen MSS; *Ohio Statesman*, Jan. 31, 1845. Bartley to Medill, Jan. 27, 1845, Medill MSS. Bartley to Allen, Jan. 25, 1845, Allen MSS. Bartley to Tappan, Mar. 16, 1845, Tappan MSS, Ohio Historical Society. *Ohio Statesman*, Feb. 1, 1845. On Hamilton Company meeting see: ibid., Feb. 4, 1845. *Cadiz Sentinel*, in

ibid., Feb. 3, 1845. Disney's speech, in ibid., Feb. 5, 1845. *See also*: *Toledo Blade*, in *Ohio State Journal*, Jan. 23, 1845. [The vote on repeal is in *Ohio House Journal*, 1845: 851-52.]

52. Holt, "Party Politics in Ohio": 562-69. Wolcott to Tappan, Sept. 22, 1844, Tappan MSS, Library of Congress. *Ohio Statesman*, July 7, 1845. Democratic meeting of Hamilton County resolutions are reprinted in Huntington, "Banking and Currency in Ohio": 428, n. 13. On Democratic opinion see: Knapp to Tappan, Sept. 2, 1845, Tappan MSS, Library of Congress; Barker to Medill, Jan. 18, 1845, Flood to Medill, Apr. 17, 1845, Medill MSS; Goodfellow to Allen, Jan. 20, 1845, Wolcott et al. to Allen, Mar. 11, 1845, Medary to Allen, Apr. 29, 1845, Allen MSS.

53. *Ohio State Journal*, 1845 issues, especially for Oct.

# Chapter 5

1. *Democratic Review* 29 (July 1851): 3. *See also*: Bayrd Still, "An Interpretation of the Statehood Process, 1800 to 1850," *MVHR* 23 (Sept. 1936): 189-204.
2. *Democratic Review* 29: 5, 15.
3. *Democratic Review* 13 (Dec. 1843): 563-76; ibid., 18 (Apr. 1846): 243-56; ibid.: 18 (June 1846): 403-20; ibid., 19 (Nov. 1846): 339-48; ibid., 20 (Mar. 1847): 195-204. *Dayton Empire*, Sept. 2, 1847, in *Speeches, Arguments, Addresses and Letters of Clement L. Vallandigham* (New York: J. Walker and Co., 1864): 548.
4. Louise Phelps Kellogg, "The Admission of Wisconsin to Statehood," and Frederic L. Paxson, "Wisconsin—A Constitution of Democracy," in Milo M. Quaife, ed., *The Movement for Statehood, 1845-46* (Madison: State Historical Society of Wis., 1918): 18-29, 30-52.
5. *Frontier State*, 407-9; *Debates of 1847*: i-xix; Charles Kettleborough, ed., *Constitution Making in Indiana* (Indianapolis: Ind. Historical Commission, 1916) 1: xv-ccxli.
6. Kettleborough, *Constitution Making in Indiana*: xxvi-lxxxiii.
7. Frederick W. Stevens, *Michigan Constitutional Convention of 1850* (n.p.).
8. *Passing of the Frontier*: 478-79; Carl Wittke, ed., *The History of the State of Ohio*, vol. 4, Eugene H. Roseboom, *The Civil War Era, 1850-1873*: 124-35.
9. *Ind. State Journal*, Jan. 5, 1847.
10. *Dayton Empire*, Sept. 2, 1847, in *Clement L. Vallandigham Speeches*: 547. *Western Review* (1846): 208, quoted in Henry C. Hubbart, *The Older Middle West* (New York: Russell and Russell 1963): 11.
11. *Milwaukee Courier*, Nov. 18, 1846, reprinted in Milo M. Quaife, ed., *The Struggle Over Ratification, 1846-1847* (Madison: State Historical Society of Wis., 1920): 200-2. *Ind. Doc. Journal*, 1847, pt. 1: no. 7.
12. These and the following generalizations are based on numerous issues of the Democratic and Whig newspapers, the addresses of the mid-

western governors, and speeches made in the conventions. Only specific references will be cited. The views of midwestern Democrats varied little from the views expressed in the articles in the *Democratic Review* cited above in n. 3. Compare them with the articles of "Jehu Bickerstaff" in the *Chicago Democrat*, Mar. 23 and 30, Apr. 6, 1847.

13. This was no mandate for executive leadership as some historians following Schlesinger, *Age of Jackson*, have charged; it reflected a view of the executive as a peoples' tribune. A. B. Johnson, "The Veto Power of the President," *Democratic Review* 28 (Mar. 1851): 243-47, represents the same view of executive power on the national level as was expressed by Democrats in these conventions in relation to governors' powers.

14. *Cleveland Plain Dealer*, Feb. 27, 1850, quoted in Roseboom, *Civil War Era*: 127.

15. Robinson to Medill, Oct. 9, 1847, Medill MSS. Helfenstein to Strong, Dec. 2, 1846, Strong MSS; for party platforms see: *Ohio Statesman*, Jan. 8 and 9, 1846; *Ill. State Register*, May 5, 1848; Paul A. Randall, "Gubernatorial Platforms for the Political Parties of Michigan (1834-1864)" (A.M. thesis, Wayne State Univ., 1937): 66; *Milwaukee Courier*, Dec. 30, 1846; Quaife, *Struggle Over Ratification*: 204-7. For governors' messages see: *Governors' Messages*, 2: 173-75; *Ill. House Journal*, 1846-47: 8-17.

16. For the state conventions see: *Ind. Doc. Journal*, 1845, pt. 1: no. 4, and 1848, pt. 1: no. 6; *Ind. State Sentinel*, Mar. 19, May 28, 1846, Jan. 11, 1849. *Goshen Democrat*, Dec. 27, 1848, in *Ind. State Sentinel*, Jan. 31, 1849. *Ind. State Sentinel*, Jan. 1, 1850.

17. *Governors' Messages*, 2: 173. For comment on the misinterpretation of French's 1846 position, see: Ficklin to French, Dec. 30, 1846, French MSS. *Ill. House Journal*, 1849: 8-17. French's message, Jan. 6, 1851, in *Ill. Governor*, 1846-53. *Ohio Press*, July 23, 1847, quoted in C. C. Huntington, "A History of Banking and Currency in Ohio Before the Civil War," *OAHS* 24 (1915): 434.

18. *Daily Lafayette Courier*, Mar. 1, 1850, reprinted in Kettleborough, *Constitution Making in Indiana*: 212-13. [The Democratic point of view is expressed in the histories of Weisenburger, Holt, Roseboom, Esarey, Kettleborough, Pease, Cole, Paxson, Streeter, and Hubbart. While it is not difficult to see why Indiana Democrats would make charges such as those that appeared in the *Daily Lafayette Courier*, it is rather surprising that these historians have believed them.]

19. In "A Case Study of Party Formation: Michigan, 1835," *MA* 50 (Apr. 1968): 83-107, and in *Mass Political Parties*, Ronald P. Formisano has shown the importance of the "citizen suffrage" issue, something often misunderstood by historians, although it was noted by contemporaries (see *Ill. Journal*, Sept. 16, 1847).

20. Quoted in Logan Esarey, *A History of Indiana* (Fort Wayne, Ind.: Hoosier Press, 1924), 1: 513, n. 10. *See also: Ind. Journal*, Jan. 7, Mar. 23, 1850.

21. *Madison Express*, July 28, quoted in Quaife, *The Movement for State-*

*hood*: 154-56. Ibid., Aug. 4, 1846, quoted in Quaife, *Movement for Statehood*: 157-59.

22. *Milwaukee Sentinel and Gazette*, Oct. 9, 1846. King to Tweedy, Nov. 1, 1846, Tweedy MSS. Milo M. Quaife, ed., *The Constitution of 1846* (Madison: State Historical Society of Wis., 1919): 185-86, for Tweedy's attempt to include free banking, and app. 1, roll call no. 17, for the vote defeating the measure.

23. For reports of contemporary politicians, see: Whiton to Tweedy, Nov. 4, 1846, Tweedy MSS; Darling to Tenney, Mar. 20, 1847, Tenney MSS; Knapp to Strong, Mar. 21, 1847, Strong MSS. Baker to Strong, Mar. 20, 1847, ibid., Ryan to Strong, Feb. 18, 1847, ibid. Bover to Tenney, Apr. 13, 1847, Tenney MSS.

24. *Debates of 1847*: 169-70.

25. *Debates of Ohio*, 1: 707-8; quotation: 708.

26. Ibid., 1: 708. *Debates of Ind.*: 221. *Debates of Mich.*: 692.

27. Quaife, *Convention of 1846*: 85. *Debates of 1847*: 124.

28. *Debates of Mich.*: 582-83. Ibid.: 581.

29. *Debates of Ohio*, 1: 707. Ibid., 2: 525, 406. On Reemelin see: Charles Reemelin, *Life of Charles Reemelin, In German Carl Gustav Rümelin. From 1814-1892* (Cincinnati: Weier and Daiker, 1892).

30. *Debates of Ohio*, 1: 708. *Debates of 1847*: 88.

31. *Debates of Mich.*: 569-70. *Debates of Ohio*, 2: 799-800.

32. *Madison Wisconsin Argus*, Nov. 24, 1846, reprinted in Quaife, *Struggle Over Ratification*: 155-56.

33. *Debates of Ohio*, 1: 708. Ibid., 2: 800.

34. *Debates of 1847*: 654.

35. *Debates of Ind.*: 1481.

36. *Debates of Ohio*, 1: 260. Ibid., 1: 158-62; *Debates of Ind.*: 1469-73, 1511-17.

37. *Debates of Ohio*, 1: 162. Ibid., 1: 475. *Debates of 1847*: 656, 328. *Debates of Mich.*: 570. *Debates of Ind.*: 1442.

38. *Debates of Ohio*, 2: 539-45; 1: 408-709. [The latter includes the Whig "Minority Report on Currency and Banking."]

39. *Debates of Ind.*: 690, 648, 1474-78, 1647, 1436-40. On classical political economy see: Lionel Robbins, *The Theory of Economic Policy in English Classical Political Economy* (London: Macmillan and Co., 1952), and Jacob Viner, "Adam Smith and *Laissez Faire*," in John Maurice Clark et al., *Adam Smith, 1776-1926* (Chicago: Univ. of Chicago Press, 1928). [Examples of contrasting views of Whig policies are: Sidney Fine, *Laissez Faire and the General-Welfare State* (Ann Arbor: Univ. of Mich. Press, 1956): 3-25; Louis Hartz, *The Liberal Tradition in America* (New York: Harvest Books, 1955): 89-142; Dexter Perkins, "William H. Seward," *N. Y. History* 15 (Apr. 1934): 160-74; Major L. Wilson, "The Concept of Time and The Concept of Political Dialogue in the United States, 1828-48," *American Quarterly* 19 (winter 1967): 619-44.]

40. *Debates of Ind.*: 1475. Ibid.: 1646.

41. Ibid.: 1647. Ibid.: 647.

42. *Debates of Ohio,* 1: 709. *Debates of Ind.:* 1539.
43. Dodge to Strong, Oct. 10, 1846, Strong MSS. Quaife, *Convention of 1846:* app. 1, roll calls 15, 17, 19. Milo M. Quaife, ed., *The Attainment of Statehood* (Madison: State Historical Society of Wis., 1928), app. 1, roll call 108. For Democratic opinion see: Crawford to Strong, Oct. 15, 1846, Helfenstein to Strong, Mar. 15, 1847, Knapp to Strong, Mar. 21, 1847, Strong MSS; Tenney to Tenney, Jan. 12, Feb. 25, 1847, Noonan to Tenney, Feb. 26, 1847, Darling to Tenney, Mar. 20, 1847, Tenney MSS.
44. Quaife, *Struggle Over Ratification:* 698, for the popular vote. On the early development of Wisconsin see the excellent studies by Joseph Schafer, *The Wisconsin Lead Region* (Milwaukee, Wis.: State Historical Society of Wis., 1932), and "The Yankee and the Teuton in Wisconsin," *Wis. Magazine of History* 6 (Dec. 1922-June 1923): 125-45, 261-79, 386-402: 7 (Sept. 1923, Mar. 1924): 3-19, 148-71.
45. *Debates of 1847:* 101-3, 808.
46. The conflict of these subcultures in Indiana and Illinois is the subject of Richard Lyle Power's *Planting Corn Belt Culture: The Impress of the Upland Southerner and the Yankee in the Old Northwest* (Indianapolis: Ind. Historical Society, 1953), and Carrie Prudence Kofoid, "Puritan Influences in the Formative Years of Illinois History," *Trans. of the Ill. State Historical Society for the Year 1905* (1906): 261-338.
47. *Debates of Ohio,* 2: 412-13, 423-24.
48. In this analysis I have drawn on *Jacksonians Versus the Banks:* 160-89, an excellent discussion of Ohio illustrating the importance of the German element in the opposition to banks. In the continuing argument about the political allegiance of the Germans in the 1850s, no one denies the Germans' overwhelming earlier support of the Democracy. This is clear in the letters of the politicians of the time; see, e.g., Schmit to Corwin, Aug. 3, 1850, Corwin MSS, Library of Congrss. Walter Stix Glazier, "Cincinnati in 1840: A Community Profile" (Ph.D. diss., Univ. of Mich., 1968), shows the strong German and Irish support for the Democratic party. Thomas A. Flinn, "Continuity and Change in Ohio Politics," *Journal of Politics* 24 (Aug. 1962): 521-44, emphasizes the importance of the "ethnic-sectional basis for Ohio Politics."
49. *Debates of Ind.:* 1446-47, 1524, 1526. Harvey Lewis Carter, "A Decade of Hoosier History, Indiana, 1850-1860" (Ph.D. diss., Univ. of Wis., 1938), is extremely helpful on the distribution of the Indiana population.
50. These descriptions of the economic and occupational bases of the parties are from Glyndon G. Van Deusen, *The Jacksonian Era, 1828-1848* (New York: Harper Row Publishers, 1959): 92-93, and *The History of Indiana,* vol. 3, Emma Lou Thornbrough, *Indiana in the Civil War Era, 1850-1880* (Indianapolis: Ind. Historical Bureau, 1965): 43. Nearly every book on the subject accepts this class explanation for party action. Van Deusen's and Thornbrough's books are cited to show the acceptance of this explanation by the most recent scholarship. In all fairness to most authors, it must be said that they usually hedge.

Edgar A. Holt says of the Whigs that they were "essentially conserva-tive" and "generally men of wealth and standing in their communities." Except on the questions concerning Negro rights, they were the party of the "*status quo.*" He also says, however, "But not all members of the Whig party were reactionary. A large portion consisted of farmers and day laborers, and the party in its appeal for support throughout the decade had never lost sight of the needs of the common man" ("Party politics in Ohio, 1840-1850," *OAHP* 37 (July 1928): 589-90). Similarly, *Jacksonians Versus the Banks* accepts the importance of cul-tural factors in the case of the Germans, although Sharp basically re-turns to an economic formulation of the problem. *See also*: Frank Otto Gatell's survey of recent writings, "Beyond Jacksonian Consensus," in Herbert J. Bass, ed., *The State of American History* (Chicago: Quad-rangle Books, 1970): 358-59.

51. Lewis E. Atherton, "The Pioneer Merchant in Mid-America," *Univ. of Mo. Studies* 14 (Apr. 1839): 23-26, Alexandra McCoy, "Political Affiliations of American Economic Elites: Wayne County, Michigan, 1844, 1860, As a Test Case" (Ph.D. diss., Wayne State Univ., 1965), and Glazier, "Cincinnati in 1840," are the only quantitative studies concerning the affiliations of midwestern businessmen, and their con-clusions are slightly different. My examination of the lawyers in the constitutional conventions of Illinois and Wisconsin shows a slightly larger percentage of lawyers among Whigs, but the difference is too small to be at all significant. McCoy's sample includes more Whig than Democratic lawyers, but the latter make up a larger proportion of their party's representation. Further study might show that those lawyers who mainly dealt with businessmen tended to be Whigs while those who dealt with large landholders tended to be Democrats. This is suggested in Charles G. Sellers, "Who Were the Southern Whigs?" *AHR* 59 (Jan. 1954): 335-46.

52. *Michigan Political Parties*: 20. Williams to Woodbridge, Aug. [?], 1838, Woodbridge MSS.

53. McCoy, "Political Affiliations": ch. 5, chart 10. [Unfortunately the number of bankers in McCoy's sample is extremely small. Frank Otto Gatell's study "Money and Party in Jacksonian America: A Quantita-tive Look at New York City's Men of Quality," *Political Science Quar-terly* 82 (June 1967): 235-52, clearly demonstrates the drift of the very rich from the Jacksonian party in New York; Gatell quite plausibly ascribes this to Jacksonian financial policy. Unfortunately he does not include matedial on occupation. According to Lee Benson, *The Concept of Jacksonian Democracy* (Princeton: Princeton Univ. Press, 1961): 159-60, New York State bankers split evenly between the parties in 1844. While this may not seem logical, it also fits the Michigan situation. Sharp in *Jacksonians Versus the Banks*: 189, repeats the traditional ar-gument in his discussion of Ohio and refers to the case of Micajah T. Williams described in Harry N. Scheiber, "Entrepreneurial and West-ern Development: The Case of Micajah T. Williams," *Business History Review* 37 (winter 1963): 345-68. One could point to David Disney,

however, one of Williams's partners in the Ohio Life Insurance and Trust Company, as an example of a banker who remained a Democrat serving in the state legislature in the mid-1840s and playing a leading role in the party in the state (see Holt, "Party Politics in Ohio": passim). A comparison of these individual cases with the bankers listed in Glazier, "Cincinnati in 1840": 267-97, suggests further problems. Disney is listed as a hardware merchant and a Whig. Williams is listed, but without either occupation or political affiliation. Of the 25 bankers included, 10 are Whigs and none Democrats. Obviously the majority of Cincinnati bankers did not involve themselves in partisan matters. A reconsideration of the whole question is in order. Formisano in *Mass Political Parties* complicates this by showing convincingly the primacy of citizen suffrage over financial policy in party formation in Michigan and by suggesting its importance elsewhere.]

54. Lawrence Howard Sabbath, "Analysis of the Political Leadership in Wayne County, Michigan, 1844" (A.M. thesis, Wayne State Univ., 1965) is the only study of midwestern party leadership. Formisano's study of Michigan, *Mass Political Parties*, grew out of his dissertation, "The Social Basis of American Voting Behavior: Wayne County, Michigan, 1837-1852, As a Test Case" (Wayne State Univ., 1966). Formisano spent more effort destroying the economic interpretation in his dissertation than in his book, which stresses his own interpretation. There is need for quantitative studies of the political leadership in all states. The conclusions of Sabbath's study conform to those of Benson, *Jacksonian Democracy*: 64-85; Grady McWhiney, "Were the Whigs a Class Party in Alabama?" *Journal of Southern History* 23 (Nov. 1957): 510-22; Thomas Alexander et al., "Who Were the Alabama Whigs?" *Ala. Review* 16 (Jan. 1963): 5-19; and W. Wayne Smith, "Jacksonian Democracy on the Chesapeake: Class, Kinship and Politics," *Md. Magazine of History* 63 (Mar. 1968): 55-67. Milton Henry, "Summary of Tennessee Representation in Congress from 1845-1861," *Tenn. Historical Quarterly* 10 (June 1951): 140-48, draws different conclusions from similar data. There is little reason to believe that the as yet unexamined states of the Old Northwest would show a drastically different pattern.

55. For examples of explicit appeals to particular economic groups, see: *Debates of Ohio*, 1: 709, and 2: 795-800; *Debates of 1847*: 270-72, 274, 280, 653; *Debates of Mich.*: 560, 569, 575-76, 691-92, 734; *Debates of Ind.*: 689, 694, 995, 1440, 1452-53, 1456, 1471, 1490, 1503, 1525. *Milwaukee Sentinel and Gazette*, Oct. 17, 1846.

56. Van Deusen, *Jacksonian Era*: 96. Corwin to Greene, June 16, 1846, in L. B. Hamlin, ed., "Selections from the William Greene Papers I," *Quarterly Publications of the Historical and Philosophical Society of Ohio* 13 (Jan.-Mar. 1918): 15-16. *See also:* Glyndon G. Van Deusen, "Some Aspects of Whig Thought and Theory in the Jacksonian Period," *AHR* 63 (Jan. 1958): 305-22; Thomas B. Alexander et al., "The Basis of Alabama's Ante-Bellum Two-Party System," *Ala. Review* 19 (Oct. 1966): 243-76; Wilson, "Concept of Time": 619-44; Joel H. Silbey,

*The Shrine of Party: Congressional Voting Behavior, 1841-52* (Pittsburgh: Univ. of Pittsburgh Press, 1967): passim; Herbert Ershkowitz and William G. Shade, "Consensus or Conflict? Political Behavior in the State Legislatures during the Jacksonian Era," *Journal of American History* 58 (Dec. 1971): 591-621.

57.  *Mass Political Parties*: 101-36; Benson, *Jacksonian Democracy*: 198-207; Rodney Owen Davis, "Illinois Legislators and Jacksonian Democracy" (Ph.D. diss., Univ. of Iowa, 1966): 293-317; Ershkowitz and Shade, "Consensus or Conflict": 606-11, 615-17. *See also*: Ralph Barton Perry, *Puritanism and Democracy* (New York: Vanguard Press, 1944), Marvin Meyers, *The Jacksonian Persuasion* (Stanford: Stanford Univ. Press, 1957), and Clifford S. Griffin, *Their Brother's Keepers* (New Brunswick, N. J.: Rutgers Univ. Press, 1960), which shed some light on this question. *Mass Political Parties* contains a convincing interpretation of the relationship between religion and attitudes toward government, which seems to fit my further research on Illinois. The concepts of "commercial-mindedness" and "agrarian-mindedness" are developed by Lee Benson in *Turner and Beard* (Glencoe, Ill.: Free Press, 1960): 214-28. Like Benson, I have used them not to "denote classes, socio-economic status groups, or occupations—[but] . . . ways of thinking": 216.

58.  Meyers, *Jacksonian Persuasion*: vii.

# Chapter 6

1.  Maurice O'Rear Ross, "An Analysis of Commercial Banking in the State of Indiana" (Ph.D. diss., Univ. of Chicago, 1936): 57-58. C. C. Huntington, "History of Banking and Currency in Ohio Before the Civil War," *OAHS* 24 (1915): 346. For Michigan see: Joseph Gantz, "A History of Banking Legislation and Currency in Michigan, 1835-1865" (A.M. thesis, Wayne State Univ., 1936): 74. [Alice E. Smith, *George Smith's Money* (Madison: State Historical Society of Wis., 1965), deals with the career of one of the most interesting private bankers in the area.]

2.  For the Democratic platforms see: *Ohio Statesman*, Jan. 10, 1850, July 7, 1851; *Ind. State Sentinel*, Feb. 2, 1850; *Ill. State Register*, May 5, 1848; *Waukesha Democrat* (Wis.), Sept. 18, 1849. *See also*: an Indiana party hack's statement of his "political creed," Kyle to Wright, May 10, 1852, Wright MSS. [The Democratic platforms in Michigan merely referred to John Barry's record (Paul A. Randall, ed., "Gubernatorial Platforms for the Political Parties of Michigan [1834-1864]" [A.M. thesis, Wayne State Univ., 1937]: 83-84, 88-90).]

3.  *Governor's Messages*, 2: 161-75, 180-206, for Barry's messages of Jan. 7, 1850, and Feb. 5, 1851; quotation: 185.

4.  French's message of Jan. 2, 1849, in *Ill. House Journal*, 1849: 8-17; quotation: 16. Dewey's messages of Jan. 10, 1850, and Jan. 9, 1851, in *Wis. Senate Journal*, 1850: 12-30, and *Wis. Assembly Journal*, 1851:

19-40. *See also*: Rubin Wood's message of Dec. 12, 1850, in *Ohio Doc.*, 1845-50: no. 7. [Joseph Wright's messages are silent on this issue, but see James Witcomb's messages of Jan. 11, 1848, and Dec. 6, 1848, in *Ind. Doc. Journal*, 1847, pt. 1: no. 7, and 1848, pt. 1: no. 6.

5.  *Wis. Assembly Journal*, 1851: 25-26. Thompson (n.d.), Wright MSS. For Wright's personal views *see also*: Mather to Wright, May 7, 1859, Wright MSS, and his messages from the mid-1850s discussed below.

6.  *Kalamazoo Gazette*, in *Detroit Daily Free Press*, Jan. 17, 1850. *Madison Daily Democrat*, Jan. 11, 1851. *See also: Daily Free Press*, Jan. 8, 16, and 17, 1850; *Adrian Watchtower* and *Niles Republican*, in ibid., Jan. 17, 1850; *Ohio Statesman*, Dec. 10, 1850, for examples of support.

7.  These generalizations are based on my reading of Wentworth's *Chicago Democrat* during these years, Stanley Llewellyn Jones, "Anti-Bank and Anti-Monopoly Movements in Illinois, 1845-1862" (Ph.D. diss., Univ. of Ill., 1926): 67-76, and Don E. Fehrenbacher, *Chicago Giant: A Biography of "Long John" Wentworth* (Madison: American History Research Center, 1957): 73-74. Quotations are from the *Chicago Democrat*, Mar. 21, Aug. 29, 1848. [There was some disparity between rhetoric and practice. Wentworth was a big land speculator. As Fehrenbacher notes, "In the very period that the *Democrat* cried out most angrily against 'land monopoly' its editor was laying the foundation of a large fortune by purchasing land for speculative purposes" (112-113). In later years Wentworth also became a Chicago "booster."

8.  Speech delivered in the Wisconsin legislature, in *Madison Daily Democrat*, Feb. 25, 1851. For the hard money Democrats concept of free banking, see: Samuel Medary, *The New Constitution* (Columbus, 1849): 234-35; *Ohio Statesman*, Mar. 3, 1851; *Waukesha Democrat*, Mar. 9, 1852.

9.  *The Centennial History of Illinois*, vol. 3, Arthur Charles Cole, *The Era of the Civil War* (Chicago: A. C. McClurg & Co., 1922): 94-95.

10. Huntington, "Banking and Currency in Ohio": 436. Jones, "Movements in Illinois": 77-79; Bessie Louise Pierce, *A History of Chicago* (New York: Alfred A. Knopf, 1937), 2: 118-19. *Ind. Journal*, Feb. 2 and 9, 1852.

11. *Detroit Daily Free Press*, Jan. 1, 1851. Ibid., Mar. 5, 8, 15, 17, 20, and 24, 1851. *See also: Detroit Daily Advertiser*, Mar. 10 and 18, 1851.

12. *Detroit Daily Free Press*, Mar. 25 and 26, 1851. *Mich. House Journal*, 1851: 364.

13. James to Corwin, Dec. 18, 1850, Corwin MSS, Library of Congress; *Jacksonians Versus the Banks*: 157-58; Huntington, "Banking and Currency in Ohio": 436-38.

14. For Whig views see: *Ohio State Journal*, Mar. 13 and 16, 1850; *Eaton Register*, in ibid., Mar. 18, 1850.

15. *Ohio Statesman*, Mar. 3, 4, and 22, 1851. *See also: Cincinnati Enquirer*, Mar. 26, 1851.

16. Jones, "Movements in Illinois": 79-83. Reddick to French, Nov. 27, 1848, French MSS.

17. *Ill. State Register*, June 27, 1850, in particular. *Chicago Democrat*, Feb.

16, Dec. 14, 1850. Petition of W. C. Mathews and Theodore Grant, in Jones, "Movements in Illinois": 86-87.

18. Ibid.: 86. *Rock Island Advertiser*, in *Ill. State Journal*, Jan. 3, 1850. *Tazwell Mirror*, in *Ill. State Journal*, Oct. 12, 1850. *Ill. State Journal*, Jan. 3, Oct. 12, Nov. 23, Dec. 19, 1850. Ameda Ruth King, "The Last Years of the Whig Party in Illinois, 1847-1856," *TISHS*, 1925 (n.d.): 128. *Chicago Tribune*, in *Ill. State Journal*, Oct. 12, 1850.

19. *Ill. Governor*, 1846-53, for French's message of Jan. 6, 1851.

20. *Peoria Democratic Press*, in *Ill. State Journal*, Jan. 3 and 17, Feb. 22, Mar. 17, 1851. Ibid., Jan. 3 and 8, Feb. 21 and 24, Mar. 3 and 7, 1851. *Chicago Daily Democrat*, Jan. 6, Feb. 11, 12, 14, 18, and 20, May 8, 1851. Wilcox to French, Jan. 27, 1851, French MSS. *See also: Morgan Journal*, in *Ill. State Journal*, Mar. 18 and 19, 1851.

21. *Ill. State Journal*, Jan. 10, Apr. 21 and 24, 1851. Jones, "Movements in Illinois": 88-89. *Ill. House Journal*, 1851: 62, 292-93. *Ill. Senate Journal*, 1851: 330-31.

22. *Ill. House Journal*, 1851: 474-77.

23. George William Dowrie, "The Development of Banking in Illinois, 1817-1863," *Univ. of Ill. Studies in the Social Sciences* 2 (Dec. 1913): 135-38.

24. *Ill. House Journal*, 1851: 478-79; *Ill. Senate Journal*, 1851: 421. See the issues of Jan., Feb., and Mar. 1851 for the exchange between the *Ill. State Register* and the *Ill. State Journal*. For analyses of the vote, see: Jones, "Movements in Illinois": 91; King, "Whig Party in Illinois": 129. For reports of northern county representatives, see: Ames to French, Apr. 12, Dec. 16, 1851, Sweat to French, Dec. 22, 1851, French MSS.

25. Dowrie, "Banking in Illinois": 138; Jones, "Movements in Illinois": 90-102. *Chicago Daily Democrat*, May 8, 1851. Woodward to French, May 7, 1851, French MSS; *Ill. State Register*, Oct. 20, 1851. *Rock Island Weekly Republican*, Oct. 8, 1851, quoted in Jones, "Movements in Illinois": 91. [Aside from the *Ill. State Register* and other papers Jones mentions, articles from the *Benton Standard, Joliet Signal*, and *Charleston Globe*, reprinted in *Ill. State Journal*, Mar. 10 and 21, 1851, show that these papers opposed the law.]

26. *Ill. State Register*, Feb. 13, 1851. Manly to French, Mar. 2, 1851, French MSS. *Benton Standard*, in *Ill. State Journal*, Mar. 10, 1851. *See also: Ill. State Register*, Apr.–May and Sept.–Oct. 1851 issues for articles attacking the free banking bill or banks.

27. *Galena Jeffersonian*, quoted in Jones, "Movements in Illinois": 98, n. 88.

28. Judge William Thomas to the *Morgan Journal*, in *Ill. State Journal*, Feb. 22, 1851. *Chicago Daily Journal*, in *Ill. State Journal*, Apr. 21, 1851. *Ill. State Journal*, Aug. 7, 1851.

29. *Chicago Commercial Advertiser*, in *Ill. State Journal*, Mar. 3, 1851.

30. *Ill. State Journal*, Jan.–Apr. and Sept.–Oct. 1851, nearly every issue. Two articles from the *Chicago Journal*, in ibid., Feb. 22, Apr. 21, 1851.

31. *Ill. State Journal*, Mar. 1, 1851. Ibid., Apr. 9, 1851. Ibid., Apr. 16 and

19, 1851, for "Mechanic" letters; *Ill. State Register*, Apr. 17, 1851, for response to "Mechanic." *See also*: *Ill. State Journal*, Apr. 16 and 19, 1851.

32. Cole, *Era of the Civil War*: 96-97; *Chicago Daily Democrat*, Nov. 5, 1851. [In the article here cited, aside from analyzing the vote, Wentworth disassociated his paper from the law that he opposed.]

33. Richard Lyle Power, *Planting Corn Belt Culture* (Indianapolis: Ind. Historical Society, 1953): passim; Carrie Prudence Kofoid, "Puritan Influence in the Formative Years of Illinois History," *Trans. of the Ill. State Historical Society for the Year 1905* (1906): passim; Henry Clyde Hubbart, *The Older Middle West, 1840-1880* (New York: Russell and Russell, 1963): 30-52. Thomas Ford, *History of Illinois* (Chicago: S. C. Griggs and Co., 1854): 280. *Alton Tri-Weekly Telegraph*, Nov. 20, 1851, quoted in Jones, "Movements in Illinois": 105. *Peoria Democratic Press*, Mar. 10, 1847. *See also*: Harry E. Pratt, ed., "Illinois As Lincoln Knew It: A Boston Reporter's Record of a Trip in 1847," *Papers in Ill. History and Trans. for the Year 1937* (1938): 153, 166-67; *Ill. State Register*, Feb. 21, 1851; *Cairo Sun*, Nov. 20, 1851.

34. On migration into Illinois, see: *Frontier State*: 1-32, 173-93; Cole, *Era of the Civil War*, 1-26; Lois Kimball Mathews, *The Expansion of New England: The Spread of New England Settlement and Institutions to the Mississippi River, 1620-1865* (New York: Houghton Mifflin and Company, 1909): 171-221; William V. Pooley, *The Settlement of Illinois from 1830 to 1850* (Madison: Univ. of Wis., 1908).

35. On economic behavior see: Ford, *History of Illinois*: 100, who describes different responses to the market, and Stanley Elkins and Eric McKitrick, who relate the existence of numerous small towns to the "market-conscious population" in their essay "A Meaning for Turner's Frontier: Part I, Democracy in the Old Northwest," *Political Science Quarterly* 69 (Sept. 1954): 341. On response to social questions, see: Cole, *Era of the Civil War*: 204-11, 230-35; Kofoid, "Puritan Influences": passim; Herbert Wiltsee, "The Temperance Movement, 1848-1871," *Papers in Ill. History* (Springfield: Ill. State Historical Society, 1938): 82-92; John Pullman, "Changing Attitudes Toward Free Public Schools in Illinois," *History of Education Quarterly* 7 (summer 1967): 191-208.

36. Lee Benson, *The Concept of Jacksonian Democracy* (Princeton: Princeton Univ. Press, 1961), and *Mass Political Parties* have disputed the notion of a monolithic foreign-born vote; and Sharp's analysis in *Jacksonians Versus the Banks* suggests German opposition to banks. Both *Jacksonian Democracy* and *Mass Political Parties* found the "New British" to be strongly Whiggish and to share many of the Yankees' economic and social attitudes. *See also*: Rowland Tappan Berthoff, *British Immigrants in Industrial America, 1790-1950* (Cambridge, Mass.: Harvard Univ. Press, 1953), passim; Charlotte Erickson, "British Immigrants in the Old Northwest, 1815-1860," in David M. Ellis, ed., *The Frontier in American Development* (Ithaca, N. Y.: Cornell Univ. Press, 1969): 323-56.

37. For the opinion of northern Democrats, see: Rust to French, Nov. 27,

1851, Ames to French, Dec. 2 and 16, 1851, Sweat to French, Dec. 22, 1851, French MSS. Douglas to Lanphier, Dec. 30, 1851, in Robert W. Johannsen, ed., *The Letters of Stephen A. Douglas* (Urbana: Univ. of Ill. Press, 1961): 235. *See also*: McRoberts to Koerner, Dec. 6, 1851, in Evarts B. Greene, ed., "Letters of Gustav Koerner, 1837-1863," *TISHS*, 1907 (1908): 241-43.

38. *Waukesha Democrat*, Nov. 20 and 27, Dec. 13, 1849. *Milwaukee Commercial Advertiser*, Nov. 27, 1849. *Milwaukee Daily Sentinel and Gazette*, Jan. 21, 22, 26 and 31, Feb. 2 and 5, 1850.

39. The positions of Strong and the other Democrats are expressed in the *Daily Democrat*, Feb. 7 and 25, 1851. *Daily Sentinel and Gazette*, Jan. 29, 1851. For the position of Whig papers, see: *Milwaukee Daily Sentinel and Gazette*, Jan. 7, 9, and 29, Feb. 24, 1851; *Mineral Point Tribune*, in ibid., Jan. 20, 1851. For the position of Democratic papers, see: *Waukesha Democrat*, Feb. 4, Mar. 25, 1851; *Madison Daily Democrat*, Jan. 14; *Potosi Republican*, in *Daily Sentinel and Gazette*, Jan. 29, 1851.

40. *Daily Sentinel and Gazette*, Sept. 29, Oct. (nearly every issue), Nov. 4, 1851; *Mineral Point Tribune*, in ibid., Oct. 25, 1851.

41. Upham to Strong, Oct. 10, 1851, Strong MSS (printed); *Daily Sentinel and Gazette*, Oct. 7, 1851. *Waukesha Democrat*, Mar. 25 and Nov. 4, 1851; *Daily Wis.*, in *Waukesha Democrat*, Oct. 21, 1851.

42. *Wis. Senate Journal*, 1852: 10-26. *Madison Daily Argus*, Jan. 16, 1852. Strong to Brown, Feb. 2, 1852, Strong MSS (printed). *See also*: *Madison Daily Argus*, Jan.-Apr. 1852 passim; *Waukesha Democrat*, Mar. 9, 1852.

43. *Wis. Assembly Journal*, 1852: 667; *Wis. Senate Journal*, 1852: 669. *See also*: *Daily Sentinel and Gazette*, Apr. 17, 1852, for a contemporary analysis.

44. *Potosi Republican*, in *Daily Sentinel and Gazette*, Oct. 27, 1852; *Waukesha Democrat*, Dec. 2, 1852; *Madison Democrat and Argus*, Dec. 4 and 31, 1852; *Daily Sentinel and Gazette*, Oct. 20 and 27, Nov. 2 and 6, 1851. The vote is given by county in the *Daily Sentinel and Gazette*, Dec. 22, 1852. On the German and Irish response to the banks, see: *Daily, Sentinel and Gazette*, Jan. 7, 1851; Baird to Tweedy, Nov. 7, 1847, Tweedy MSS. On Germans and Irish-Catholics, *see also*: Crawford to Strong, Oct. 15, 1846, Helfenstein to Strong, Dec. 2, 1846, Mar. 15, 1847, Knapp to Strong, Mar. 21, 1847, E. G. Ryan to Strong, Feb. 18, 1847, Strong MSS.

45. Logan Esarey, "State Banking in Indiana, 1814-1873," *Ind. Univ. Studies* 10 (Apr. 1912): 278-81. *Ind. Journal*, Feb. 9, 1852.

46. *Ind. House Journal*, 1851: 340, for the committee and its report. *Ind. Journal*, Feb. 25, 1852. *Ind. Senate Journal*, 1851: 1018-19; *Ind. House Journal*, 1851: 1058.

47. Philip M. Crane, "Governor Jo Wright: Hoosier Conservative" (Ph.D. diss., Ind. Univ., 1963): 160-64. *Ind. State Sentinel*, Feb. 2, 1850, Dec. 30, 1852, Aug. 22, 1854. Elliot to Wright, May 27, 1852, Wright MSS. *Ind. Doc. Journal*, 1852, pt. 1: no. 2, 23-27.

48. See Harvey Lewis Carter, "A Decade of Hoosier History, Indiana, 1850-1860" (Ph.D. diss., Univ. of Wis., 1938): 1-46, on settlement patterns and cultural conflict.

49. *Ind. Journal*, Jan. 29, Feb. 2 and 9, Apr. 30, 1852. Hudson's speech supporting the free banking law, in ibid., Feb. 25, 1852.

50. This is clear in the confused discussion in Ross's otherwise good dissertation, "Commercial Banking in Indiana": 59. One set of problems caused by this confusion is the subject of William G. Shade and Ronald P. Formisano, "The Concept of Agrarian Radicalism," *MA* 52 (Jan. 1970): 3-30.

51. This conception of Jacksonian behavior is similar to what Richard Hofstadter and others have called "status politics." See: Richard Hofstadter, *The Paranoid Style in American Politics and Other Essays* (New York: Alfred A. Knopf, 1965); Daniel Bell, ed., *The Radical Right* (Garden City, N. Y.: Doubleday and Company, 1963); Joseph R. Gusfield, *The Symbolic Crusade: Status Politics and the American Temperance Movement* (Urbana: Univ. of Ill. Press, 1963). These extremely important works err in assuming the "reality" or concreteness of economic issues in contrast to those involving "simply" ethnic or religious differences. This study insists that the importance of economic issues is often primarily symbolic and denies that conflicts over values and cultural styles are "unreal."

52. Milton M. Gordon, *Assimilation in American Life: The Role of Race, Religion and National Origins* (New York: Oxford Univ. Press, 1964), is extremely suggestive; but assimiliation ideologies in the nineteenth century deserve far greater study.

# Chapter 7

1. The general development of the American economy in this period is treated in Henry David et al., *The Economic History of the United States*, vol. 4, George Rogers Taylor, *The Transportation Revolution, 1815-1860* (New York: Holt, Rinehart and Winston, 1951): 345-51, and Douglass C. North, *The Economic Growth of the United States, 1790-1860* (New York: W. W. Norton and Company, 1966): 206-15. While Taylor comments on "Wealth and Income" (392-95), an extensive analysis is presented in Ralph Andreano, "Trends in Economic Welfare, 1790-1860," in idem, ed., *New Views on American Economic Development*, (Cambridge, Mass.: Schenkman Publishing Company, 1965): 131-67.

2. Taylor, *Transportation Revolution*: 79, table.

3. David, *Economic History*, vol. 3, Paul W. Gates, *The Farmer's Age* (New York: Holt, Rinehart and Winston, 1960): 156-99, 171, table; North, *Economic Growth*: 135-56. Willis Dunbar, *Michigan* (Grand Rapids, Mich.: William B. Eerdmans Publishing Company, 1965): 349-91.

4. C. C. Huntington, "A History of Banking and Currency in Ohio Before

the Civil War," *OAHS* 24 (1915): 438. On Indiana see: *Banks and Politics*: 617-22. *Chicago Banks*, 2: 215-18. Berry, *Western Prices*: 510.

5. McRoberts to Koerner, Dec. 6, 1851, in Evarts B. Greene, ed., "Letters to Gustav Koerner, 1837-1863," *TISHS*, 1907 (1908): 214-43; Stanley Llewellyn Jones, "Anti-Bank and Anti-Monopoly Movements in Illinois, 1854-1862" (Ph.D. diss., Univ. of Ill., 1947): 121-24. Some Democrats' reactions to the bill appear in: Rust to French, Nov. 27, 1851, Ames to French, Dec. 2 and 16, 1851, Sweat to French, Dec. 22, 1851, Wake (?) to French, Dec. 27, 1851, Breese to French, Jan. 5, 1852, and (?) to French, Jan. 21, 1852, French MSS; Douglas to Lamphier, Dec. 30, 1851, in Robert W. Johannsen, ed., *The Letters to Stephen A. Douglas* (Urbana: Univ. of Ill. Press, 1961): 235.

6. *Ind. Doc. Journal*, 1852, pt. 1: no. 2 (mislabeled pt. 2: no. 1).

7. Huntington, "Banking and Currency in Ohio": 438, 456-61, and Carl Wittke, ed., *The History of the State of Ohio*, vol. 4, Eugene H. Roseboom, *The Civil War Era, 1850-1873* (Columbus: Ohio State Archaeological and Historical Society, 1944): 136-37, discuss this period in general.

8. James L. Bates, *Alfred Kelley, His Life and Works* (Columbus: privately printed, 1888): 143-71; Kelley is quoted on 153, the Democrat on 151.

9. *Ohio Statesman*, Jan. 10, 1850.

10. Huntington, "Banking and Currency in Ohio": 458, 462; Roseboom, *Civil War Era*: 138. *Cincinnati Enquirer*, Apr. 11 and 13, 1856. *Ohio State Journal*, Jan. 18, Feb. 14, 20, and 21, Mar. 18 and 22, 1856; quotation, Feb. 14, 1856, issue.

11. Harold M. Somers, "The Performance of the American Economy before 1860," in Harold F. Williamson, ed., *The Growth of the American Economy: An Introduction to the Economic History of the United States* (New York: Prentice-Hall, 1946): 334-35; Margaret G. Myers, *The New York Money Market: Origins and Development* (New York: Columbia Univ. Press, 1931): 140; *Western Prices*: 510-17.

12. Most suggestive on the rise of the Republican party are: Joel H. Silbey, *The Transformation of American Politics, 1840-1860* (Englewood Cliffs, N. J.: Prentice-Hall, 1967); Andrew Wallace Crandall, *The Early History of the Republican Party, 1854-1856* (Gloucester, Mass.: Peter Smith, 1960); Michael F. Holt, *Forging a Majority: Pittsburgh, 1848 to 1860* (New Haven, Conn.: Yale Univ. Press, 1969); Eric Foner, *Free Soil, Free Labor, Free Men: The Ideology of the Republican Party Before the Civil War* (New York: Oxford Univ. Press, 1970); Henry C. Hubbart, *The Older Middle West, 1840-1880* (New York: Russell and Russell, 1963): 1-29, 88-116; *Mass Political Parties*: 217-331; *Mich. Political Parties*: 100-253; Roseboom, *Civil War Era*: 255-312; *The History of Indiana*, vol. 3, Emma Lou Thornbrough, *Indiana in the Civil War Era, 1850-1880* (Indianapolis: Ind. Historical Bureau, 1965): 1-84; Harvey Lewis Carter, "A Decade of Hoosier History, Indiana, 1850-1860," (Ph.D. diss., Univ. of Wis., 1938); Charles Zimmerman, "The Origin and Rise of the Republican Party in Indiana

from 1854 to 1860," *Ind. Magazine of History* 13 (Sept. 1917): 211-69, and (Dec. 1917): 349-412; a series of articles by Roger Van Bolt: "Indiana in Political Transition, 1851-1853," *Ind. Magazine of History* 44 (June 1953): 131-60, "Fusion out of Confusion," ibid. (Dec. 1953): 353-90, and "The Rise of the Republican Party in Indiana, 1855-1856," ibid., 51 (Sept. 1955): 185-220; *The Centennial History of Illinois*, vol. 3, Arthur Charles Cole, *The Era of the Civil War* (Chicago: A. C. McClurg & Co., 1922): 101-52; Don E. Fehrenbacher, *Prelude to Greatness: Lincoln in the 1850's* (New York: McGraw-Hill Book Company, 1964): 1-47; and Aaron Morey Boom, "The Development of Sectional Attitudes in Wisconsin, 1848-1861" (Ph.D. diss., Univ. of Chicago, 1948).

13.  Aside from the above-mentioned books, the issue of nativism is treated in detail in Sister M. Evangeline Thomas, *Nativism in the Old Northwest* (Washington, D.C.: Catholic Univ., 1936); Eugene H. Roseboom, "Salmon P. Chase and the Know Nothings," *MVHR* 25 (Dec. 1938): 335-50; Carl Fremont Brand, "The History of the Know Nothing Party in Indiana," *Ind. Magazine of History* 18 (1922): 47-81, 177-206, 266-306; and John P. Senning, "The Know Nothing Movement in Illinois from 1854-56," *Journal of the Ill. State Historical Society* 7 (Apr. 1914): 7-33. Don E. Fehrenbacher's "Illinois Political Attitudes, 1854-1861" (Ph.D. diss., Univ. of Chicago, 1951), is generally helpful, particularly on nativism: 165-82. Especially helpful for the nativist position are the letters in the Hamilton MSS for these years.

14.  The economic aspects of this question are emphasized in Madison Kuhn, "Economic Issues and the Rise of the Republican Party in the Northwest" (Ph.D. diss., Univ. of Chicago, 1940): 1-132. The antisouthern, rather than simple antislavery, aspects of the Kansas-Nebraska Act are indicated by Fehrenbacher in his biography of John Wentworth, *Chicago Giant* (Madison: American History Research Center, 1957), as well as the two works cited in notes 11 and 12. On negrophobia see: Eugene H. Berwanger, *The Frontier Against Slavery: Western Anti-Negro Prejudice and the Slavery Extension Controversy* (Urbana: Univ. of Ill. Press, 1967); and Ronald P. Formisano, "Attitudes to Colored Suffrage, Michigan, 1835-1861," *Mich. History* 41 (spring 1972): 58-89.

15.  Paul A. Randall, ed., "Gubernatorial Platforms for the Political Parties of Michigan (1834-1864)" (A.M. thesis, Wayne State Univ., 1937): 113. *Ohio State Journal*, Oct. 6, 1856. [Foner, *Free Soil*: 168-72, asserts that the Republicans dropped the bank issue in the interest of party unity.]

16.  Sigler to Davis, Jan. 22, 1855, quoted in Philip M. Crane, "Governor Jo Wright" (Ph.D. diss., Ind. Univ. 1963): 169. Indiana banking questions are covered in ibid., 166-80, and in Logan Esarey, "State Banking in Indiana, 1814-1873," *Ind. Univ. Studies* 10 (Apr. 1912): 283-96.

17.  Hugh McCulloch, *Men and Measures of Half a Century* (New York: Scribner's Sons, 1888): 127-28. [Esarey, "State Banking in Indiana": 288-96, tried to unravel the question of corruption in the legislature,

but was unconcerned with the party affiliation of the men involved. The above conclusions resulted from a check of the party affiliations of those the investigation showed to have been part of the "syndicate" and to whom "bribes" had been offered. Some of the "bribes" merely promised branches for the districts of those bribed or an extension of an opportunity to purchase stock. *See also:* Fletcher Diary, Jan.-Feb. 1855, for the attitudes of the bankers who opposed the politicians on the rechartering of the state bank, and the *Journal of the Bank Investigating Committee, A Select Committee of the Indiana Senate, 1857* (Indianapolis: Joseph J. Bingham, State Printer, 1857).]

18.  Esarey, "State Banking in Indiana": 297; McCulloch, *Men and Measures:* 128-30. [For the opinion of a man who believed he was cheated, see Law to Wright, May 26, 1856, Wright MSS.]

19.  *Ind. House Journal,* 1855: 764, and *Ind. Senate Journal,* 1855: 551, for the votes. *Ind. Senate Journal,* 713-16, for Wright's veto. Hunt to Wright, Aug. 18, 1856, Hall to Wright, Feb. 29, 1856, Wright MSS.

20.  *Ind. Doc. Journal,* 1854, pt. 1: no. 2. [*Ind. Journal,* Feb. 7 and 17, 1855, shows a shift from free banking, but this reflected the new publisher's attitudes rather than a shift in party policy.]

21.  *Ind. State Sentinel,* Aug. 22, 1854. Crane, "Governor Jo Wright": 168. *Ind. Doc. Journal,* 1854, pt. 1: no. 5.

22.  Esarey, "State Banking in Indiana": 286-87. *Ind. House Journal,* 1855: 230-31, for introduction of the bill, and ibid.: 614 and *Ind. Senate Journal,* 1855: 616 for the vote. [In both houses 21 Democrats (40%) opposed banks of any sort, and 7 more opposed free banks but voted for the Bank of the State of Indiana. Among the Fusionists 5 (7%) opposed all banks and 14 opposed free banks and voted for the Bank of the State of Indiana.]

23.  *Ind. State Sentinel,* Mar. 15, 1855. *Ind. Senate Journal,* 1855: 721-24, for veto.

24.  Ibid.: 720 for vote on repeal. [The party affiliations of two men opposed to free banking are not known. This interpretation is based on my reading of the letters in the Wright MSS in which a conflict between Indianapolis and the rest of the state is suggested and his veto is applauded.]

25.  Commentary on the Democratic response can be found in: Hall to Wright, Feb. 29, 1856, Conduitt to Wright, June 23, 1856, Hunt to Wright, Aug. 5 and 19, 1856, Wright MSS. *Ind. Doc. Journal,* 1857, pt. 1: no. 5. [The letters from Hunt to Wright in the Wright MSS are extremely interesting. Hunt was Wright's antislavery, banker cousin who opposed the free banking system and suggested ways to reform it. He bitterly opposed the Bank of the State of Indiana, but seems to have been one of those who was "persuaded" to support it. These letters, like Fletcher's Diary, show how complex the attitudes of a man who might be categorized simply as "banker" could be.]

26.  *Ohio Doc.,* 1853-54: no. 9. Ibid., 1855-56: no. 1. *Cincinnati Enquirer,* Oct. 14, 1855, Jan. 17, 1856.

27.  On Chase's gubernatorial candidacy see: *Cincinnati Enquirer,* Oct. 14,

1855; Roseboom, "Salmon P. Chase and the Know Nothings": 345-46; *Cincinnati Gazette*, July 18, 1855, quoted in ibid.: 346, n. 44. *See also*: Taylor to Chase, May 10, 1855, Chase MSS, Library of Congress.

28. For Democratic and Free-Soil views on Chase's position, see: *Ohio Statesman*, Feb. 22, 1849; Miller to Chase, Jan. 21, 1850, Taylor to Chase, Feb. 9, 1850, Chase to (?), July 18, 1850, Chase MSS, Library of Congress. Chase to Sutliff, Dec. 20, 1850, in American Historical Association, "Diary and Correspondence of Salmon P. Chase," *Annual Report of the American Historical Association for the Year 1902* (1903), 2: 226. *Ohio Doc.*, 1855-56: no. 4.

29. Roseboom, *Civil War Era*: 314; Huntington, "Banking and Currency in Ohio": 465. *Cincinnati Enquirer*, Jan. 17 and 26, Mar. 28, Apr. 13, 1856.

30. *Massillon News*, in *Ohio State Journal*, Jan. 18, 1856. *Ohio State Journal*, Feb. 20, 1856. Ibid., Apr. 2, 1856. *See also*: Ibid., Jan. 18, Feb. 5, 6, 8, and 9, Mar. 22 and 24, 1856.

31. *Ohio State Journal*, Oct. 19, 21, 22, and 23, 1856.

32. Huntington, "Banking and Currency in Ohio": 465-66. *Ohio Doc.*, 1856-57: no. 10. *Ohio State Journal*, Dec. 30, 1856, Jan. 13 and 23, 1857; *Ohio Statesman*, in ibid., Jan. 15, 1857.

33. Joseph Gantz, "A History of Banking Legislation and Currency in Michigan, 1835-1865" (A.M. thesis, Wayne State Univ., 1936): 77-78, 85. *Governors' Messages*, 2: 238-39. *Detroit Daily Advertiser*, Dec. 15 and 16, 1852, Jan. 6, 1853, Jan. 1, 1855.

34. *Pontiac Jacksonian*, Dec. 2, 15, and 22, 1852; *Detroit Daily Free Press*, May 27, 1853, Apr. 25, 1854; *Lansing Journal*, in ibid., Apr. 30, 1854; *Ionia Gazette*, in *Detroit Daily Free Press*, May 3, 1854. *Governors' Messages*, 2: 221-42.

35. *Governors' Messages*, 2: 259. *See also*: Justin E. Walsh, "Radically and Thoroughly Democratic: Wilbur F. Storey and the Detroit *Free Press*, 1853-1861," *Mich. History* 47 (Sept. 1963): 193-225.

36. Walsh: "Wilbur F. Storey": 281-301.

37. Gantz, "Banking Legislation": 85-86. *Governors' Messages*, 2: 302-21.

38. *Daily Advertiser*, Nov. 24, 26 and 28, Dec. 1 and 13, 1856, Jan. 24 and 27, 1857. *Monroe Commercial*, in ibid., Dec. 22, 1856. *Daily Advertiser*, Dec. 27, 1856. Ibid., Feb. 2, 1857. *See also*: *Marshall Statesman*, in ibid., Dec. 25, 1857.

39. *Mich. Senate Doc.*, 1857: nos. 2, 15, 16. [A comparison of the names on the "monster" petition and the men listed in Alexandra McCoy's study, "Political Affiliations of American Economic Elites" (Ph.D. diss., Wayne State Univ., 1965) yields the political affiliations (for 1860) of 34 signers: 22 Republicans, 6 Democrats, 1 Constitutional Unionist, and 5 "no party" men. In the McCoy sample there are 56 Republicans, 48 Democrats, 4 Constitutional Unionists, and 25 "no party" men. Her figures on the occupations of the elite undermine any interpretation arguing that Republicans supported free banking because of banker influence. Of the 11 bankers in her 1860 sample, 5 are Republicans and 6 are Democrats. However, it can be argued that those people who

most wanted expanded credit and banking services, such as merchants and capitalists, were more likely to be Republicans than Democrats.]

40. *Daily Free Press,* Dec. 12, 1856. Ibid., Dec. 11, 1856. *See also: Lansing Journal,* in ibid., Dec. 28, 1856. [The issues of the paper from Oct. 2 to Dec. 1, 1856, are lost, but there are indications in the *Daily Advertiser* and subsequent issues of the *Free Press,* particularly a letter signed "E.C.B." in the Dec. 2, 1856, issue, that the paper bitterly attacked the free banking system during these months.]

41. *Jackson Patriot,* in *Daily Free Press,* Dec. 27, 1856. *Daily Free Press,* Dec. 2, 1856, Jan. 3, 10, 14, 20, 22, 23, and 24, 1857. *Ann Arbor Argus,* in ibid., Dec. 15, 1856.

42. *Daily Free Press,* Feb. 11, 1857.

43. *Mich. House Journal,* 1857: 339, 512-13. *Mich. Senate Journal,* 1857: 25, 248. *Governors' Messages,* 2: 340. *Daily Advertiser,* Feb. 3, 1857. *Daily Free Press,* Feb. 15, 1857. *See also:* ibid., Feb. 18, 1857.

44. Gantz, "Banking Legislation": 142-43, lists the vote for governor and the banking law. [It should be noted that two Democratic counties, Genesee and Wayne, turned in large votes for the bill. Genesee was generally Whig and later Republican, although it gave a majority to Democrat Charles Stuart in 1858. Wayne was the most rapidly developing commercial area in the state and turned Republican in 1860. For the long-term affiliations of the counties in Michigan, see W. Dean Burnham, *Presidential Ballots, 1836-1892* (Baltimore: Johns Hopkins Press, 1955): 191-93.]

45. *Chicago Banks,* 1: 238-39; George William Dowrie, "The Development of Banking in Illinois, 1817-1863," *UISSS* 2 (Dec. 1913): 144-45. Matteson's message of Jan. 1, 1855, in *Ill. Governor,* 1853-57.

46. Bissell's inaugural of 1857, in *Ill. Governor,* 1857-60. Dowrie, "Banking in Illinois": 148-49; *Chicago Banks,* 1: 241-43.

47. See especially two essays by Mildred C. Stoler: "The Democratic Element in the Republican Party in Illinois," *Papers in Ill. History and Trans. for the Year 1942* (1944): 32-72, and "The Democratic Element in the New Republican Party in Indiana," *Ind. Magazine of History* 36 (Sept. 1940): 185-207; and Van Bolt's essay, "Republican Party in Indiana": 209. [My own examination of Illinois and Indiana state legislators indicates a high degree of continuity. In these legislatures 64 men stayed through this period (43 Democrats and 21 Whigs). Of this group only 5 Democrats switched to the new party and only 1 Whig became a Democrat.] Orth to Colfax, July 4, 1854, and Orth to Colfax, Nov. [?], 1854, in J. Herman Schauinger, ed., "The Letters of Godlove S. Orth, Hoosier American," *Ind. Magazine of History* 40 (Mar. 1944): 54, 56, give some insight into Whig attempts at first to remain in the background without giving up control.

48. This is based on percentages computed from Burnham, *Presidential Ballots:* 248, using the same method employed by William O. Lynch in "The Convergence of Lincoln and Douglas," *TISHS,* 1925 (n.d.): 155-73, but applying it to a longer time period and exclusively to the five states dealt with in this study. Lincoln's remark is in Lincoln to

Trumbull, June 7, 1856, in Roy P. Basler, ed., *The Collected Works of Abraham Iincoln* (New Brunswick, N. J.: Rutgers Univ. Press, 1953), 2: 342-43.

49. Burnham, *Presidential Ballots*: 176-80, 208-10, on voting shifts of Indiana, Illinois, and Ohio counties; ibid.: 532 and McCoy, "Political Affiliations": chart 14 and passim, on Wayne County, Michigan. Certainly articles in the Democratic press such as "Conservatism and Radicalism," *Cincinnati Enquirer*, Oct. 23, 1855, were direct appeals to the conservative Whigs.

50. See the extremely interesting debate in the *Milwaukee Daily Sentinel* and *Daily Milwaukee News* during Feb. 1863 that was set off by S. S. Cox's speech "Puritanism and Politics." The most suggestive works on ethnoreligious conflict at this time are: Richard Lyle Power, *Planting Corn Belt Culture* (Indianapolis: Ind. Historical Society, 1953); Carrie Prudence Kofoid, "Puritan Influence in the Formative Period of Illinois History," *Trans. of the Ill. State Historical Society for the Year 1905* (1906); Joseph Schafer, "The Yankee and the Teuton in Wisconsin," *Wis. Magazine of History* 6 (Dec. 1922-June 1923): 125-45, 261-79, 386-402, and 7 (Sept. 1923, Mar. 1924): 3-19, 148-71; idem, "Who Elected Lincoln?" *AHR* 47 (Oct. 1941): 51-63; McCoy, "Political Affiliations"; *Mass Political Parties*: 217-331; two unpublished papers by Harvey Lewis Carter: "The Origins of Political Patterns in the Older Middle West, 1856-1864," and "Persistent Political Patterns in Indiana Presidential Elections."

51. *Ind. State Journal*, Nov. 27, 1856. *Ohio State Journal*, Nov. 24, 1856. Samuel A. Brimblecom to Elihu B. Washburn, Jan. 24, 1860, quoted in Kuhn, "Rise of the Republican Party": 30.

52. Logan Esarey, *A History of Indiana* (Fort Wayne, Ind.: Hoosier Press, 1924), 2: 604-8; Power, *Planting Corn Belt Culture*: 40-42; Carter, "Origins of Political Patterns": 4-5.

53. Clifford S. Griffin, *Their Brother's Keepers* (New Brunswick, N. J.: Rutgers Univ. Press, 1960): 219-41, adds a dimension to understanding Republican attraction to the "isms." A most insightful essay by Richard Hofstadter, "Abraham Lincoln and the Self-Made Myth," in *The American Political Tradition and the Men Who Made It* (New York: Alfred A. Knopf, 1948): 93-136, has helped me formulate my interpretation of the Whigs and Republicans.

# Chapter 8

1. George Tucker, "Banks or No Banks," *Hunt's Merchants' Magazine* 38 (Feb. 1858): 147. [These years are treated in greatest detail in Allan Nevins, *The Emergence of Lincoln*, 2 vols. (New York: Charles Scribner's Sons, 1950).]

2. Unless otherwise noted the material on the Panic of 1857 is from: George W. Van Vleck, *The Panic of 1857* (New York: Columbia Univ. Press, 1943); Charles Franklin Dunbar, *Economic Essays*, O. M. W.

Sprague, ed. (New York: Macmillan Company, 1904): 266-94; Henry David et al., eds., *The Economic History of the United States*, vol. 4, George Rogers Taylor, *The Transportation Revolution, 1815-1860* (New York: Holt, Rinehart and Winston, 1951): 345-51; and Nevins *Emergence of Lincoln*, 1: 176-228.

3. *Western Prices. New York Herald*, Jan. 4, 1858, quoted in Van Vleck, *Panic of 1857*: 84. For the panic's economic impact on the Old Northwest, see: *Western Prices*: 517-29; Madison Kuhn, "Economic Issues and the Rise of the Republican Party in the Northwest" (Ph.D. diss., Univ. of Chicago, 1940): 133-54; *Mich. Political Parties*: 257-61. *See also*: McCulloch to Hamilton, Sept. 3, 1857, Hamilton MSS; McCulloch to McCulloch, Sept. 5, 1857, McCulloch MSS.

4. Kuhn, "Rise of the Republican Party": 134.

5. Leonard Bayliss Krueger, *History of Commercial Banking in Wisconsin* (Madison: Univ. of Wis., 1933): 68. *Bureau County Republican*, Sept. 15, 1859, quoted in Kuhn, "Rise of the Republican Party": 134. *New York Tribune*, Feb. 4, 1860, quoted in Nevins, *Emergence of Lincoln*, 1: 193. *Washington County Democrat*, Dec. 20, 1857, quoted in Van Vleck, *Panic of 1857*: 84.

6. *Grand Rapids Enquirer and Herald*, Dec. 16, 1857, quoted in *Mich. Political Parties*: 260. *Chicago Banks*, 1: 270. On Cincinnati see: Nevins, *Emergence of Lincoln*, 1: 294.

7. *Banks and Politics*: 621. *Ind. Doc. Journal*, 1859, pt. 2: no. 5.

8. Van Vleck, *Panic of 1857*: 65. C. C. Huntington, "A History of Banking and Currency in Ohio Before the Civil War," *OAHS* 24 (1915): 471-77. *Ohio Doc.*, 1857: no. 8.

9. Krueger, *Commercial Banking in Wisconsin*: 56-65; Theodore A. Anderson, *A Century of Banking in Wisconsin* (Madison: State Historical Society of Wis., 1954): 34-36.

10. *The Centennial History of Illinois*, vol. 3, Arthur Charles Cole, *The Era of the Civil War* (Chicago: A. C. McClurg & Co., 1922): 100; George William Dowrie, "The Development of Banking in Illinois, 1817-1863," *Univ. of Ill. Studies in the Social Sciences* 2 (Dec. 1913): 151-54. Bissell's speech of Jan. 3, 1859, is in *Ill. Governor*, 1857-60.

11. *Western Prices*: 521; *Chicago Banks*, 1: 264-68. Wis. Bank Comptroller, *Report*, 1860, quoted in Frederick Merk, *Economic History of Wisconsin During the Civil War Decade* (Madison: State Historical Society of Wis., 1916): 190-91. Dunbar, *Economic Essays*: 322-24.

12. Dowrie, "Banking in Illinois": 155; *Chicago Banks*, 1: 270-72, 259 (table 6), 260 (table 7); Joseph Gantz, "A History of Banking Legislation and Currency in Michigan, 1835-1865" (A.M. thesis, Wayne State Univ., 1936): 90; Dunbar, *Economic Essays*, 296-98, 316.

13. The "Crisis of 1860" is discussed at length in Dunbar, *Economic Essays*: 294-314.

14. *Chicago Banks*, 1: 277-85; Cole, *Era of the Civil War*: 361-62.

15. Merk, *Economic History of Wisconsin*: 191-200; Krueger, *Commercial Banking in Wisconsin*: 77-85.

16. *Chicago Tribune*, Aug. 8, 1861. [The *Tribune*, as will be seen in chap-

ter 9, was in the vanguard of demands for a national banking system and had little use for the state banks. Yet on Jan. 30, 1862, it called on the Illinois constitutional convention to construct a sound banking system for the state.]

17. For an analysis of the general reaction to the panic, see: Van Vleck, *Panic of 1857*: 80-104; Samuel Rezneck, "The Influence of Depression Upon American Opinion, 1857-1859," *JEH* 2 (May 1942): 1-23. *New York Herald*, Sept. 29, 22, and 25, 1857, quoted in Rezneck, "Influence of Depression": 5.

18. James D. Richardson, comp., *A Compilation of the Messages and Papers of the Presidents* (Washington, D.C.: By Authority of Congress, 1900), 5: 436-41; quotations: 437, 441.

19. Ibid.: 441. Ibid.: 438. [Interestingly enough, Buchanan also praised a policy of the Bank of England, that of keeping a special reserve of one-third liabilities (ibid.: 438). Any favorable mention of the Bank of England 20 years earlier would have cast doubt upon the sincerity of Buchanan's "Democracy."]

20. *New York Herald*, Sept. 28, 1857, quoted in Albert J. Beveridge, *Abraham Lincoln, 1809-1858* (New York: Houghton Mifflin Co., 1928), 2: 524. Amassa Walker, "The Commercial Crisis of 1857," *Hunt's Merchants' Magazine* 37 (Nov. 1857): 531-34. William Gouge, "The Banks of the United States," *Bankers' Magazine and Statistical Register* 14 (July 1859): 3-9 (hereafter cited as *Bankers' Magazine*). Daniel Hundley, "The Causes of Western Failures," *Hunt's Merchants' Magazine* 37 (Oct. 1857): 444-45. Richard Sully, "Money and Banking," ibid., 38 (Mar. 1858): 287-92. Peter Cooper, "Remarks on the Present Currency System," *Bankers' Magazine* 14 (Aug. 1859): 81-85. [There are numerous articles by Walker in *Hunt's Merchants' Magazine* during these years and his book *Political Economy* was serialized in 1857 and 1858. He also published in 1857 *The Nature and Uses of Money and Mixed Currency with a History of the Wickaboag Bank* (Boston: Crosby Nichols and Co., 1857). *Hunt's Merchants' Magazine* did print both sides of the debate. In contrast to the antibank articles by Walker, Edmund Dwight, George Dutton, and Charles H. Carroll were those of Ezra C. Seaman and George Ward defending banks and the credit system.]

21. Stevens to Douglas, Nov. 25, 1857, Huntington to Douglas, Nov. 29, 1857, Douglas MSS. John Hunt, "A Sound Currency, What is It?" *Bankers' Magazine* 14 (July 1859): 1-3; *Ill. State Register*, Nov. 2, 1875. Stanley Llewellyn Jones, "Anti-Bank and Anti-Monopoly Movements in Illinois, 1845-1862" (Ph.D. diss., Univ. of Ill., 1947): 132-33. *See also*: Disney to Douglas, n.d., Wick to Douglas, Dec. 8, 1857, George to Douglas, Dec. 11, 1857, Douglas MSS.

22. *Ohio Statesman*, Oct. 10, 1857. Carl Whittke, ed., *The History of the State of Ohio*, vol. 4, Eugene H. Roseboom, *The Civil War Era, 1850-1873* (Columbus: Ohio State Archaeological and Historical Society, 1944): 325-29.

23. Bolton to Chase, July 12, 1858, Chase MSS, Historical Society of Pa.;

Roseboom, *Civil War Era*: 139-40; Huntington, "Banking and Currency in Ohio": 462-63. *Ohio Statesman*, Feb. 11 and 14, May 27, 1859.

24. *Ind. Doc. Journal*, 1859, pt. 2: no. 5.

25. Kenneth M. Stampp. *Indiana Politics During the Civil War* (Indianapolis: Ind. Historical Bureau, 1949): 31-67; quotation is from the *New Albany Weekly Ledger*, Nov. 28, 1860, quoted in ibid.: 54. *Ind. Doc. Journal*, 1860, pt. 1: no. 3. [This trend can be followed in the *Indianapolis Daily State Sentinel* from July 1860 to Mar. 1861, especially in Oct. 17, 1860, issue.]

26. Don E. Fehrenbacher, *Chicago Giant* (Madison: American History Research Center, 1957): 188-95; quotations are from the *Chicago Daily Democrat*, July 2, 1860, and *Chicago Post*, Feb. 20, 1861, quoted in ibid.: 191-92, 193. *See also*: Barney to Chase, Oct. 11, 1855, Bolton to Chase, July 12, 1858, Chase MSS, Historical Society of Pa.

27. Jones, "Movements in Illinois": 161-76; quotation: 176.

28. O. M. Dickerson, "The Illinois Constitutional Convention of 1862," *UISSS* 1, no. 9 (1905): 3-6; quotation is from the *Urbana Weekly Democrat*, Aug. 24, 1861, quoted in ibid.: 6. *Ill. State Register*, July 20 and 27, Aug. 13 and 16, Oct. 3, Nov 17, 1861.

29. *Ill. State Journal*, Nov. 23, 1861; Dickerson, "Illinois Constitutional Convention": 7-9; Cole, *Era of the Civil War*: 266-67; Stanley L. Jones, "Agrarian Radicalism in Illinois' Constitutional Convention of 1862," *Journal of the Ill. State Histrocial Society* 48 (autumn 1955): 274-75. [While Wentworth represented an old Jacksonian attitude toward banks, the same could not be said of Campbell. He was an old Whig and from the small minority of that party that favored a national currency, opposing the financial interests that "robbed" the workingman by charging interest. These men advocated a flexible, paper currency issued by a national agency. Campbell's ideas are expressed in his "Report on Treasury Notes," *Journal of the Constitutional Convention of the State of Illinois Convened at Springfield, January 7, 1862* (Springfield, Ill.: Charles H. Lanphier, Printer, 1862): 181-87. Although there is no doubt that he opposed local banks (see vote in ibid.: 355), he neither voted on the bank article in the constitution (see votes in ibid.: 662-63, 938) nor signed the final document (see vote to accept in ibid.: 1114-15). His resolution to instruct the Illinois members of Congress to vote for the legal tender bill was defeated (*Ill. State Register*, Feb. 15, 1862).]

30. Dickerson, "Illinois Constitutional Convention": 15-17, 41-48; Cole, *Era of the Civil War*: 268-69; *New Constitution of the State of Illinois . . . with an Address to the People of Illinois* (Springfield, Ill.: Charles H. Lanphier, Printer, 1862): 23, 27-28, 53-54; *Journal of the 1862 Constitutional Convention*: 10, 143, 662-63, 938. [Wentworth was on the Committee on Banks and Corporations (ibid.: 45) and generally agreed with the article. However, he did present a minority report arguing that the issue should be submitted to the people and that if they were in favor of banks, a guarded free banking system should be pro-

vided for (ibid.: 144-46). The makeup of the convention and attitudes of its leaders on corporations and money are the subject of Ronald P. Formisano and William G. Shade, "The Concept of Agrarian Radicalism," *MA* 52 (Jan. 1970): 3-30.]

31. Cole, *Era of the Civil War*: 269-70; Dickerson, "Illinois Constitutional Convention": 48-52. *Ill. State Journal*, Jan. 7 and 14, 1862. Yates to Trumbull, Feb. 14, 1862, Trumbull MSS, Library of Congress. *See also*: Palmer to Trumbull, Mar. 26, 1862, Rankin to Trumbull, June 4, 1862, Notestine to Trumbull, June 24, 1862, ibid.

32. *Chicago Tribune*, Jan. 30, 1862. Ibid., Feb. 13, 1862. *Aurora Beacon*, Apr. 24, 1862, quoted in Cole, *Era of the Civil War*: 269. *Chicago Post*, in *Ill. State Journal*, June 16, 1862. *See also: Ill. State Journal*, Mar. 27, 1862; *Havana Battle Axe*, in ibid., Apr. 4, 1862. [There were obvious cultural overtones to this Republican argument; see: Frank L. Klement, *The Copperheads in the Middle West* (Chicago: Univ. of Chicago Press, 1960): passim.]

33. Dickerson, "Illinois Constitutional Convention": 17; Jones, "Movements in Illinois": 177; Fehrenbacher, *Chicago Giant*: 195; Cole, *Era of the Civil War*: 70. *Peoria Union*, in *Ill. State Register*, May 16, 1862. *Ill. State Register*, May 8, 1862.

34. Dickerson, "Illinois Constitutional Convention": 23-24; Cole, *Era of the Civil War*: 271; Jones, "Agrarian Radicalism": 281-82. Zayne to Trumbull, June 22, 1862, Trumbull MSS, Library of Congress. [Although it is just conjecture, the shifts in voting in traditionally antibank areas might be accounted for by changes in the settlement pattern and economic growth fostered by the railroad, which altered the pattern of population and wealth. See: Douglass C. North, *The Economic Growth of the United States, 1790-1860* (New York: W. W. Norton and Company, 1966): 135-55, especially the maps on 147 and 149; and William E. Dodd, "The Fight for the Northwest, 1860," *AHR* 16 (July 1911): 774-88.]

35. *Ohio Doc.*, 1857: no. 8. Chase also called for a Democratic reform: the elimination of small notes.

36. *Wis. Senate Journal*, 1858: 30-38. Merk, *Economic History of Wisconsin*: 188–90; Krueger, *Commercial Banking in Wisconsin*: 71-74.

37. *Wis. Senate Journal*, 1859: 11-12, 1860: 15-17; Merk, *Economic History of Wisconsin*: 209; Krueger, *Commercial Banking in Wisconsin*: 79-80.

38. *Chicago Banks*, 1: 272-74; Dowrie, "Banking in Illinois": 150-53, 158-60. Bissell's speech of Jan. 3, 1859, in *Ill. Governor*, 1857-60. *Chicago Tribune*, Jan. 5, 1860.

39. *Chicago Banks*, 1: 274-75. Bessie Louise Pierce, *A History of Chicago* (New York: Alfred A. Knopf, 1937), 2: 127-29. Wood's address of Jan. 7, 1861, in *Ill. Governor*, 1860-61.

40. Cole, *Era of the Civil War*: 200. Yates's message of Jan. 14, 1861, in *Ill. House Journal*, 1861: 84-103.

41. *Bankers' Magazine* 15 (Jan. 1861): 543, 584-85; ibid. (Apr. 1861): 793-804; Dowrie, "Banking in Illinois": 164-65. *Ill. House Journal*,

1861: 115, 371, 473-79, 536; *Ill. Senate Journal*, 1861: 383. [The vote
was 21-4 in the senate and 59-12 in the house.]

42.  *Ohio Doc.*, 1860, pt. 1: nos. 39, 549. Ibid., 1861, pt. 1: no. 26. Ibid.:
no. 35.

43.  Gantz, "Banking Legislation": 91-92. *Governor's Messages*, 2: 403,
430-31. *Detroit Dilay Advertiser*, Feb. 7 and 8, 1861. *Mich. Senate
Doc.*, 1861: nos. 8, 18.

44.  Dowrie, "Banking in Illinois": 165-66; *Bankers' Magazine* 15 (Apr.
1861): 777-92. *Ill. House Journal*, 1861: 543: *Ill. Senate Journal*, 1861:
478. [The vote was 15-9 in the senate and 58-7 in the house.]

45.  Merk, *Economic History of Wisconsin*: 200-11.

46.  *Ohio Doc.*, 1860, pt. 1: no. 39, 548.

# Chapter 9

1.  Charles Franklin Dunbar, "The Crisis of 1860," in *Economic Essays*,
ed. O. M. W. Sprague (New York: Macmillan Company, 1904); Emerson D. Fite, *Social and Industrial Conditions in the North During the
Civil War* (New York: Frederick Unger Publishing Co., 1963): 105-14;
Robert T. Patterson, "Government Finance on the Eve of the Civil
War," *JEH* 12 (winter 1952): 35-44.

2.  Chase to Denison, Mar. 6, 1861, reprinted in J. W. Schuckers, *The Life
and Public Services of Salmon Portland Chase* (New York: D. Appleton
and Co., 1874): 207-8.

3.  Chase to Wilson, Dec. 13, 1860, reprinted in American Historical Association, "Diary and Correspondence of Salmon P. Chase," *Annual
Report of the American Historical Association for the Year 1902* 2
(1903): 293-95.

4.  Robert P. Sharkey, *Money, Class, and Party: An Economic Study of
the Civil War and Reconstruction* (Baltimore: Johns Hopkins Press,
1959): 16-20; Henry David et al., eds., *The Economic History of the
United States* (New York: Holt, Rinehart and Winston, 1945-  ), vol.
6, Edward C. Kirkland, *Industry Comes of Age*: 13-15; Wesley C.
Mitchell, *A History of the Greenbacks with Special Reference to the
Economic Consequences of Their Issue* (Chicago: Univ. of Chicago
Press, 1903): 3-43. *Senate Executive Doc.*, 37th Cong., 1st sess., no. 2.

5.  Doolittle to Chase, Sept. 13, 1861, Chase MSS, Library of Congress.
"The Causes of Bank Failure," *Bankers' Magazine* 11 (July 1861): 5.
[The handling of these loans is treated in detail in Fritz Redlich, *The
Molding of American Banking* (New York: Hafner Publishing Company, 1947), 2: 85-95.]

6.  See the following articles by Charles H. Carroll: "Congressional Movement in the Currency Question," *Hunt's Merchants' Magazine* 42 (Apr.
1860): 443-47; "Mr. Lowell vs. Mr. Hooper on Banking and Currency,"
ibid. (May 1860): 575-85; "Financial Heresies," ibid. (Sept. 1860):
317-21; "Currency of the United States," ibid. (Nov. 1860): 574-83.

7.  John Jay Knox, *United States Notes: A History of the Various Issues*

*of Paper Money By the Government of the United States* (New York: Charles Scribner's Sons, 1885): 40-79. Jackson to Dawson, Nov. 4, 1842, Jackson-Dawson MSS, Cincinnati Public Library. "The Fiscal System of the United States," *Democratic Review* 7 (Jan. 1840): 53. [I must thank one of my students, James Obenshain, for a typed copy of the letter from Jackson to Dawson.]

8. Richard H. Timberlake, Jr., "The Specie Standard and Central Banking in the United States Before 1860," *JEH* 21 (Sept, 1961): 318-41; George Tucker, "Banks or No Banks," *Hunt's Merchants' Magazine* 38 (Feb. 1858): 147-57. Coe to Chase, Dec. 12, 1861, Chase MSS, Library of Congress.

9. The most complete presentation of Kellogg's ideas is Edward Kellogg, *A New Monetary System,* ed. Mary Kellogg Putnam (New York: Rudd and Carleton, 1861), which is a later edition of his *Labor and Other Capital,* first published in 1849. His plan is discussed in Sharkey, *Money, Class, and Party:* 187-91; Chester McArthur Destler, *American Radicalism, 1865-1901* (New York: Octagon Books, 1963): 50-77; and Irwin Unger, *The Greenback Era: A Social and Political History of American Finance, 1865-1879* (Princeton, N. J.: Princeton Univ. Press, 1964): 95-97. [Some Democrats may have been interested in a national paper currency. A letter from Don Eaton to French, Jan. [?], 1851, French MSS, requests French, the antibank Democratic governor of Illinois, to sign a petition to have Congress establish a national paper currency based on the credit of the United States. Eaton's political affiliation is unknown, but the idea was generally supported by Whigs (Stanley Llewellyn Jones, "Anti-Bank and Anti-Monopoly Movements in Illinois, 1845-1862" [Ph.D. diss., Univ. of Ill., 1947]: 80-81). Eaton referred for authority to "Alison the historian" rather than Kellogg. This is a reference to Archibald Alison, the Scottish historian of the French Revolution, whom Unger connects with the ideas of Henry Carey (*Greenback Era:* 51, n. 42). There was also an unsigned proposal for a national paper currency in *Bankers' Magazine* 4 (Dec. 1849): 421-29.]

10. L. Bonnefoux, "Financial Policy of the Government," *Bankers' Magazine* 11 (Dec. 1861): 417-50. Frank H. Severance, ed., "Millard Fillmore Papers, Volume One," *Publications of the Buffalo Historical Society* 10 (1907): 282. [The relation of the Fillmore report and the national banking system is traced in Redlich, *American Banking,* 2: 101-2.]

11. *Washington Union,* quoted in Bonnefoux, "Financial Policy": 433. *Ill. State Register,* Oct. 30, 1849. Tappan to Tappan, Oct. 9, 1843, Tappan MSS, Ohio Historical Society. *Racine Advocate,* July 21, 1846, reprinted in Milo M. Quaife, ed., *The Movement for Statehood, 1845-46* (Madison: State Historical Society of Wis., 1918): 286-89. *Democratic Review* 24 (Feb. 1849): 101-2. [Bonnefoux claimed that the *Democratic Review* praised his ideas. The *Democratic Review* 22 (June 1848): 508, praised him in an article supporting the New York free banking system. However, this was not an endorsement of his ideas on a national currency.]

12. Joseph Dorfman, *The Economic Mind in American Civilization, 1606-1865* (New York: Viking Press, 1946), 2: 789-826. Bonnefoux, "Financial Policy": 417-50. Putnam to Sherman, Feb. 14, 1862, Sherman MSS.

13. Carey to Chase, Sept. 14 and 25, Dec. 7, 1861, Chase MSS, Historical Society of Pa. Campbell to Chase, June 22, 1861, Doolittle to Chase, Sept. 13, 1861, Chase MSS, Library of Congress. Medill to Chase, Nov. 25, 1961, Chase MSS, Historical Society of Pa. *See also*: Martin to Chase, Aug. 12, 1861, Gunkel to Chase, Oct. 3, 1861, Caldwell to Chase, Oct. 22, 1861, Chase MSS, Library of Congress. [Campbell praises Kellogg in his major work, *The True American System of Finance* (Chicago: Evening Journal Book and Job Print, 1864): 7. On Campbell's Influence, see: Sharkey, *Money, Class, and Party*: 191-95; *Destler, American Radicalism*. 8-9, 60, 61, 76; Unger, *Greenback Era*: 97-101. Campbell's ideas in early 1862 are expressed in *Journal of the Constitutional Convention of the State of Illinois Convened at Springfield, January 7, 1862* (Springfield, Ill.: Charles H. Lanphier, Printer, 1862): 51, 181-87. While he clearly opposed Chase's suggestion of a national banking system, his main interest lay in defending the issue of legal tenders as a better method of financing the war than the Gallatin plan put forth by the bankers of Boston, New York, and Philadelphia. Campbell seems not to have read Kellogg until some time after the appearance of *A New Monetary System* in 1861.]

14. *Ohio Doc.*, 1855-56; no. 4; ch. 7 above. Potter to Chase, Aug. 19, 1861, Chase MSS, Library of Congress. [Chase was hardly a "primitive bullionist Democrat," as Unger describes him in *Greenback Era*: 14.]

15. U.S., Dept. of the Treasury, *Report of the Secretary of the Treasury on the State of Finances for the Year Ending June 30, 1861* (Washington, D.C.: U.S. Government Printing Office, 1861): 7-29; quotation: 17-18.

16. Ibid.: 18.

17. Ibid.: 19.

18. Ibid.: 13-19; Chase to Jesse Baldwin, May 18, 1864, reprinted in Robert B. Warden, *An Account of the Private Life and Public Services of Salmon Portland Chase* (Cincinnati: Wilstack, Baldwin and Co., 1874): 409-10.

19. Cooper to Chase, Dec. 10, 1861 (misdated 1862), Chase MSS, Historical Society of Pa. Bush to Chase, Dec. 28, 1861, Chase MSS, Library of Congress. Martin to Chase, Dec. 31, 1861, ibid. Taylor to Chase, Dec. 24, 1861, ibid., Taft to Chase, Dec. 11, 1861, ibid. [Andrew McFarland Davis, *The Origin of the National Banking System* (Washington, D.C.: U.S. Government Printing Office, 1910): 44-51, gives summaries of many such letters in both collections of the Chase MSS.]

20. Elbridge Gerry Spaulding, *History of the Legal Tender Paper Money Issued During the Great Rebellion . . . Being a Loan Without Interest and a National Currency* (Buffalo: Express Printing Company, 1869): 13.

21. Ibid.: 14. [Concerning Chase's decision to demand specie, Redlich, *American Banking*, 2: 92-93, tends to defend the secretary, while Hammond condemns him in *Banks and Politics*: 720-21, and "The North's

Empty Purse, 1861-1862," *AHR* 67 (Oct. 1961): 1-18. Sharkey, *Money, Class, and Party*: 21-23, is closer to Redlich than Hammond.]
22. Spaulding, *Legal Tender Paper Money*: 12-13, 18-21, 27. [Among the several letters reprinted herein is one from Chase to Spaulding, Jan. 22, 1862, expressing his views. *See also*: Chase to Bryant, Feb. 4, 1862, reprinted in Warden, *Account of Chase*: 409; and U.S., Dept. of Treasury, *Report of the Secretary of the Treasury on the State of Finances for the Year Ending June 30, 1862* (Washington, D.C.: U.S. Government Printing Office, 1863): 8.]
23. *Cong. Globe*, 2d sess.: 633-36 (Conkling), 630-31 (Morrill), 614-15 and app.: 42-46 (Vallandigham); 549-51 (Pendleton).
24. Ibid.: (*opposing*) 663-65 (Horton, Ohio), 684-85 (Riddle, Ohio), 691 (Lovejoy, Ill.); (*supporting*) 636-40 (Bingham), 679-81 (Kellogg), 685-86 (Blake), 690 (Shellabarger), 771-75 (Sherman), 774 (Chandler, Mich.), 796-97 (Howard, Mich.), app.: 51-56 (Howe, Wis.), app.: 56-58 (Doolittle, Wis.).
25. Ibid., 2d sess.: 775 (Sherman). Ibid.: 636 (Bingham). Ibid.: 679 (Kellogg). Ibid.: 686 (Blake). For votes see: ibid., 695 (Senate), 800 (House). [The bill in its final form gained the votes of 93 representatives and 30 senators.]
26. There was no change among western senators on the two votes. The House figures are on the final vote. Riddle, who spoke against the bill, voted for it on the final vote. An Indiana Democrat, Knapp, voted for retaining the legal tender provision and against the bill. Sharkey, *Money, Class, and Party*: 42, seem to have miscounted the western votes in his analysis.
27. Spaulding, *Legal Tender Paper Money*: 154-63. *Cong. Globe*, 2d Sess.: 617. John Sherman, *Recollections of Forty Years in the House, Senate and Cabinet* (New York: Werner Company, 1895), 1: 282-85. Wilmer C. Harris, *Public Life of Zachariah Chandler, 1851-1875* (Lansing: Mich. Historical Commission, 1917): 71. [Sherman voted against the increase in Greenbacks. Chandler spoke against it but did vote for it. Both actively championed the national banking system.]
28. Chase to Spaulding, Jan. 30, 1862, reprinted in Spaulding, *Legal Tender Paper Money*: 46. American Historical Association, "Diary and Correspondence of Salmon P. Chase": 76. Chase to Bigelow, Oct. 7, 1862, reprinted in Warden, *Account of Chase*: 501-4.
29. Davis, *National Banking System*: 56-57. Fawn M. Brodie, *Thaddeus Stevens: Scourge of the South* (New York: W. W. Norton and Company, 1959): 171-75. Chase to Trowbridge, reprinted in Schuckers, *Life of Chase*: 292.
30. James D. Richardson, comp., *A Compilation of the Messages and Papers of the Presidents* (Washington, D.C.: By Authority of Congress, 1900), 4: 129-30.
31. *Report of the Secretary of the Treasury . . . 1862*: 1-30; quotations: 17, 21.
32. Chase to Fessenden, Jan. 7, 1863, reprinted in Spaulding, *Legal Tender Paper Money*: 182. Richardson, *Presidential Messages and Papers*, 4: 149-50.

33. Davis, *National Banking System*: 75. Cooke to Cooke, Jan. 23, Feb. 12, 1863, reprinted in Ellis Paxson Oberholtzer, *Jay Cooke, Financier of the Civil War* (Philadelphia: George W. Jacobs and Company, 1907), 1: 332-33. Walker to Sherman, Jan. 31, 1863, Sherman MSS. Guthrie to Wade and Sherman, Feb. 11, 1862, ibid. [Sherman's actions in 1862 give no reason to discount his explanation in *Recollections*, 1: 284.]

34. *Cong. Globe*, 3rd sess.: 504, 820-26, 840-46, 874-77. Sherman, *Recollections*, 1: 298.

35. *Cong. Globe*, 3rd sess.: 840-46 (Sherman). Ibid.: 877 (Chandler). Ibid.: 881-82 (Doolittle).

36. Ibid.: 296-97 (Morrill). Ibid.: 869-74 (Collamer). Ibid.: 341-42 (Gurley). Ibid.: 1117 (Harrison).

37. Ibid., 2d sess., app.: 43; ibid., 3rd sess.: 1143.

38. Ibid.: 897 (Senate), 1148 (House). [Trumbull did not vote on the first legal tender act, but voted against the second. Either his Jacksonian background or increased pressure from Illinois Democrats who had just replaced Orville H. Browning with Democrat William A. Richardson must have influenced him. Unfortunately his latest biographer (Mark Krug, *Lyman Trumbull* [New York: A. S. Barnes and Company, 1965]) does not deal with his attitudes on the financing of the war.]

39. "Report of the Comptroller of the Currency," in *Report of the Secretary of the Treasury . . . 1863* (Washington, D.C.: U.S. Government Printing Office, 1864): 49-61; quotation: 56.

40. Redlich, *American Banking*, 2: 108; Frederick Merk, *Economic History of Wisconsin During the Civil War Decade* (Madison: State Historical Society of Wis., 1916): 213-14; "Report of the Comptroller of the Currency [Nov. 25, 1864]," in *Report of the Secretary of the Treasury . . . 1864* (Washington, D.C.: U.S. Government Printing Office, 1865): 46-55.

41. *Report of the Secretary of the Treasury . . . 1863*: 1-27; Richardson, *Presidential Messages*, 4: 183; "Report of the Comptroller of the Currency [Nov. 28, 1863]," in *Report of the Secretary of the Treasury . . . 1863*: 49-61. Hugh McCulloch, *Men and Measures of a Half Century* (New York: Scribner's Sons, 1888): 163-70. Davis, *National Banking System*: 88-104.

42. *Detroit Daily Advertiser*, Jan. 18, 1862. *Cincinnati Gazette*, in *Milwaukee Daily Sentinel*, Feb. 10, 1862. *Milwaukee Daily Sentinel*, Jan. 25 and 27, Feb. 15 and 26, 1862. *Chicago Tribune*, Feb. 8, 1862. [The support of western Republicans for the Civil War financial measures is discussed in: Davis, *National Banking System*: 17-18, 25-26, 44-53, 63-66, 69-70, 98; *Chicago Banks*, 1: 307, 315, 329, 338-67; Joanna Elizabeth Schneider, "The Reaction of Michigan Republicans to Civil War Financial Legislation" (A.M. thesis, Wayne State Univ., 1963): passim.]

43. Day to Sherman, Feb. 11, 1862, Sherman MSS. Guthrie to Wade and Sherman, Feb. 11, 1862, ibid. For reports see: Buchanan to Sherman, Feb. 11, 1862, ibid.; Montigue to Wade, Feb. 21, 1862, Wade MSS; Taylor to Chase, Dec. 24, 1861, Chase MSS, Library of Congress. *Milwaukee Daily Sentinel*, Feb. 10, 1862. Resolutions of Chicago Board

of Trade in Clary to Browning and Trumbull, Feb. 10, 1862, Trumbull
MSS Library of Congress.

44. Pennington to Washburne, Mar. 6, 1862, Washburne MSS. *See also*:
Worthington to Wade, Jan. 12, 1862, Wade MSS. [This conclusion is
based on casual references to farmers in some of the previously cited
letter and the absence of contradictory evidence. More systematic study
may necessitate the modification of these conclusions.]

45. McCulloch, *Men and Measures*: 135-38. Corwith to Washburne, Jan.
3 and 23, 1862, Washburne MSS. Scammon to Trumbull, Feb. 5, 1862,
Trumbull MSS, Library of Congress. Mitchell to Washburne, Jan. 18,
Feb. 11, 1862, Washburne MSS. [John Jay Knox, "A Uniform National
Currency," *Hunt's Merchants' Magazine* 48 (Jan. 1863): 29, says that
the legal tender bill was "opposed by the bank interest." Knox, himself
a banker, supported the legislation, however. It is quite possible that
the banking community of the West was split on the issue. Certainly
this is true of the New York banking group, although it seems clear
that most bankers in the city opposed the legal tenders. See: Woodman
to Washburne, Feb. 18, 1862, Washburne MSS; Lanier to Sherman,
Jan. 18, 1862, Sherman MSS; Opdyke to Chase, Feb. 8, 1862, Chase
MSS, Library of Congress; Cisco to Chase, Dec. 10, 1862, Chase MSS,
Historical Society of Pa. Eastern and western bankers had clashed on
the earlier issue of treasury notes (A New York bank officer, "Objections to Government Demand Notes," *Bankers' Magazine* 11 [Nov.
1861]: 353-57, and the *Cincinnati Gazette*, in ibid. [Oct. 1861]; 313).]

46. Sturgis to Chase, Jan. 20, 1862, Chase MSS, Library of Congress.
Medill to Chase, May 30, 1862, Chase MSS, Historical Society of Pa.
Worthington to Wade, Jan. 12, 1862, Wade MSS. *See also*: Medill to
Trumbull, June 25, 1862, Trumbull MSS, Library of Congress; Medill
to Chase, Dec. 28, 1862, Chase MSS, Historical Society of Pa.; Carson
to Chase, Feb. 9, 1862, Chase MSS, Library of Congress.

47. Campbell's position is concisely stated in Campbell to Washburne, Feb.
18, 1863, Washburne MSS. Young to Chase, Feb. 11, 1862, Chase MSS,
Library of Congress. Dorsey to Sherman, Jan. 9, 1863, Sherman MSS.
Armstrong to Sherman, Jan. 22, 1863, ibid. *See also*: Ball to Chase,
Feb. 23, 1862, Chase MSS, Library of Congress; Armstrong to Sherman,
Jan. 21, 1863, Sherrard to Sherman, Jan. 23, 1863, Sherman MSS.

48. Medill to Washburne, Feb. 18, 1863, Washburne MSS. Medill to Trumbull, Jan. 28, 1863, Trumbull MSS, Library of Congress. Preston to
Sherman, Feb. 4, 1863, Sherman MSS. *See also*: Medill to Trumbull,
June 25, 1862, Trumbull MSS, Library of Congress; Hildt to Sherman,
n.d., Ball to Sherman, Jan. 27, 1863, Sherman MSS. [There are a number of such letters in the Sherman and Chase collections.]

49. Knox, "Uniform National Currency": 28-34. Dorsey to Sherman, Jan.
9, 1863, Sill to Sherman, Jan. 28, 1863, Stone to Sherman, Jan. 29,
1863, Ballard to Sherman, Feb. 10, 1863, Ellis to Sherman, Feb. 11,
1863, Sherman MSS. For suggestions on the tax structure, see: Baker
to Sherman, Apr. 8, May 31, 1864, Moss to Sherman, May 9, 1864,
ibid. [Again, western bankers were split on the issue (Heaton to Chase,

Jan. 24, 1863, Chase MSS, Library of Congress). McCulloch, *Men and Measure*: 163-68, discusses his conversion from opposition to support of the measures and why many bankers opposed the bill. The letters from eastern bankers in the Chase and Sherman MSS show that they were also split, the majority being opposed to the plan. There hardly seems to have been a united response by bankers to the Chase plan, and their perception of the issue was probably as much a function of party affiliation as occupation. If Alexandra McCoy's sample is typical ("Political Affiliations of American Economic Elites" [Ph.D. diss., Wayne State Univ., 1965]), bankers were about evenly divided in their political affiliations in 1860. Further systematic research on this problem is certainly needed.]

50. For Republican legislators' support see: Walker to Chase, Dec. 12, 1862, Meyers to Chase, Feb. 16, 1863, Zinn to Chase, Feb. 24, 1863, Chase MSS, Library of Congress. *Chicago Tribune*, Jan. 18, 1862. *Detroit Daily Advertiser*, Feb. 8, 1862. *Milwaukee Daily Sentinel*, Feb. 16, 1863. *Detroit Advertiser and Tribune*, Jan. 10, 1863. *Indianapolis Daily Journal*, Feb. 9, 1864. See also: *Chicago Tribune*, Jan. 2, 15, and 16, 1862, Feb. 7 and 13, Mar. 7, 1863; *Detroit Daily Advertiser*, Jan. 7, 9, 10, and 18, 1862; *Milwaukee Sentinel*, Jan. 7 and 21, Feb. 11, 1862; *Detroit Advertiser and Tribune*, Feb. 16 and 23, 1863.

51. Snethen to Chase, Feb. 21, 1863, Chase MSS, Library of Congress. *Philadelphia Press*, in *Ill. State Register*, Feb. 10, 1863. Wilder to Chase, Dec. 7, 1861, Chase MSS, Library of Congress. See also: Smith to Chase (n.d., probably Feb., 1863, but filed at the end of Dec. 1862), ibid.; Johnson to Chandler, July 15, 1862, Chandler MSS; Yates's message, Jan. 5, 1863, in *Ill. Governor*, 1861-65; Sherman, *Recollections*, 1: 289-90, 298-300; McCulloch, *Men and Measures*: 169-70.

52. *Chicago Times*, in *Indianapolis State Sentinel*, Jan. 11, 1862. [On the *Times* and its colorful editor, Wilbur F. Storey, during this period, see: L. E. Ellis, "The Chicago *Times* During the Civil War," *TISHS, 1932* (n.d.): 135-81; and Donald Bridgeman Sanger, "The Chicago *Times* and the Civil War," *MVHR* 17 (Mar. 1931): 557-80. [Opposition of the western Democrats to the Civil War financial legislation is discussed in: Kenneth M. Stampp, *Indiana Politics During the Civil War* (Indianapolis: Ind. Historical Bureau, 1949): 189-91, 266-68; *The History of Indiana*, vol. 3, Emma Lou Thornbrough, *Indiana in the Civil War Era, 1850-1880* (Indianapolis: Ind. Historical Bureau, 1965): 194-96; and Frank L. Klement, *The Copperheads in the Middle West* (Chicago: Univ. of Chicago Press, 1960): 73, 83-84.]

53. *New York Express*, in *Daily Milwaukee News*, Jan. 4, 1862. *Detroit Free Press*, Jan. 11, 1862. *Chicago Times*, Jan. 30, 1862, quoted in Ellis, "Chicago *Times*": 162. *Daily Milwaukee News*, Feb. 5, 1862. *Indianapolis State Sentinel*, Jan. 30, 1862. Judge Perkins is quoted in Thornbrough, *Indiana in the Civil War Era*: 195. [An argument similar to that of Perkins was advanced in the *Chicago Times* (Sanger, "Chicago *Times* and the Civil War": 574).]

54. *Daily Milwaukee News*, Feb. 10, 1863. *Chicago Times*, June 19, 1862.

quoted in Ellis, "Chicago *Times*": 162. *See also: Daily Milwaukee News,* Nov. 11, 1862. [Some Democratic papers were more moderate in their criticism. "Brick" Pomeroy's *La Crosse Weekly Democrat,* Mar. 1, 1862, thought "the ablest Senators of both parties opposed" the measure and hoped their worst fears would not be realized. The *Detroit Free Press,* which opposed the issue of treasury notes, did defend the legal tender clause because it thought it necessary to prevent the country's being "surrendered, bound hand and foot, to the money speculators" (Feb. 8, 1862).]

55. Stampp, *Indiana Politics*: 190. *Cincinnati Daily Enquirer,* Feb. 24, 1863, quoted in Klement, *Copperheads*: 84.
56. *Indianapolis State Sentinel,* Oct. 27, 1863. Ibid., May 12, 1865. *Chicago Times,* Sept. 30, 1863, quoted in Ellis, "Chicago *Times*": 163. *Crisis,* July 6, 1864. *See also:* ibid., Mar. 4 and 18, 1863.
57. *Daily Milwaukee News,* Dec. 12, 1861. *Ill. State Register,* Feb. 10, 1863. *Daily Milwaukee News,* Feb. 25, 1863. *Indianapolis State Sentinel,* May 12, 1865. *Albany Argus,* in *Daily Milwaukee News,* Dec. 18, 1861. *New York Express,* in *Daily Milwaukee News,* Dec. 7, 1862. *Daily Milwaukee News,* Dec. 16, 1862.
58. On Seymour see: *Daily Milwaukee News,* Jan. 10 and 11, 1863; *Ill. State Register,* Jan. 9, 1863. For anti-Yankee remarks see: *Daily Milwaukee News,* Feb. 14, 1863; *Chicago Times,* in *La Crosse Weekly Democrat,* May 2, 1862; *Chicago Times,* Jan. 19, 1863, quoted in Ellis, "Chicago *Times*": 161; *Ill. State Register,* July 9, 1861, May 2 and 3, 1862, Jan. 2 and 9, Feb. 25, 1863. *New York Express,* in ibid., Jan. 23, 1863. *Daily Milwaukee News,* Mar. 5, 1863. [Frank Klement in *Copperheads* argues that this was basically a sectional response to economic problems, although he is aware of the cultural overtones. It seems to me that he ignores the attitudes of western Republicans and eastern Democrats that undermine his thesis. Other than the many clippings from eastern papers printed by the western Democratic journals, the speeches and pamphlets of easterners in the 1864 election show the uniformity of Democratic thought. See: *Official Proceedings of the National Democratic Convention, Held in 1864 at Chicago* (Chicago: Times Steam Book and Job Printing House, 1864); James Gallatin, *Address by the Hon. James Gallatin Before the Democratic Union Association, October 18, 1864* (n.p., n.d.); and *Lincoln Catechism Wherein the Eccentricities and Beauties of Despotism Are Fully Set Forth. A Guide to the Presidential Election of 1864* (New York: J. F. Feeks, 1864).]
59. Samuel S. Cox, "Puritanism in Politics," in *Daily Milwaukee News,* Jan. 20, 1863. *Ill. State Register,* Feb. 10, 1863. *New York Express,* in *Daily Milwaukee News,* Dec. 7, 1862. *La Crosse Weekly Democrat,* Sept. 5, 1864. [There is an intriguing exchange on Puritanism in the *Milwaukee Daily Sentinel* and the *Daily Milwaukee News* during February and early March, 1863. All of these papers feature blatant appeals to the Irish and the Germans and intimate that the Republican party was merely the revived Know-Nothing party. V. Jacque Voegeli, *Free*

*But Not Equal: The Midwest and the Negro During the Civil War* (Chicago: Univ. of Chicago Press, 1967), and Forrest G. Wood, *Black Scare: The Racist Response to Emancipation and Reconstruction* (Berkeley: Univ. of Calif. Press, 1970), deal with racism. That this was not merely a sectional phenomenon is clear from *Lincoln Catechism* and *Abraham Africanus I. Mysteries of the White House*, (New York: J. F. Feeks, 1864). The former mixes racism with attacks on Republican financial policy.]

# BIBLIOGRAPHY

## Manuscripts

William Allen Papers. Library of Congress, Washington, D.C.
Sidney Breese Papers. Illinois State Historical Library, Springfield, Ill.
Lewis D. Campbell Papers. Ohio Historical Society, Columbus, Ohio.
Zachariah Chandler Papers. Library of Congress, Washington, D.C.
Salmon P. Chase Papers. Historical Society of Pennsylvania, Philadelphia, Pa.
Salmon P. Chase Papers. Library of Congress, Washington, D.C.
Thomas Corwin Papers. Library of Congress, Washington, D.C.
Thomas Corwin Papers. Ohio Historical Society, Columbus, Ohio.
David Davis Papers. Illinois State Historical Library, Springfield, Ill.
James R. Doolittle Papers. Library of Congress, Washington, D.C.
Stephen A. Douglas Papers. University of Chicago, Chicago, Ill.
John Ewing Papers. Indiana State Library, Indianapolis, Ind.
Alpheus Felch Papers. Burton Historical Collection, Detroit Public Library,
    Detroit, Mich.
Calvin Fletcher Diary. Indiana State Historical Society, Indianapolis, Ind.
Augustus C. French Papers. Illinois State Historical Library, Springfield, Ill.
Allen Hamilton Papers. Indiana State Library, Indianapolis, Ind.
Illinois Executive File. Illinois Archives, Springfield, Ill.
Illinois Executive Records. Illinois Archives, Springfield, Ill.
Illinois Governor's Letter Books. Illinois Archives, Springfield, Ill.
Samuel Judah Papers. Lilly Library, Indiana University, Bloomington, Ind.
Hugh McCulloch Papers. Lilly Library, Indiana University, Bloomington,
    Ind.
George W. Manypenny Papers. Library of Congress, Washington, D.C.
Stevens T. Mason Papers. Burton Historical Collection, Detroit Public Li-
    brary, Detroit, Mich.
Samuel Medary Papers. Ohio Historical Society, Columbus, Ohio.
William Medill Papers. Library of Congress, Washington, D.C.
Samuel Merrill Papers. Indiana State Historical Society, Indianapolis, Ind.
Samuel Milroy Papers. Indiana State Historical Society, Indianapolis, Ind.
Noah Noble Papers. Indiana State Library, Indianapolis, Ind.
Ohio Governors' Papers. Ohio Historical Society, Columbus Ohio.
Robert Owen Papers. Indiana State Historical Society, Indianapolis, Ind.
Robert Owen Papers. Indiana State Library, Indianapolis, Ind.
John M. Palmer Papers. Illinois State Historical Library, Springfield, Ill.
John Sherman Papers. Library of Congress, Washington, D.C.

Moses M. Strong Papers. Wisconsin State Historical Society, Madison, Wis.
Benjamin Tappan Papers. Library of Congress, Washington, D.C.
Benjamin Tappan Papers. Ohio Historical Society, Columbus, Ohio.
Horace A. Tenney Papers. Wisconsin State Historical Society, Madison, Wis.
Allen G. Thurman Papers. Ohio Historical Society, Columbus, Ohio.
Lyman Trumbull Papers. Illinois State Historical Library, Springfield, Ill.
Lyman Trumbull Papers. Library of Congress, Washington, D.C.
John W. Tweedy Papers. Wisconsin State Historical Society, Madison, Wis.
Martin Van Buren Papers. Library of Congress, Washington, D.C.
Benjamin F. Wade Papers. Library of Congress, Washington, D.C.
Elihu B. Washburne Papers. Library of Congress, Washington, D.C.
John R. Williams Papers. Burton Historical Collection, Detroit Public Library, Detroit, Mich.
William Woodbridge Papers. Burton Historical Collection, Detroit Public Library, Detroit, Mich.
Joseph Wright Papers. Indiana State Library, Indianapolis, Ind.

# Public documents

The journals of the state legislatures bear lengthy titles, which often changed slightly from year to year. I have thus used the briefer citations under which they can be found in a card catalog.

*Illinois Governor.* [The addresses of the governors of Illinois are collected under this title in the Illinois State Historical Library. They also appear in the journals.]
*Illinois Legislature. House Journal.*
*Illinois Legislature. Senate Journal.*
*Indiana Legislature. Documentary Journal.*
*Indiana Legislature. House Journal.*
*Indiana Legislature. Senate Journal.*
*Journal of the Bank Investigating Committee, a Select Committee of the Indiana Senate, 1857.* Indianapolis: Joseph J. Bingham, State Printer, 1857.
*Journal of the Constitutional Convention of the State of Illinois Convened at Springfield, January 7, 1862.* Springfield, Ill.: Charles H. Lanphier, Printer, 1862.
*Journal of the Constitutional Convention of the State of Michigan 1850.* Edited by John Swegles, Jr. Lansing, Mich.: R. W. Inglas, 1850.
*Michigan Legislature. House Documents Accompanying Journal.*
*Michigan Legislature. House Journal.*
*Michigan Legislature. Senate Documents Accompanying Journal.*
*Michigan Legislature. Senate Journal.*
*New Constitution of the State of Illinois . . . with an address to the People of Illinois.* Springfield, Ill.: Charles H. Lanphier, Printer, 1862.
*Ohio Legislature. Documents . . . of the State of Ohio.*
*Ohio Legislature. House Journal.*

315

*Ohio Legislature. Senate Journal.*

*Report of the Debates and Proceedings of the Convention for the Revision of the Constitution of the State of Indiana, 1850.* Reported by H. Fowler. Indianapolis: A. H. Brown, Printer, 1850.

*Report of the Debates and Proceedings of the Convention for the Revision of the Constitution of the State of Ohio, 1850–51.* Columbus: S. Medary, Printer to the Convention, 1851.

*Report of the Proceedings and Debates in the Convention to Revise the Constitution of the State of Michigan. 1850.* Lansing, Mich.: R. W. Ingals, State Printer, 1850.

U.S., Bureau of the Census, *Historical Statistics of the United States. Colonial Times to 1957.* Washington, D.C.: Government Printing Office, 1967.

U.S., Congress, *Congressional Globe*, 37th Cong.

U.S., Congress, Senate, *Executive Documents*, 37th Cong., 1st sess., 1861, no. 2.

U.S., Dept. of the Treasury, *Report of the Secretary of Treasury . . .* , 1861–1865.

*Wisconsin Legislature. Assembly Journal*

*Wisconsin Legislature. Senate Journal*

# Newspapers and periodicals

During this period newspapers made no pretense of objective journalism and served as blatant party organs. Two papers, one from each party, have been chosen. Each reflected the "party line" in its state. Other papers and journals of special importance are also included.

*Annals of Cleveland*
*Bankers' Magazine and Statistical Register*
*Chicago Democrat*
*Chicago Tribune*
*Cincinnati Advertiser and Journal*
*Cincinnati Advertiser and Ohio Phoenix*
*Cincinnati Enquirer*
*Columbus Ohio State Journal*
*Columbus Ohio Statesman*
*Columbus The Crisis*
*Columbus The New Constitution*
*Detroit Advertiser and Tribune*
*Detroit Daily Advertiser*
*Detroit Daily Free Press*
*Detroit Democratic Free Press*
*Hunts' Merchants' Magazine*
*Indianapolis Daily Journal*
*Indianapolis Indiana Democrat*
*Indianapolis Indiana Journal*

*Indianapolis Indiana State Sentinel*
*La Crosse* (Wis.) *Weekly Democrat*
*Madison Daily Argus*
*Madison Daily Democrat*
*Madison Democrat and Argus*
*Milwaukee Daily Milwaukee News*
*Milwaukee Daily Sentinel*
*Milwaukee Daily Sentinel and Gazette*
*New York Daily Tribune*
*New York Merchants' Magazine and Commercial Review*
*New York United States Magazine and Democratic Review*
*Springfield Illinois State Journal*
*Springfield Illinois State Register*
*Springfield Sangamo Journal*
*Vandalia Illinois Advocate and State Register*
*Vandalia Illinois State Register and Peoples' Advocate*
*Waukesha* (Wis.) *Democrat*

## Contemporary books and pamphlets

*Abraham Africanus I. Mysteries of the White House, Diabolism—Seward Necromancer—Lincoln in the Trance—Reveals his Secret History.* New York: J. F. Feeks, 1864.

Adams, Charles Francis. *Further Reflections Upon the State of the Currency of the United States.* Boston: William D. Ticknor, 1837.

Appleton, Nathan. *Remarks on Currency and Banking.* Boston: Charles C. Little and James Brown, 1841.

Bank Director, A. *An Examination Into the Prospective Effects of the National Banks Upon the Public Welfare.* New York: Hall, Clayton and Medole, 1863.

*Banks, Notes, and Specie Concerned as Circulating Medium.* Boston: C. C. P. Moody, 1856.

Benton, Thomas Hart. *Thirty Years' View.* 2 vols. New York: D. Appleton and Co., 1854.

Brass, William. *A Lecture Before the Mechanics Institute of the City of Chicago.* Chicago: Langdon and Rounds, 1852.

Byrdsall, F. *The History of the Loco-Foco or Equal Rights Party . . . .* New York: Clement and Packard, 1842.

Campbell, A[lexander]. *The True American System of Finance; The Rights of the Labor and Capital and the Common Sense Way of Doing Justice to the Soldiers and their Families. No Banks: Greenbacks the Exclusive Currency.* Chicago: Evening Journal Book and Job Print, 1864.

Citizen of Boston, A. *A New System of Paper Money.* Boston: I. R. Butts, 1837.

Committee of New Jersey State Bank Officers, A. *An Appeal to the Congress of the United States on the Subject of Bank Tax and Bank Currency.* Trenton, N. J.: "True American" Office, 1864.

Curtis, George Ticknor. *Address of the Hon. George Tickner Curtis at Philadelphia, Sept. 30, 1864. Campaign Document No. 10,* n.p., n.d.

Dean, Henry Clay. *Crimes of the Civil War, and Curse of the Funding System.* Baltimore: J. Wesley Smith and Bro., 1869.

*Equality.* West Brookfield, Mass.: O. S. Cook and Co., 1849.

Evans, Eastwick [The Belarius of Cymbeline]. *Work (in Six Numbers) in Favor of the Constitutionality of a National Bank.* Washington, D.C.: L. Towers and Co., 1862.

Ford, Thomas. *History of Illinois.* Chicago: S. C. Griggs and Co., 1854.

Gallatin, James. *Address by Hon. James Gallatin Before the Democratic Union Association, October 18, 1864. George B. McClellan as a Patriot, a Warrior and a Statesman. Course of the Administration, State of the Finances, etc., etc.,* n.p., n.d.

———. *Letter to Hon. Wm. P. Fessenden, Senator of the United States, From James Gallatin of New York. The Proposed United States Banking System and Further Issues of Legal Tender.* New York: John W. Amerman, Printer, 1863.

Gibbons, J. S. *The Banks of New York, Their Dealers, The Clearing House and the Panic of 1857.* New York: D. Appleton and Co., 1858.

Gouge, William M. *An Inquiry into the Expediency of Dispensing with Bank Agency and Bank Paper in the Fiscal Concerns of the United States.* Philadelphia: William Stavely, 1837.

———. *A Short History of Paper Money and Banking in the United States . . . .* Philadelphia: 1833.

Hammond, Jabez D. *The History of Political Parties in the State of New York.* 3 vols. Cooperstown, N. Y.: Hard E. Phinney, 1844.

Hooper, Samuel. *An Examination of the Theory and the Effect of Laws Regulating the Amount of Specie in Banks.* Boston: Little, Brown and Company, 1860.

Hubbard, Bela. *Memorials of a Half-Century.* New York: G. P. Putnam's Sons, 1887.

Kellogg, Edward [Godek Gardwell]. *Currency: The Evil and the Remedy.* New York: 1884.

———. *A New Monetary System.* Edited by Mary Kellogg Putman. New York: Rudd and Carleton, 1861.

Lanier, J. F. D. *Sketch of the Life of J. F. D. Lanier.* New York, 1870.

Lewis, Joseph J. *Letter to a Member of Congress on the National Currency.* Philadelphia: King and Baird, Printers, 1865.

*Lincoln Catechism Wherein the Eccentricities and Beauties of Despotism Are Fully Set Forth. A Guide to the Presidential Election of 1864.* New York: J. F. Feeks, 1864.

Lord, Eleazar. *Six Letters on the Necessity and Practicability of a National Currency, and the Principles and Measures Essential to It.* New York: Anson D. F. Randolph, 1862.

McCulloch, Hugh. *Men and Measures of a Half Century.* New York: Scribner's Sons, 1888.

*Official Proceedings of the Democratic National Convention Held in 1864 at Chicago.* Chicago: Times Book and Job Printing House, 1864.

318

*Record of the Democratic Party, 1860-1865*, n.p., n.d.

Seaman, Ezra C. *Argument of E. C. Seaman on Judicial Legislation, and the General Banking Law of Michigan*. Detroit: O. S. Galley and Co., 1844.

Sherman, John. *Recollections of Forty Yeas in the House, Senate and Cabinet*. 2 vols. New York: Werner Company, 1895.

Spaulding, E. G. *History of the Legal Tender Paper Money Issued During the Great Rebellion . . . Being a Loan Without Interest and a National Currency*. Buffalo: Express and Printing Company, 1969.

*Spirit of the Chicago Convention. Extracts From All the Notable Speeches Delivered in and out of the National "Democratic" Convention . . .*, n.p., n.d.

Spooner, Lysander. *A New System of Paper Currency*. Boston: A. Williams and Co., 1861.

Steams, George L. *A Few Facts Pertaining to Currency and Banking, Adapted to the Present Position of Our Finances*. Boston: A. Williams and Co., 1864.

Stevens, Frederick W. *Michigan Constitutional Convention of 1850*, n.p., n.d.

Tallmadge, Nathaniel P. *Remarks of Mr. Tallmadge in Defense of New York Against the Charge of Bank Influence in the Result of their Election*. Washington, D.C.: Madisonian, 1838.

Voorhees, Daniel W. *The Financial Policy of the Government. The Public Debt and Frauds in Public Expenditures Inequality in Distribution of the Burdens of Government. Speech By Hon. Daniel W. Voorhees, in Congress, May 21st, 1862*, n.p., n.d.

———. *The Political Issues in Indiana. Speech of Hon. D. W. Voorhees Delivered in the Academy of Music, Indianapolis, March 31, 1870*, n.p., n.d.

———. *Public Finances and the Public Debt Monopoly and Privilege vs. the Laborer—Fiction and Fraud in Creating the Debt The Burdens and Inequalities of Taxation—The Wrongs of the National Banking System—Plans for Payment of Public Debt—A Plea in the Interest of the Laborer. Speech of Hon. D. W. Voorhees in the United States House of Representatives, January 28, 1870*, n.p., n.d.

———. *Silver and Gold Must Be Our Coin Standard. Speech of Hon. Daniel W. Voorhees of Indiana In the Senate of the United States, Tuesday, August 22, 1893*, n.p., n.d.

Walker, Amassa. *The Nature and Uses of Money and Mixed Currency with a History of the Wickaboag Bank*. Boston: Crosby Nichols and Co., 1857.

Wright, Charles [Mountaineer]. *Our Political Practice. The Usurpations of Vice Through the Popular Negligence*. Boston: Alfred Mudge and Son, Printers, 1864.

Wright, Joseph A. *An Address Delivered at the Installation of Rev. W. M. Daily, D. D. as President of the Indiana University, August 2, 1854*. Indianapolis: Journal Monmoth Steam Printing Establishment, 1854.

———. *An Address Delivered by Gov. Joseph A. Wright on the 6th Day of October, 1853, At Livonia, Washington County, Indiana to the District*

319

*Agricultural Society Composed of the Counties of Washington and Orange.* Indianapolis: Austin H. Brown and Co., 1854.

———. *Addresses Delivered By Gov. Wright and Pres't. Berry at the Indiana Asbury University, July 16, 1850.* Indianapolis: John D. Defrees, 1850.

———. *Speech of Governor Joseph A. Wright on the Bank Fraud Case in the Senate March 9, 1857,* n.p., n.d.

# Printed collections of letters, papers, and debates

Adams, Henry, ed. *Writings of Albert Gallatin.* Philadelphia: 1879.

American Historical Association. "Diary and Correspondence of Salmon P. Chase." *Annual Report of the American Historical Association for the Year 1902,* vol. 2 (1903).

Basler, Roy P., ed. *The Collected Works of Abraham Lincoln.* New Brunswick, N. J.: Rutgers Univ. Press, 1953.

Bassett, John Spencer, ed. *Correspondence of Andrew Jackson.* Washington, D.C.: Carnegie Institute of Washington, 1931.

Blau, Joseph L., ed. *Social Theories of Jacksonian Democracy.* New York: Liberal Arts Press, 1954.

Burnham, W. Dean. *Presidential Ballots, 1836-1892.* Baltimore: John Hopkins Univ. Press, 1955.

Carter, Clarence Edwin, ed. *The Territory of Michigan,1829–1837. The Territorial Papers of the United States,* vol. 12. Washington, D.C.: U.S. Government Printing Office, 1945.

Cole, Arthur Charles, ed. *The Constitutional Debates of 1847.* Springfield: Illinois State Historical Library, 1919.

Coleman, Charles H., ed. "Three Vallandigham Letters, 1865." *Ohio Archaeological and Historical Publications* 43 (1934): 461–64.

Commager, Henry Steele, ed. *Documents of American History.* New York: Appleton-Century-Crofts, 1949.

Commons, John R. et al., eds. *Documentary History of American Industrial Society.* New York: Russell and Russell, 1958.

Dorr, Harold M., ed. *The Michigan Constitutional Conventions of 1835–36: Debates and Proceedings.* Ann Arbor: Univ. of Michigan Press, 1940.

Fuller, George N., ed. *Messages of the Governors.* Lansing: Michigan Historical Commission, 1925-26.

Greene, Evarts B., ed. "Letters to Gustav Koerner, 1837–1863." *Transactions of the Illinois State Historical Society for the Year 1907* (1908): 222-46.

Greene, Evarts B., and Thompson, Charles M., eds. *Governor's Letter Books, 1840–1853.* Springfield: Illinois State Historical Society, 1911.

Hamlin, L. Belle, ed. "Selections from the Follett Papers, II." *Quarterly Publications of the Historical and Philosophical Society of Ohio* 9 (July–Sept. 1914): 72–100.

———, ed. "Selections from the Follett Papers, III." *Quarterly Publications of the Historical and Philosophical Society of Ohio* 10 (Jan.–Mar. 1915): 4–33.

# INDEX

325